Empowerment Practice in Social Work

Developing Richer Conceptual Foundations

edited by
Wes Shera
and
Lilian M. Wells

Canadian Scholars' Press Inc.   Toronto   1999

Empowerment Practice in Social Work: Developing Richer Conceptual Foundations
edited by Wes Shera and Lilian Wells

First published in 1999 by
Canadian Scholars' Press Inc.
180 Bloor Street West, Ste. 1202
Toronto, Ontario
M5S 2V6

We acknowledge the financial support of the Government of Canada through the Book Publishing Industry Development Programme for our publishing activities.

Canadian Cataloguing in Publication Data

Main entry under title:
    Empowerment practice in social work: developing richer conceptual
    foundations

Includes bibliographical references.
ISBN 1-55130-146-6

1. Social service. I. Shera, Wes, 1946- . II. Wells, Lilian M.

HV40.E46 1999   361.3'2   C99-931195-6

Page layout and cover design by Brad Horning

We dedicate this book to our families
who continue to teach us good things about families
and empowering relationships.

Caroline, Emily and Matthew Shera

Gordon Wells and Russell Blair

CONTENTS

INTRODUCTION

The primary intent of this volume is to review the current base of knowledge regarding empowerment practice in social work and to identify directions for future development and research. The Faculty of Social Work at the University of Toronto hosted an invitational think-tank of leading scholars in the area to engage in this process. Participants brought expertise in the development and study of empowerment from an international perspective and had previously published in this domain. They each prepared an original paper for the think-tank, revised it after the meetings and submitted it for consideration for this volume. This book is divided into four major sections that address pivotal issues in empowerment practice. The conclusion synthesizes what we have learned and identifies areas for future development and research.

Over the past 20 years, the use of the concept of empowerment has become widespread. At the political level, it is being used by all sides—right and left—in the social welfare debate. At academic and professional levels, in the social work, social psychology, health and mental health, and administration/organization literature, the concept is used with increasing frequency—yet there is not a firm consensus as to what the concept and its application in practice represent (Lee, 1994; Simon, 1994).

The literature on empowerment (Coyne, 1987; Israel, Checkoway, Schultz and Zimmerman, 1994; Swift and Levin, 1987) describes interventions that actively involve consumers and their significant others in determining what will work. Rather than viewing the client as a passive receptacle for intervention, the professional works collaboratively with the client and shares responsibility for the design, implementation, monitoring and evaluation of interventions (Boker, 1992; Corrigan, Liberman, and Engel, 1990; Coyne, 1987).

Empowerment has been described as a multi-level construct that emphasizes health promotion, self and mutual help and multiple definitions of competence (Fairweather and Fergus, 1993; Israel, Checkoway, Schulz and Zimmerman, 1994). Gutiérrez (1990) defines empowerment as a process of increasing personal, interpersonal or political power so that individuals can take action to improve their life situation. A systematic operationalization of this construct is still emerging (Gutiérrez, Parsons and Cox, 1998; Miley, O'Melia and DuBois, 1998; Parsloe, 1996). There has also been a significant growth in the literature on the use of empowerment in various phases or fields of social work practice, including child welfare (Hegar and Hunzeker, 1988); women of colour (Gutiérrez, 1990); Asian immigrants (Hirayama and Cetingok, 1988); families (Dunst, Trivette and Deal, 1988); and the severely mentally ill (Rose, 1992).

Some central features of the emerging empowerment paradigm in social work practice include: clients are treated as subjects rather than objects; the focus is on clients' strengths rather than pathology; clients actively participate throughout the helping process; resources are seen as the total community rather than just formal services; emphasis is placed on the rejuvenation or creation of informal social networks; and monitoring, evaluation and advocacy are done in a collaborative fashion. This approach has also influenced practice in organizations (Shera and Page, 1995; Wells, Singer and Polgar, 1992) and communities (Mondros and Wilson, 1994).

The core of this book is divided into four major sections, each of which addresses a central question in exploring this area of practice.

- What are the major theoretical approaches employed as frameworks for empowerment practice and what conceptual struggles have been encountered in moving forward?
- How is empowerment practice operationalized in different fields of practice (e.g., child welfare, gerontology, mental health)?
- What are some of the critical issues encountered in the implementation of empowerment practice (e.g., group work, spirituality, consumer involvement, responding to diversity, empowering organizations)?
- What is the future of empowerment practice and research, and what are the implications for social work education?

These questions provide a framework for each of the sections.

SECTION ONE: THEORETICAL PERSPECTIVES

This section includes theoretical approaches that have been employed as frameworks for empowerment and identifies some of the conceptual struggles encountered in moving forward. Key questions addressed in this section include:

- While empowerment is frequently described as a multi-level construct, how is this operationalized?
- What are some of the theories and concepts that are useful in conceptualizing empowerment at different levels?
- Is empowerment practice reserved only for identified disenfranchised and oppressed groups?

Several topics that are discussed include: empowerment practice and generalist social work; the contributions of theories of participation; the dynamics of individual and collective empowerment; the limits to empowerment; and the importance of understanding power relations.

SECTION TWO: FIELDS OF PRACTICE

In this section we examine how empowerment practice is operationalized in different fields of practice. The areas of disability, mental health, child welfare, women in poverty, minorities and gerontology are addressed. Some of the key questions focused on in this section include:

- What is unique about empowerment practice in specific fields?
- Are the technologies and strategies of empowerment practice transferable across specific fields of practice?
- Where are the opportunities for service users to define empowerment?
- How can empowerment be operationalized in areas where social control is a predominant concern?

Core concepts in this section include the importance of a strengths perspective, of partnerships with clients and the centrality of consumer voice in defining empowerment. The need for attention to the special needs of particular populations, an historical understanding of stigma, discrimination and oppression and the importance of strategies of collective empowerment are pertinent themes.

SECTION THREE: CRITICAL ISSUES IN EMPOWERMENT PRACTICE

The third section expands on a number of critical issues, which tend to cut across fields of practice and practice in different countries. Key questions posed in this section include:

- How do diversity and different world views impact on empowerment practice?
- What special role does group work play in an empowerment context?
- What are some of the barriers and best practices in the area of user/ consumer involvement in services?
- How can we deal with professional and organizational factors that impede empowerment practice?

The impact of broad socio-political changes such as globalization, dismantling of the traditional welfare state and neo-conservatism are considered. Redefining our organizational contexts, the role of group work, ethnicity and culture and the importance of spirituality and religion are areas that are also examined.

SECTION FOUR: RESEARCH AND EDUCATION

The fourth section examines research issues in empowerment and the implications of an empowerment perspective for social work education. Questions addressed in this section include:

- What kind of research is needed to further our understanding of empowerment practice in specific fields of practice?
- Can we conduct research as an empowering process?
- How can concepts and principles of empowerment be utilized in education?

The need to conduct research based on principles of empowerment, facilitating genuine consumer involvement in research and modelling empowerment practice in the learning enterprise are all themes that permeate this section.

CONCLUSION

The final chapter provides an in-depth synthesis, on a section by section basis, of the key issues addressed in the book. It makes an overall assessment of the contributions of an empowerment perspective to social work and concludes by identifying some of the challenges for further development in the conceptualization of empowerment practice and in the nature of research needed to document its effectiveness.

The papers gathered for this volume were submitted by leaders in this field of scholarship from four different countries (USA, Canada, UK and Israel). Collectively they represent some of the best thinking in the area and will no doubt stimulate further debate and inquiry in the field. It is our hope that this volume will make a significant contribution to our understanding of empowerment practice in social work and spur further research in this important area.

REFERENCES

Boker, W. (1992). A call for partnership between schizophrenic patients, relatives and professionals. *British Journal of Psychiatry*, 161 (suppl. 18.), 10-12.

Corrigan, P.W., Liberman, R.P. and Engel, J.D. (1990). From noncompliance to collaboration in the treatment of schizophrenia. *Hospital and Community Psychiatry*, 41, 1203-1211.

Coyne, J.C. (1987). The concept of empowerment in strategic therapy. *Psychotherapy*, 24, 539-545.

Dunst, C.J., Trivette, C.M. and Deal A.G. (1988). *Enabling and empowering families.* Cambridge, MA: Brookline Books.

Fairweather, G.W. and Fergus, O.F. (1993). *Empowering the mentally ill.* Austin, TX: Fairweather Publishing.

Gutiérrez, L.M. (1990). Working with women of color: An empowerment perspective. *Social Work*, 35, 149-153.

Gutiérrez, L., Parsons, R. and Cox, E. (1998). *Empowerment in social work practice: A sourcebook.* Pacific Grove: Brooks/Cole.

Hegar, R.L. and Hunzeker, J.M. (1988). Moving toward empowerment-based practice in public child welfare. *Social Work*, 33, 499-502.

Hirayama, H. and Cetingok, M. (1988). Empowerment: A social work approach to Asian immigrants. *Social Casework*, 69, 41-47.

Israel, B.A., Checkoway, B., Schulz, A. and Zimmerman, M. (1994). Health education and community empowerment: Conceptualizing and measuring perceptions of individual, organizational, and community control. *Health Education Quarterly*, 21(2): 149-170.

Lee. J. (1994). *The empowerment approach and social work practice*. New York: Columbia University Press.

Miley, K., O'Melia, M. and DuBois, B. (1998). *Generalist social work practice: An empowering approach*. Boston: Allyn & Bacon.

Mondros. J. and Wilson, S. (1994). *Organizing for power and empowerment*. New York: Columbia University Press.

Parsloe, P. (1996). *Pathways to empowerment*. Birmingham: Venture Press.

Rose, S.M. (1991). Strategies of mental health programming: A client-driven model of case management. In C. Hudson and A. Cox (Eds.), *Dimensions of state mental health* (pp. 139-154). New York: Praeger.

Rose, S.M. (1992). *Case management and social work practice*. New York: Longman.

Shera, W. and Page, J. (1995). Creating more effective human service organizations through strategies of empowerment. *Administration in Social Work,* 19(4), 1-15.

Simon, B.L. (1994). *The empowerment tradition in American social work*. New York: Columbia.

Swift, C. and Levin, G. (1987). Empowerment: An emerging mental health technology. *Journal of Primary Prevention,* 8, 71-95.

Wells, L. M., Singer, C. and Polgar, A.T. (1992). *To enhance quality of life in institutions: An empowerment model of social work practice*. Toronto: Canadian Scholars' Press.

Section 1

Theoretical Perspectives

Chapter 1

EMPOWERING PROCESSES
FOR SOCIAL WORK PRACTICE

Karla Miley
Department of Social and Behavioral Studies
Black Hawk College, Moline, IL
Brenda DuBois
School of Social Work
St. Ambrose University, Davenport, IA

Social work practitioners and educators must be able to present a clear definition of empowerment, cogently explicate its underlying assumptions and integrate these assumptions into meaningful practice models and social work processes. This paper offers a perspective on empowerment, delineates practice assumptions about human systems, change and empowerment; presents a practice framework based on these assumptions; and describes the implementation processes of activating client system resources, creating alliances that facilitate change and expanding opportunities in the resource structures in society.

PERSPECTIVES ON EMPOWERMENT

Empowerment refers to both process and outcome. Empowerment is the "process of increasing personal, interpersonal, or political power so that individuals, families, and communities can take action to improve their situations" (Gutiérrez, 1994, p. 202). Empowerment, as *process*, implies exercising psychological control over personal affairs, as well as exerting influence over the course of events in the socio-political arena. With respect to empowerment as *outcome*, it defines the end state of achieving either personal or political power. As such, empowerment refers to a state of mind, such as feeling worthy and competent or perceiving power and control; and it also refers to a reallocation of power that results from modifying social structures (Swift and Levin, 1987). Rappaport (1987) says empowerment:

suggests both individual determination over one's own life and democratic participation in the life of one's community, often through mediating structures such as schools, neighborhoods, churches, and other voluntary organizations. Empowerment conveys both a psychological sense of personal control or influence and a concern with actual social influence, political power, and legal rights. It is a multilevel construct applicable to individual citizens as well as to organizations and neighborhoods; it suggests the study of people in context. (p. 121)

Empowerment implies access to power. Gutiérrez (1991) describes power as: "the ability to get what one needs; the ability to influence how others think, feel, act, or believe; and the ability to influence the distribution of resources in a social system such as a family, organization, community, or society" (pp. 201-202). Personal power refers to individuals' abilities to control their destiny and influence their surroundings. Political power manifests in the ability to change systems, redistribute resources, expand opportunity structures and create social change through social action (Hartman, 1990).

EMPOWERMENT AND SOCIAL WORK PRACTICE

Empowerment-oriented social workers base their practice on an understanding that clients' issues result from an imbalance between the pool of available personal, interpersonal and societal resources and the necessity of these resources for meeting the demands of daily living. To address this incongruity, social work practitioners and clients develop multi-level strategies that enrich self-efficacy, enhance skills, increase the awareness of the links between personal difficulties and public issues, forge alliances with others within the social service delivery network, and implement actions to foster changes in the socio-political arena (Breton, 1994a, 1994b; Cox and Parsons, 1993; Gutiérrez, 1994; Lee, 1994; Simon, 1994; DuBois and Miley, 1999; Miley, O'Melia and DuBois, 1998).

Assumptions about empowerment in social work practice emerge from practice assumptions about human systems and about change.

Assumptions About Human Systems
- All people deserve acceptance and respect.
- Clients know their situations best.
- All human system behaviour makes sense in context.

- All human system behaviour is motivated.
- Challenges emerge from transactions between human systems and their physical and social environments rather than reside in clients themselves.
- Strengths are diverse including personal feelings of worth, cultural pride, successful relationships and resourceful interdependence within a community (Miley, O'Melia and DuBois, 1998, p. 99).

Assumptions About Change
- Change is not only possible, it is inevitable.
- A small change in one part of the ecosystem may initiate a chain of beneficial changes.
- Challenges are likely to have many solutions.
- You don't have to solve a problem to find a solution.
- Enduring change builds on strengths.
- Strengths and the potential for growth characterize all human systems.
- Given niches and opportunities, human systems cultivate competencies.
- Collaborative relationships stimulate feelings of power and lead to actions.
- Cultural differences are resources offering broader perspectives, additional options, and possibilities of synergistic solutions (Miley, O'Melia and DuBois, 1998, p. 100).

Assumptions About Empowerment
- Empowerment is a collaborative process, with clients and practitioners working together as partners.
- The empowering process views client systems as competent and capable, given access to resources and opportunities.
- Clients must perceive themselves as causal agents able to effect change.
- Competence is acquired or refined through life experiences, particularly experiences affirming efficacy, rather than from circumstances in which one is told what to do.
- Multiple factors contribute to any given situation, and therefore effective solutions are necessarily diverse in their approach.
- Informal social networks are a significant source of support for mediating stress and increasing one's competence and sense of control.
- People must participate in their own empowerment; goals, means and outcomes must be self-defined.
- Level of awareness is a key issue in empowerment; information is necessary for change to occur.

- Empowerment involves access to resources and the capacity to use those resources effectively.
- The empowering process is dynamic, synergistic, ever-changing and evolutionary.
- Empowerment is achieved through the parallel structures of personal and socio-economic development (DuBois and Miley, 1999, p. 25).

For empowerment-based social work practice, "the empowerment concept links individual strengths and competencies, natural mutual aid systems, and proactive behaviors to social action, social policy, social change, and community development" (Anderson, 1992, p. 7). Social workers engage clients as partners in activities related to enhancing the client system's competence as well as in efforts directed at creating responsive networks of resources that are beneficial to the client.

EMPOWERING PROCESSES FOR SOCIAL WORK PRACTICE

The challenge for practitioners and social work educators is to translate the assumptions of empowerment, human systems and change into processes that provide a framework for day-to-day social work practice. Miley, O'Melia and DuBois (1998) propose an empowering approach to generalist social work practice that incorporates elements of dialogue, discovery and development (see Table 1):

> Through dialogue, workers develop collaborative partnerships with clients, articulate the aspects of challenging situations, and define the purposes of the work. In discovery, practitioners and clients implement processes to locate resources on which to construct plans for change. For development, workers and clients activate interpersonal and institutional resources, forge connections with other persons and systems, and create new opportunities to distribute the resources of a just society. (p. 24)

To focus discussion, let us consider three implementation strategies in the development phase of the social work process that, in general, parallel micro-, mid- and macrolevel change: activating resources, creating alliances and expanding opportunities.

Table 1: An Empowering Approach to Generalist Practice

Phase	Process	Activities
Dialogue	Forming Partnerships	Building empowering social worker-client relationships that acknowledge clients' privileges and respect their uniqueness
	Articulating Partnerships	Assessing challenging situations by responding to validate clients' experiences, add transactions dimensions and look toward goals
	Defining Directions	Determining a preliminary purpose for the relationship to activate client motivation and guide the exploration for relevant resources
Discovery	Identifying Strengths	Searching for client strengths in general functioning, coping with challenging situations, cultural identities and overcoming adversity
	Analyzing Resource Capabilities	Exploring resources in clients' transactions with the environment including connections to family, social groups, organizations and community institutions
	Framing Solutions	Constructing an achievable plan of action by mobilizing available resources through consultancy, resource management and education
	Creating Alliances	Forging empowering alliances among clients, within clients' natural support networks and within the service delivery system
	Expanding Opportunities	Developing new opportunities and resources through program development, community organizing and social action
	Recognizing Success	Evaluating the success of the change efforts to recognize achievements and inform continuing actions
	Integrating Gains	Wrapping up the change process in ways that resolve the relationship, celebrate success and stabilize positive changes

Used with permission of the authors from "Applying an Empowerment Process in Social Work Practice," B. DuBois, K. Miley and M. O'Melia, 1993. Cited in Miley, O'Melia and DuBois, 1998.

ACTIVATING RESOURCES

Activating resources involves empowerment-oriented activities that enhance client systems' access to their own personal resources and to the resources available in their social environments. In activating resources, clients access personal, interpersonal and institutional resources. Social workers consult with clients about strategies for coordinating and managing resources. Possible activities include:

- Enhancing personal efficacy
- Fostering interpersonal competence
- Promoting consciousness-raising
- Building on strengths
- Motivating change
- Drawing upon cultural resources
- Exercising personal power

The activities associated with activating resources often result in an enhanced sense of personal competence and efficacy, significant personal characteristics of empowerment. However, focusing solely on personal competence fails to measure up to the standard of empowerment as both personal and political. Furthermore, an individualized focus on self-efficacy and personal adaptation also fails to consider the transactional nature of empowerment. Breton (1994a) contends that a narrow focus on the personal domain ignores the central point of empowerment.

The development of a critical consciousness ensures that connections are made between the personal and political (Moreau, 1990; Simon, 1994; Parsons, 1991; Breton, 1994a; Lee, 1994; Gutiérrez, 1994; Pinderhughes, 1997). Consciousness-raising contextualizes experiences, reduces self-blame and "helps group members to take account of the nature and impact of their own choices and actions and to take responsibility for them" (Simon, 1990, p. 35). Critical reflection leads to understanding the social origins of personal actions and to recognizing the changeability of institutional structures and policies (Young, 1994). When this reflective dialogue occurs in a group context, group members form a base for collective actions to change social policies and modify social structures.

CREATING ALLIANCES

By *creating alliances*, social workers and clients align the efforts of clients in empowerment groups, strengthen the functioning of clients within their natural support networks and organize the service delivery network. These alliances bring emotional support to clients and build bases of power. Key techniques for discussion include:

- Forming empowerment groups
- Developing a critical consciousness
- Aligning natural support networks
- Creating responsive social service delivery systems
- Constructing client-service alliances
- Maximizing interpersonal power

Many contend that working with clients in groups is a major vehicle for empowerment-based social work (Hirayama and Hirayama, 1986; Cox, 1988, 1991; Parsons, 1991; Mullender and Ward, 1991; Staub-Bernasconi, 1991; Simon, 1990, 1994; Breton, 1994a, 1994b; Lee, 1994; Gutiérrez, 1994, Cox and Parsons, 1996). According to Dodd and Gutiérrez (1990), work in small groups "is the perfect environment for raising consciousness, engaging in mutual aid, developing skills, problem solving, and experiencing one's own effectiveness in influencing others" (p. 71).

The alliances social workers create also extend to their work with community coalitions, interagency networks and case management teams. These alliances with professionals, client advocates and service consumers provides bases of power for promoting collective social action, advocating policy change and restoring order in a fragmented social service delivery system. Involving clients in these types of alliances gives them opportunities to represent their own views and protect their rights.

EXPANDING OPPORTUNITIES

Social workers and clients join to expand opportunities in the social fabric of society. Expanding opportunities through social reform, policy development, legislative advocacy and community change efforts is directly related to the professional mandate to ensure a just distribution of resources and to develop just social policies. Related techniques and strategies include:

- Recognizing environmental opportunities and risks
- Engaging in community empowerment and development
- Promoting social activism and social advocacy
- Championing social justice
- Exercising socio-political power

Collective action that seeks to reallocate power and resources, to redress social inequities and to benefit disenfranchised and oppressed populations leads to socio-political empowerment. Social action is an appropriate strategy for both the macropractitioner and the direct service worker who advocates on behalf of clients to influence policies and encourage clients to speak in their own voices in efforts to effect social and political change (Lee, 1994; Simon, 1994; Zippay, 1995; Weil, 1996; McInnis-Ditterich, 1997; Miley, O'Melia and DuBois, 1998).

CONCLUSION

Numerous questions emerge as we consider implementing empowerment-based social work practice, including:

- Is a philosophical orientation to empowerment sufficient to ensure its application to practice?
- What techniques and skills are associated with empowerment-based implementation at the micro-, mid- and macrolevels of practice? Can we retrofit techniques or are we compelled to craft new skills and techniques consonant with empowerment? If we can draw upon the resources of tradition, what are the screening criteria for ensuring a "fit" with empowerment-based practice?
- Are all social work clients, by virtue of being social work clients, considered to be oppressed and disenfranchised in some way or does the generic application of empowerment to the whole of social work dilute its potency to work with identifiable "at-risk" population groups?
- How can empowerment-oriented social workers survive in an organizational culture and managed care environment that is counterproductive to the empowerment of clients?

To address these questions, we need to effectively translate the know-what of empowerment into the know-how of social work practice; however, there are no quick and easy answers. On the one hand, one might hold that a particular way of thinking is sufficient to direct one's way of doing. On the other hand, we believe that a philosophical orientation to empowerment needs to be buttressed by strategies and methodologies consonant with empowerment. So, while a philosophical orientation toward empowerment is critical in screening and selecting various approaches to one's work with clients, we may need to work harder to create methodologies that are directly consistent with an empowerment-based practice. In creating such new models for practice, let us heed what researchers tell us. Empowerment-oriented research suggests the importance of systemic change and group work and community-based models for social work practice. These practice venues afford opportunities to explore change in both the personal and the political. Clearly, personal and political empowerment counters the deleterious effects of oppression and discrimination for clients and society. But, rather than further labelling clients as "oppressed" and "disenfranchised," we believe it is more productive to challenge oppressive and discriminatory human systems. Finally, we recognize that the social service delivery context of practice imposes its own values and culture on the nature of the social worker-client relationship, the identification of problems and concomitant development of solutions, and the selection of preferred processes of change. An empowerment practice orientation implies that social workers must strive, most especially in the face of managed care and other cost-containment strategies, to create humane and empowering environments for the delivery of services and resources to clients.

REFERENCES

Anderson, J. D. (1992, March). *Between individual and community: Small group empowerment practice in a generalist perspective.* Paper prepared for Council on Social Work Education's Annual Program Meeting. Kansas City, MO.

Breton, M. (1994a). Relating competence-promotion and empowerment. *Journal of Progressive Human Services*, 5(1), 27-44.

Breton, M. (1994b). On the meaning of empowerment and empowerment-oriented social work practice. *Social Work with Groups*, 17(3), 23-37.

Cox, E. O. (1988). Empowerment of the low income elderly through group work. *Social Work with Groups*, 11(4), 111-125.

Cox, E. O. (1991). The critical role of social action in empowerment oriented groups. *Social Work with Groups*, 14(3/4), 77-90.

Cox, E. O. and Parsons, R. (1993). *Empowerment-oriented social work practice with the elderly.* Pacific Grove, CA: Brooks/Cole Publishing Company.

Cox, E. O. and Parsons, R. (1996). Empowerment-oriented social work practice: Impact on late life relationships of women. *Journal of Women and Aging*, 8(3-4), 129-143.

Dodd, P. and Gutiérrez, L. (1990). Preparing students for the future: A power perspective on community practice. *Administration in Social Work*, 14(2), 63-78.

DuBois, B. and Miley, K. K. (1999). *Social work: An empowering profession* (3rd ed.). Boston: Allyn & Bacon.

Gutiérrez, L. M. (1989, March). *Empowerment in social work practice: Considerations for practice and education.* Paper presented at the Council on Social Work Education Annual Program Meeting, Chicago, IL.

Gutiérrez, L. M. (1991). Empowering women of color: A feminist model. In M. Bricker-Jenkins, N. R. Hooyman and N. Gottlieb (Eds.), *Feminist social work practice in clinical settings* (pp. 199-214). Newbury Park, CA: SAGE Publications.

Gutiérrez, L. M. (1994). Beyond coping: An empowerment perspective on stressful life events. *Journal of Sociology and Social Welfare*, 21(3), 201-219.

Hartman, A. (1990, October). *Family-based strategies for empowering families*. Paper presented at the Family Empowerment Conference of the University of Iowa, School of Social Work, Iowa City, IA.

Hirayama, H. and Hirayama, K. (1986). Empowerment through group participation: Process and goal. *American Journal of Community Psychology*, 15, 353-371.

Lee, J. A. B. (1994). *The empowerment approach to social work practice*. New York: Columbia University Press.

McInnis-Ditterich, K. (1997). An empowerment-oriented mental health intervention with elderly Appalachian women: The women's club. *Journal of Women and Aging*, 9(1/2), 91-105.

Miley, K., O'Melia, M. and DuBois, B. (1998). *Generalist social work practice: An empowering approach*. Boston: Allyn & Bacon.

Moreau, M. M. (1990). Empowerment through advocacy and consciousness-raising: Implications of a structural approach to social work. *Journal of Sociology and Social Welfare*, 17(2), 53-67.

Mullender, A. and Ward, D. (1991). Empowerment through social action group work: The self-directed approach. *Social Work with Groups*, 14(3/4), 125-139.

Parsons, R. J. (1991). Empowerment: Purpose and practice principle in social work. *Social Work with Groups*, 14(2), 7-21.

Pinderhughes, E. B. (1997). The interaction of difference and power as a basic framework for understanding work with African Americans: Family theory, empowerment and educational approaches. *Smith College Studies in Social Work*, 67(3), 323-347.

Rappaport, J. (1987). Terms of empowerment/ exemplars of prevention: Toward a theory for community psychology. *American Journal of Community Psychology*, 15(2), 121-144.

Simon, B. L. (1990). Rethinking empowerment. *Journal of Progressive Human Services*, 1, 27-39.

Simon, B. L. (1994). *The empowerment tradition in American social work: A history*. New York: Columbia University Press.

Staub-Bernasconi, S. (1991). Social action, empowerment and social work—An integrative theoretical framework for social work and social work with groups. *Social Work with Groups*, 14(3/4), 35-51.

Swift, C. and Levin, G. (1987). Empowerment: An emerging mental health technology. *Journal of Primary Prevention*, 8(1/2), 71-94.

Weil, M. O. (1996). Community building, building community practice. *Social Work*, 41(5), 481-499.

Young, I. (1994). Punishment, treatment, empowerment: Three approaches to policy for pregnant addicts. *Feminist Studies*, 20(33+) [on line]. Available: http://www.elibrary.com [1996, July].

Zippay, A. (1995). The politics of empowerment: Empowerment of low-income populations as a component of social work and community development practice. *Social Work*, 40(2), 263-267.

Chapter 2

EMPOWERING THROUGH PARTNERSHIP— THE RELEVANCE OF THEORIES OF PARTICIPATION TO SOCIAL WORK PRACTICE

Monica Barry
Social Work Research Centre
University of Stirling, Scotland
Roger Sidaway
University of Edinburgh, Scotland

There is a certain tendency among humans to identify power with the capacity for victory, that is, overcoming some other person, will or institution. (Boulding, 1990, p. 16)

Current political initiatives to tackle poverty and social exclusion in the UK and to give people more power to deal with environmental problems at the local level in the USA (so-called "civic environmentalism") call for an urgent re-examination of the concepts of empowerment and participation (see Wicks 1997; Teles, 1997). Although the concepts may not have been subject to a formal analysis, there have been close parallels between advocating for empowerment in the social work field and community participation in environmental planning. Both draw on similar ideals and are part of a longstanding debate taking place at similar times about access to and redistribution of resources. Both sets of literature contain similar critiques that initiatives often result in no more than a tokenistic response from government and other agencies, and that marginal improvements being made in decision-making processes make few changes that might improve the lot of the "have-nots" in society.

Our aim in this chapter is to focus on empowerment in the social work field and to draw on a wider range of theory from environmental planning and rural development. Our contention is that each "world" can learn from the other, and this chapter will concentrate on ways in which such theory can be developed.

THE CONCEPTS OF EMPOWERMENT AND COMMUNITY PARTICIPATION

The concepts of empowerment and community participation, particularly the latter, have their origins in the fight against poverty. Initiatives to eliminate poverty as a social problem are not new. Wicks (1997), in commenting on the most recent initiative, has pointed out the parallels both in aim and in language with community development initiatives in the UK in the 1970s and the earlier war on poverty legislation in the US in the 1960s. Wicks contends that such initiatives must address both economic and social agendas, reducing family insecurities and dependencies as well as providing jobs by coordinating social, educational and employment services.

The dictionary definition of the word empowerment is "to give authority to," implying a delegation if not a transference of power. But the term has taken on a new meaning since the late 1980s, when empowerment has become common parlance within social work. The term has been given educational connotations: a process which enables people "to engage in significant learning. To be empowered is to be able to connect with others in mutually productive ways" (Shrewsbury, 1987, p. 8). It has also been related to personal and social development: "the act of strengthening an individual's beliefs in his or her sense of effectiveness" (Conger, 1989, p. 18), or "an interactive process through which less powerful people experience personal and social change, enabling them to achieve influence over the organisations and institutions which affect their lives, and the communities in which they live" (O'Brien & Whitmore, 1989, in Morley, 1995, p. 3). More recently, Robinson (1994, in Morley, 1995, p. 3) states that "empowerment is a personal and social process, a liberatory sense of one's own strengths, competence, creativity and freedom of action, to be empowered is to feel power surging into one from other people and from inside, specifically the power to act and grow." The focus on personal development has been criticized for losing the emphasis on political radicalism and social change (that many now consider the concept to imply) and becoming more process- rather than outcome-oriented. Morley describes such definitions of empowerment as somewhat evangelical, and suggests instead that empowerment is a "manipulative strategy, designed to disguise the harsh consumer-oriented market values of New Right policies in the public and voluntary sectors" (1995, p. 4). Morley also suggests that empowerment "appears part of the manipulative, victim-blaming ideology suggesting that oppressed groups have the power to change their material circumstances through psychological restructuring" (1995, p. 8). It is indeed ironic, and probably no coincidence, that empowerment as a concept to denote personal responsibility, resources and motivation entered the arena of social policy and social welfare in the UK during the Thatcher era.

There are parallels to be drawn between initiatives which address social problems and those that focus on environmental issues in terms of participatory or empowering practice. The term participation, while on the surface politically neutral—in the sense of "taking part in"—gained more exact, political connotations in the 1960s. Indeed, the response of the French government to the Paris riots in 1968 was an initiative entitled "Participation" (Oxford, 1989). The war on poverty legislation in the USA in 1964, which encouraged "maximum feasible participation of the poor" in anti-poverty strategies, heralded a burgeoning of grass-roots community action which left the local elites decidedly nervous about the extent of empowerment such participation might engender. The outcry from existing power-holders over how much participation was either maximum or feasible led to a subsequent U-turn by the instigators of the legislation, who tried to reassure the establishment "that the intent was simply to encourage citizen participation, not to turn over control of the programme to [the local communities], nor to by-pass local political structures" (Gaventa, 1998, p. 52).

In a review of rural development and development aid projects, Baxter (1996) has traced the increasing emphasis on community participation. In the 1950s and 1960s, community development projects were geared to the contribution that local people could make to the economic development of their areas. But the goals of development projects were determined by professionals, and community participation was seen as a strategy towards the sharing of material benefits rather than the empowerment or capacity building of local people. Key components of capacity building, which contain several common elements with empowerment, have been identified by Cernea (1992). These are:

- mobilising local resources;
- self-definition of interests, recognising that people have the best knowledge of their own problems and interests;
- community diagnosis of priorities and local structures;
- local priorities must be integrated into regional and national systems;
- iterative planning, i.e., starting where people are at and moving forward in incremental stages rather than with radical solutions;
- information dissemination. (Cernea, 1992, in Baxter, 1996, p. 4)

Over the last 20 years there has been a move from top-down towards bottom-up approaches, which attempt to integrate conservation and development projects and which recognize the need for grass-roots support, but these still exclude local people from project design with "little discernible shift in the balance of power" (Baxter, 1996, p. 5). Recent environmental initiatives promoting sustainable development place a strong emphasis on participation, capacity building and empowerment, for example, by advocating:

> [a] focus on empowerment of local and community groups through the principle of delegating authority, accountability and resources to the most appropriate level to ensure that the programme will be geographically and ecologically specific. (United Nations Conference on Environment and Development, 1992, *Agenda 21*, Section 3.5a)

Following a review of a sample of World Bank projects, Paul (1987) suggested that participation was only appropriate in certain contexts, which, to Paul, were only relevant to community participation when such participation was defined as:

> ....an active process by which beneficiary/client groups influence the direction and execution of a development project with a view to enhancing [their] well being in terms of income, personal growth, self-reliance or other values they cherish. (Paul, 1987, in Baxter, 1996, p. 139)

By 1994, however, the World Bank was more actively advocating participation, suggesting that such development was "a process through which stakeholders influence and share control over development initiatives, and the decisions and resources which affect them" (World Bank, 1994, p. i).

In effect, the concepts of empowerment and participation have virtually become one and the same, as the definitions from O'Brien and Whitmore (1989) and the World Bank (1994) demonstrate, with their common emphasis on the less powerful gaining influence over their own lives. Perhaps the most widely quoted analysis of participation, namely, that of Arnstein (1969), recognizes the close links with empowerment. She defines participation as:

> the redistribution of power that enables the have-not citizens, presently excluded from the political and economic processes, to be deliberately included in the future. It is the strategy by which the have-nots join in determining how information is shared, goals and policies are set, tax resources

are allocated, programs are operated and benefits like contracts and patronage are parcelled out. In short, it is the means by which they can induce significant social reform which enables them to share in the benefits of the affluent society. (Arnstein, 1969, p. 71-72)

BROADENING THE CONCEPT OF COMMUNITY PARTICIPATION

Following on from Arnstein, other writers have also identified the links between empowerment and participation. For example, Wilcox (1994, p. 4) suggests that "understanding participation involves understanding power: the ability of the different interests to achieve what they want," and Barry (1996, p. 3) has further suggested that "empowerment cannot be achieved without having participation as a precursor." It is at this point that the literature on community participation can provide the most helpful pointers.

The aspect of Arnstein's work that has attracted the most attention is her typology of participation, which she devised to describe community development issues in the USA and which she recognized might be provocative in being overtly political in nature. By presenting the typology as "a ladder of participation," she infers that there are hierarchical degrees of participation, and, by inference, that one can progress either up or down the ladder. The "rungs" of such a ladder define stages which range from manipulation and therapy (non-participation), through informing, consultation and placation (degrees of tokenism) to partnerships, delegated power and finally citizen control (degrees of citizen power, i.e., empowerment). The typology suggests an outcome-oriented rather than a process-oriented approach to participation, in that an increase in power allows greater control of both resources for action and decision-making for implementation. There have been various attempts to develop or refine Arnstein's ladder of participation, which is displayed in Table 1 alongside some of the derivative or variant typologies.

What each of the other typologies attempts to recognize are some of the finer distinctions of decision-making and control, what has already been determined, and the relationships between practitioners and participants; in other words, who has the autonomy to decide, and whether as privilege or by right. There may be additional stages suggested within the hierarchy (e.g., TPAS, 1989; Pretty, 1994) or inferences that the distinctions between them may be blurred or overlap (TPAS, 1989). In the same way that Arnstein drew the distinction between degrees of citizen power and degrees of tokenism, Pretty highlighted the likelihood of tokenistic participation by concluding that "if

Table 1: Alternative Hierarchies of Participation

	Arnstein, 1969	TPAS, 1989	Pretty, 1994	World Bank, 1994	Wilcox, 1994
Degrees of Citizen Power	*Citizen Control*	*Control*	*Self-mobilization*: take initiatives, may challenge initiatives	*Empowering*: (mechanisms) self-management	*Supporting independent community interests*: [in doing what they want]
	Delegated Power	*Choice* *Joint management*	*Interactive*: joint analysis and control of local decisions	*Collaborative*: joint working, taking responsibility	*Acting together*: deciding and forming partnerships to carry out plans
	Partnerships			*Shared decision-making*: participatory planning and conflict resolution	*Deciding together*: providing ideas before a joint decision
		Dialogue	*Functional*: meet pre-determined objectives once major decisions taken	*Joint assessment*: participatory assessment	

Degrees of Tokenism	*Placation*		*Material incentives:* provide resources only		
	Consultation	*Consultation* / *Listening*	*Consultation:* provide views, professionals not obliged to change proposals	*Consultative:* meetings, field visits and interviews	*Consultation:* offering options for feedback
	Informing	*Seeking information* / *Providing information*	*Information giving:* survey information but no influence	*Information sharing:* dissemination	*Information [giving]:* tell them what is planned
Non-participation	*Therapy*		*Passive participation:* unilateral decisions		
	Manipulation				*Exclusion:* unaware of the decision

development is to be sustainable, then nothing less than 'functional participation' will suffice." (Pretty, 1994, in Baxter, 1996, p. 132). Wilcox (1994) also implies degrees of empowerment within the top three categories of his framework, grouping them as substantial participation—roughly equating with Arnstein's degrees of citizen power.

Arnstein's framework has been criticized on a number of counts, for example, in ignoring the possible need for expertise in the exercise of power through decision-making (Kasperson and Breitbart, 1974). Richardson (1983) suggested that Arnstein's typology failed to recognize the potential for consensus as well as conflict and that the interests of citizens are often congruent with, rather than in conflict with, the interests of the more powerful. Hallett (1984, p. 22) states that Arnstein's typology is useful in asserting "that power is central to an understanding of participation; both the nature and extent of *formal powers* present in various participatory mechanisms and the degree of *actual power* and influence exerted." However, Hallett also infers that even though power may be formally ascribed, it does not necessarily mean that it is effectively exercised.

Van Til and Van Til (1970), in a review of urban renewal and community action programs in the US, move away from the uni-dimensional model of Arnstein by proposing a two-dimensional typology based on the scope (range of citizens involved) and focus (their respective activities) of participation, a typology which Kasperson and Breitbart (1974) suggest deals more adequately with the complexity and relational property of participation. This analysis is particularly helpful as it focuses on the distributional issues of who participates and who benefits.

Van Til and Van Til identify three groups of participants—elites only, elites and non-elites and non-elites only—and focus on two sets of concerns— administrative concerns only (questions of means or modifications to the existing system) or political and administrative concerns (questions of ends or more radical changes to the system). This matrix results in six categories of participation: elite coalition, citizen advice, client participation, in the first set of concerns, and politics of renewal, pluralist participation and grass-roots participation in the second. They use examples from the programs to demonstrate that even in the first set, where aspirations were limited, elites tended to become incorporated into the system, citizen advisors serve as buffers between the poor and the affluent society and the representatives of non-elites utilized the participation of the poor to make individual bids for power. The threat of political change reduced the effectiveness of participatory initiatives, participation became tokenistic and the poor became weary of the cycle of stalemate and retreated back into non-participation. Notwithstanding this depressing history, the Van Tils advocate the development of fully democratic pluralism.

USING THEORY TO INFORM PRACTICE

Our analysis leads us away from further refinement of the definitions of empowerment and participation to an examination of the issues raised by Van Til and Van Til. Once again there are parallel developments in the analysis of social welfare and rural development projects. Both Hallett (1984), in a review of participation in personal welfare services, and Baxter (1996), in a review of rural development programs, suggest that there are very similar key issues, which provide a convenient framework in which to review initiatives in empowerment in social work. These are:

- who participates;
- for what purpose (aims);
- by which means (process); and
- to what ends (outcome).

Tabel 2: A Typology of Meanings of Citizen Participation in Social Policy

	Participation focuses on	
Participation is by	Administrative concerns only	Political and administrative concerns
Elites only	Elite coalition: elites tend to become incorporated	Politics of reform
Elites and non-elites	Citizen advice: advisors serve as buffers between the poor and the affluent	Pluralist participation
Non-elites only	Client participation: representatives of the non-elites make individual bids for power	Grassroots participation

Source: Van Til and Van Til, 1970, p. 317.

However, it must be recognized that these issues are interrelated, not least because of the power relationships between different sections of the community, and are not necessarily easy to disentangle in any formal analysis. While the distinction between means and ends appears clear, participation is often seen as both a means of achieving a product (outcome) and as an end in itself (process).

The aims of a participatory initiative can clearly vary depending upon whether the primary concern is the needs of the community as a whole, the needs of disadvantaged sectors of the community or the managerial needs of an organization irrespective of whether it is operating in the public interest to secure a public good. Therefore, the crucial issue becomes who initiates participation, whether a member of the community or a practitioner, and with what aim, which in turn raises issues of their authority, motive and stance. Van Til and Van Til's (1970) analysis suggests that the preoccupation of the powerful (agencies, administrators, managers) is to retain power and that the price of their participation is to retain control of the process. Even advocates of participation can take a de-facto managerial stance. For example, Wilcox (1994) considers that organizations promoting participation should take a clear stance on the level of involvement that is appropriate for different interests within an initiative. In other words, participation processes are designed *for* rather than *by* participants.

It is with these considerations in mind that we now examine recent initiatives within social work intervention and support. The question of how to involve those most affected in the fight against disempowerment and disaffection has gained momentum in many spheres of social work practice, for example, in mental health, community care, youth work and disability. This chapter focuses on two developments in youth work over the last two decades, namely, social action and social crime prevention. The former deliberately uses empowerment to mobilize and support disadvantaged young people; the latter focuses on the concerns of young people in relation to the prevention and/or reduction of crime.

SOCIAL ACTION AND SOCIAL CRIME PREVENTION INITIATIVES

While the origins of the term "social action" are unclear, it has nevertheless developed over the last two decades as a method of group work used predominantly in the UK with young disadvantaged people that allows them to set the agenda in working together as a group towards alleviating pressures or problems in their lives. Based on the writings of Freire (1972), the emphasis is on collective action towards social change, although Freire's original intention was on the instruction of potential revolutionary leaders within oppressed societies in order that they may: "consider seriously ... ways of helping the people to help themselves critically perceive the reality which oppresses them" (Freire, 1972, p. 134).

The method adopted by some social action proponents in the UK (see, for example, Mullender and Ward, 1991) could be argued to be equally instructive, concentrating as it does on the process of engagement of young people in order that they can better understand their predicament. The method is cyclical— young people come together, with the support of workers, to identify and understand the issues of concern to them, they act collectively to address those issues, they reflect back on the process of learning as a result of such action and then identify new areas of concern. However, different types of youth work and community development work use different approaches to social action, all of which can be seen to be both justified and effective in light of the term's uncertain origins and definition.

Social action aims to encourage the participation and empowerment of young people through replacing the pathological victim-oriented approach, so prevalent in much traditional social work intervention, with the perspective of young people as consumers or users of services and as key players in identifying their own needs. One of the main aims of social action is for workers to facilitate young people in questioning and understanding why their situation is as it is, prior to contemplating change. Only by tackling the question of why such problems arise in the first place can young people then participate fully in addressing how to resolve those problems (Fleming and Ward, 1997).

Williamson (1995, p. 8) also stresses the need for young people to explore causes as a precursor to full participation and empowerment, when he defines the objective of social action as being: "... to enable young people to understand those aspects of their lives about which, given motivation and encouragement as well as information and ancillary and professional support, they may be able to effect some change."

But the limitations on scope for change implied in this definition suggest that in the UK social action tends to be about understanding the processes of power and social exclusion and possibly gaining some influence within the system. In the USA—as demonstrated by the definitions of participation emanating from there—social action goes beyond the process orientation towards radical outcomes: the transference of power and change to the system. From a US perspective, Mondros and Wilson (1994) describe social action as "self-generated groups of people which are organized to wrest power resources from established individuals and institutions and create change" (p. 1). Thus, Mondros and Wilson envisage that it is the transfer of power (defined as 'a process of accruing and maintaining influence') rather than the transfer of functions/tasks that motivates the people involved. They identify four main aims of social action: to create practical change; to develop leadership skills; to develop a group's resources and skills; and to educate the public about both the issue and the organization.

They see empowerment as gaining a psychological sense of competence, control or entitlement, but such action is still seen as politically motivated because the participants work on public issues rather than private troubles.

Social action in the UK, in the context of encouraging disadvantaged young people to understand the causes of their plight, also implies young people's politicization, but the issues of who sets the agenda for such politicization and whether young people actually feel the need for such political action have recently fuelled a growing debate (see, for example, Barry, 1996; Breen, 1995). The extent to which social change should be strictly defined by the young people themselves (through allowing them to set the agenda) and thus risk being non-political in nature, or the extent to which it should be defined by the professionals who may want to politicize or raise the consciousness of oppressed groups—which suggests a top-down approach— is a mute point worthy of further investigation. There is a risk that the goals of professionals are not consistent with the more limited aspirations of young group members. Feedback from group participants suggests that awareness-raising attempts may push them beyond their years—"we're getting on better with him now—he wanted us to grow up and we didn't want to" (Centre for Social Action, 1995)—or may serve the covert agenda of the workers—"they [the young people] felt the workers were wanting them to do, say or think certain things, and they did not understand what, how or why" (Barry, 1995, p. 29).

Social crime prevention—the second initiative that we wish to consider— has its origins in more top-down than bottom-up methods of participation, but is still participative in the sense of interested parties coming together to effect change. In the UK, social crime prevention initiatives developed rapidly in the 1980s in response to the need to address the issues for young people which arise from crime and criminality. Also known as criminality prevention, social crime prevention concentrates on offenders (predominantly young offenders), their families and social backgrounds. It seeks to influence young people's behaviour by reducing the factors most likely to exacerbate their offending, for example, poor parenting, educational under-achievement and unemployment. Social crime prevention arose as a complementary approach to more traditional forms of [situational] crime prevention: better security and increased surveillance, which attempt to make it more difficult for crimes to be committed. Both situational crime prevention and social crime prevention have, over the last decade or so, developed multi-agency approaches to crime reduction, involving those seen as key stakeholders in the fight against crime—namely, the police, local authority housing and social work departments, businesses, community groups and voluntary organizations. While crime prevention had originally been the sole domain of the police, increasingly in the late 1980s and 1990s greater emphasis has been placed on a community-wide response to crime and criminality, again reflecting the need to listen to and involve the consumer.

However, inter-agency crime prevention panels, while claiming to be increasingly representative of the communities they cover, have never claimed to be empowering of young people as stakeholders within such initiatives. To date, there has been little if any effort put into having lay community representatives on such panels, let alone involving representative young people themselves—who are, after all, the predominant focus of such preventative work. It is ironic that such panels are keen to ensure that appropriate ethnic and gender representation is secured on these panels, but fail to encourage youth representation. Liddle (personal communication, 1997) has suggested that one would be hard pressed to find examples of young people being involved in formal partnerships: agencies are not comfortable with lay representatives. Young people are often consulted in the initial audit of local resources, but rarely are they involved actively in the process of initiating change. Liddle and Gelsthorpe (1994) emphasize that consultation with not only local agencies but also the local community is crucial if crime prevention work is to be sustainable and accountable, and that a lack of consultation can lead to a disparity between public concerns and agency goals, with a consequent directing of resources to issues "which are of less (or no) concern to those affected" (1994, p. 23).

In an attempt to compensate for the apparent lack of representation of young people on such panels, many voluntary organizations in Britain (for example, Crime Concern, NACRO and the Scottish Community Education Council) have developed youth fora and social crime prevention programs which are often run by and for young people who are concerned about their own or others' criminal behaviour. These organizations have, as a basic tenet of their philosophies, the aim of securing a multi-agency partnership approach to crime reduction with young people as equal partners in such initiatives. The Scottish Community Education Council (SCEC), for example, runs a national initiative—Connect Youth—to promote greater involvement of young people in the planning and delivery of appropriate youth services. While adopting a social action approach, in that young people are encouraged to set the agenda for implementing appropriate change, SCEC also stresses the need for a strategic approach to the agendas of the various interested parties—mainly social work, housing, the police, community education and local businesses. NACRO and Crime Concern have also recently involved young people in the setting up of youth councils, which again use social action methods to empower young people in the process of crime prevention and reduction.

TOWARDS AN EVALUATION OF EMPOWERMENT PRACTICE

To our knowledge, no literature on social crime prevention and social action exists that presents adequate data on which to base a rigorous assessment of current practice. Although our assessment is necessarily qualitative and indicative, by utilizing the Van Tils's typology we are able to consider the extent of participation (who participates) and the purposes (means and ends). In Table 3 we map out the location of recent UK social work initiatives within the social action and social crime prevention fields alongside those in the rural development and land management fields, according to the Van Tils's dimensions of participation. In this classification, social crime prevention initiatives within the statutory sector equate with an elite coalition in that they involve elites only and focus on administrative concerns. Initiatives taken by voluntary organizations in this field are somewhat more pluralist in participation techniques but nevertheless, in practice, tend to focus on administrative concerns. If the focus of participation (horizontal) dimension of the typology were adapted to consider the extent to which initiatives attempted to achieve change within or alternatively to the system, social crime prevention initiatives generally work with the grain and do not challenge the status quo.

Social action projects may equate with grassroots participation and may appear to be more radical in their aspirations, if their rhetoric is to be believed. However, the lack of empirical evidence for their effectiveness suggests that their concentration on process rather than outcome tends to leave the system itself undisturbed, and consequently, such projects may be more accurately classified as dealing only with administrative concerns. Furthermore, as their membership is confined to non-elites, the transfer of power is less likely.

Within the field of environmental planning, most initiatives have been top-down, merely consulting with non-elites on the proposals of elites, although more recent initiatives have encouraged wider participation (Sidaway, 1997b), though on a micro scale.

Table 3: Effective Participation in Social Action/Crime Prevention, Land Management and Rural Development

Participation is by	Participation focuses on	
	Change *within* the system	Change *of* the system
Elites only	Official social crime prevention initiatives (SCP) Consultation-based land management projects (top-down)	
Elites and non-elites	SCP by voluntary organizations Participatory land management plans	Community-initiated rural development
Non-elites only	Social action projects (Actual)	Social action projects (Rhetoric)

Following their analysis of social policy initiatives, Van Til and Van Til (1970) advocate a model of pluralist participation. This entails participation by elites and non-elites and a focus on both political and administrative concerns (i.e., means and ends). After decades of experimentation, the sponsors of rural development projects have come to a similar conclusion by recognizing the importance of involving the whole community and cooperating with existing social structures, if they are to achieve their aims (World Bank, 1996). Effective community-based development needs to involve well-functioning community groups, which:

- address a felt need and a common interest;
- provide benefits of cooperative working which outweigh the costs;
- are embedded in the local social organization;
- have the capability, leadership, knowledge and skills to manage the task in hand; and
- own and enforce their rules and regulations (Narayan, 1995 in World Bank, 1996, p. 56).

In our view, this amounts to a partnership (Lister, 1998; ATD, 1996) between the powerful agency and the community, resulting in shared control and responsibility over important decisions. Both partners gain more through cooperation, but it requires the agency to have the self-confidence to enter into negotiation and to delegate certain responsibilities. We would argue that this provides a solution which is preferable to the familiar recurring cycle of initiatives which Van Til and Van Til describe as the cycle of stalemate. Those interventions that are concerned only with process lead to false promises, disillusionment and social exclusion. Social inclusion requires the transfer of appropriate elements of power through the broadening of decision-making processes and an increase in the level and quality of participation of all stakeholders.

THE PROFESSIONAL AS THE FACILITATOR OF PARTNERSHIP

Participatory planning in the environmental field and social action in the social work field both aim to empower the relatively powerless and to redistribute power. Very similar discussions occur about the propriety of both professional planners and social workers attempting to redistribute power and whether their role should be strictly neutral, leaving empowerment to political activists (see, for example, Forester, 1987).

Baxter (1996) stresses the need to change the prevalent culture of professionalism among agencies involved in community participation techniques. Knowledge and expertise are not the sole preserve of the professional to the exclusion of local people, and approaches need to be more people-oriented than technically focused. He contrasts those situations where development has evolved from local people and participation is a natural, inherent characteristic of the process, with those where participation is problematic because of an externally induced, often government-led program.

Ter Haar (1979) suggests that the roles of different parties are quite different within different planning philosophies and during the different stages of the planning process. Within planning methods it is possible to distinguish between the approaches of:

- ad hoc planning: based on political pressure of interest groups;
- standards planning: where quality standards are used;
- investigative planning: using demand/supply models or the capacity approach;
- participatory planning: with and by the interest groups.

While these different planning approaches may not be mutually exclusive, certainly the first will reflect the power base of the powerful, while the second and third depend on technical assessment and therefore will tend to put power into the hands of the professionals. Only the fourth recognizes the learning that can be gained from tapping into the expertise and experience of the recipients of such developments.

Social work, by tradition, has always been an interventionist profession, dealing as it does with the least powerful and most vulnerable of society's members. Intervention was originally missionary, as in the early charitable organizations in the nineteenth century, to more recently being reactive in times of depression or crisis. Now it seems to be moving more towards an emphasis on proactive intervention based partly on consumer choice/need. The social worker is increasingly expected to respond to the needs of the client as directed by the client rather than as diagnosed by the worker, particularly in the field of disability (Oliver, 1990) and community care (Wilson, 1998). With this newly found opportunity to have their voice heard, various client groups are becoming more vocal: social work services are now increasingly needs-led in their development and often user-led in their management (Evans and Fisher, 1997, although see also Clarke and Newman, 1997). Advocacy groups have evolved as a result of the increase in social service provision by private and voluntary sectors and the latter's need (in a competitive climate) to consult with and listen to the consumers of such services. This development has created an increased demand for, involvement in and control over such provision by service users (Evans and Fisher, 1997).

Social action groupwork is grounded in value-based considerations: "its underpinning rationale is one of handing back the power over decision-making to service users" (Mullender and Ward, 1989, p. 25). However, the role of the professional in social action work is seen as pivotal and essential to the success of the groupwork method of empowerment. Williamson (1995) sees that role as: "to enable young people to learn about the collective nature of their condition and to support young people in taking collective action to address it" (p. 5), and Smale and Tuson (1993) equate the role of the social worker with that of a "broker" between the providers and those in need (p. 29). Nevertheless, there are limitations in the ability of social work professionals to facilitate the empowerment of others. In certain cases, their statutory responsibilities in relation to the client may mean that they cannot play the neutral role that is required. In other situations, their ability to transfer power is inhibited by their own position within a hierarchical power structure. Worker empowerment in the social work field, while outside the scope of this chapter, is a key consideration when facilitating client empowerment, especially in the current economic and political climate of globalization, downsizing, accountability and restructuring (see, for example, Nagda, 1997; Shera, 1997; Wilson, 1998).

DISCUSSION

It is our contention that social action methods of empowerment and community participation are preoccupied with the "why" question propounded by Fleming and Ward (1997), to the virtual exclusion of the "what next" question, i.e., how is change to be effected. We argue that it is crucial to simultaneously address the "why" and "what next" questions through partnership with the powerful. Such an approach would move us from Freire's stage one of conscientization and transformation of oppression to his stage two of "becoming a pedagogy of all men [sic] in the process of permanent liberation" (Freire, 1972, p. 31).

Autonomy of decision-making by one faction over another is not what should be strived for, but partnership within a negotiated and cooperative process. Social action techniques that are enabling in a personal development sense, and which give the semblance of control or autonomy, are not empowering in the sense of enabling the non-elites to share power with the elites and to redistribute resources equitably.

In our review of empowerment theory and practice, we advocate social work initiatives based on partnership, but we have also recognized the fallacy of assuming that transfers of power are easily achieved. Traditionally, transfers of power have been achieved by political struggle and have used adversarial rather than cooperative means, although much attention has recently focused on mediated negotiation as a form of conflict resolution, which may only occur when power is evenly balanced (Sidaway, 1997a)

Exercises in empowerment are perceived as threats to the status quo (Van Til and Van Til, 1970). We argue that this demonstrates a misconception on the part of the powerful about the basis of the negotiation in which they may be engaged. The powerful perceive power as a zero sum commodity, i.e., a finite quantity, and that any concession to the relatively powerless will diminish the amount of power held by the powerful. The transaction between the powerful and the powerless, such as it is, is equivalent to positional bargaining (Fisher and Ury, 1981) and at best, therefore, can only be a compromise between the powerful and powerless in which a fixed amount of power is redivided. However, certain Native American studies, among others, argue that power distribution need not be limited and adversarial (as often viewed by many Western European and white American cultures), but can be limitless and shared cooperatively (Lowery and Mattaini, 1997). We would also argue that, in effect, empowerment of the powerless would increase the total amount of power available without diminishing the amount held by the powerful. This is particularly important when the powerful are agents of the state, whether a social work department or an environmental agency, which have statutory mandates and responsibilities for which they are accountable and where they have to exercise power in the course of their duties. Yet there are many dimensions to power, and allowing the powerless to have influence over decisions that affect the distribution of resources does not necessarily diminish the responsibility or authority of the statutory agency. Arguably it increases their legitimacy and authority.

Indeed, we argue that the principal weakness of typologies of participation has been their concentration on a single dimension of power when power has several dimensions. Boulding (1990) distinguishes between three dimensions of power:

- political power, which can be used destructively when exercised as a threat or by coercion;
- economic power, which may be creative and productive; and
- social power, which is concerned with relationships and can be integrative.

We suspect that elites are concerned largely with maintaining political power within hierarchical structures, hence their resistance to the empowerment of non-elites. Yet the latter may be seeking the economic and social power that is rightfully theirs. By broadening the dimensions of the exchange to cover all three dimensions, it should be possible to devise the win-win solution in which all parties gain (Fisher and Ury, 1981).

This suggests that the role of the social work professional should be akin to that of the mediator assisting in the transference of power within a partnership. In terms of social action and empowerment, it is important to reconcile the agendas of young people with the professional responsibilities and goals of the host organization (Williamson, 1995). Social action cannot operate in a vacuum with young people setting their own agendas and workers facilitating that process uncritically: "All social life is subject to negotiation and governed by regulation" (Williamson, 1995, p. 5) and "both professional workers and young people live and work within the constraints of wider social realities" (Fryman, 1995, p. 99-100). It is therefore imperative that these wider social constraints are taken into account when facilitating the empowerment and participation of people who have widely varying degrees of influence and power.

We anticipate that further work on typologies that incorporate multi-dimensional theories of power will be more revealing than previous approaches to theories of empowerment and participation. We envisage that frameworks of empowerment that incorporate disparities in power and changes in the process, i.e., from adversarial to negotiative participatory decision-making as suggested by Sidaway (1997b), can be used to depict cycles of stalemate identified by the Van Tils. The major advantage of this formulation is that it removes one of the major constraints of ladders of participation, i.e., that social groups move either up or down. We conceive a structure, a chessboard perhaps, where social groups can move sideways or diagonally as well, depending on the context and circumstances, but more importantly perhaps, depending on their definition of the problem. A partnership cannot fully develop without taking into account the varying perspectives of all the key stakeholders.

In terms of research and evaluation, both social action and social crime prevention initiatives could be criticized for not fully exploring the views and aspirations of the key stakeholders—in particular, young people themselves. Much documented evidence on participatory processes has been written by professionals or academics, reflecting a top-down and strongly ideological approach. There is little material written by the participants themselves, especially in the environmental field, which gives their views and aspirations about the processes in which they have been involved (Baxter, 1996), such information being accessible only through interviews or group discussions. Likewise in the social work field more generally, little documented evidence is available on the user perspective, although this is growing in the field of community care and disability in particular (Beresford and Wilson, 1998; Evans and Fisher, 1997). Social crime prevention prides itself on undertaking an initial audit of local resources and opinions to gauge the views and experiences of local people about crime and criminality in their communities; but all too often, this is where such people's involvement ends.

In terms of their longer-term aim, for example, of reducing offending and guiding young people towards constructive activity, the effectiveness of social action and social crime prevention approaches is less certain. On a local scale, these programs seem to be successful in at least temporarily diverting young people from crime and criminality. However, while NACRO (1997) has identified several problem areas in its work with young people using social action methods (for example, involving older teenagers, helping young people to grasp the concept of empowerment, maintaining viable attendance levels and securing adequate funding), there is little, if any, documented evidence that such work is actually effective in the longer term in addressing its aims: namely, reducing crime, meeting the needs of young people, building partnerships with other agencies and empowering young people through a process of change.

Admittedly, crime prevention and social action programs with young people in trouble are notoriously difficult to evaluate because of the many confounding variables which affect a young person's propensity to resist engaging in crime over time. However, this should not preclude professional workers and researchers from asking questions about such factors as recidivism rates, attitudinal and behavioural change or changes in social circumstances. In terms of social action, independent evaluations undertaken by neutral, external researchers are comparatively rare. It seems that there have been no documented evaluations of the technique *per se* in relation to its appropriateness and effectiveness in facilitating the empowerment of marginalized and powerless groups.

Much of the philosophy of empowerment becomes mere rhetoric without empirical data to substantiate it. However, part of the problem of evaluating, for example, social action projects, must surely relate to the concentration on process rather than outcome and to the lack of suitable strategies for change— given that change is one of the underlying objectives of social action and social crime prevention work. Our priority would be for theory-led evaluation of initiatives in empowerment that cover not only the perspective of the non-elite participant and that of the practitioner but also that of the existing power holder whose views are equally crucial if a true partnership is to develop.

CONCLUSIONS

In conclusion, we return to the framework of key questions suggested by Hallett (1984) and Baxter (1996) as the basis of a rigorous analysis of participation, namely: who participates; for what purpose (aims); by which means (process); and to what ends (outcome).

We advocate the Van Tils's pluralistic partnership of elites (the powerful) and non-elites (the powerless) as the goal for empowerment, with the aim of an effective sharing of resources between the powerful and the powerless. The process should be inclusive and fully participatory and the outcome should be genuinely, rather than tokenistically, empowering of all interested parties.

As the chapters within this book clearly demonstrate, there is an ongoing debate over the extent to which a process of empowerment or participation should politicize, radicalize or merely socialize those involved. In terms of aims, both individual and social agendas need to be addressed in a negotiation that is concerned with the social and economic, as well as the political dimensions of power. Power sharing must extend to control of the process to ensure initiatives are designed with, rather than for, all stakeholders. Thus, we would argue that it is not power *per se* that is at issue, so much as the delegation of functions and tasks, which—if shared within a partnership—can motivate and empower those involved. The concept of partnership should include outcomes as well as process, i.e., unless both political and administrative concerns are addressed, as depicted by the Van Tils's typology, there is a high probability that initiatives will be tokenistic and consequently ineffectual.

Finally, we return to the role of the social work professional. A partnership between the already powerful and those currently without influence within the social welfare field requires mediation and negotiation on the part of all parties, where skills and resources which will benefit all sides are identified and shared. Within this partnership, the role of the social work professional becomes that of facilitator, an honest broker who links and develops dialogue between the interested parties so as to address common concerns. It is therefore essential that social workers are encouraged to develop the skills to become honest brokers, namely, in negotiation, facilitation and conflict resolution, without which their clients are unlikely to become empowered in the process of change.

REFERENCES

Arnstein, S. (1969). A ladder of citizen participation. *Journal of the American Institute of Planners*, 35(4), 215-224.

ATD Fourth World. (1996). *Talk with us, not at us: How to develop partnerships between families in poverty and professionals*. London.

Barry, M. (1995). Young people in the care/justice system in Scotland. In H. Williamson (Ed.), *Social action for young people*. Lyme Regis: Russell House Publishing.

Barry, M. (1996). The empowering process: Leading from behind? *Youth and Policy,* 54, 1-12.

Baxter, S. H. (1996). *Experiences in participation: A review of current practice in rural development programmes* (Report). Perth: Scottish Natural Heritage.

Beresford, P. and Wilson, A. (1998). Social exclusion and social work: Challenging the contradictions of exclusive debate. In M. Barry and C. Hallett (Eds.), *Social exclusion and social work: Issues of theory, policy and practice*. Lyme Regis: Russell House Publishing.

Boulding, K. E. (1990). *Three faces of power*. Newbury Park: Sage Publications.

Breen, K. (1995). Social action: Practice and theory—a personal reflection. In H. Williamson (Ed.), *Social action for young people*. Lyme Regis: Russell House Publishing.

Centre for Social Action. (1995). *Review of social action projects in Bradford: Allerton social action project*. Leicester.

Cernea, M. (1992). *The building blocks of participation*. Washington, D.C.: The World Bank.

Clarke, J. and Newman, J. (1997). *The managerial state*. London: Sage.

Conger, J. (1989). Leadership: The art of empowering others. *The academy of management executive*, 3(1), 17-24.

Evans, C. and Fisher, M. (1997). User controlled research and empowerment, working paper, Faculty of Social Work, University of Toronto.

Fisher, R. and Ury, W. (1981). *Getting to yes: Negotiating agreement without giving in.* London: Hutchinson Business Books.

Fleming, J. and Ward, D. (1997). Research as empowerment: The social action approach, working paper, Faculty of Social Work, University of Toronto.

Forester, J. (1987). Planning in the face of conflict: Negotiation and mediation strategies in local land use regulation, *Journal of the American Planning Association*, 53(3): 303-314.

Freire, P. (1972). *Pedagogy of the oppressed*. London: Penguin.

Fryman, L. (1995). Bypass building design in Bolton: Involving young people. In H. Williamson (Ed.), *Social action for young people*. Lyme Regis: Russell House Publishing.

Gaventa, J. (1998). Poverty, participation and social exclusion in north and south. *IDS Bulletin*, 29(1), 50-57.

Hallett, C. (1984). *Participation in personal welfare services* (Working Papers and Research). Western Australia: The Welfare Community Services Review.

Kasperson, R. E. and Breitbart, M. (1974). *Participation, decentralization and advocacy planning* (Commission on College Geography, Resource Paper No. 25). Washington, D.C.: Association of American Geographers.

Liddle, A.M. and Gelsthorpe, L.R. (1994). *Inter-agency crime prevention: Further issues* (Police Research Group, Supplementary Paper to CPU Series Paper No. 52 and 53). London: Home Office Police Department.

Lister, R. (1998). In from the margins: Citizenship, inclusion and exclusion. In M. Barry and C. Hallett (Eds.), *Social exclusion and social work: Issues of theory, policy and practice*. Lyme Regis: Russell House Publishing.

Lowery, C. and Mattaini, M. (1997). The co-construction of empowerment cultures in social work, working paper, Faculty of Social Work, University of Toronto.

Mondros, J. B. and Wilson, S. M. (1994). *Organizing for power and empowerment*. New York: Columbia University Press.

Morley, L. (1995). Empowerment and the New Right. *Youth and Policy*, 51, 1-10.

Mullender, A. and Ward, D. (1989). Challenging familiar assumptions. *Groupwork*, 2, 5-26.

Mullender, A. and Ward, D. (1991). *The practice principles of self-directed groupwork: Establishing a value-base for empowerment.* Leicester: Centre for Social Action.

NACRO. (1997). *Youth empowerment scheme: Progress report.* Walsall: NACRO.

Nagda, B. A. (1997). A social relationships approach to worker empowerment: Similarities and differences across race and gender, working paper, Faculty of Social Work, University of Toronto.

Narayan, D. (1995). *Designing community-based development* (Participation Series, Environment Department Paper No. 7). Washington, D.C.: World Bank.

O'Brien, M. and Whitmore, E. (1989). Empowering women students in higher education. *McGill Journal of Education*, 24(3), 305-320.

Oliver, M. (1990). *The politics of disablement*. Basingstoke: Macmillan.

Oxford English Dictionary. (1989). Oxford: Oxford University Press.

Paul, S. (1987). *Community participation in development projects*. Washington, D.C., World Bank.

Pretty, J. N. (1994). Alternative systems of inquiry in sustainable agriculture. *IDS Bulletin*, 25(2), 37-38.

Richardson, A. (1983). *Participation*. London: Routledge & Kegan Paul.

Robinson, H. A. (1994). *The ethnography of empowerment: The transformative power of classroom interaction*. London: Taylor and Francis.

Shera, W. (1997). Constructing and deconstructing organizations: An empowerment perspective, working paper, Faculty of Social Work, University of Toronto.

Shrewsbury, C. (1987). What is feminist pedagogy? *Women's Studies Quarterly*, XV (3 & 4), 6-14.

Sidaway, R. (1997a). Outdoor recreation and conservation: Conflicts and their resolution. In B. Solberg and S. Miina (Eds.), *Conflict management and public participation in land management*. Joensuu: European Forestry Institute.

Sidaway, R. (1997b). Policy implementation and planning in coastal zones: The potential limitations of a top-down approach. In J. M. Drees (Ed.), *Coastal dunes: Recreation and planning*. Proceedings of a European Seminar. Leiden: European Union for Coastal Conservation.

Smale, G. and Tuson, G. (1993). *Empowerment, assessment, care management and the skilled worker*. London: HMSO.

Teles, S. (1997, August 22). Think local, act local. *New Statesman*, 28-31.

Ter Haar, E. (1979). Het Beslissingproces [The decision-making process]. In J. C. Van der Perk and J. L. M. Van der Voet, *Stedelijkle recreatie [Urban recreation]* (Rapport, 7). Lelystad: WIRO.

TPAS. (1989). *Tenant participation in housing management*. Salford: Institute of Housing, Coventry and Tenant Participation Advisory Service.

United Nations Conference on Environment and Development. (1992). *Agenda 21*. Rio de Janeiro, Brazil.

Van Til, J. and Van Til, S. (1970). Citizen participation in social policy: The end of the cycle? In *Social Problems*, 17, 313-323.

Wicks, M. (1997, August 22). Let's sort poverty this time. *New Statesman*, 11.

Wilcox, D. (1994). *The guide to effective participation*. Brighton: Partnership and Joseph Rowntree Foundation.

Williamson, H. (Ed.). (1995). *Social action for young people: Accounts of SCF youth work practice*. Lyme Regis: Russell House Publishing.

Wilson, G. (1998). Staff and users in the postmodern organisation: Modernity, postmodernity and user marginalisation. In M. Barry and C. Hallett (Eds.), *Social exclusion and social work: Issues of theory, policy and practice.* Lyme Regis: Russell House Publishing.

The World Bank. (1994). *The World Bank and participation.* Washington, D.C.: The World Bank.

The World Bank. (1996). *Participation sourcebook.* Washington, D.C.: The World Bank.

Chapter 3

COLLECTIVE EMPOWERMENT:
CONCEPTUAL AND PRACTICE ISSUES

Shulamit Ramon
School of Community Health and Social Sciences
Anglia Polytechnic University, Cambridge

Empowerment is defined as:

> .. a process, or a mechanism, by which people, organisations
> and communities gain mastery over their affairs. (Wolff, 1987)

This working definition includes a collective dimension, even though it does not point out the differences in the process or in the mechanism by which empowerment may be achieved at the different levels. Most of the current Anglo-Saxon debate of empowerment, however, usually remains at the individual level of the concept, despite the fact that its origins rest at the collective level. Barbara Solomon (1976) is referred to as the first person to use the term to describe oppressed communities, not individuals. Friere's (1972) work with Brazilian peasants, which took place under the banner of consciousness-raising, was also concerned primarily with collective rather than with individual empowerment.

What is the difference between consciousness-raising and empowerment? The objective of the first seems to be more modest in that it aims at changing people's perspectives of their lives, their abilities and the impact of others on it, yet is perhaps more paternalistic than empowering. Berger (1974) criticized Friere for not taking into account the fact that the peasants he was working with knew more than him about a number of matters, despite the built-in assumption of their hidden abilities and potential that exist in his framework.

Empowerment is more encompassing than consciousness-raising, as it can apply to any mastery and does not assume ignorance of those empowered. Nor is there an in-built assumption as to whether or not people need others to become empowered or only themselves. Yet this lack of specification turns it into a more nebulous concept.

Is it a reflexive activity, as Simon (1990) has proposed? Is it one in which "spoiled," or "threatened" identities (Goffman, 1961; Breakwell, 1986) overcome the spoiling or threatening features to become "unspoilt"? Is it a process of re-creating identities, biographies and histories (Rees, 1991)? Is it about taking action as a way to assert control for oneself and for a collective (Brandon, Brandon and Brandon, 1995)?

What are the goals of empowerment? According to Rees (1991) these include: positive discrimination; increasing liberty and increasing equality—all taking place within non-exploitative relationships. If we accept these goals, then the mastery element mentioned above in the definition would become an instrument to achieving greater social justice rather than an aim in its own right. Furthermore, within such a framework, reflexivity, re-built identities and greater autonomy are also relegated to being means with which to achieve greater personal and social justice. It would therefore seem that there is tension between the achievement of power by people who have been hitherto denied it and the purposes for which power is achieved, or for which the exercise of power is necessary.

Controlling one's life, or for a group to control its own destiny, is usually about promoting greater equality and liberty. Yet it is also about achieving coherence as an aim in its own right, securing a valuable place in the world and contributing to it, enhancing self/group esteem and that of others towards oneself/group, being able to determine priorities and to use potentials which have been either devalued or previously repressed.

In exploring collective empowerment, we need to look at:

1. The differences and similarities concerning empowerment at the levels of individuals, groups and communities. Does the difference in level require a different outlook, analysis, tools; are they interdependent?
2. Why is the current debate in the Anglo-Saxon world focusing more on individuals and less on collectives and why is this not the case in either Southern Europe or Southern America?
3. Does empowerment offer a universal currency? What are the issues involved in its cross-cultural transfer? Does the context matter?
4. What is the place of collective empowerment within social work?
5. What is the relationship between empowerment and research?

Table 1 highlights the differences rather than the similarities between the two levels of empowerment. This is perhaps because the tools for achieving autonomy and mastery differ at each level. Furthermore, it would seem that collective empowerment can enhance individual empowerment, but not vice versa.

This is not only due to the fact that collective empowerment takes usually the form of group activity but also because individuals fulfil different roles within it, from the few activists, through the regular helpers, the occasional helpers, the passive members, those excluded and the excluders (Chanan, 1992).

EMPOWERMENT AT THE INDIVIDUAL AND THE COLLECTIVE LEVELS

Ideologically, individual empowerment comes from the liberal tradition, whereas collective empowerment comes more from a conflict model of society, notably from Marxism. Although Durkheim focused on solidarity as a means of combating anomie, he did not explore this further (Durkheim, 1897, 1952). He viewed solidarity as a product of a well-integrated society rather than as a means of achieving greater integration and a tool for those largely excluded from mainstream society.

Table 1: The Distinct Features of Individual and Collective Empowerment

	individual	collective
user	autonomy	solidarity
	mastery	shared understanding
	re-working	shared action
	biography	pressure group
		advocacy
		empowering individual members
carers	respect	as for users
	support	
	treated as partner	
workers	autonomy	as for users
	mastery	
	pride	
	more responsibility	
	empowering others	
community		as for users

It is the nature of the power which collectives can generate that accounts for their greater potential for empowerment. This lies not simply in the larger numbers involved but in the effect of shared forces and expertise which a group has at its disposal and which it can develop. Yet it needs to be remembered that collectives can be oppressive and have a greater potential for disempowerment than most one-to-one relationships possess. Consequently, to achieve empowerment higher investment is needed in a collective than in an individual process.

Interdependency, rather than autonomy, is a central feature in both individual and collective empowerment. Acknowledging interdependency and perceiving it as a positive rather than a constraining feature of human co-existence is long overdue in a cultural climate that celebrates the mythical value of independence. The overemphasis on independence is directly linked to the overemphasis on individualism without collectivism which prevails in the New Right ideology.

Imagery and understanding are as crucial to both individual and collective empowerment as is concrete action. This is a common thread that runs throughout any branch of social psychology and sociology as well as through examples and analysis of empowerment. Friere's focus on words and literacy, the women's movement emphasis on re-worked biographies, the disability movement's focus on disablism as a social attitude rather than on direct support to people with disability (Oliver, 1995), the value of slogans such as "Black is Beautiful" all attest to the intuitive significance of imagery and understanding.

I am currently working with a research assistant on a project titled "Seamless Services and Re-Building Identities." We are embarking on the pilot phase of charting the career and subjective experience of young people recently discharged from a psychiatric admission, including their relatives' and key workers' perspectives. The young woman who is the research assistant has herself been recently discharged from a secure psychiatric unit; she is likely to receive a grant from a mental health charity and begin her Ph.D. on an aspect of this project. We have conducted a focus group of users whom we asked to share with us their experiences of discharge and post-discharge living, as well as their ideas about how to conduct this research.

I would argue that without a considerable collective attitudinal shift in viewing her—and others like her—as being able to be both an ex-patient and a researcher, it would not have been possible for me to entertain the idea of employing her and it would not have been possible for her to consider all of this as a realistic option. Furthermore, she had to modify her own view of herself. As Goffman (1961) has suggested, master identities are internalized, and this internalization reinforces their hold on us. Thus my research assistant represents a hybrid identity. She is one of the increasing number of people in a postmodern world who live with more than one master status/identity (Werbner, 1996).

This fulfils a function for the rest of us in broadening our horizon, in allowing us to recognize and re-consider our own different identities. As a result, some previously repressed identities have been allowed to re-surface in society, notwithstanding the ambiguity and ambivalence that the re-surfacing has created for both the holders of the hitherto repressed identities and the rest of us. Sexual minority identity is a prime example of this process.

At the same time, some other identities continue to be repressed by the collective. For example, as a member of the collective I do wish that paedophiles will continue to repress this identity and let their other identities become master identities. Some identities make people the butt of hatred and negative discrimination by substantial segments of the societies in which they live, as we have witnessed recently in the former Yugoslavia.

COMPARATIVE PERSPECTIVES

Looking at publications on empowerment (Parsloe, 1996) it would seem that most of the literature in the Anglo-Saxon world focuses on individual empowerment, whereas parallel literature from Southern Europe, South America and South Africa focuses more on collective empowerment. This perhaps reflects the degree to which casework is developed as a major social work tool. Indeed, it is more widespread in the Anglo-Saxon world than elsewhere. However, the focus on casework already echoes a greater emphasis on individuals than on groups or communities.

Conversely, the rest of the world—some of which includes the so-called less developed world—provides less casework and more community work, reflecting either lack of investment in individuals and casework, lack of belief in its usefulness, and/or greater emphasis on communities as the social work arena. Even countries classified as developed, such as France and the Netherlands, have retained more community work than the Anglo-Saxon world has.

The lack of balance between the value given to individuals and that given to communities typifies the values of the New Right, which has been more prominent in the Anglo-Saxon world than in other societies. Although other societies have adopted capitalism as their predominant mode of economic production, this has not implied the adoption of capitalism as the guide for social co-existence. The way the Volvo factory in Sweden is managed, highlights more successful potential possibilities in which empowering the collective leads to more and better quality production.

As you know, we in Britain are emerging from the Thatcherite era. During that period it was politically incorrect to use the following words: collective, conflict, contradiction, class, consciousness-raising, identity, social exclusion, solidarity, socialism. It was politically correct to use the words: choice, consumers, challenge, individuals, families, capitalism, market (free or quasi), enterpreneurial, investing in people, cost-effective, total quality management.

Ward and Mullender (1991) have suggested that the use of empowerment during that period acted as a social 'aerosol' covering up the disturbing smell of conflict and conceptual division. If this has been/is the case, then we need to be aware of why this is so.

In the context of this paper I would like to suggest that the term collective threatened Thatcherite hegemony because:

- of its clear connotation with power and the political;
- of the implicit assumption in it that collectives exist (at one point Lady Thatcher went as far as to suggest that society does not exist, only individuals and families do);
- groups have a will of their own; and
- groups may become political protagonists, which may challenge the legitimacy of the ruling group to its taken-for-granted hegemony.

Thus the promise—or the threat—of collective empowerment lies in its socio-political dimension, its potential to generate collective thought, action and research.

Given the recent repression outlined above, it seems to me that the Anglo-Saxon world has much to learn from the rest of the world in terms of understanding and operating collective empowerment. This is not to deny that it has also its own useful examples to learn from. However, some of the conceptual and practice features of empowerment taken for granted in the Anglo-Saxon world could do with a critical re-examination (e.g., the abiding need to enshrine any initiative in formalities and formal structures).

The issue of the universal currency of empowerment has been raised recently by Kwong (1996) in the context of Hong Kong. He has argued that this is yet one other concept brought in from the West, more in evidence in professional discourse than in everyday practice and thus part of a fashion fad. Kwong is hinting, rather than developing, the likely tension between a

Western tradition of focus on individualism and an Eastern tradition of favouring collectives, such as extended families, communities and regions.

The focus on collectives within the Eastern tradition does not imply necessarily that the favoured collective forms were/are empowering, or were set up to be empowering. However, the existence of such a tradition implies that if introduced, empowerment has a better chance to be understood and accepted via a collective route.

It is of relevance to note at this junction that the post-Communist countries of Central and Eastern Europe are more interested in developing individualized rather than community work, and that for them empowerment sounds unrealistic and not particularly desirable. This is likely to be a response to years of enforced and imposed collective existence, and living within an authoritarian tradition, long before Communism was introduced. It is also a response to their interpretation of what capitalism is about, namely:

- a highly competitive and exploitative system from which a minority profits enormously;
- a system in which the collective, largely represented by the state, has no principled responsibility towards individuals and families.

The above brief discussion demonstrates that the context does matter to both the conceptualization and the practice of empowerment. Therefore, it should be taken into account in any analysis of this theme.

THE PLACE OF COLLECTIVE EMPOWERMENT WITHIN SOCIAL WORK

If the creation of professional social work in the UK dates to the Charity Organisation Society in the late nineteenth century and to parallel developments in the US, then collective empowerment did not feature either as an objective, a method, or a value at that stage. This is hardly surprising given the underlying liberal ideology of social work, in which individualism took the centre stage alongside the belief in an harmonious model of social co-existence.

Although social work was committed to serve vulnerable and stigmatized populations from its beginning, the root of this vulnerability and stigmatization was then assumed to be located in their own activities, with and without individual responsibility for it. Collective empowerment within this framework can be at best a method, rather than an underlying principle.

It is only when social work includes structural injustice, inequality in opportunities and active oppression of some social groups as being at the root of its users' problems of living (without excluding the place of motivation and responsibility in the equation), coupled with the belief in people's unfulfilled potential, that a space is created for the concept and principle of empowerment and for collective empowerment.

This shift in world view took place during and especially after World War II, when taken-for-granted assumptions about a harmonious world and about the belief in the overriding personal responsibility of individuals for the impact of social ills were put to rest—or so it seemed.

The ideology underlying the New Right since the 80s has challenged these beliefs in the source of social ills, and in collective responsibility for the impact of these ills, as well as collective responsibility for personal ills brought upon people by themselves (Bosanquest, 1988; Glennerster, 1989; Hutton, 1995, 1997). The challengers have argued that it is up to individuals to fend for themselves and to achieve a powerful place for themselves in the world. The role of the collective is to prevent interference in this "natural" process, in which those who manifestly fail to achieve a secure and valued social place have mostly themselves to blame for this failure. The New Right accepts that there will be always some cases without personal responsibility for failure—such as serious physical illness or disability—and that the collective will have to take care of such instances. These obligations have been:

a. relegated into a much more residual social position than before, as reflected in eligibility-proven and means-tested services;
b. put more and more within the domain of the family rather than the collective; and
c. preferably provided within a for-profit setting run by an individual who has no obligation to the collective.

This re-interpretation of the place of the collective in our lives and of the relationships between individuals in trouble and the rest of us has profound implications for the value base of social work.

The emerging prominence of empowerment within Western social work can be seen as a reaction to the New Right by those who disagree with its ideological premises yet recognize that we cannot—and should not, for a number of good reasons which cannot be expanded upon in this text—go back in time to the 40s-70s era. It is a reaction which also builds on developments external to social work, such as the impact of the women's and black people's movements, and more recently the disability movement and the wider postmodern context. All of these movements have challenged the New Right consistently, without moving back to the statism and impersonal services typical of the earlier period.

Kwong (1996) asserts that empowerment plays more a part of the professional discourse and less in its practice in Hong Kong and the rest of the social work world. I would go further to suggest that empowerment has penetrated the professional discourse as a slogan rather than as a serious conceptual and practice development. Apart from a few pockets, collective empowerment—as distinct from individual empowerment—has yet to enter British social work.

Together with Liz Sayce, the national policy officer of Mind (the largest mental health voluntary organization in Britain), I have outlined the fears and hopes of social workers from collective user involvement in mental health (Ramon and Sayce, 1993). The list highlighted the need for attitudinal change, as well as the acquisition of knowledge and skills by social workers if collective empowerment were to be a reality. This is the case even though social workers have pioneered user involvement in British mental health services.

For empowerment to become part of everyday practice, social workers would need to begin to think about their clients through the collective perspective. In practice this would mean:

- re-including groupwork and community work as everyday methods of social work;
- supporting people in pursing employment and education opportunities rather than the current focus of living on benefits.
- actively working on connecting people to networks.

There are good examples of both conceptual and practice developments around collective empowerment in Britain, such as the work of the Social Action Centre (initially based in Nottingham and now in Leicester) (e.g., Mullender and Ward, 1991), citizen involvement (e.g., Croft and Beresford, 1993), advocacy (Brandon et al., 1995) and mental health (Milory and Hennelly, 1989). There is systematic work at the level of European Community collaborative projects in which the British participate too (Chanan, 1992), where the issues of social exclusion and inclusion are at the conceptual and practice core. However, most of this is taking place outside mainstream British social work.

The empowerment of social workers has been regarded as a necessary condition for their ability to support users' and carers'/relatives' empowerment.

At the collective level, British social workers' empowerment has been nose-diving in terms of increased gagging, being bureaucratically controlled, engaging in controlling statutory activities—all supported by a negative public opinion. We need to consider seriously whether such an empowerment is indeed a pre-condition to users' empowerment or not.

I, for one, am not sure. Empowerment of one group may or may not lead to its readiness to act as a catalyst for the empowerment of another, and more disempowered group, especially when some elements of the power of the first group come via the control it has over the second group. The answer would lie in the content and format that empowering social workers would take, and the extent to which users' empowerment is an integral part of the message of social work empowerment.

COLLECTIVE EMPOWERMENT AND RESEARCH

Research is a central tool in elaborating and testing conceptual developments, as well as in evaluating practice. When collective empowerment is taken seriously, it has implications for the type of research to be conducted. New paradigm research (Reason, 1995) and participatory action research (Hart and Bond, 1995), in which the participants are not treated as subjects but as contributors to the formulation of the research aims and methodology, fit in with collective empowerment. Incorporating the experiential level of knowledge is one further (complicated) step within this framework which has come to us mainly via feminist research (Borkman, 1990).

Involving users, carers and workers as partners in the research is a logical extension of the principle of empowerment, as is employing users and carers as researchers. For many researchers in social work such a shift would require a parallel shift in their attitudes, knowledge and skills. Historically, these researchers have worked within a research paradigm in which clients are subjects, rather than participants who can contribute beyond information. The notion of empowering research would strike many of them as unscientific and ideologically biased. The debate about research as an empowering tool within social work is in its infancy. It is important to emphasise that the issues at stake cannot be equated with the quantitative-qualitative divide, but with the more fundamental issue of what is valid knowledge in social work.

REFERENCES

Berger, P. (1974). *Pyramids of sacrifice: Political ethics and social change.* New York: Basic Books.

Borkman, T. (1990). Experiential, professional and lay frames of references. In T. J. Powell (Ed.), *Working with self-help.* Washington: NASW Press.

Bosanquest, N. (1988). *The new right.* London: Heinmann.

Brandon, D., Brandon, A. and Brandon, T. (1995). *Advocacy: Power to people with disabilities.* Birmingham: Venture Press.

Breakwell, G. (1986). *Coping with threatened identities.* London: Methuen.

Chanan, G. (1992). *Out of the shadows: Local community action and the European community.* Brussels: European Foundation for the Improvement of Living and Working Conditions.

Croft, S. and Beresford, P. (1993). *Citizen involvement: A practical guide for change BASW.* Basingstoke: Macmillan.

Durkhiem, E. (1897). *Le suicide: Etude sociologie.* Paris: Felix Arcan.

Durkhiem, E. (1952). *Suicide: A sociological study.* London: Routledge.

Friere, P. (1972). *Pedagogy of the oppressed.* Brighton: Sheen and Ward.

Glennerster, H. (Ed.). (1989). *Welfare in a cold climate.* London: Heinmann.

Goffman, I. (1961). *Stigma: Notes on the management of spoiled identity.* Harmondsworth: Penguin.

Hart, E. and Bond, M. (1995). *Action research in health and social care.* Milton Keynes: Open University Press.

Hutton, W. (1995). *The state we're in.* London: Vintage.

Hutton, W. (1997). *The state to come.* London: Vintage.

Kwong W. M. (1996). Empowerment practice in social work: The case of Hong Kong. In P. Parsloe (Ed.), *Pathways to empowerment* (pp. 41-65). Birmingham: Venture Press.

Milory, A. and Hennelly, R. (1989). Changing our ways. In A. Bracx (Ed.), *Crisis in mental health.* London: Pluto Press.

Mullender, A. and Ward, D. (1991). *Self-directed groupwork.* London: Whiting and Birch, London.

Oliver, M. (1995). *Understanding disability: From theory to practice.* Basingstoke: Macmillan.

Parsloe, P. (Ed.). (1996). *Pathways to empowerment.* Birmingham: Venture Press.

Ramon, S. and Sayce, L. (1993). Collective user participation: Implications for social work education and training. *Issues in Social Work Education,* 13(2), 53-70.

Reason, P. (1988). Human inquiry in action: Developments. In *New paradigm research.* London: Sage.

Rees, S. (1991). *Achieving power.* London: Allen and Unwin.

Simon, L. (1990). Rethinking empowerment. *Journal of Progressive Human Services,* 1(1), 27-39.

Solomon, B. (1976). *Black empowerment: Social work in oppressed communities.* New York : Columbia University Press.

Werbner, P. (Ed.). (1996). *Debating cultural hybridity.* London: Zed Press.

Ward, D. and Mullender, A. (1991). Empowerment and oppression: An indissoluble paring for contemporary social work. *Critical Social Policy,* 39, 21-30.

Wolff, T. (1987). Community psychology and empowerment: An activist's insight. *American Journal of Community Psychology,* 15, 151-166.

Chapter 4

EMPOWERMENT:
A CRITICAL VIEW

Kenneth Macdonald
Applied Social Studies, Nuffield College, Oxford
Geraldine Macdonald
School for Political Studies, University of Bristol

A standard way in to a discussion would be to begin by defining terms. Unfortunately empowerment has "different meanings to different people" (Servian 1996, p. 17) so defining can rapidly degenerate into list making (see also Adams, 1996, p. 1-50). And indeed empowerment can be argued for from many perspectives: as way in to confidence (Challis 1986, p. 326); as a device to ensure professionals do not restrict need to available services (Sinclair, O'Connor, Stanforth and Vickery, 1988, p. 158); as a basic human need (e.g., of autonomy Gough and Doyal 1984); as a device to enhance effectiveness in service delivery (e.g., Griffiths 1988); and as a device to avoid routinized, non-individuated, approaches to clients (e.g., to older people, Biehal 1993, p. 454). Kondrat (1995, p. 425-426) provides an annotated list of some of the literature, and observes:

> In short, the empowerment perspective has been described as applicable to practice with virtually every client group social workers encounter in the course of practice. (1995, p. 413)

But the perspectives vary across practice, and the particular ground from which empowerment is defended (Baistow, 1994) will matter sharply when its achievements are assessed—and the ground also defines how empowerment is to be measured. As well as being of concern to the consumer or client, the empowerment discussion has extensive implications for the profession itself.

As Howe (1986, p. 160) observes: "Social work has no essential nature. Its existence, its characteristics and style are a product of time, place and the balance of power between those occupations interested in tackling certain types of behaviour and social concerns." Add the recipients of our services into that equation and the equilibrium becomes more unstable, less predictable.

Consideration of this diversity, and the extent to which the interpretation of empowerment is determined by prior political ideology leads Parsloe (1995, p. 1) to suggest that "*power sharing* might be a more honest, albeit more difficult, aim for social work." We have much sympathy with this as a strategy, enabling the specification of tasks for intervention. As Perkins (1995, p. 765) observes: "The popularity, and subsequent ambiguity, in the use of empowerment has created an even greater need for re-assessment in the applied context than in the theory and research literatures." Parsloe's resolution has the merit of addressing both contexts. But in this chapter we take a different strategy, examining the notion of empowerment from within the theoretical and research literatures. Our end point will be that some empowerment is straightforwardly about intra-organizational power; but some—what might be called deep empowerment, where empowerment is seen as defining of the self—can only be consistently and non-evaluatively read as skill and knowledge acquisition. To set out to make another free is arrogant and dangerous. To set out to provide another with knowledge and skills is a more modest—though not an easy—task. And it may make them free.

DEFINING POWER

We begin from a consideration of power, since empowerment is itself too variously understood; however all interpretations of empowerment must presuppose some understanding of what power might be. Beginning from power we may get some leverage on the rescuable components of empowerment.

Some early definitions of power are simply capacities to act. For Hobbes, power is "present means, to obtain some future apparent Good" (*Leviathan*, Bk 1 Ch. 10) and life itself is a "perpetual and restless desire of power after power that ceaseth only in Death" (Bk. 1 Ch. 11); for Hamilton: "What is power, but the ability or faculty of doing a thing?" (*Federalist* No 33). This sense of power as capacity to act is clearly present in some deployments of empowerment—as in Furlong's (1989) report of a project to empower older adults to use computer technologies to enhance their lives through network connections, where to empower merely translates to "provide the ability or faculty of doing a thing." But a more extended, and now common, usage of power refers to some oppositional component. For Weber, power involves the probability that one actor in a social relationship will carry out his will against the resistance of others; for Dahl (1957, p. 203) power becomes one actor's ability to make another do something that the latter "would not otherwise do." Whilst the introduction of such a clause is intelligible (it is unclear what it would mean to *make* you do something that you would anyway do, and very unclear how a researcher would observe this act taking place), the clause itself introduces complications. These also affect the understanding of empowerment, since it is clear that at least some of the community-care usages encapsulate this conflictual usage of power.

The uses—and possibly abuses—of power can be seen in Lukes's (1974) lively and influential analysis. Lukes works within a general concept of power which involves getting another to do what they would otherwise not do. The interesting feature of his approach—and the feature that makes it particularly pertinent to a study of empowerment—is his presentation of the varying social contexts within which power can be exercised (and empowerment sought). At the simplest we have straightforward coercive acts—Lukes calls these man with gun scenarios, a one-dimensional view of power. More complex are those situations where those well placed in the hierarchy determine the terms of the debate, set the agenda, structure the discussion (Hugman, 1991, presents telling instances of this in the caring professions). Lukes labels this a two-dimensional view of power; the social situations described are classically ones within which empowerment is attractive. Thirdly we have subtle situations where people, apparently willingly, acquiesce in their own subjugation—women are happy to be mere housewives, the elderly accept their lot uncomplainingly—where one might wish to say that they were disempowered and might equally wish to intervene to empower them. This final move, responsible for much of the appeal of Lukes analysis, is very seductive. And some of the empowerment literature operates in this area, with a desire to empower those so trapped into roles that they do not even see themselves as unfree. We, in contrast, shall be arguing against the applicability of power, and straightforwardly interpreted empowerment, to such situations. Lukes labels the analysis of power in these subtle situations the three-dimensional view of power. The dimensional terminology is *not* in fact a worked-through metaphor, and serves simply to reflect the assumption that the usages are of increasing complexity. So in what follows we drop the dimension image and refer simply to the first, second and third views of power, where the third is the most complex.

There are perhaps three noteworthy components in Lukes's position— though our concern here is not to explicate or criticize Lukes specifically but to use his introduction as a familiar framework to launch some general points. Firstly, the book presents power as ineradicably evaluative and so an essentially contested concept, so that the choice of analytic interpretation becomes itself a political (and perhaps power-related) act. Secondly, and following from this, he develops the concept from straightforward conflictual exercises to his third, overtly radical, view of power. Thirdly, along the way he picks up and emphasizes the conflictual component in the definition. We wish to take issue with all three moves and show how they impact upon empowerment.

It is likely that some view of power and hence empowerment as being essentially contestable underlies our collective willingness to use empowerment while leaving its meaning unreconciled (for on this view, disagreement is appropriate to the term, not something to be expunged). Lukes's view runs thus: "I shall argue for a view of power (that is, a way of identifying it) which is radical in both the theoretical and political senses (and I take these senses in this context to be intimately related). The view I shall defend is ... ineradicably evaluative and 'essentially contested' ..." (1974, p. 9). The notion of essentially contested is defined by reference to Gallie (1955) and although the above quotation may be ambiguous, Lukes's later usage makes clear that he is claiming that it is the concept of power (and not his metatheoretic statement about it) that is essentially contested.

For the record, since essentially contested has reached common discourse, it may be worth noting that this is a move away from the original usage (Macdonald, 1976). Gallie was concerned with evaluative terms where we could see "the derivation of any such concept from an original exemplar whose authority is acknowledged by all the contestant users of the concept" (1955, p. 180) but where the boundaries and definition were unclear (good cricket might be a trivial example). This model (agreement on exemplar, disagreement on definition) is not quite the picture deployed by subsequent writers. Gellner (1967), for example, is ill at ease with Gallie's talk of an original exemplar, but agrees that defining a concept as essentially contested locates disputes within the concept: "Gallie's central point is that a kind of inner turbulence, a permanent disequilibrium between various elements within a complex concept, is an essential and inherent part of the very life of certain important concepts" (1967, p. 55).

Of course power is politically charged, but perhaps it is a mistake to locate that political charge within the concept. Consider a fairly standard definition: "I have defined the concept of power by saying that A exercises power over B when A affects B in a manner contrary to B's interests" (Lukes, 1974, p. 34). Certainly definitions can be examined. For example, one might argue that "exercise" is an intentional verb while Lukes (1974, p. 39) accepts that the affecting may be unconscious, and would hence have to talk of A exercising power even when A's actions affected B in a way explicitly not intended by A.

Again, the formal definition is agnostic as to whether there are plural and incompatible interests, and, were there such, we have the problem that any affecting (i.e., presumably any interaction) could be contrary to some of B's interests. Such discussion is characteristic of any definition of any term. Since these are technical discussions, which can be carried out in a non-evaluative mode, this does not reflect an inner turbulence of the concept. The turbulence enters with the term "interests" (which does most of the work in the proffered definition).

We can define power; and that definition invokes the concept of interest. And that concept is contestable and value laden. Very.

THE THIRD VIEW OF POWER—AND EMPOWERMENT: PROBLEMS

Location of what constitutes the contentiousness of power is important because it affects our understanding of the problems of (with) empowerment. It makes clear that one central difficulty is being clear what people's interests might be.

Lukes's own, and subsequently popular, extension of power to the third view brings this out. The first view of power is simply one individual overtly coercing another (the robber with the gun). This—the argument runs— obviously misses the more subtle ways in which we are coerced. The powerful within a community set the agenda and terms of debate, so that certain options are not considered. The parents leaving the case conference feeling that their plans have not been seriously considered might be victims of power on the richer, second view, where A affects B by mobilization of bias. Problems of intentionality may begin to creep in around here (if the chair of the case conference kept the parents disenfranchised not out of clear strategy but simply out of incompetence, does this remain an exercise of power?). But at least interests remain well defined—the robbed and the disenfranchised are aware of what they would have wanted. The goal of increasing their power— of empowering them—is intelligible and specifiable, though, since interests of actors are interconnected, it may remain an open question whether increasing power maximizes welfare (more on this later). But both the first and second view fail to handle the more subtle and interesting cases where people apparently collude in their own exploitation and act against their objective interests. The poor, women, lower castes in a stratified society all have been at times willingly exploited. To capture this Lukes introduces his third view of power where individuals act against their own objective interests—they do what, without socialization and conditioning, they would not otherwise do.

The problems of exploitation pointed to are, at both the global and the individual level, crucial and in need of resolution. It is obviously in this area that some of the fascination of empowerment lies. But the difficulties are perhaps so large as to be intractable.

Notice that power is here no longer intentional—writers, in this tradition, writing about the power of patriarchy need make no claims about male intention, either jointly or severally. This may be to stretch the metaphor of power (with its associated attributions of responsibility). One might feel that part of the analytic force of power is precisely the intentionality that permits allocation of responsibility—"To locate power is to fix moral responsibility" (Isaac, 1987, p. 5); in the absence of intentionality, the phenomena may be better seen through a different analytic filter. It may, for example, be that gender inequalities are best not analyzed in power terms (when, for example, it is not self-evident that men should choose men as their interest group as opposed to, say, their children or their immediate family), and that to handle the systemic asymmetry in resources by gender we were better to understand the structural constraints upon both sexes. Historically and adventitiously, the abuse of power has provided a more radical rhetoric than has the understanding of structural constraints; but this association is contingent, not necessary and arguably an understanding of the structural constraints might entail a more radical restructuring of human affairs. If power ceases to be a good metaphor for the complexities, then it follows that empowerment equally becomes an unsatisfactory metaphor.

But the most intractable difficulty faced by the extension of power to these arenas where the disadvantaged collude in violation of their true interests lies precisely in identifying true interests. For an individual, at first blush it may seem straightforward enough to determine what I would otherwise have done had I not been subject to some quite targeted socialization/indoctrination. To unthink the impact of the deodorant industry (given what we now know about the informational importance of pheromones in mammalian selection of viable mates) may be straightforward enough. But the truly interesting exploitations lie deeper than that. For example, I have to ask myself what would I otherwise have done had I not been reared within one particular Protestant tradition. And these counter-factuals strip away layers of socialization that are defining of me as a person; it becomes unclear who I am. To ask for my true interests when the effects of my socialization are removed is to ask a question with no empirical content, for I then have no expressible interests. The observer may posit my true interests, but these are no more than the value judgments of the observer. It is here that the third view of power, though introduced as radical and liberating, becomes dangerous. Equally, deep empowerment becomes imposition, not liberation (and this is not an idle worry: the current 1997 version of the *Code of*

Ethics of the British Association of Social Workers imposes the task of enabling the self-realization of clients).

In fact this is a variant of the classic problem of freedom, as popularized by Berlin (1969). The pure negative liberty of Mill, where individuals are free to do whatever does not damage others, though a useful defence against intrusion, can be seen to generate a thin view of the free life. Surely freedom is a more positive thing? But once we make that move—to a view of positive freedom, a view that true freedom consists in positively doing certain things (not just refraining from doing some things)—we are, says Berlin, embarked upon the Gaderene slope towards forcing others to be free. And forcing others to be free is one of the recurrent hallmarks of tyranny.

The claim we are making is that if we consider the subjectively interesting areas of empowerment it would seem that there is no reasonably neutral intervention available. Any action—depending as it does from this power perspective on the location of true interests—is too dependent upon the value system of the empowerer to count as empowerment.

So we have argued that, while on the first and second views of power empowerment can plausibly be seen as a good to be pursued, this plausibility dissolves at the more ideological third level. For these issues the metaphor of power (and hence empowerment) ceases to be an adequate descriptor of the social processes at work. Further—and perhaps for our present project even more pertinent—it is only possible to empower at this level by deciding for another what their best interests might be—so disempowering them.

Yet the issues pointed to seem real: people voluntarily act in ways that may not be optimal (for them, for others), and the radical view has a certain attraction. So, if the issues are real, but the solution of giving power does not work (because we can not define what then is to be given), what is the way forward?

KNOWLEDGE AS THE RESOLUTION

Our suggested resolution is the generation and dissemination of knowledge. We can provide knowledge and skills without settling on the true interests, and yet these inputs may unsettle patterns of existing exploitation. There is a case to be made (Macdonald, 1980) that many—not all, but many—apparently evaluative statements are disguised consequentialist claims. If asked to defend our views on abortion, rights of children or the role of natural parents, we unpack these claims into alleged consequences of particular behaviours. Insofar as this is true, fresh information about the complexities of social interaction, about the historical and comparative position of women, may well unsettle previously unquestioned world views. It is, we suggest, reasonable to provide such knowledge (though one could legitimately disagree) whereas it would not be reasonable to impose a particular stance in relation to it. If you believe in an omnicompetent deity, it may be reasonable to expect that you be roughly familiar with what the fossil record has to say about the emergence of life; it would be unreasonable to require that you see this as destroying your faith. To provide actors with knowledge and understanding of social processes does not solve the true interest problem—actors can have here no better insight into their true interests than external observers—but may provide the route forward for critical reflection. For example, a better understanding of the cognitive processes involved in understanding risk can lead to clearer decision-making (Macdonald and Macdonald, 1999)

A parallel may help. Preston (1984), considering the notion of freedom within capitalist markets concludes:

> For my purpose here, the most valuable contribution of recent philosophical writing on freedom is the rather clear suggestion of what must be possible if individuals are to exercise free choice. Free decisions and actions are identified as those in which an agent's conscious deliberation has played an essential role.... [Difficulties in identifying this] can be avoided if we assess *indirectly* the presence of deliberate choice by examining whether individuals possess, before decision and action, the relevant capacities and conditions for deliberate choice regarding the particular matter under consideration. (1984, p. 961)

In our account, knowledge is occupying the role of capacities and conditions for deliberative choice. For us, as for Preston, the impossibility of ascertaining or providing, without imposition, free choice (or, as we might say, empowerment) forms good grounds for removing it here from active consideration.

This knowledge-focused resolution, of the problems generated by the third view of power, shapes the structure of the remainder of this chapter. Though the first and second views of power generate some sustainable implications simply in terms of empowerment, we are also concerned to note that problem resolution will require more than empowerment. There is a need for competency-based, skill-related social work. That naturally leads to a discussion of whether such social work is compatible with those aspects of empowerment we would wish to retain—we hope to show that on a proper understanding of respect for persons that behavioural social work, despite its bad press, scores well. Knowledge requires research, more intensive research than into social work practice than is currently undertaken. Indeed social work we would argue should properly be a more continuously self-monitoring activity than it is (Macdonald, 1997a, 1997b). But this in turn leads to consideration of the appropriate safeguards to protect users against research exploitation (where our answer is again knowledge rather than empowerment, for a full discussion see Macdonald and Macdonald, 1995).

Unfortunately for our argument there also exists a literature noting (properly) the social processes at work in science and research but arguing beyond that to the view that all knowledge is socially constructed. This, if accepted, would undermine our strategy of appealing to knowledge as a way forward in an uncertain world: if knowledge is as socially constructed as interest, we gain nothing in moving from one to the other. It will come as no surprise that we are unpersuaded by the strong version of that thesis, and spend some time later in this chapter setting out some of the grounds. We wish, while acknowledging the social, to argue that the pursuit of knowledge is not purely socially determined.

FIRST AND SECOND VIEWS OF POWER AND EMPOWERMENT: PROBLEMS

We have been sceptical of empowerment on the third view of power. However, if we restrict attention to the first and second views—where interests and possible actions corresponding to an exercise of power are identifiable—we see some force in the choice of empowerment as a goal.

Providing power, enabling, empowering—or simply attenuating the abuses of the power of others—have been an important part of the history of human development. For Marshall, writing in 1949: "one of the main achievements of political power in the nineteenth century was to clear the way for the growth of trade unionism by enabling the workers to use their civil rights collectively" (1949, p. 116). In contrast, in Britain during the Thatcher years the governmental view was

> that unions should bargain at a local level and have no national political role especially a confederated one. The irony is that if the government is successful in achieving this they may re-create the conditions under which the trade unions originally (successfully) fought a liberal state. (Lewis and Wiles 1984, p. 87)

Whatever the outcome—and British New Labour has yet to work through in practice its perspectives on unions—the debate around the power of the shopfloor is, despite the outdated metaphor, a major issue that substantively affects the lives of many.

But notice also that these analyses are not uncontentious. Some argue that many actions that appear to be motivated by a concern for power are perhaps better understood as concerned with culture. For example, some have noted that participants in anti-pornography movements tended to be individuals whose low investments (low status, education) were coupled with high returns (high status, income), and argued that their reaction took the form of a symbolic crusade intended to maintain a societal status quo; as Wood and Hughes (1984, p. 88) comment:

> The crux of the matter is that the manifest goals of social movements based in status discontent are not concerned with social position and power, but instead with the "cultural baggage" ... of the groups or individuals suffering deprivation.... Thus, while Protestant fundamentalism has often provided the universe of discourse for American preservatist right-wing movements, this is ultimately a matter of coincidence....

Others have argued that what looked like cultural conflicts were in fact power conflicts. For example, Bordin (1981, p. 162) re-evaluated the role of women in the US post Civil War temperance movement thus: "In the latter part of the nineteenth century at least it could be argued that temperance represented a 'symbolic crusade' not of Protestant status discontent, but of women's lack of control over their lives and their efforts to secure that same control."

Examples could be multiplied. The point is that enthusiasts for the efficacy of empowerment have to take care that, in any individual case, an apparent exercise of power is what is at issue.

But these examples also raise a further—and substantial—problem. Though empowerment is often regarded as an unequivocal good, it is clear from these examples that not all seizures of power by the people produce outcomes that we would unhesitatingly endorse. Pro-life activists and advocates of abortion-on-demand may well think of themselves as empowered. Our view of anti-pornography movements, however populist, will vary depending upon their (and our) level of acceptable offence. A classic European example of incontestably unlovely populism—the rise of support for Hitler and German National Socialism—is open to differences of narrative interpretation. For example, one of the most persistent theories of the electoral base of German National Socialism—status discontent experienced by the lower middle class—has been challenged by Hamilton (1982) who found that support for GNS varied directly with the class level of the district, and whose review of previous literature revealed almost no supporting data for the status discontent theory. But whatever the narrative, the outcome of this particular empowerment was no credit to humanity:

> We tend nowadays to associate democracy with tolerance.... We also tend to imagine that democracies are by nature lenient in punishment and reluctant to take the lives of their own citizens. If we have made this assumption, the conduct of the classical Athenian democracy will sometimes surprise us.... There does not seem to have been any limit ... to the community's rights over the property and lives of the individuals who composed it. (Dover, 1974, p. 288-9)

These examples of the (arguably) malevolent or maleficent activities of the empowered mean that we cannot treat empowerment as a simple intrinsic good. And that means that it cannot simply be taken (as, for example, Hartman, 1993 or Furlong, 1987 have taken it) as the goal of practice. We have to attend to the consequences of empowerment, not just empowerment. And if we make that move, perhaps we could dispense with the concept of empowerment and concentrate instead on skill and competence acquisition.

Though we introduced it in terms of maleficent and malevolent empowerment, the problem recurs even when no perverse motives are assumed. One way of forcing the problem into the open is to ask: What is the point of social science? What does it add to our untutored intuitions? An influential set of answers to that query has focused on the location of unexpected outcomes. Karl Popper in *Conjectures and Refutations* claims that "the main task of the theoretical social sciences ... is to trace the unintended social repercussions of intentional human action" (Popper, 1969, p. 342). Boudon's view is that "it would not be at all excessive to assert that [perverse effects] are present everywhere in social life and that they represent one of the fundamental causes of social imbalances and social change" (1982, p. 1). Perverse effects are, by their very definition, not part of the intentionality of the empowered actors.

Examples are easy to come by. For example, Pritchard (1993, p. 645) claims: "The most crucial issue for the child protection services is how successful or otherwise they are in their ability to prevent the deaths of children." This seems on first inspection a reasonable goal for the social worker, but it can be shown (Macdonald 1995) to generate unacceptable implications for the overall activity of social work. Though in this example the perversity inheres in the model of prediction that would have to be assumed to operationalize the task, the commonest source of the non-intentional repercussions arises around the activity of aggregating from individual to collective decisions.

We can not assume coherent interests within even quite small and local groups; so that the notion of empowering them becomes ill-defined. Some of the community work literature reads to the outsider as if, were we to manage to transfer power to the people, the people would know what to do with it. Certainly on some specific issues there may be well-defined local interests, and power-to-the-people would produce clear and (for these people at least) benign outcomes. But it would be a fallacy to assume that reducing decision-making to small units of itself resolves conflicts or generates fairer solutions to conflicts. In ethnic community work, for example, divergences of interest between immigrant elders and their non-immigrant offspring are not reduced by reducing the scale of groupings. Writing about user participation in mental health provision, Ramon and Sayce (1993, p. 60) explain: "Unlike many of our American colleagues we do not see the relatives' perspective as being as central as that of the users.... This position is informed by the often conflicting perspectives between users and relatives and our primary commitment to the identified client." One might wonder why the happenstance of being an identified client confers such a degree of moral primacy, but that is an issue for another day. Our current point here is the obvious one—empowered users and their relatives may have differing interests, and their empowerment does not generate a solution.

Notice that conflictual interests are problematic not simply because they may entail conflict; they are problematic because it is not always transparent how—even with infinite goodwill—we should resolve the conflicts. We may have been brought up to regard majority decision-making as sensible or even intrinsically good. But imagine three friends, or three social groups, ranking goods A, B, C (the goods could be films to see this evening or expenditure targets for health, education, defence). Person (or group) one prefers A to B to C. Person (group) two prefers B to C to A, while number three prefers C to A to B. Being democratically minded they decide to proceed by majority voting. The majority prefers A to B. The majority prefers B to C. So, a clear rank-order has emerged (A before B before C)? Not so. If we vote on C against A the majority prefers C to A. Individually coherent preferences do not aggregate to a coherent preference. Empowering the actors does not generate a solution.

Another aggregation problem arises from the fact that individually rational (empowered) responses need not cumulate to provide aggregate rationality. One set of paradoxical outcomes centres around so-called positional goods. Hirsch (1977) uses the example of standing on tiptoe to see better in a crowd to introduce discussion of this class of goods, where if we all acquire them, none of us receive the benefit; allocation of these is not best left to individual decision. But counter-intuitive outcomes also appear in relation to economic goods, when there is a collective outcome but individuals have access only to individual action. Recently the English public spent, it is estimated, some £25 million (*The Times*, London, 9/9/97, p. 5) buying individual floral tributes to the late Diana, Princess of Wales. The resulting floral carpets on the ground outside the Royal Palaces in London were impressive if short lived. Whether individuals would have voted to spend £25 million to obtain them is a separate matter, but the decision did not present in that form. The classic economic example, involving straightforward goods, is Hardin's tragedy of the commons, where it is rational (in terms of benefits and costs) for the individual villager to place an extra cow upon the common; overgrazing then effectively denies the common to all. Though the textbook examples may be somewhat stylized, for the users of social services the problems are real. Many are locked into complex interpersonal networks where individuals following their interests are unable to find a way forward out of present difficulties. It is not necessary (though it may happen) that empowering all the actors (enabling them to better articulate their interests) will free the log-jam, it may lock it tighter. In such situations it might not be misplaced to suggest that what people want is a solution to their problem. Of course we could describe such a resolution as empowering of the actors, but it would be misdescription to say that the social work task is empowerment (Dingwall, 1988). The task here would be problem resolution.

None of this is novel, the so-called voters' paradox has been around for some time. But it is as if those in favour of empowerment had forgotten these things and saw a world full of empowered individuals as unproblematic and unproblematically good.

Issues become even less straightforward on the side of empowerment if we move from individual-level social work to interventions at the level of social policy. Some of those concerned with the spectacle of excess rural to urban migration in sub-Saharan Africa have sought to address the problem by increasing the wages of the rural poor (in a sense, empowering them); the poor then used their increased resources to buy transport to the towns. An issue which has exercised the British polity in recent years is the family, and specifically the incidence of single parents. In the sociology of the family the best explanatory frameworks are quasi-economic, e.g., Becker, Landes and Michael (1977) on contract under uncertainty, and this assumes that shifting incentives will affect outcomes. Now if you think family unity useful for socializing what Parsons called the "continual influx of Barbarians"—or even have some narrative about household finance and risk-sharing—that perhaps entails that the state/society/collective-we has an interest in maintaining families. This would then involve shifting the economic incentives towards intact households, tightening the contract-under-uncertainty (making stiffer break clauses, for it has been observed that currently marriage is the most defeasible contract any of us enter). You might then growl as you are coerced (by a contract too costly to break) into devising some minimally acceptable *modus vivendi* with your rebarbative spouse; your consoling thought would be that your children would benefit (in education and career terms) by being reared in a traditional family. The weight of the current (1997) British evidence is certainly so read. (Though, it should be noted that the evidence is open to interpretation—there are, unsurprisingly, no RCTs and we may be witnessing the effects of material resources adventitiously associated with single parenthood, rather than some intrinsic characteristic of that parenting; we may be misreading what the children of such households seek to maximise and so forth). Our concern is not (here) with where the balance on this issue should lie; the point is that the discussion around what should be done is a proper discussion and one that is not answerable simply by empowering (or even by giving power to) individual actors.

Again, as with the other issues in this section, many of the—apparently straightforward, involving only the first and second views of power—situations in which we might be tempted to deploy empowerment can not be assessed simply in terms of empowerment. Resolution of these problems requires the application of knowledge, not the liberation of the participants.

IS POWER BAD?

Part of the attraction of empowerment is some underlying assumption that exercises of "power over" are *prima facie* bad. Such a conclusion flows from the "contrary to B's interests" clause in the general definition of power. We have seen why such a clause might be introduced. And, with such a clause in place, the defence of empowerment (particularly as freeing from the power of others) becomes straightforward—freeing B from being significantly affected against her best interest must be a good. But the definition is too narrow. Surely the significant affecting need not be contrary to the subject's interests:

> imagine a physician remonstrating with her reluctant patient
> to try to persuade him to stop smoking; or a teacher telling a
> student to read and ponder the meaning of a particular poem.
> If successful, each exercises power in that they cause these
> people to do something they would not otherwise do ...
> They are no less exercises of power for bringing some sort
> of benefit to the reluctant recipients. (Ball, 1995, p. 550-551)

Lukes himself sees the force of this argument; he asks whether rational persuasion is a form of power: "For what it is worth, my inclination is to say both yes and no" (1974, p. 33). Despite Lukes's ambivalence (for his intuition that teaching is indeed powerful runs counter to his formal definition of power), the answer should surely be yes. But if so, then not all acts of power are bad (nor, analogously, all acts of empowerment good). So the evaluation of empowerment will depend on content and outcome.

We have deliberately used Ball's examples, which he appears to regard as uncontentious. Some may well regard these exercises of power as intrinsic bads (doing what Doctor says, force-fed culture)—which can at best be justified as least bads—so empowerment in relation to these would be a good. We are, therefore, aware that the positioning of the boundary is disputable, but nevertheless suggest that there will be exercises of rational persuasion that involve significant affecting but are benign (both benevolent and beneficent). And for these, empowerment is not self-evidently the good to be sought.

Now none of this forms a knockdown argument against empowerment as a goal. At one level it merely says that sometimes things are just a bit confused in the long term; but advocates of empowerment can cling to empowerment as being, if not the last word, at least the first word?

But. If we are always having to evaluate empowerment in terms of its consequences, then perhaps it is these consequences which matter. So at least some empowerment is not a primary good, and if evaluation is to be in terms of consequences perhaps these should be directly maximized—we may be able to dispense with the intermediate goal of empowerment.

Another assumption that, we suspect, underpins standard expressions that, other things being equal, power and the use of power is to be avoided, is an assumption that equality—of opportunity at least—is straightforwardly a good. There is an egalitarian pedigree behind some support for empowerment. But equality is an awkward notion. We may well agree that inequality is undesirable—that does not entail that equality in itself is desirable. Equality as a goal suffers from the logical problem of being unobtainable. If we set up an exactly equal society, but then iterate it to the next generation—unless we impose draconian interventions upon individual freedom and liberty— inequalities will emerge. At the very least, if we permit people to trade and take advantage of natural skills, if we admit that individuals will chose to deplete their individual resources differently, then this will differentially advantage their children, and the second generation will display inequalities. To avoid such inter-generational transfers one would have to impose sharper segregation between procreation and child-rearing than existed even in the early days of the kibbutz movement (and that segregation was sustained by the sharp economic necessity of getting adults to work in the fields (see Bettleheim

1969)). While we may be sceptical that you will ever find a human society in which everyone is virtuous, there is no internal inconsistency manifest in the imagining of such a society. To imagine (other than at a single time point) an equal society requires suspension of human interaction.

Some theorists have addressed this issue (the wish to oppose extreme inequality while equality is not a sustainable goal) by positing a more complex notion of fairness. Walzer (1983, p. 16), citing Pascal's observation that "The nature of tyranny is to desire power over the whole world and outside its own sphere .... Tyranny is the wish to obtain by one means what can only be had by another. We owe different duties to different qualities," suggests we should focus on this notion of cross-sphere dominance as defining power-to-be-opposed: "I want to argue that we should focus on the reduction of dominance ... this line of argument, though it is not uncommon historically, has never fully emerged in philosophical writing" (1983, p. 17). The thought is that, say, wealth inequalities *per se* are acceptable provided they are generated appropriately; what is unacceptable is the use of wealth to purchase, say, political power. Conversely, inequalities in political power provided they are appropriately acquired (say through democratic electoral means) are acceptable; what is unacceptable is the use of political power to acquire, say, wealth. This analysis also matches our initial postulate: societies with, for example, extreme inequalities in wealth merit disapprobation because it is precisely in such situations that we see wealth being translated to political power.

We are not presenting this analysis as a resolution to all problems. The analysis for example relies heavily upon the social definition of appropriate spheres. Walzer's account is on his own admission "particularist" (Walzer 1983, p. xiv) for "Men and women do indeed have rights beyond life and liberty, but these do not follow from our common humanity; they follow from shared conceptions of social goods; they are local and particular in character" (Walzer 1983, p. xv). For example, suppose we inhabit (as we do) a culture within which purchasing private education for our children would be seen as cross-sphere purchase (buying educational advantage), but if we purchase goods which facilitate child-rearing—buy time (dishwashers, child-care, transport) and facilities (books, toys, music lessons, computers, travel)—these are commendable and appropriate within-sphere parental purchases. Is that social definition the end of the matter? Or can we raise the question "should this be so—is this consistent—appropriate?" If, as we suspect, the question is proper, then shared concepts of social goods can not settle the matter, so accounts of justice must be more than radically particularistic. Notice also of course that, in our example, social attitudes towards private education would vary within the UK; this practical difficulty of locating shared conceptions in turn becomes an in-principle objection to its deployment as a definition. (Our earlier point about the proper second order question may gain more bite from this particular ambivalence within the UK towards private education, but it does not depend upon that ambivalence.)

The existence of an account such as Walzer's reminds that an argument can be made that certain power relations are defensible (with a consequent diminution of a claim to propriety of the associated empowerment moves).

Also at this level of generality—and as was implicit in our earlier aside around democracy—the assumption that empowered action is intrinsically superior to disempowered is not beyond dispute. There is a famous dictum of T.H. Green to the effect that the state ought not to do for an individual what the individual could do for itself (so states provide for defence, since the individual action will not bring about nuclear deterrence, but collective child-care after the fashion of kibbutzim is contra-indicated), and some of the ideology of the Thatcher years in Britain was in this mould. People, it was held, should take responsibility for their health and their relatives; part justification was what might be called the house-owner analogy—the individual owning its own house takes more care than of a dwelling rented from the state; part was some—semi mystical—notion that responsibility is good for people. But it is worth noting that the obverse of Green's position is not absurd: the individual ought not to waste her time doing things the state could do for her. Leave the state (ourselves at work) to worry about pensions and health care and such, freeing our real lives to focus on more interesting interpersonal, creative matters.

We are not (here) concerned to defend one interpretation or the other, but to note that the issue is real and not closed and that depending upon your view of it you will take very different views of empowerment.

DO PEOPLE WANT EMPOWERMENT?

This is a variant of the "is empowerment a good?" (against the provision of which social work is to be assessed) question. Of course on the third view of power one can always disregard the answers, but that, as we have tried to suggest, is to embark on a very slippery slope.

We are clear that in some arenas an emphasis upon empowerment has been constructive. In the general field of support for the variously disabled, a stress on empowerment (see, for example, Simons, 1995; Corker, 1993) has acted as a constructive antidote to much historical prejudice; also, since here empowering translates into specifiable actions within an organizational framework, the concept can be seen to work and can be assessed in its effects. There are other places where empowerment is being used as an empty word (such as Stevenson and Lennie's 1992 article, "Empowering school students in developing strategies to increase bicycle helmet wearing"). In between are usages where, we have argued, whether welcomed by participants or not, more scepticism is in order than is customarily displayed.

The preceding paragraph, the reader will have noted, does not really address the question of whether people want empowerment (though it makes judgments as to whether they should). Partly because the information is lacking. And part reason for that, which in turn becomes a further criticism of empowerment, is that it is not obvious how such information could be obtained. Empowerment is not, as such, something about which most people have formulated views, and, as we indicated at the beginning of this chapter, the diversity of the professional usages renders any operational definition implausible. So we leave this section as an mainly unfilled marker, but before leaving it wish to make two points.

Firstly, we once heard a Spanish-American activist say, with some feeling: "What we want is not empowerment but power." Partly, as he spelt out, he had in mind that power is more actual, less revocable. Partly that empowering carries paternalist overtones—it assumes an asymmetry between recipient and empowerer—whereas ceding power can be a transaction between equals. (Notice that this is first cousin to Parsloe's 1995 power sharing as an honest, overt aim.) Further, it could be argued, if the point of empowerment is to give people the power to get things done, why not focus on power rather than the intermediate empowerment (confidence derives from the capacity to take decisions, not conversely—we give our students skills so that they can be confident, not confidence so that they can be skilful). Palpably our bias throughout this chapter has been to sidle away from power towards knowledge and consequences as conditions for effective action. But a citizen wishing to run a narrative within the power mode of discourse might be more likely to adopt power than empower.

Secondly, consider this tale: our aging relative takes his encroaching cataract to a specialist. She—properly alert to empowerment—spends her time setting out the options, ending with "You decide." He wanting sight, not empowerment, thinks she—the specialist—should decide. And we can understand the force of both stances. There are, obviously, some medical decisions (Nicholson and Matross, 1989; Lupton, 1994) one would—as subject—wish to take (dying with dignity at home in one month against undignifiedly in hospital in six). But equally there is force in a desire for effective intervention, not empowerment. We know how little information even the young and sharp-of-hearing retain from relatively simple GP consultations; information givers may well mislead themselves on the extent to which they can inform users. In the sense that the specialist has a more detailed appreciation of the options and the weight of their side-effects than can be transmitted to the non-expert in a ten-minute consultation, asking the specialist to balance the costs may be an entirely rational strategy for our aged relative. Of course user empowerment, as monitoring professionals' decisions, may have some effect on quality control (it may also help pay the salaries of lawyers), but (as we have argued in relation to control of research, Macdonald and Macdonald, 1995) there are other ways of arranging quality control.

This illustration was intended to stand for cases where it would be rational for users to leave the decision in the hands of the professionals, because the professional has objectively a higher probability of locating the right answer (so perhaps restricted to instances where the right answer is well defined). Nevertheless there are other instances where no such claim for expert superiority is made, but where the individual may choose not to invest the resources needed for empowerment. Confronted with our tax problems we have no desire to be empowered to fill in tax returns; we want an accountant to do it for us. We may well have sufficient arrogance to believe that, did we take the time to inform ourselves on taxation regulations, we would do as good a job as the accountant, but we have other priorities.

The concerns in previous sections have been "in principle" concerns, following from the logic of the terms. The present worry is highly contingent upon the facts of the case—it may, for example, be that the problems of the overwhelming majority users of social services are less isolatable than the Macdonalds' tax worries, so for them empowerment matters as attenuating future as well as present problems. All we are doing is raising the possibility that users may have rational grounds (both true and manifest) for declining to be empowered. How many do is a factual question to which we do not have the answer.

ASSESSING THE EVIDENCE FOR EMPOWERMENT

Underlying all the preceding issues, and in turn dependent on the answers to them, is the question of the research data on which the assessment of empowerment is to be made. Outcome assessment in as complex a field as social work is always difficult, but empowerment presents particular problems.

For example, Biehal (1993) provides a sensitive discussion of the some of the issues around client participation in relation to community care of the elderly, and some useful descriptive accounts of how social workers actually comport themselves when thinking about participation (or as we might say empowerment) with elderly clients. Such descriptive work is helpful in understanding what people do and in appreciating the street-level constraints on service delivery. What it does not do is address the issue of effectiveness. It is all too easy for individuals to find that those clients whom they have successfully engaged in participation are also those who have been most effectively helped, and then to move to regarding participation as effective. The obvious problem is that the elderly who are good at participation may well be precisely those elderly who are good at profiting from proffered help, so empowerment *per se* is not generating the outcome, so it is not effective. The need for some randomized controlled trials (RCTs), with careful definition of what is participation and what is the justification and desired outcome, is obvious. But though we say obvious, Biehal (1993) manages to discuss these issues without once considering such a research strategy.

Empowerment—by being tied to human capacity—is even more in need of the astringency of RCTs than more external interventions. For those, if we permit groups to assemble themselves as treatment (and possibly control), we may be liable to unspecified bias in the group composition. For empowerment we know that if we leave the assemblage of the experimental group uncontrolled we are very liable to attract the empowerable, and their subsequent performance is likely to have more to do with their prior personal character than with any of our empowering. This ready assemblage of positive feedback may be why all of us, as individuals, feel positively towards empowerment. Research, in contrast, might be described as the battle against the bewitchment of our understanding by immediate experience, and RCTs form a powerful tool in that armoury. As a profession we remain very short on hard research evidence for the efficacy of empowerment.

The general reluctance of social work to deploy RCTs (Macdonald, 1997b) may be partly to blame. In fairness—though this in turn becomes a criticism of empowerment as a viable concept—some of the blame may inhere in the particularly difficult nature of the research question. We have earlier raised the concern as to whether, if our concern is with the skill or capacity acquired, we might be able to dispense with empowerment and move directly to the outcome. So the appropriate comparison is between someone who has been empowered to acquire the skill (and has acquired it?) and someone who has simply been provided with the skill (where that is not empowerment). (You may feel that giving skills is empowerment; but if so we can forget about empowerment and just talk about skills.).

This delicacy of the research task also affects terms such as self-efficacy and self-esteem, which share some of the logical structure of empowerment. Collins's (1982) study, along with a number of others discussed by Bandura (1984, 1993), provide support for the claim that self-efficacy is a good predictor of performance. However this leaves unresolved its status in the causal sequence. Collins's results demonstrate that children with high perceived mathematical self-efficacy perform well at such things as solving arithmetic problems, persisting with attempts to solve problems and getting more problems right. However, it could be argued that their high levels of self-perceived efficacy are the result of these other abilities (e.g., arithmetic ability, persistence) and that these (having been previously reinforced) and not self-efficacy account for the better results eventually obtained by these children. Similar criticisms pertain to the other areas of more direct relevance to social work, such as health (eating disorders, substance misuse). Here, perceived self-efficacy is shown to be "a reliable predictor of who will relapse and the circumstances of each person's first slip" (O'Leary 1985, p. 437). This would be unproblematic were it not for the fact that both O'Leary and others (Bandura, 1984; Peterson, Maier and Seligman, 1993) go on to claim a causal link between perceived self-efficacy and differences in health, recovery from illness and stress management. They may be right, but such claims go beyond the evidence which supports no more than a correlation between perceived self-efficacy and these physical and cognitive differences. Such criticisms indicate why seductive variables such as self-efficacy and self-esteem should be treated with caution: they appear to carry more meaning that they do.

What we observe is more likely to be skill and confidence than empowerment and self-esteem. One last example. Brown and Harris's (1978) seminal study of the social origins of depression among women, after a very thoughtful analysis of the role of severe events in precipitating depression, located four vulnerability factors lying between severe events and the onset of depression (there is legitimate disagreement over whether the factors are correctly seen as intervening—see, for example, McKee and Villhjalmsonn, 1986—but that does not affect our present point). They are an odd assortment:

> loss of mother before eleven, presence at home of three or more children under fourteen, absence of a confiding relationship, particularly with a husband, and lack of a full- or part-time job.... We suggest that low self-esteem is the common feature behind all four and it is this that makes sense of them. There are several terms other than self-esteem that could be used almost interchangeably—self-worth, mastery, and so on. In the end we chose it because it was a term sometimes used by the women themselves (although they more often talked of lacking confidence). (1978, p. 236)

This finding (that self-esteem mediates between severe events and depression) is now routinely reported in the secondary literature as robust (and it has clear practical implications for the conduct of social work). But notice the ease with which Brown and Harris have succumbed to the temptation to move beyond their data. Confidence is a task specific, assessable attribute—we can specify how it might be measured—and is in part given us by the data; self-esteem is a much more nebulous concept, and its measurement is underspecified. Brown and Harris, like some enthusiasts for empowerment, might have done better to stick at the level of explanation their data support. (Notice, though extraneous to our present story, that the odd assortment could equally be read as measures of available social support—remember mothers' part in maintaining affective kinship links—showing that social, not personal, resources mediate between severe events and the onset of depression).

In its most basic form, empowerment presents, in sharp relief, the difficulties of interpreting data outside the framework of RCTs, for in most of the published literature, selection into empowerment is not random. If the empowered go on to display marked benefits, we do not know if this is because they were empowered or whether simply those receptive to empowerment are also those skilled at taking advantage of other opportunities. At a more general level, if empowerment is claimed as any variety of intrinsic (non-instrumental) good, there remain non-trivial problems of measurement of such a good (and these may feed directly back into our first, philosophical worry).

IS SKILL-RELATED BEHAVIOURAL SOCIAL WORK DISEMPOWERING?

If skills and competencies are the rescuable interpretation of deep empowerment, there is a case for asserting that behavioural social work, broadly defined, has the best track record at imparting such skills. It has also been open, in popular perception, to the charge that it is unduly impersonal, intrusive and has enthusiasms that run counter to concerns to empower clients. This charge is, we consider, misplaced. The argument is important both in its own right and as further clarifying what is defensible and indefensible within the empowerment rubric.

How then do behavioural approaches compare with other, non-technical and avowedly non-directive approaches? It might be argued that the latter, their interaction with their clients, offers nothing prescriptive or offers a number of alternatives each of which is presented without any particular value-judgment or recommendation. Consider this possibility.

The simplest (most apparently straightforward) example of a non-directive approach would be helping a person to make their mind up about something. It requires considerable skill not to indicate, even non-verbally, one's own preferences and biases and, even when done well, one cannot control for the client's second guessing and misinterpretation, for instance taking the worker's reminding him about one particular consequence (which he may be consistently forgetting) as indicative of the worker's preference for this. Skinner has debated the issue of control with an equally famous humanist therapist, Carl Rogers. In fact both agreed that therapists aimed to influence their client. Rogers stated: "We are deeply engaged in the prediction and influencing of behaviour, or even the control of behaviour" (Rogers and Skinner, 1956). Rogers's contention, however, is that this is best and most appropriately done via a process that he describes as self-actualization. Skinner, on the other hand, maintains that this is naïve—and Hugman's (1991) review lends some support to his views. The crux of the matter is that people are subject to all sorts of control, some structured and explicit (the law), others arbitrary and unpredictable (income, resources, health). What Skinner wishes to do is alter the balance, bringing more of the arbitrary factors of control under control. Contrary to his critics' views, Skinner is concerned that this is the only way we can ensure the compassionate treatment of groups with little or no power such as the poor, the elderly and the handicapped.

This seems to summarize the most significant difference between directive and non-directive approaches to intervention. Research on client-centred therapies such as Rogers's has demonstrated quite categorically that workers do respond to clients' statements in ways which indicate approval or disapproval, enthusiasm or distance, and that these responses affect the clients' subsequent behaviour, as suggested above. And of course, most social work activities are considerably more complex than helping people to make decisions, and the opportunities for exerting a determining influence on clients' lives are considerably greater. We would therefore maintain that it is a fallacy that less technical, less directive approaches influence clients less or empower them more. What they may do is influence clients in less predictable and therefore less useful ways. More overtly influential approaches are in a position to control these influences most effectively—or at least be aware of their effects and to use them in a planned way to achieve goals determined by the client.

We would hope that an approach which can be defended in respect of its ability to empower people, and to offer them effective help in an acceptable way, would be seen to be tantamount to recognizing (acknowledging) their importance and, *ipso facto*, their worth and dignity. The allegation is often made that behavioural social work is incompatible with such goals because of its instrumental nature and its relative disattention to life-story narratives. People's problems, indeed their lives, it is said, are reduced to so many behaviours (that could be anyone's) to be manipulated: how can such an approach safeguard or even recognize and acknowledge and empower the unique value and dignity of every human being?

Behavioural social work does indeed break down problems into identifiable and manageable proportions: behaviours, their antecedents and consequences.

Certain problems do have features commonly complained of by the sufferer: for instance it is often the case that a depressed person will complain of sleep disturbance. But to identify and itemize these is not to depersonalize the problem. Such an itemization is a very detailed and personalized assessment leading to equally personalized intervention plan, which will reflect the client's uniqueness. Notice that Brown and Harris, in the study already mentioned, who carried out their own PSI measurement on the women in their sample, found many women in the community who were clinically depressed, though they themselves reported nerves or not coping. Though it has become conventional to regard medical labels as disempowering, as attempts by the professionals to control the world, for these women provision of an appropriate diagnostic label might well have been empowering—providing them with tools to externalize and handle their problems

The intellectual appeal of broadly behavioural approaches to social work lies primarily in the empirical status enjoyed by learning theories and the proven value of the intervention strategies derived from them. It is because we consider social work to be essentially a skill-based and knowledge-based occupation, rather than one which takes ethics or values as its *raison d'être*, that we place such emphasis on an empirical approach to knowledge. An interventionist discipline must plead effectiveness to justify intervention—if we cannot justify what we do in terms of its likely utility (effectiveness) compared with other options, then we surely fall foul of "the peculiar repulsiveness of those who dabble their fingers self-approvingly in the stuff of other people's souls" (Wootton, 1959, p. 279, quoting Virginia Woolf). Effectiveness is the linchpin of ethical social intervention, and this should hold regardless of ideological orientation. We agree with Ivanoff, Robinson and Blythe (1987) that empirically based approaches are empowering to both sexes and an ethical requirement of good practice, and are not at odds with feminist perspective (see also Oakley, 1989). To disregard this and view social work as intrinsically ethical would entail (if it is to be other than vacuous) that the decisions made by social workers would properly differ with the differing ethical principles of the decider; it is not at all clear where this would leave the interests of the client (akin to the point made earlier on the third view of power). Put it another way: power is ineluctably part of social work interactions—no amount of moral emphasis can dissolve that away—but a view of social work as evidence-based introduces a strong form of accountability, both for individuals and the agencies in which they work (see Macdonald, 1990). And for those of us involved in the training of social workers, the remit of evidence-based social work provides a clear specification for a coherent course. We can give our students skills (empower them), not act as thought police.

Of course behavioural social work has moved forward since Skinner's original insights. But it is worth emphasizing that, even at its most astringent, behaviourism carried a more humanist moral force than the demonology might suggest. One of Skinner's most powerful messages is that to refrain from intervening in the contingencies governing human behaviour, to refrain from enabling groups and individuals to see how their difficulties are created and maintained, is to abandon them to those contingencies. *Beyond Freedom and Dignity* is, in essence, a treatise on empowerment. Understanding what determines our behaviour, and that of others, provides an important first step to change. This, for behaviourists, is what insight is about. It is rarely a sufficient condition for change, and not always a necessary one—and this is why it behoves us to think carefully about how, as well as whether, we should use any influence we are lucky enough to have.

Finally, social work is not just a caring profession, and social work agencies do not have the subtitle rent-a-friend, even though befriending and caring may be important aspects of social work. The already cited *Code of Ethics* of the British Association of Social Workers contains an exhortation not to lose concern for clients' suffering even when unable to help; that misapplies an obligation of friendship to an inappropriate setting. (Social workers characteristically need help to close cases, not encouragement to fret when they can do nothing.) And it may be that empowering falls better within the role of friend and political activist than it does as a goal of social work. Though it should be clear from what has gone before that we are unpersuaded of its unqualified pertinence even to the activist.

KNOWLEDGE DEFINES POWER, NOT POWER KNOWLEDGE

We are—particularly in trying to make sense of the third view of power, in examining what social work might do and whether that empowers—relying quite heavily upon the importance of empirically based (ideally experimentally based) knowledge. As we noted earlier, there exists an active intellectual tradition which would reverse the entailments we propose and see knowledge as determined by power relations.

Kondrat (1995) provides an insightful analysis of some aspects of empowerment, and the analysis leads to conclusions, with some of which we would agree.

> The framework advocated here suggests one alternative to psychodynamic interpretations in the supervision of students. In this framework, self-awareness as a

psychological concept becomes superseded by the notion of critical discernment.... If practised correctly, critical discernment as a supervisory tool has the potential to keep student supervision and self-reflection within the arena of learning (as opposed to therapy), where, in most cases, it appropriately belongs. (Kondrat, 1995, p. 421)

But her route involves invoking Habermas and the sociology of science. Some sociology of science has moved from an awareness of the social forces at work in science, to a claim that all knowledge is socially constructed

So, while not discarding the insights of the sociology of science, we take the route to independence from ideology to be scientific, not ideological. Better understanding of the nature and extent of the evidence (which involves understanding of the logic of evidence) is the route to freedom of thought. And, in that sense, to empowerment.

CONCLUSION

This chapter has been critical of many facets of the concept empowerment. We have tried, perhaps not always successfully, to refrain from scoring points against individual authors and to avoid taking advantage of the diversity of voices in playing one view off against another. But the chapter has also a positive purpose, displaying, we would argue, a clear role for professional technical competence, sensitively applied. We have argued that, even in straightforward instances of empowerment, knowledge of social consequences is necessary before the empowerment can be efficacious. We have argued that apparently directive empirically based social work is the most empowering. And we have argued that the provision of knowledge is the only defensible route to empowerment when dealing with the third view of power. Exactly 400 years ago Francis Bacon published his assertion that 'knowledge itself is power.' The content and acquisition strategies of knowledge have altered in the intervening period—perhaps the most marked change being the realization that knowledge is continually adapting and developing. With these provisos, we share Bacon's admiration of knowledge. It is cumulative, and in that sense irreversible (others cannot take it away once it has been given), and irremediably open-ended. Come to think of it, that might not be a bad definition of empowerment.

REFERENCES

Adams, R. (1996). *Social work and empowerment*. London: Macmillan.

Baistow, K. (1994). Liberation and regulation?: Some paradoxes of empowerment. *Critical social policy* 14(3), p. 34-6.

Ball, T. (1995). Power. In R. E. Goodwin and P. Pettit (Eds.), *A companion to contemporary political philosophy*. Oxford: Blackwell.

Bandura, A. (1984). Recycling misconceptions of perceived self-efficacy. *Cognitive Therapy and Research*, 8(2), 31-55.

Bandura, A. (1993). Perceived self-efficacy in cognitive development and functioning. *Educational-psychologist*, 28(2), 117-148.

Becker, G. S., Landes, E. M. and Michael, R. T. (1977). An economic analysis of marital instability. *Journal of Political Economy* 85, 1141-1187

Berlin, I. (1969). *Four essays on liberty*. Oxford: Oxford University Press.

Bettelheim, B. (1969). *The children of the dream*. London: Thames and Hudson.

Biehal, N. (1993). Participation, rights and community care. *British Journal of Social Work* 23, 443-458.

Bordin, R. (1981). *Woman and temperance: The quest for power and liberty, 1973-1900*. Philadelphia: Temple University Press.

Boudon, R. (1982). *The unintended consequences of social action*. London: Macmillan.

Brown, G. and Harris, T. (1978). *Social origins of depression*. London: Tavistock.

Challis, D. (1986). Case management and consumer choice: The Kent Community Care scheme. In D. Clode, C. Parker and S. Etherington (Eds.), *Towards the sensitive bureaucracy: Consumers, welfare and the new pluralism*. Aldershot: Gower.

Collins, J. (1982). *Self-efficacy and ability in achievement behaviour*. Paper presented at the meeting of the American Educational Research Association, New York.

Corker, M. (1993). Integration and deaf people: The policy and power of enabling environments. In J. Swain, V. Finkelstein, S. French and M. Oliver (Eds.), *Disabling barriers—enabling environments*. Milton Keynes: OUP.

Dahl, R. A. (1957). The concept of power. Reprinted in R. Bell, D. V. Edwards and R. H. Parekh (Eds.), (1969). *Political power: A reader*. London: Collier Macmillan.

Dingwall, R. (1988). Empowerment or enforcement: Some questions about power and control in divorce mediation. In R. Dingwall and J. M. Eckelaar (Eds.), *Divorce mediation and the legal process*. Oxford: Clarendon Press.

Dover, K. J. (1974). *Greek popular morality, in the time of Plato and Aristotle*. Oxford: Blackwell.

Furlong, M. (1987). A rationale for the use of empowerment as a goal in casework. *Australian Social Work* 40, 25-30.

Furlong, M. S. (1989). Crafting an electronic community: The seniorNet story. *International Journal of Technology and Ageing*, 2, 125-134.

Gallie, W. B. (1955). Essentially contested concepts. *Proceedings of the Aristotelian Society*, LVI, 167-168.

Gellner, E.(1967). The concept of a story. *Ratio*, ix , 49-66.

Gough, I. and Doyal, L. (1984). A theory of human needs. *Critical Social Policy* 10, 6-38.

Griffiths, R. (1988). Does the public service serve? The consumer dimension. *Public Administration*, 66, Summer.

Hamilton R. (1982). *Who voted for Hitler?* Princeton: Princeton University Press.

Hartman, A. (1993). The professional is political. *Social Work* 38, 365-6.

Hirsch, F. (1977). *Social limits to growth.* London: Routledge & Kegan Paul.

Howe, D. (1986). *Social workers and their practice in welfare bureaucracies.* London: Gower.

Hugman, R. (1991). *Power in caring professions.* London: Macmillan.

Isaac, J. (1987). *Power and Marxist theory: A realist view.* Ithaca, NY: Cornell University Press.

Ivanoff, A., Robinson, E. A. R. and Blythe, B. (1987). Empirical clinical practice from a feminist perspective. *Social Work,* May, 417-423.

Kondrat, M. E. (1995). Concept, act and interest in professional practice: Implications of an empowerment perspective. *Social Service Review* 69, 405-428

Lewis, N. and Wiles, P. (1984). The post-corporatist state? *Journal of Law and Society* 11, 65-90

Lukes, S. (1974). *Power: A radical view* (pp. 9). London: Macmillan.

Lupton, D. (1994). Power relations and the medical encounter. In *Medicine as culture: Illness, disease and the body in Western societies.* London: Sage.

Macdonald, G. M. (1990). Allocating blame in social work. *British Journal of Social Work*, 20, 525-546.

Macdonald, G. M. and Macdonald K.I. (1995). Ethical issues in social work research. In D. Smith and R. Hugman (Eds.), *Ethical issues in social work* (pp. 46-64). London: Routledge.

Macdonald, G. (1997a). Social work: Beyond control? In A. Maynard and I. Chalmers (Eds.), *Non-random reflections on health services research. On the 25th anniversary of Archie Cochrane's effectiveness and efficiency.* Plymouth: BMJ Publishing Group.

Macdonald, G. (1997b). Social work research: The state we're in. *Journal of Interprofessional Care*, 11(1), 57—65.

Macdonald, K. I. (1976). Is "power" essentially contested? *British Journal of Political Science*, 6, 380-382.

Macdonald, K. I. (1980). Time and information in political theory. In M. Freeman and D. Roberston (Eds.), *The frontiers of political theory* (pp. 140-172). Brighton: Harvester Press.

Macdonald, K. I. (1995). Comparative homicide and the proper aims of social work: A sceptical note. *British Journal of Social Work*, 25, 489-497.

Macdonald, K. I. and Macdonald, G. (1999). Perceptions of risk. In P. Parsloe (Ed.), *Risk assessment in social care and social work: Research highlights.* London: Jessica Kingsley.

Marshall, T. H. (1949). Citizenship and social class, [Lecture, Cambridge 1949]. In *Sociology at the crossroads and other essays* (pp. 67-127). Ch IV.

McKee, D. and Villhjalmsonn. (1986). Life stress, vulnerability and depression: A methodological critique of Brown et al., *Sociology*, 20, 589-600.

Nicholson, B. L. and Matross, G. (1989). Facing reduced decision-making capacity in health care: Methods for maintaining client self-determination. *Social-Work*, 34, 234-238.

Oakley, A. (1989). Who's afraid of the randomised controlled Trial? Some dilemmas of the scientific method and "good" research practice. In *Women and Health*, 15, 25-59.

O'Leary, A. (1985). Self-efficacy and health. *Behaviour Research and Therapy*, 23, 437-451.

Parsloe, P. (1995). The concept of empowerment in social work practice. *Hong Kong Journal of Social Work*, 29, 1-11.

Perkins, D. D. (1995). Speaking truth to power: Empowerment ideology as social intervention and policy. *American Journal of Community Psychology*, 23, 765-794

Peterson, C., Maier, S. and Seligman, M. E. P. (1993). *Learned helplessness: A theory for the age of personal control.* New York: Oxford University Press.

Popper, K. (1969). *Conjectures and refutations: The growth of scientific knowledge*, third edition. London: Routledge & Kegan Paul.

Preston, L. M. (1984). Freedom, markets, and voluntary exchange. *American Political Science Review*, 78, 959-970.

Pritchard, C. (1993). Re-analysing children's homicide and undetermined death rates as an indication of improved child protection: A reply to Creighton. *British Journal of Social Work*, 23, 645-652.

Ramon, S. and Sayce, L. (1993). Collective user participation in mental health: Implications for social work education and training. *Issues in Social Work Education*, 13(2), 53-70.

Rogers, C. R. and Skinner, B. F. (1956). Some issues concerning the control of human behavior: A symposium. *Science*, 124, 1057-1066.

Servian, R. (1996). *Theorising empowerment: Individual power and community care.* Bristol: Policy Press.

Simons, K. (1995). Empowerment and advocacy. In N. Malin (Ed.), *Services for people with learning disabilities.* London: Macmillan.

Sinclair, I., O'Connor, P., Stanforth, I. and Vickery, A. (1988). *Bridging two worlds— Social work and the elderly living alone.* Aldershot: Gower.

Stevenson, T. and Lennie, J. (1992). Empowering school students in developing strategies to increase bicycle helmet wearing. *Health Education Research*, 7, 555-566.

Walzer, M. (1983). *Spheres of justice.* New York: Basic Books.

Wood, M. and Hughes, M. (1984). The moral basis of moral reform: Status discontent vs. culture and socialization as explanations of anti-pornography social movement adherence. *American Sociological Review*, 49, 86-99.

Wootton, B. (1959). *Social science and social pathology.* London: Allen Unwin.

Chapter 5

A DIALECTIC DISCOURSE AS A
STRATEGY FOR EMPOWERMENT

Salvatore Imbrogno
College of Social Work
The Ohio State University

The importance of empowerment arises whenever the disparity between opposing values increases exponentially in favour of one and need arises to consider ways to modify the power relations. A power relation exists between those who make critical decisions in social policy and those affected by them— a situation referred to as "deep empowerment" in contrast to "structural and behavioral empowerment" discerned in social work practice models.

The later attempts to decrease the degree of inequities between extreme sets of values by consciousness-raising; by nurturing, facilitating, mediating, mobilizing and/or becoming social and organizational reformers. In this context, empowerment is perceived as an supportive and enabling concept. However, power implies confrontation and argumentation and, therefore, is encapsulated with negative connotations of coercion, intimidation and conflict.

An apparent strategy to structural/behavioural empowerment is to gain access to people and institutions whose positions enable them to mitigate and meliorate the problems of social, political or economic disparity. The population usually involves the most vulnerable and least empowered; namely, the oppressed and those living in poverty. A desirable outcome is to have a need, want or desire met in segments, even if this means that the problem that created the situation is not solved. Implicit in this strategy is to acquire a social benefit or service without solving the problem; or changing the problematic situation and/or power relation. By maintaining and preserving the system, the hope is that serial and fragmentary increments will limit or lessen the disparity between the haves and have nots.

Viewed from a power perspective, when the need for empowerment arises and precipitates claims and demands on the system, it suggests an impending social crisis that might jeopardize the existing power relations. In turn, this will mean changing the norms and values that set rules and regulations for engagement. It can be said that the empowerment movement has produced the following insights:

1. Empowerment arises as a societal reaction to social exclusion bordering a social crisis.
2. Empowerment by its very nature is problem focused and conflict oriented.
3. Empowerment, however way defined in process, content or product, is contingent upon those in power who make critical decisions that determine the conditions under which changes or modifications are possible.

This inquiry pursues a search for an explanation as to why social work distinguishes between deep power or structural empowerment in practice. It begins with an apparent commitment to a paradigm; a world view as to how best a constituency can meet its needs, wants and desires without disrupting the system's equilibrium. Given this world view of working within the established norms of the system, consensus becomes a tactical outcome for empowerment; namely, a constituency is empowered when it can realize incremental adjustments to disparities in relations with others while still maintaining and preserving the system. Hence, the recent interest in empowerment is viewed by some as not a paradigmic shift but rather a "conceptual deodorant" for a movement in the 90s (Adams, 1996; Page, 1992; Baistow, 1994).

Conversely, a constituency strives for consensus in power relations as a means to realize social changes to the values and norms of that system. This represents a transformation of focus from empowerment as resolution, remedy, restitution and restoration to empowerment as a process by which power is acquired, developed and used for equalizing and democratizing the power relations. In this view, the key to empowering practice is to seek changes not only through winning power but through transforming it (Adams, 1996) into new patterns and relations.

The first stage to this inquiry is to establish the meaning given to these two world views; namely, incremental and rational consensus. This serves as a means to consider the possibility of a paradigmic shift while providing an analytical framework for establishing distinctive meaning to power and empowerment. The second stage reflects on how each conceptualizes and specifies problems that precipitate the need for empowerment and/or power in the first place. Empowerment is a response and/or reaction to social issues and/or social policy problems that are initiated by social workers as a professional practice. When power is introduced in the human and social problematic situations, action, interaction and transactions are generated for change.

The common core to empowerment or power are matters of value choices (what do you want to change, where do you want to go, what do you need and how will you get there?) related to the structuring of problems. A third stage in this inquiry is a comparative analysis of incremental and rational consensus. This leads to the strategies and tactics for initiating, participating and contributing in a dialectic discourse. This becomes the principle means for achieving a rational consensus. A paradigmic shift requires new ways of knowing that affects conventional professional role and function.

EXISTING AND EMERGING PARADIGMS: INCREMENTAL AND RATIONAL

Consensus is an outcome of a group solidarity in a unanimity over a value, sentiment or belief. Values perceived as a shared symbolic system serve as criteria or standards for selecting among an array of alternatives. A social consensus, therefore, becomes a parsimonious process to confront the clustering of values characterized in opposing positions. An incremental consensus has a utility value in a plurality of diverse interest. It is an expedient and pragmatic process by which to resolve clashes and move away from a social ill. Small change in increments that are serial, remedial and fragmentary are accepted as a desirable outcome in a clash of values.

It is assumed in social work practice models that empowerment can only be attained through an incremental consensus; that is, when opposing values over a desirable state are at odds, pragmatism and expediency demand compromise. An incremental consensus ought not to be viewed as sacrosanct to resolving a clash of values. In fact, it can evolve into a bargaining and compromise process that is exceedingly coercive, intimidating and, at the least, disingenuous.

In contrast, a rational consensus begins with a premise that a clash of values in pluralistic systems is a positive occurrence and a vital ingredient for change in human and social activity. Critical reasoning expressed through a

Socratic method of a dialectic discourse takes the view that opposing values can be intellectually investigated through an unconstrained dialogue. This discourse leads to rational consensus: a more advanced terminal goal state at a higher and richer level of social and intellectual communication.

A rational consensus is genuine: a discursively achieved consensus that becomes a standard for a critique of distorted communication represented by the parochial positions taken by conflicting and contradictory positions. Other forms of consensus are established under coercive conditions; for example, to fight, surrender or flee. Incremental and rational consensus characterize different world views and provide different specifications on how decisions for equity and equality ought to be structured and analyzed for social change.

POWER, THE CRITICAL COMPONENT TO EMPOWERMENT

At this point, it would be propitious to define the meaning of power as it relates to rational consensus. It is not viewed to mean that when confronted with an opposing value one must fight to the end with violence, coercion and intimidation. Nor does it suggests that those not in power acquiesce to those in power (surrender), willingly or unwillingly. It obviates too against viewing power as belonging to those who can create the conditions for non-decisions, that is, eliminate, omit or restrict critical issues from being placed on the agenda. All of these dimensions to power prevail at given times, places and actors in similar and different situations.

Here the acquisition and utilization of knowledge, information, technology and communication is power (knowledge is power)—a form most conducive to the ethics, goals and objectives of professional social work practice.

There seems to be a general awareness that power and empowerment are intertwined. In this regard, and without any conscious realization, the acquisition and use of power for effecting social change is being reintroduced into social work practice. Even with a positive interpretation of deep empowerment, the propensity is to resort to the stereotyped and routine supportive methods and techniques designed to adjust the individual, group or community to the exigencies of their situation. For example, the conventional modes of intervention such as negotiating, advocating and mediation are used by practitioners to assist and involve constituents in the problem solving processes by giving support and expertise about problems and systems; using empowerment as a group and community approach (Lee, 1994).

When the acquiring power is taken seriously, it is translated to mean influencing and persuading those in power to be benevolent on behalf of an "oppressed people;" always within the context of the existing rules of the game prescribed by those with authority and power: "Oppressed people need the power to persuade the people with the power to make the right decisions" (Richan, 1991, p.3).

This modern interpretation of empowerment does not come close to an earlier version of social and community action programs where the social worker's knowledge skills were vital in mobilizing, organizing and managing a constituency for a decisive course of action. It is difficult to discern what is new and different about contemporary social work empowerment practices: "This approach [empowerment] is the beginning of a new way to practice social work" (Lee, 1994, p.xiii) and "how social action organizations pursue and apply power... shape our view of organizing as exercising power"(Mondrous and Wilson, 1994, p. 47).

The Mobilization for Youth, as the forerunner to the Office of Economic Opportunity, is an excellent example of an earlier version of empowerment where public funds were made available to community groups as the primary means to make demands and claims on government. If this unique experience in public sector ends through private sector means were built upon in social work practice, empowerment would have transgressed into power. That is, strategies of involvement in power relations (ends) and tactics for intervention in political processes (means) would have produced profession knowledge "in and about" power as the focal point to social work practice skills for social change.

Modern interpretations of empowerment have not strengthened or reinforced the primordial mission of social work nor accumulated knowledge, skills and competence to actively engage comfortably and successfully in the dynamics of power and politics. This requires two major accomplishments:

1. Social work must colonize its knowledge so as to reach a point of expertise and specialization in the use of "knowledge is power."
2. Since to date this has not been achieved, social work must retract and build a theoretical conceptualization, an epistemological foundation with methodological directives that can integrate empowerment and power.

EMPOWERMENT AND A MOBILIZATION OF BIAS

The combinatorial, causal and cumulative effects of plurality, utilitarianism and incrementalism have become the mainstay to social work empowerment practice. The outcome is disjointed incrementalism or social adjustments to periodic social perturbations between competing and conflicting groups. Increments are remedial, serial and fragmentary (Braybrooke and Lindblom, 1963). It requires a constituency to make a claim or demand on the system within prescribed conditions; that is, conforming and complying to the rules of the game. This is a

> ...mobilization of bias a set of predominant values, beliefs, rituals and institutional procedures (rules of the game) that operate systematically and consistently to the benefit of certain persons and groups at the expense of others. (Barchrach and Baratz, 1970, p.43)

Incremental decisions for empowerment strengthen and reinforce conventional thinking about next steps. Clients or a client group are expected to make daily life more rewarding by "sharing in power partnership with others" or to foster clients' use of their own strengths in the process of searching for and consolidating enhanced self-esteem, health, community, security and personal and social power (Weick, 1982, 1990; Cook, 1992).

No doubt it is vital to mobilize and organize for mutual reinforcement and supportive gatherings of constituents working toward a tangible social change. The personal and political ought to be linked to overcome the internalized oppression that characterizes marginalized people. The sharing of grief and, above all, friendship are sources of comfort with great potential for culminating into power (Bishop, 1994). Perhaps all of this is a source of strength, security, protection and even a consciousness-raising against oppression. Deep empowerment, however, requires acquiring and using power as a means of producing qualitative social change.

Empowerment as conceived in social work empowerment models must be transformed into power; that is, using rational consensus to create a syncretic construct:

> ...a model which seeks to reconcile competitive paradigms by raising the subject of inquiry to a higher level of abstraction. In general, a syncretic construct builds on restricted (parochial) perspectives and attempts to procure broader paradigm ... by eliminating the a priori predicates that underlie the several competing constituents, thus isolating the grounds available for complementation. (Sutherland, 1978, p.313)

To acquire power and to be empowered means having equal access to information that is affected and being affected by all those parties to a dispute. Each position to a dispute is expected to contribute and participate in an open and free exchange of this information. It is through a critical dialogue that we can discover new ways of knowing and to justify claims and demands on any social policy issue or problem. In sum, engaging directly in power relations as an equal participant changes both the basis for power and the problem itself. Hence, what is sorely needed is understanding and accepting the sets of assumptions governing a syncretic construct.

THE RELATION BETWEEN POWER AND EMPOWERMENT

Power, authority and influence constitute the critical components of being empowered. Social workers are reluctant to impose sanctions or use coercive measures in a direct frontal confrontation. And rightly so. Social work relies heavily upon persuasion and influence to resolve policy problems. As noted earlier, the empowerment models rely heavily on traditional social work tactics of mediation, facilitation, advocacy, negotiation and education, the characteristics of a utilitarian, pluralistic and incremental approach to social work theory and practice (Connaway and Gentry, 1988).

Reconciling opposing positions predicated upon influence and persuasion, as defined by proponents of empowerment, is effective if juxtaposed toward changing the basis and nature of the existing the power relation. Social work has historically placed a self-imposed limitation on reaching this "degree of confrontation" by substituting its professional authority in favour of persuasion. This has been the case in spite of a rich body of literature that would indicate otherwise (Piven and Cloward, 1971).

Perhaps it is inevitable that social work should focus on being empowered rather than becoming powerful because of its heavy reliance on professional authority to justify its actions (i.e., the achieved or ascribed statuses of its workers' expertise; its social network of information and use of communication); its professional ethics about the rightness or wrongness, goodness or badness of policies and their consequences (i.e., mode of "value critical"); and finally, its professional methods and techniques (mode of analycentric) that are regarded as valuable and adaptable to desirable courses of action. In sum, social work analycentric methods for empowering are claims on the basis of assumptions about the validity and reliability of methods and techniques used by social workers.

Unlike medicine and perhaps law, social work has been unable to colonize its knowledge, the epitome to acquiring authority (i.e., knowledge is power).

And by concentrating on methods, social work has become rich in modes of treatment that have produced an eclectic set of techniques but without their integration into a unified knowledge foundation. More specifically, influence and authority, in and of themselves, are not directly aimed at changing the existing power relation or its structure. Nor does the foregoing statement, if reflective of the general thinking in social work, encourage or prepare social workers for institutional leadership roles or functions in social change. Social workers need not "be visible or responsible for all action tasks. Instead they can consciously motivate people and help them to take their own action" (Mondrous and Wilson,1994, p.185).

Social work empowerment models must go beyond being enabling, supporting and facilitating to acquire and use knowledge as power to determine the where, what and how things can, will and must change; to develop knowledge skills in use of information and adopting social communication networks that strengthen and reinforce critical thinking. This is vital for creative decisions for complex problem solving.

EMPOWERMENT AND POWER AS A RESPONSE TO ISSUES AND PROBLEMS

It can be argued that the disparity in the power relations is a natural state of social and human affairs. For example, determining the basis for social allocations, the nature of social provisions, methods of financing and the structuring of the human service system are unresolved social policy issues and problems. Disputes over which end of the pendulum society ought to adopt has created social perturbations (i.e., social insurance or public assistance programs). Positions taken on what is thought to be right or wrong and good and bad invariably generate the need for action, reaction, interaction and sometimes, proaction.

Exercising power or to be empowered is always contingent upon the relative importance of conflicting and opposing values in the mind of the social worker, the constituency and others and always evolves within the context of a power relation. Knowledge skills and competence "in and about" the policy process are steps in the right direction but they are no guarantee that one has acquired power: "If practitioners and beneficiaries, professionals and recipients, workers and clients apply skills to analyze the processes whereby policy comes into being, they are empowered" (Flynn, 1992, p.1).

Knowledge about content and outcome is equally important. Knowledge of process should be interlinked with improving and advancing the quality of content relative to achieving more desirable and higher level outcomes. It takes access to the power relation to create a synergy of content, process and outcomes. Acquiring this capability allows the social worker to contemplate the "know where" of desirable outcomes, the "know what" of design and resources needed to get there and the "know how" to get it done.

When defined as an adversarial struggle and when one group is in a position to coerce, intimidate and punish another with sanctions for non-conformity, power is oppressive and a possession of the elite. Some would argue that the elite power and/or the oligarchy of the elite are supposed to be a natural state in human relations:

> ... In all societies—from societies that are very meagerly developed and have barely attained the drawings of civilization, down to the most advanced and powerful societies—two classes of people appear—a class that rules and a class that is ruled. The first class, always the less numerous, performs all political functions, monopolizes power and enjoys the advantages that power brings, whereas the second the more numerous class, is directed and controlled by the first. (Mosca, 1939, p.50)

This is not necessarily the case in democratic societies where opposing positions need not be an antagonistic and competitive struggle in which only a fight to the end determines the winner. Opposing positions can be expressed in a dialogue where the intent is to ensure growth and development through a mutual exchange of ideas, knowledge and information. In the process, both sides are engaged in a process of conceptualizing and specifying the problem situation; what are their expectations and perceptions of policy goals; what are their sources of information necessary for scrutiny; and finally, what are their motivations for actions to be taken. This is a search to discover and justify varying positions in an open discourse free of recrimination: "every human being is capable of looking critically at his [her] world in a dialogical encounter with others ... each wins his [her] own right to say his own world, to name the world" (Freire, 1973, p.11).

In our view there are three ways to confront policy issues and problems. The first two are committed to either incremental or rational consensus, the last to a ruling elite: (1) one can approach problem situations with an attitude that attempts reconciliation as desirable realizing the prospects of changing the power relation is limited; (2) one can engage in a dialogue that builds on the restricted idiosyncratic positions in an attempt to reach a higher and more advanced level of problem solving; (3) the oppressor and oppressed are in continuous conflict, in which case a discontinuity in the power relation becomes inevitable. There is a winner and loser.

STRUCTURING POLICY PROBLEMS

Social and policy problems are serious disputes about the definition, classification, explanation and evaluation of asocial policy problems.

If social work empowerment practice is problem oriented and focused on the specific needs, wants and desires of a constituency, then a strategy ought to enable us to conceptualize and specify the policy problems based entirely on idiosyncratic interests and parochial values (i.e., a self-interest world view ideology). If, however, a constituency decide to structure problems so that they are viewed as affecting and being affected by problems of different constituencies, then the key lies in accepting the position that one's world views on problems are inseparable and unmeasurable apart from the whole "system of problems" of which they are interlocking parts (Dunn, 1981, p.99). This minimizes, if not eliminates, group self-interest.

Policy issues and problems conceived within an empowerment conception, separately or collectively, involve value dilemmas or value conflicts either over the preferred ends (i.e., the normative and desired ends of policy) and/or the feasible means (i.e., human, social and material provisions) necessary for implementing the means in a project striving toward a solution. The functions of social work range from the subjective value judgments of policy formulation (macro), the subjective/objective transformation in the use of resources (meso) to rational objectives of implementation in concrete services (micro).

The first stage to any social work empowerment practice model is to know the variations possible to structuring the right policy problems to solve: "Successful problem solving requires finding the right solution to the right problem. We fail more often because we solve the wrong problem than because we get the wrong solution to the right problem" (Ackoff, 1974, p.15). For example, realizing that there are four variations to the conceptualization of a desired end and feasible means, each produces different social work strategies for involvement and tactics for intervention:

1. The desired ends or terminal state of a problem and the feasible means are known and agreed upon. Decisions derived from power relations are precise and orderly.

2. The desired ends are not in agreement, but the feasible means are known and in agreement. The ends are uncertain and decisions by both sides must be compromised and bargained.
3. The ends are in agreement, but the feasible means are unknown or in disagreement. Decisions are heuristic and will change in development.
4. Both means and ends are complementary. Decisions derived from this interactive process produce an outcome that is different from each decision taken separately regarding the ends and/or means.

Structuring policy problems is contingent upon the analysts' conceptions of a world view and the manner in which human, material and social resources are mobilized, organized and managed. And since choices in these dimensions are value laden, the manner in which social policy problems are structured will determine the degree and extent to which empowerment ought, will and can be acquired and used.

SOCIAL DIMENSIONS OF CHOICE

The preceding discussion highlights that policy problems in human and social systems are permeated with value dilemmas and value conflicts.

> … In pluralistic ideologies, high priority is attached to values that are recognized to be in frequent even intense, conflict with each other. Important values often point to contradictory policies (i.e. I value social equality but dislike making economic sacrifices to pay for it). (Tetlock, 1986, p. 280)

There exist multiple and diverse values, interests and belief systems as, for example, deciding between the worthy versus the unworthy; lump sum payments versus per capita; in cash versus in kind etc. It is virtually impossible in a "value multiplicity" to achieve unanimity on any one or combination of values (Tropman, 1989. p.21). Hence, this is one reason why there is no beginning or end to policy problems. Another reason is the increasing multiplicity and complexity of social and policy problems.

A common core to value dilemmas and value conflicts is the matter of choice: do we choose to empower a constituency to assume leadership in policy-making; do we empower constituents to assume a technological and managerial capability to determine the distribution or redistribution of resources and/or do we strive to empower a constituency to acquire control and management of the delivery of human services?

Empowerment deals with the policy problems of choice relative to the three levels of social work practice: policy planning and development; program planning and management and project planning and operations. (Project planning and operations on a micro-level of practice entail community organization, planning, action and development). On each level, social workers simply segregate some piece of the choice problem to establish either the purpose and direction, the "know where;" the resources needed, the "know what" or how empowerment is to be targeted, the "know how."

There are as many different interpretations to the terms of being and becoming empowered as there are social workers involved in defining it for practice. Numerous value choices are made in the helping process from categorizing the number of phases and stages to establishing the procedures of the psychosocial process; emphasizing the formation of action systems and ways to exercise influence. Others expound the professional knowledge skills needed in these phases, and still others choose the worker as the inquirer and clarifier and the client/teacher and as learner (Germain and Gitterman, 1995; Hepworth and Larsen, 1986; Hollis and Woods, 1981; Lum, 1986; Pincus and Minahan, 1973; and Schulman, 1991.)

Choices are made in each multi-level social work function:

1. Macro-level practitioners act upon problems emanating from social allocations and social provisions and focus on how to engage constituents to change institutional norms and values—empowerment over ideas, values and perceptions.
2. Meso-practitioners are involved in the design, structure and resources of human services and are engaged in empowering constituents to ensure their effective delivery. This is referred to as empowerment over matter, the instruments of power.
3. Finally, micro-level practitioners are expected to choose efficient means to the implementation for services and goods. This is empowerment over the control and management of people.

If choice is the focus to determine the stages and phases, the procedures, processes and actions for implementation, they can be divided into three social dimensions. Each spells out the where, what and how of empowerment; namely, the normative, structural and behavioural dimensions.

The normative deals with values and norms influencing the choice which ought to be made. The structural considers the patterns and relations of social action; the relationships among individuals. The normative/structural dimensions are external to the individual and place restrictions, limitations and omissions on his or her choices. The significance of which is often overlooked by micro-level practitioners. The behavioural analyzes the choices individuals in fact do make and the reasons for their selection of particular choices. In sum, the normative and structural dimensions define what choices are available; the behavioural dimension involves the selection among alternatives presented by the other two dimensions.

When considering empowerment, macro-level practitioners ought to focus on policy ideologies and norms, particularly those expressing the moral and ethical basis for power and the properties of rulership in terms of their adverse effect on equity and equality. An ideological paradigm determines what is right, good and best; values that are institutionalized into the cultural system. Meso-practitioners are concerned about empowering a social class, namely, unserved and underserved, to elevate their status by involving them in the intra- and inter-organizational structure and allocation of resources as a means to decide how these services and goods are to be distributed. Micro-level practitioners are preoccupied with the individual's psychological and social functioning relative to empowering the individual to engage in personal and social change.

These three dimensions are predisposed toward different strategic modes of involvement and tactical modes of intervention. Although empowerment cuts across all three levels of social work practice, each level has adopted its own idiosyncratic meaning of empowerment. For example, the strategy and tactics for empowerment lie in policy knowledge skills regarding interest groups and legislature. As for the meso-level, strategies and tactics are designed to empower a constituency to make demands and claims on the administration to meet its responsibilities and to be more responsive to their needs. Finally, the strategies and tactics for micro-level practitioners are lodged in mobilizing, organizing and managing community in social action.

In sum, to enable, encourage and create opportunities for empowering differs for developing knowledge skills and competence in the "know where" of policy; from the "know what" of organization and finally, the "know how" of practice. Multi-level social work functions, along with their possible variations for empowerment, can be identified and defined. What is needed is their integration into a unified and overarching strategy for involvement and related tactics of intervention.

MAINSTREAM PERSPECTIVES ON CONFRONTING OPPOSITION

Let us review the sets of assumptions underlying our two paradigms for empowerment: incremental and rational consensus. They are seen as the primary means to confront opposition where the consequences are either value dilemmas or value conflicts. Both paradigms see consensus, not surrender or fight, as the principle means to solve problems. One advocates problem solving within the confines of a mobilization of bias; the other within the boundaries of a syncretic construct. Each paradigm represents the internal referents and systemic boundaries by which the choices to empowerment are made.

There are six basic postulates that govern an incremental consensus predicated upon the following concept.

> ...if analysts cannot agree on the value themselves, they can, and do agree on the principles, rules, or procedures for their reconciliation. (Braybrooke and Lindblom, 1963. p.34)

1. The basic values that structure power relations must be preserved and maintained, and to be empowered means acquiring the ability and capability of satisfying a specific need, want or desire, preferably of a quantifiable nature, without adversely effecting the underlying norms and values that govern the power relation.
2. An unmet need, desire or want is considered to be a problem when it results in a social perturbation; that is, when it jeopardizes the existing value system and, consequently, power structure. An external value input can be integrated only within the body of an existing value system. Hence, the unmet need, want and desire are reshaped, reorganized and reformed to "fit into" the original value system. Empowerment remedies and restores a problematic situation that has caused an actual or potential disruption of the power relation.
3. Value dilemmas must be resolved through compromise and bargaining as a critical means to avoid conflict to "move away" from a social perturbation. Only those external values that are marginal and dependent upon the existing value system can enter the negotiating process.
4. Problems are mitigated through mediation of opposing positions (i.e., those making claims on the norms and values of the system) agree to concede some aspect of their position for reasons of expediency or pragmatism.
5. The existing values and norms are given an embodiment of purpose and direction; whose integrity must be protected and values promoted. Each value input is treated as an external perturbation and is uniquely treated as a fragmentary aberration on the system requiring remedial actions (disjointed incrementalism).

6. The system adapts to external value demands by adjusting human service delivery to include a material distribution of a social service, program or activity. The intrinsic qualitative values of the system are preserved and maintained while a concrete, tangible service or benefit is offered in distributive service.

The original conception and specification of a problem situation structured by each opposing position undergoes major modifications through a process of mutual adjustments through serial, fragmentary and remedial decisions in resolving differences. The idea is to move away from a social ill rather than to solve it.

Social work practitioners have a long history of serving as brokers or advocates in securing, protecting and promoting the human and social rights of an affected constituency (Connaway and Gentry, 1988). These mainstream social work intervention modalities perceive opposing values, interests and belief systems as requiring social adaptations and adjustments. Social work's primary role in this problem solving framework is to facilitate adjustments through education, information and referral, mediation, environmental manipulation, coalition formations etc. that could otherwise be used in a rational consensus.

NON-RATIONAL STATE OF A DIALECTIC DISCOURSE

An incremental consensus can be labelled as "irrationality of formal rationality." The self-imposed rules of the game become the norm and acquire a logical connotation that makes the process inadvertently exclusive. It is a formidable defense for the conditions required for participation and contributions. Some would argue it excludes the oppressed and exploited population unable to fend for themselves under these conditions for participation (i.e., lack of empowerment).

A rational consensus begins with a "nonrational state" of irreconcilable opposition between oppressor and the oppressed. That is, both positions are determinant perturbations, in which case both positions are made subject to the rational conditions imposed by a dialectic discourse. Confrontation and argumentation generates logical and rational explanations resulting in a new configuration of the power relation.

Both paradigms are in agreement that "people who are vulnerable, oppressed and living in poverty" need to be empowered. However, conventional social work empowerment practice models address the isolated and fragmentary needs of a vulnerable and oppressed population almost always to remedy past social ills. This is usually attained through distributive adjustments; namely, social adjustments in the distribution of resources in housing, welfare benefits, health etc. This stands in contrast to a rational consensus where emphasis is placed on redistribution of resource allocations, which generates quantitative impact on the qualitative values of the system:

> ... the actions of agents involved are coordinated not through egocentric calculations of success but through acts of reaching understanding. In communicative action participants are not primarily oriented toward their own successes; they pursue their individual goals under the condition that they can harmonize their plans of action on the basis of common situation definitions. (Habermas, 1984, p. 286)

Four primary conditions must be put in place to avoid the idiosyncratic and parochial pitfalls that often become the motivating force behind the self-interest of an individual, group or community:

1. The purpose of a syncretic construct is to advance the common interests and universal values of groups of individuals.
2. Recognition that groups of individuals also have purely individual interests different from those of the group; hence, the necessity to focus on a system of problems.
3. That the participation and contribution of groups of individuals must make a difference in power relations.
4. Finally, only action derived from a dialectic discourse will impact favourably on the power relations.

A syncretic discourse is needed which seeks to reconcile competitive paradigms by increasing the level of inquiry to a higher level of abstraction, observation and generalization. It is designed to provide opposing positions opportunity to present, defend and justify their claims on all levels of practice. A syncretic discourse is a dialectic process that is uncoerced and where unlimited discussion between free and equal human agents prevails in unconstrained dialogue to realize a rational consensus (Guess, 1981; Benhabib, 1986).

Let us now present five principles of a syncretic construct that govern the conditions for meaningful individual and small group participation and contribution and, if these principles are accepted, a commitment to social change:

1. Conditions prevail that are non-deprivative, non-coercive and where information is not withheld or distorted and is made available and subject to scrutiny by all participants. It is the analyst's responsibility to create and ensure this climate in a social agency and community. Secondly, key to effective social work empowerment practice is the skill to acquire, utilize and share usable information for analysis, evaluation and development.

2. Optimal conditions for a dialogue must be created that go beyond open and free environments to include skills and methods of communicating information effectively and efficiently. This is what is meant by formulating a rational explanation or consensus of genuine expressions in an integration of parochial positions.

3. Social work would be expected to provide information and knowledge skills enabling constituents to organize, formulate and present their positions as they can concurrently unravel the complexities of opposing value positions in problem solving.

4. It is within an open climate of airing obstacles and hindrances to understand that participants can establish optimal conditions to realize desired courses of action. Professionals are expected to acquire knowledge in the dynamics of individual and small group decision-making within the context of a dialectic process.

5. A search for the optimal conditions can only be realized through a rational comprehensive process in which real values and interests are explicated for consensus. A pursuit toward optimal conditions sweeps in parochial perspectives and idiosyncratic positions. Hence, social work empowerment practice becomes a process by which the worker actively observes and participates in a group process of synthesis; an optimal condition for creative rationality.

A concept of equal and unconstrained dialogue eliminates the either/or competitive and rivalry positions that too often are taken as inevitable rather than as complementary.

COMPARATIVE ANALYSIS OF INCREMENTAL AND RATIONAL

A unity of opposites in a rational consensus model differs from a meliorative and distributive process in incremental consensus. Rational consensus is not designed to be pragmatic in the sense of expediency or to mitigate a problematic situation over the short or long run. Coalition formations, like many other modes of intervention applied in practice, structure policy problems for the main purpose of mitigating and meliorating a problem.

Opposing positions within a syncretic construct or rational consensus are seen as both bipolar complementary and as mutually inclusive or harmonious. As a result, positions taken by opposing groups converge to reach a higher level of inquiry and discourse. Changes in macro-micro practices result from a continuous interaction of contrasting similar forces for self-maintenance and creative growth. An interaction of opposing forces evolves into an interrelated and interdependent process. This produces both continuity and transformation of the social structure, function and process while it increases the problem solving capability of its participants.

In direct contrast to incremental consensus, a rational consensus views diametrically opposing positions not as social disorganization or deviance, necessitating reactive behaviour, but rather as source of energy, generating new and different values necessary for social change. In contrast to the facilitating/mediating role, an analyst in a dialectic discourse would create an open, non-coercive environment in which opposing and competing ideals and ideas on issues, problems or conflicts are expressed. A dialectic discourse seeks to reconcile competitive paradigms by reinforcing and then building new dimensions to parochial perspectives.

Social work empowerment practice would, therefore, build on parochial and restricted perspectives by enabling participants to converge their opposing positions to a new and higher level of discourse in an environment of harmonious complementarity.

METHODS AND PROCEDURES FOR A RATIONAL CONSENSUS

It is now timely to enumerate the conditions governing a rational consensus. The following basic practice skills and methods for problem solving are established: a capability of responding to various modes of argumentation or advocacy claims; attention and sensitivity to individual and group motivations; a program designed for purposeful participation, contributions and commitment and, finally, the means to address the interdependence and interrelatedness to complex macro-meso-micro levels of practices.

1. Each participant, individual and/or small group must be given equal opportunity to impact by participating in the setting of an agenda for argumentation; share in determining a course and direction for deliberations agreed on; a length of time for communication and to be informed who is to be represented as the affected constituents.

2. Each participant and small group must be open for confrontation raising questions; demanding justifications for claims made and providing explanations within the context of a discourse.

3. Each participant(s) must be given equal opportunity to express their needs, interests, desires and expectations without any internal or external constraints on discourse. A climate must be created where participants know that they will be heard. An open and free discourse encourages genuine and sincere interactive exchange of information.

4. Each participant(s) knows that they play a major role in determining the purpose and direction of a problem solving process and that the norms built in by a social agency structure do not become ends in and of themselves.

5. Individuals, small groups and communities must have equal access to information in an organization or community, particularly where it is known that conflicting and contradictory claims will emerge in response to an issue or problem. This ensures equal chance to make assertions, recommendations, provide explanations and to challenge others in a thoughtful but confrontation manner. No one is exempt from questioning and criticism: all are accountable for their behaviour.

These conditions set the stage for realizing a rational consensus that transcends analytical distinctions striving for mediation and mediocrity. A rational consensus includes a process of creative synthesis in a unification of opposites. This conceptual framework deliberately sets a stage for a more enlightened, emancipated and reflective participant in the problem solving process.

SUMMARY

Intrinsic to this analysis was the selection of a dialectic discourse to problem solving as the most parsimonious, representative and propitious for social work empowerment practice. A rationale was presented for augmenting contemporary practices with a dialectic discourse as an alternative model for strategies of involvement and modes of intervention for being and becoming empowered.

REFERENCES

Ackoff, R. (1974). *Redesigning the future: A systems approach to societal problems.* New York: John Wiley.

Adams, R. (1996). *Social work and empowerment.* London: Macmillan.

Baistow, K. (1994). Liberation or regulation? Some paradoxes of empowerment. *Critical Social Policy,* 42, 78-93.

Barchrach, P. and M. Baratz. (1970). *Power and poverty.* New York: Oxford University Press.

Benhabib, S. (1986). *Critique, norm and utopias: A study of the foundation of critical theory.* New York: Plenum Press.

Bishop, A. (1994). *Becoming an ally: Breaking the cycle of oppression.* Halifax, Nova Scotia: Fernwood.

Braybrooke, D. and Lindblom, C. (1963). *A strategy of decision.* New York: The Free Press.

Connaway, R. and Gentry, M. (1988). *Social work practice.* Englewood Cliffs, NJ: Prentice Hall.

Cook, B. (1992). *Eleanor Roosevelt 1884-1933.* New York: Viking.

Dunn, W. (1981). *Public policy analysis.* Englewood Cliffs, NJ: Prentice Hall.

Freire, P. (1973). *Pedagogy for the oppressed.* New York: Seabury.

Flynn, J. (1992). *Social agency policy.* Chicago: Nelson-Hall.

Germain, C. and Gitterman, A. (1995). *Life model of social work practice.* New York: Columbia University Press.

Guess, R. (1981). *The idea of a critical theory: Habermas and the Frankfurt school.* London: Cambridge University Press.

Habermas, J. (1984). *The theory of communicative action. Vol.1, Reason and the rationalization of society.* Boston: Beacon Press.

Hepworth. D. and Larsen, J. (1986). *Direct social work practice: Theory and skill.* Chicago: Dorsey.

Hollis, F. and Woods, M. (1981). *Casework: A psychosocial therapy,* (3rd ed.). New York: Random House.

Lee, J. (1994). *The empowerment approach to social work practice.* New York: Columbia University Press.

Lum, D. (1986). *Social work practice and people of color.* Monterey, CA: Brooks/Cole.

Mondrous, J. and S. Wilson. (1994). *Organizing for power and empowerment.* New York: Columbia University Press.

Mosca, G. (1939). *The ruling class.* New York: McGraw Hill.

Page, R. (1992). Empowerment, oppression and beyond: A coherent strategy: A reply to Mullender and Ward, (CSP Issue 32). *Critical Social Policy,* 35, 89-92.

Parsons, R. (1989). Empowerment for role alternatives for low income minority girls: A group work approach. In J. Lee (Ed.), *Group work with the poor and the oppressed* (pp.27-46). New York: Haworth.

Pincus, A. and Minahan, A. (1973). *Social work practice: Model and method.* Itasca, IL: Peacock.

Piven, F. and Cloward, R. (1971). *Regulating the poor.* New York: Vantage.

Richan, W. (1991). *Lobbying for social change.* New York: Haworth.

Schulman, L. (1992). *Interactional social work practice: Toward an empirical theory.* Itasca, IL: Peacock.

Solomon, B. (1976). Social work, special issue on women. *Journal of the National Association of Social Work,* 21(6), 371-377.

Sutherland, J.(1978). *Societal systems.* New York: North-Holland.

Tetlock, P. (1986). A value pluralism model of ideological reasoning. *Journal of Personality and Social Psychology,* 50(4), 265-282.

Tropman, J.(1989). *American values and social welfare.* Englewood Cliffs, NJ: Prentice Hall.

Weick, A. (1982). Issues of power in social work practices. In A. Weick and S. Vandiver (Eds.), *Women, power and change.* Washington, D.C.: National Association of Social Work.

Section 2

Fields of Practice

Chapter 6

BUILDING AN EMPOWERMENT MODEL OF PRACTICE THROUGH THE VOICES OF PEOPLE WITH SERIOUS PSYCHIATRIC DISABILITY

Susan S. Manning
Graduate School of Social Work
University of Denver

Empowerment has become an important theme in social work theory and practice over the past decade, particularly as social, economic and political conditions further reduce the quality of life and self-determination of oppressed and disenfranchised groups (Gutiérrez, Parsons and Cox, 1998). Empowerment, as a theory and a field of practice, offers an approach that expands and extends the abilities of people to cope with and impact the systems that affect their lives. People who suffer from serious and persistent psychiatric disability (referred to in this paper as "consumers") are one of society's most disempowered groups.

Profound changes in health-care service delivery place social work in a position of leadership to develop networks of services and support that facilitate the rehabilitation of people with serious disability (Shera, 1996). Further, the involvement of consumers in the development, implementation and monitoring of services is essential. An empowerment model that reflects the consumer voice and is specific to their experience is needed to inform future innovations in the mental health service system.

Models of empowerment developed for particular groups (e.g., community groups, women receiving welfare, corporate employees) do not necessarily apply for people with mental disability. Empowerment takes different forms for different people, and is different according to the context where the individual or group is located (Zimmerman, 1995). This "contextual determinism" also will vary across the domains of life, so empowerment at work does not necessarily mean the same level of empowerment at home (p. 586). Empowerment is a dynamic construct and changes over time. Thus, these characteristics eliminate universal measures (Zimmerman, 1995). Instead population-specific understandings of empowerment that are located in the context of people's experience are needed.

Consumers in the mental health system have a unique experience: the impact of a psychiatric disability; stigma from society and within systems of intervention and care; and the unintended effects of institutionalization that require compliance, adaptation and dependency (Chamberlain, 1978; Ludwig, 1971; Deegan, 1992). Empowerment models in mental health must be relevant to, and have the capacity to address, the unique features of their experience.

Research which describes consumers' experience of empowerment and the impact on the development of an empowerment model for the mental health system will be presented in this chapter. First, a brief review of the issues of power and disempowerment in the mental health system will be presented, followed by major findings from selected empowerment research projects of the author and associates.

THE CONSUMER EXPERIENCE OF POWER AND POWERLESSNESS

For the mental health consumer, the distribution of power in their experience is embedded in the nature of their psychiatric condition and the history of psychiatry. The disease model of care, whereby the provider or "expert" administers to the patient in a passive role, creates a differential distribution of power between care provider and care receiver (Segal, Silverman and Tempkin, 1993). This model includes the necessity of diagnosis, or labelling, according to the assessment of the provider. The individual's behaviour, feelings and attitudes are interpreted through the label, which becomes a form of identity in the mental health system (Segal et al., 1993).

Most consumers with a psychiatric history have been institutionalized through inpatient hospitalizations or community treatment over many years. They experience a loss of control over their life, or "learned helplessness" (Seligman, 1975; Peterson, Maier, and Seligman, 1993). Due to a lack of control over major decisions that affect their lives, and fear of the control and power of the system, consumers experience a "central attitudinal barrier" (Deegan 1992, p. 12). This barrier is the assumption they cannot be self-determining because they have a mental disability and therefore lack sound reasoning. Further, the years of institutionalization have reinforced behaviours of compliance and adaptation, required by institutions in order to work with large numbers of disabled clients. Goldin (1990) argues that care-giving institutions:

... exercise considerable control over clients through their definitions of disability, their criteria for treatment, and through policies which segregate their clients, and create and maintain psychological, social, and economic dependency. (p.896)

Stigma from society and within the mental health system further affects consumers' ability to access and wield power. The label of "mentally ill" represents a difference from the rest of society and conveys stereotypes of dangerousness, unpredictable behaviour, etc. (Boltz, 1992). Stigma from society affects empowerment and quality of life. In a study on daily life of consumers, stigma was most bothersome to the respondents (Miller and Miller, 1991). Stigma is evident within the professional realm as well. Negative attitudes against persons with serious mental illness have been discerned in a variety of professional and paraprofessional care-givers (Wilk, 1994; Mirabi, Weinman, Magnetti and Keppler, 1985; Johnson, 1990).

The impact of mental disability also affects quality of life. Consumers evaluate their quality of life as substantially lower than the poorest groups in the general population (Lehman, Ward and Linn, 1982; Rosenfield, 1992). Poverty, in particular, has a profound effect; it is a critical barrier to accessing resources and developing relationships.

The mental condition itself is even more profound, due to the loss of self in several dimensions (Estroff, 1982, 1989). Consumers have lost their personal history. They experience a cultural and symbolic change from the impact of their disability and others' reaction to it (Chesler and Chesney, 1988; Estroff, 1982, 1989). Bachrach (1992) cites Wing and Morris (1981) and their classification of the varieties of disability. They see the primary disability as that of the illness and symptoms of the illness. Secondary disability comes not from the illness but from the experience of illness—a frightening, confusing and disturbing experience that affects people long after the symptoms have diminished. Tertiary disability is external to the consumer and comes from the community's reactions to their disability. Isolation, stigma, unemployment and loss of a social place or role are examples of this type of effect.

RESEARCH APPROACH

The findings from three research projects further the understanding of the consumer experience of empowerment and help to develop a model of intervention. All of the studies presented employed a qualitative, participative design. This approach involves consumers in the research about their own social problems (Yeich and Levine, 1992). Consumers and family members participated in defining the research question, collecting and analyzing data and interpreting results. The participatory design contributed to the empowerment of the consumer researchers (Rapp, Shera and Kisthardt, 1993) and also facilitated rich description of the context of their experience. Most importantly, the participatory design produced research, " ... more relevant, credible and meaningful to consumers" (Rogers and Palmer-Erbs, 1994, p. 9). Data were gathered in the field—from other consumers in the natural setting where the experience was located (consumer-run, drop-in centres, mental health centers, support groups, private partnership clinics, clubhouses, etc.).

CONSUMERS AS EMPLOYEES IN THE MENTAL HEALTH SYSTEM

The first study examined factors that affect the training and employment of persons with serious mental illness as case manager aides (Manning and Suire, 1996; see Sherman and Porter, 1991 for a description of the training program). Individual interviews with 16 participants about their experience as employees in the mental health system revealed data about the barriers to empowerment within the system, as well as what was empowering. The major factors affecting work included orientation, support, role definition, empowerment, stigma and agency policy. Conclusions important to this discussion are related to stigma, role definition and empowerment.

Stigma was a critical barrier to the success of a consumer in an employee role. The label of mental illness was experienced as more powerful than any other aspect of personality or ability. Stereotypical attitudes about mental illness impacted the opportunity to make decisions, give feedback, advocate for clients and participate in social activities. Frequently, [expression of opinion or information was interpreted as a manifestation of the person's disability.] This pervasive stigma reinforces the importance of self-awareness of providers about stereotypical attitudes and beliefs that impede consumer empowerment.

Role definition brought forward the boundary issues for consumers, providers and administrators who found themselves in unfamiliar territory— consumers in employee positions. There was a tendency to fall back on traditional roles and structures that denied the strengths and advantages of consumers' experience with mental illness, discussed by Paulson (1991). This finding promotes a needed strategy for innovations—the use of a developmental process, with a focus on interaction and exploration of dual roles. A feedback loop to all participants is an important communication structure to build into program change that includes changes in roles and the legitimated power attached to roles.

Empowerment was experienced by case manager aides through their own personal growth and relationships with others. Employment brought an increased awareness of capabilities, personal growth through helping others and an increased sense of personal potential. The new information about themselves contributed to enhanced self-esteem and self-confidence. The education components of employment and training contributed to conceptualizing their own disability and strengthened coping with the disability. The opportunity to be open about their illness contributed to a sense of health rather than shame. All of these factors added to new problem solving skills that increased their efficacy with clients. In addition, the material symbols associated with employment—an office, door label, salary, even tax forms— added to the sense of legitimation consumers experienced. The visible recognition of their value helped to create a role or place in society, as Estroff (1989) has discussed.

The results from this study point to the importance of working with provider and consumer attitudes and beliefs, the development of structures of communication to facilitate innovations, and the benefits to consumers of meaningful work.

THE CONSUMER EXPERIENCE OF EMPOWERMENT

The second study (Manning, Zibalese-Crawford and Downey, 1994) was an evaluation of a three-year demonstration project to empower consumers of mental health services and their family members. The grant involved providers, consumers and family members working collaboratively to develop and administer the project. Consumers and family members were hired and trained as researchers. The research question was, "What is the experience of empowerment for consumers with serious and persistent mental illness?"

Eleven group interviews were conducted with consumer and family support groups and the project steering committee (N=100+). Individual interviews were held with 17 provider, consumer and family leaders from rural, suburban and urban locations. Participant observation provided contextual immersion at three consumer drop-in centres. The triangulation of these methods provided the qualitative data for analysis.

Factors of empowerment. Results of the study provided rich description about consumers' perception of empowerment; factors that facilitate or impede empowerment in the mental health system. Major themes of empowerment included self-determination, decision-making, information/education, respect, involvement/belonging, contribution to others and "coming out."

Self-determination was described as making choices and "having control over our own lives." The opportunity to self-determine led to the possibility of success and failure, both of which were perceived by consumers as providing a level of competence and the resiliency to handle failures. Having and making choices was particularly important for consumers who have been institutionalized for many years and have lacked the opportunity to make even the most simple and basic life choices. Self-determination was described as an art that happens naturally through a nurturing environment that provides opportunities to make choices that are authentic to the individual. Self-determination is tied directly to decisions.

Decision-making was an action-oriented theme based on two components— the opportunity to decide and then action through making the decision, "doing is empowering." The process of learning happened through actual experience. Participants experienced power in two ways when in the decision-making role. First, in the sense of responsibility for the decision, and second, the access to power to make the decision. Both aided in developing skills and a sense of competency.

Information/education related to three important areas for participants— managing their condition, skill building and accessing resources. Information about psychiatric disability, medications, technologies, etc. offered consumers a better understanding of their own condition and the information necessary to advocate for themselves with providers about their own treatment. This process redistributed the power between consumer and professional. Information/education were critical to skill building and developing abilities to solve life problems. Finally, consumers experienced the information-sharing process, particularly between each other, as increasing their access to resources, validating their experiential knowledge and helping to cope with stigma.

Respect was experienced as having a voice and being heard. Respect resulted in a sense of feeling valued for their experiential knowledge and expertise. Respect developed best in a safe environment where people could tell their stories and express their values. Expression was not empowering in and of itself, but in conjunction with the perception of being listened to and heard. The expert status of providers, at times, was viewed as a barrier to being heard. Also, self-respect was a critical part of this theme. Self-respect included living their own values, being able to take a stand, advocating for self, committing to a relationship and participating in self-care and wellness activities. The interactive nature of respect, taking place within a relationship, underscores the importance of involvement with others and the type of involvement.

Involvement and belonging is about the importance of relationship and community. Consumers, because of the nature of psychiatric disability, stigma and poverty, have isolation as a constant factor in their lives. Membership in a community was viewed as critical to empowerment. Within the community there was opportunity for validation from others through interpersonal relationships. Relationships were also viewed as necessary to change perceptions about self and others. Developing competence in relationships within a community transferred to external situations, according to consumers. The community is a place for friendship that is not connected to "treatment." Some consumers saw relationship with others as more healing than medications.

Contribution to others happened as a result of membership in a group/ community. Consumers perceived helping others as an opportunity to develop and use skills and to role model for others that consumers are capable. The opportunity to give as well as receive was experienced as empowering. Consumers who were role models, and those who observed, perceived the process as contributing to hope. Consumers perceived real "work" as promoting societal acceptance and providing an entree into the greater community.

"Coming out" was identified as important. "Going public" with their disability provided relief, a sense of freedom and a feeling of empowerment. Being open about their disability confronted stigma and educated others in the process. Coming out allowed the consumer to help others through their experience. Lastly, going public was described as part of the healing process, which led to reaching out and supporting others, which in turn reduced isolation and powerlessness.

Barriers to empowerment. Consumers also discussed their perceptions of barriers to empowerment—poverty, isolation, stigma, impact of mental disability, unintended effects of institutionalization and inequitable distribution of power.

Poverty associated with mental illness was viewed as a critical factor in empowerment and an overriding theme in the study. The effects of poverty were profound. Economic status affected living conditions, social status, health and well-being and access to resources and opportunities. Basic issues such as transportation, medical and dental care, telephones and adequate food and clothing were constant problems in the lives of the consumers interviewed. People in rural areas were especially affected by lack of funds for transportation and telephones—the link to support, information, services and membership.

Isolation from others effectively severed opportunities for relationship. Isolation was precipitated by the effects of the mental disability, poverty and lack of social skills. The tendency to withdraw is pronounced, according to some consumers, and contact or outreach from peers was viewed as important.

Stigma about mental illness—from society and from professionals in the mental health system—was viewed as disempowering in two ways. First, consumers absorb the perceptions of society about mental illness and then oppress themselves through secretiveness and shame. Second, the constant perception of who they are through the lens of a label affects their sense of themselves as a person. Both professionals and consumers noted that relating through the disease metaphor, rather than as person to person, was disempowering. This category affirmed the experience of stigma discussed in the consumer case manager study.

Impact of psychiatry disability is a factor unique to this population. Consumers described different levels of awareness about the nature of their disability and different understandings about the impact of the disability on self-determination. Denial of the disability was viewed as a barrier to empowerment by consumers. Denial restricted opportunities to affect their situation through better management of the disability, thus affecting self-determination. In addition, providers, consumers and family members found it difficult to evaluate a person's ability or readiness to make decisions due to the impact of their mental illness. The "illness" provided a convenient excuse when working with difficult people or people with poor interpersonal and decision skills. A consumer noted, " ... Mental illness is used as a reason for problems that a person might have, with or without the illness." And finally, the nature of the symptoms and losses due to disability have a profound impact on empowerment.

Unintended effects of institutionalization—compliance and dependency— are especially pronounced with consumers who have spent their lives in some part of the mental health system. These effects impacted consumers' willingness and motivation to make decisions. Consumers, " ... are educated to follow the decisions and instruction of many other people, not to follow their own instincts," for decisions about their lives. Also, consumers experienced pressure to conform to the role of patient. Behaviours and attitudes suitable for a treatment environment were not conducive to empowerment.

Distribution of power between providers and consumers was perceived as unequal. Providers are viewed as having "power-over," and consumers doubted that providers were willing to share power in real ways. Consumers were afraid of providers' retribution for assertive or empowered behaviour. Consumers expressed fear of providers' power over them based on past experiences of invasive, coercive and/or involuntary treatments. Providers and consumers identified a sense of intimidation at times in the mental health system. Related to this issue, consumers identified the lack of models for a different distribution of power. Consumer-run groups and centres help with developing power in consumers, but in provider-driven programs, the traditional distribution of power is in place.

Power to decide is sometimes co-opted by providers, other consumers and family. A consumer leader noted that it is "easier to do it yourself." Second, consumers expressed the difficulty of sharing power in order to provide opportunities to others. Providers particularly experienced confusion about how to share power. Language demonstrated this confusion. Some providers implied that power rested in their hands as something to give or withhold, e.g., " ... should we *give* them more responsibility?" Traits of individuals were generalized by providers e.g., " ... *They* do not learn ... *they* lose sight ...." A consumer researcher identified " ... an intangible sense of differentiation" through this generalization that shifted the distribution of power. A related theme was the use of language and labels in the mental health system that convey the consumer as an object—the label becomes the person (e.g., "that guy is a schizophrenic," that "borderline").

Based on the above, delegation was a critical skill connected to awareness, attitudes and motivation to share power. Consumers discussed delegation as an art that takes time—to create opportunities, to pass on power. Delegation communicates a message that the consumer has potential, value and capability.

CONSUMER-RUN ENVIRONMENTS

Consumers experience their own programs as empowering. Factors described from a consumer-run environment that are useful for an empowerment model follow.

An unstructured environment was viewed as an opportunity for natural growth and change. Consumers did not feel pressured to work on treatment goals or to conform to a structure or schedule. In fact, the lack of structure allowed consumers to just be, to spend time, with acceptance and accommodations for a range of individual differences. An encouragement of discovery was experienced, whereby consumers felt free to self-actualize in their own way and at their own pace. This was especially valued by consumers who were used to structures, goals and expectations of "participation" according to provider outcomes and schedules.

Self-determination was encouraged. Consumers were free to make choices. Participation was totally voluntary. Each individual's experience was viewed as unique, and consumers did not feel categorized. Also, consumers felt valued for the experience and strengths each brought to the center.

Relationships were based on responsiveness. Consumers noted that people took time with each other. The focus of interaction was on support and common-sense problem solving of daily living. There was an exchange of "folk medicine," whereby they shared ideas, techniques and helpful hints about what helped—with medications, providers and treatment issues. Consumers saw each other as role models and experts and felt valued and hopeful through those relationships.

A CONSUMER MODEL OF EMPOWERMENT

The above results, combined with the practice elements of empowerment from Parsons's (1994) study of five empowerment-based programs (cohesive collective environment, collaborative relationship between providers and peers, strength-based assessment/focus, and educational focus), provided substantial data about the experience of consumers. The purpose of the next study (Manning, Parsons and Silver, 1997) was to develop specific descriptions of empowerment components and interventions necessary to promote empowerment grounded in the experience of consumers. The results included interventions and strategies, as well as philosophical assumptions, values, organizational environment and process issues of empowerment.

Data collection consisted of focus group and individual interviews. Groups were held with clients at four different programs with empowerment philosophy (one clubhouse and three consumer-run drop-in centres). Two focus groups with providers known in the mental health system as empowerment "experts" integrated the provider perspective. Individual interviews were also held with a peer counsellor trainer and the executive director of a clinic based on a partnership model of governance.

Three major categories emerged that describe components of an empowerment model—consciousness, learning environment and strategies. However, critical to the model are five dimensions that emerged repeatedly from the consumer experience. The dimensions capture the philosophical essence of an empowerment model in mental health. Therefore, the dimensions must be infused throughout the components of the model and evident in all aspects of programming.

The five critical dimensions necessary to an empowerment intervention model for persons with serious psychiatric disability include: authenticity, power, opportunity, relationship and connectedness.

Authenticity is the freedom to *be* and *live* according to each person's uniqueness. There is an emphasis on consumer self-awareness and self-worth. Sensitivity to the whole person and her or his physical, psychological, emotional, social and economic well-being is conveyed. Thus, quality of life according to the individual's definition is paramount. Authenticity helps to counteract the loss of self (Estroff, 1982, 1989) discussed earlier in the paper.

Power is the dimension necessary for self-determination and self-efficacy. Consumers must be afforded access to power and the skills to wield it. Further, responsibility for decisions and actions and using their own experiential knowledge are elements of this dimension. A pervasive attention to power helps to impact the stigma and unintended effects of institutionalization.

Opportunity is the "window" whereby consumers can participate, take risks and learn to govern. Creating opportunities through issues, activities or decisions creates the possibility of experience—choosing, deciding and learning. Viewing all occasions as an opportunity in the empowerment model helps to change the "central attitudinal barrier" (Deegan, 1992, p.12) and reinforce self-determination.

Relationship was emphasized as the vehicle for involvement and learning. Relationship promotes trust and facilitates taking risks. With relationship there is support and needed interpersonal skills. Consumers can interact with people with varying levels of power and benefit from the role modelling. Through relationship consumers experience community membership. Included is relationship to self. Through greater self-awareness consumers can develop self-efficacy and self-confidence.

Connectedness describes the interconnections necessary for personal, interpersonal and political well-being, the three levels of power experienced through empowerment (Gutiérrez, Parsons and Cox, 1998). Building lasting connections provides the support and resources necessary to utilize power and opportunity and provides a social support system. Understanding connections provides skills useful in managing life situations and the development of self-advocacy. The ability to be connected extends linkages beyond the mental health system to the larger community. Connectedness creates a "web" for the consumer that helps with the chronic isolation associated with psychiatric disability. Equally important, the skills in building connections enhance quality of life and self-determination through personal and political activity.

The five dimensions are the backdrop to the following discussion of components of an empowerment model.

Empowerment consciousness described the attitudes, values and role behaviour of providers, clients and family members that promote empowerment. Consciousness is the critical component of an empowerment intervention in mental health. A change in attitudes, values and role behaviour is necessary to change the distribution of power in the helping process and address the stigma documented in the literature and described by consumers in previous studies.

Attitudes. The key issue in this factor is changing the way people think about people who are clients. Consumers stressed seeing the person first, before diagnosis and symptomatology. An awareness of the diversity of individuals who experience gradations between "sick and well" is also important. A belief in consumers' potential/ability to find solutions and the promotion of self-determination are needed attitudes. Providers must also develop a critical self-awareness of disempowering attitudes and behaviours and be willing to confront their own "expert status." This means a willingness to share power.

Values/beliefs. Values that are important to consider in the hiring and training process start with valuing consumer self-help. Providers must value consumers' experiential knowledge and the importance of using that knowledge through consumer self-determination. Valuing reflection and constant assessment of the distribution of power in programs and relationships is critical. Trusting in the natural process of growth and change, connected to a value of client strengths as the focus of assessment and involvement, creates empowering relationships.

Role. The relationship between provider and consumer must be restructured to one of a partnership based on a more egalitarian distribution of power. Providers act as guides with the focus on problem solving and skill building. The relationship is person to person rather than defined through role. Language is subjective; consumers are not referred to as objects. People are "real" in the relationship—working with real issues through involvement. Partnering—"doing with" rather than "for" in activities—changes the nature of the relationship. Responsibility for the outcome of activities and decisions is shared. Goals for change include life plans as well as treatment plans. The treatment plan should support, and be congruent with, the consumer's life plan.

The learning environment describes the program/agency structures and processes that promote empowerment. The following were identified as necessary to empowerment.

Consumer governance. Consumers must have the opportunity to participate in a partnership form of governance whereby they have decision-making power and responsibility in regard to self and program issues. Two structures, at a minimum, were recommended: 1) a client centre conceptualized, administered and staffed by consumers to provide opportunity for governance, free from provider influence; 2) consumer participation and responsibility for decisions in all program areas (e.g., budget, program development, evaluation, etc.). Governance provides opportunity for leadership development and decision skills.

Consumers as helpers. Consumers as role models was a consistent theme in the empowerment studies. Employment positions such as case managers/ aides, peer counsellors and other paid positions provide opportunity for role modelling, skill development and meaningful work. Work, in turn, impacts poverty and helps develop a social place in the world. Active efforts to develop paid and volunteer opportunities for consumer leadership are important.

The collective. The structures and process of program activity are aimed at developing a sense of community where people feel valued, safe and connected. "Group" was described as the process medium to build community. Through meaningful involvement consumers develop a sense of belonging, the ability to give and receive feedback, relationship skills and contribute to the well-being of others. Group as the structural medium for program development, implementation and evaluation further creates and maintains a sense of community through ownership and responsibility. ..

Developmental perspective. Consumers stressed the importance of recognizing and using natural developmental processes. Start with where the individual and/or group is and move toward individual/group goals over time.

Feedback loops. Communication structures that provide opportunity to give and receive feedback about the nature and impact of empowerment in program activities and relationships must be formalized. Interaction contributes to development of critical awareness and moves consumers/providers forward in the empowerment process. This is particularly necessary in relation to innovative changes.

Empowerment strategies describe activities/interactions that are based on underlying principles that facilitate empowerment. Strategies have structural and process implications but are not at the level of formal program structures. Strategies create opportunities for meaningful involvement beyond the treatment aspects of a mental health program. The following are examples, but not an exhaustive list, from the data.

Leadership. Create opportunities for leading, deciding, choosing and contribution according to the capacity and choices of the consumer(s) at any given time in the program.

Client-driven. Develop activities and treatment plans in collaboration with consumers and directed toward their goals. Full participation in treatment planning, with access to read and write in the record, is important for consumer self-determination.

Education/information. Information and education about the nature and management of mental illness is primary. Skill development and access to information/education is infused into all activities.

Meaningful involvement. Activities are developed according to what is meaningful to individuals and groups in their daily life. Opportunities to participate, to make decisions, to take responsibility, to succeed and fail, to learn new skills and help others were central themes for activities.

Whole person. Strategies that contribute to the quality of life of the whole person—health/medical care, nutrition, wellness, living situations, spirituality, meaningful work, social networks, etc.—are considered necessary to empowerment. This focus helps reduce the artificial dichotomy between treatment and life.

Celebration. Rituals help to celebrate steps in recovery and validate the developmental process of growth and change. This is especially important for consumers who feel hopeless. Involvement in the development of traditions—holidays or other community events—accentuates integration into the community.

CONCLUSION

This empowerment model, based on a partnership between consumers and providers, has many features and components congruent with, and complementary to, the work of other empowerment theorists. Also, the recent definition of empowerment by Chamberlain (1997) is similar to the themes defined by consumers in the above studies. These findings from researchers across the country confirm a collective experience for consumers with serious psychiatric disability in the mental health system. Further, their experience can be the foundation of empowerment models that facilitate a greater social justice, through their own advocacy, than has been done on their behalf in the past.

Critical questions remain about the experience of empowerment for people with severe psychiatric disability and what specific empowerment approaches are most useful. Consumers currently in the mental health system tend to be younger in age and have less long-term inpatient experience in their history due to deinstitutionalization and managed care. This brings forward issues of development—young adulthood, emancipation and separation from family—and more reliance on community systems than some of their older peers have experienced. Do the developing models meet the needs of this population? Is there a need for separate or specialized programs or theories that individualize the approaches further? What is the nature of the interaction of different groups at different developmental stages in relation to empowerment?

In addition, little is known about the special empowerment needs of women, the physically disabled, people of colour, the elderly etc. who also have a serious psychiatric disability. For these groups, the experience of oppression is magnified many times over, along a number of different dimensions. For example, little exists in the area of domestic violence protection and programs for women with psychiatric disability that is directed toward their special needs.

What empowerment distinctions, if any, exist for special populations with special needs?

Finally, how do we work with the paradox of facilitating the development of consumer power within the mental health system, when many of the assumptions of the consumer activist movement, self-help etc. were based on achieving independence from that system? Are we moving in a reverse direction by developing empowerment programs within the system viewed by so many consumers as an oppressive system? Can there be true partnership models when the definers of the problem, and the associated vested outcomes, are determined by individuals in traditional roles who tend not to have a psychiatric disability?

The answers to these questions, and others, provide the challenge to researchers invested in empowerment of consumers who are involved in the mental health system. Clearly, support for action research models whereby consumers are the researchers is important. I appreciate the opportunity to dialogue with colleagues about these challenges.

REFERENCES

Bachrach, L. (1992). Psychosocial rehabilitation and psychiatry in the case of long term patients. *American Journal of Psychiatry*, 149(11), 1455-1463.

Boltz, S. (1992). *Creating partnerships with self-help: Differences in the self-help and professional roles*. [Center for Self-Help Research, working paper series.] Berkeley, CA: Center for Self-Help Research.

Chamberlain, J. (1978). *On our own: Patient controlled alternatives to the mental health system*. New York: McGraw Hill.

Chamberlain, J. (1997). A working definition of empowerment. *Psychiatric Rehabilitation Journal*, 20(4), 43-46.

Chesler, M. and Chesney, B. (1988). Self-help groups: Empowerment attitudes and behaviors of disabled or chronically ill persons. In H. Yuker (Ed.), *Attitudes toward persons with disabilities* (pp. 230-247). New York: Springer.

Deegan, P. (1992). The independent living movement and people with psychiatric disabilities: Taking back control over our own lives. *Psychosocial Rehabilitation Journal*, 15(3), 3-19.

Estroff, S. (1982). *Making it crazy*. Berkeley, CA: University of California Press.

Estroff, S. (1989). Self, identity, and subjective experiences of schizophrenia: In search of the subject. *Schizophrenia Bulletin*, 15(2), 189-186.

Goldin, C. (1990). Stigma, biomedical efficacy, and institutional control. *Social Science Medicine*, 30(8), 895-900.

Gutiérrez, L., Parsons, R. and Cox, E. (1998). A model for social work practice. In Gutiérrez, Parsons, and Cox (Eds.), *Empowerment in social work practice: A source book*. Pacific Grove, CA: Brooks-Cole.

Johnson, D. (1990). Serious mental illness and the urgent need for relevant training. In D. L. Johnson (Ed.), *Service needs of the seriously mentally ill: Training implications for psychology* (pp. 3-6). Washington, D.C.: American Psychological Association.

Lehman, A., Ward, N. and Linn, L. (1982). Chronic mental patients: The quality of life issue. *American Journal of Psychiatry*, 139, 1271-1276.

Ludwig, A. (1971). *Treating the treatment failures: The challenge of chronic schizophrenia*. New York: Grune and Stratton.

Manning, S., Parsons, R. and Silver, J. (1997). *An empowerment model for persons with serious psychiatric disability*. Denver, CO: University of Denver, Graduate School of Social Work.

Manning, S. and Suire, B. (1996). Bridges and roadblocks: Consumers as employees in mental health. *Psychiatric Services*, 47(9), 939-943.

Manning, S., Zibalese-Crawford, M. and Downey, E. (1994). *Colorado mental health consumer and family development project: Program evaluation*. Denver, CO: University of Denver, Graduate School of Social Work.

Miller, S. and Miller, R. (1991). An exploration of the daily hassles for persons with severe psychiatric disabilities. *Psychosocial Rehabilitation Journal*, 14(4), 39-51.

Mirabi, M., Weinman, M., Magnetti, S. and Keppler, K. (1985). Professional attitudes toward the chronic mentally ill. *Hospital and Community Psychiatry*, 36, 404-405.

Parsons, R. (1994, March). *Empowerment based social work practice*. Paper presented to the 41st Annual Program Meeting, Council on Social Work Education, San Diego, CA.

Paulson, R. (1991). Professional training for consumers and family members: One road to empowerment. *Psychosocial Rehabilitation Journal*, 14, 69-80.

Peterson, C., Maier, S. and Seligman, M. E. P. (1993). *Learned helplessness: A theory for the age of control*. NY: Oxford University Press.

Rapp, C., Shera, W. and Kisthardt, W. (1993). Research strategies for consumer empowerment of people with severe mental illness. *Social Work*, 38(6), 727-735.

Rogers, E.S. and Palmer-Erbs, V. (1994). Participatory action research: Implications for research and evaluation in psychiatric rehabilitation. *Psychosocial Rehabilitation Journal*, 18(2), 3-33.

Rosenfield, S. (1992). Factors contributing to the subjective quality of life of the chronic mentally ill. *Journal of Health and Social Behavior*, 33, 229-315.

Segal, S., Silverman, C. and Tempkin, T. (1993). Empowerment and self-help agency practice for people with mental disabilities. *Social Work*, 38(6), 705-712.

Seligman, M. E. P. (1975). *Helplessness: On depression, development, and death*. San Francisco, CA: Freeman.

Shera, W. (1996). Managed care and people with severe mental illness: Challenges and opportunities for social work. *Health and Social Work*, 21(3), 196-201.

Sherman, P. and Porter, R. (1991). Mental health consumers as case management aides. *Hospital and Community Psychiatry*, 42, 494-498.

Wilk, R. (1994). Are the rights of people with mental illness still important? *Social Work*, 39(2), 167-175.

Wing, J. and Morris, B. (1981). Clinical basis of rehabilitation. In J. Wing and B. Morris (Eds.), *Handbook of psychiatric rehabilitation practice*. Oxford: Oxford University Press.

Yeich, S. and Levine, R. (1992). Participatory research's contribution to a conceptualization of empowerment. *Journal of Applied Social Psychology*, 22, 1894-1908.

Zimmerman, M. (1995). Psychological empowerment: Issues and illustrations. *American Journal of Community Psychology*, 23(5), 581-599.

Chapter 7

CONSUMER EMPOWERMENT IN A MENTAL HEALTH SYSTEM: STAKEHOLDER ROLES AND RESPONSIBILITIES

Lee H. Staples
School of Social Work
Boston University

There is a general consensus in the literature that empowerment is attenuated when problems are solved for those who are powerless. The ability to redefine oneself (or one's group) and to act effectively on one's own behalf is at the core of this concept. No one fully can empower another person or group. Helping professionals who talk about "empowering my clients" are misguided at best and often are caught up in a paternalistic paradigm.

Nevertheless, there is a facilitative role that helpers can play in the empowerment process by establishing relationships, providing access to resources, furnishing opportunities, strengthening capacities and creating options which enable individuals and groups to obtain and exercise greater power to control their own lives. Likewise, organizations, agencies and even bureaucratic systems institutionally can sanction possibilities for developing empowerment through rights, laws, regulations, policies, procedures, programs, structures and authorizations. Often, the ability of consumers to empower themselves will be impacted profoundly by how well provider professionals play a facilitative role and the extent to which organizations sanction empowerment opportunities.

This paper explores how consumer empowerment can be increased in a state mental health system. It draws on the empowerment literature, a consumer-provider survey and qualitative data from interviews with members of a consumer self-advocacy organization. Three distinct instrumentalities or mechanisms for effecting empowerment are identified and discussed below for organized consumers, provider professionals and the mental health bureaucracy. These developmental, facilitating and sanctioning mechanisms provide distinct structures, processes and tools for all three stakeholders to advance empowerment. They enable both professionals and organizations to play a supportive role in an empowerment process that must be driven by consumers themselves.

Qualitative data for this paper were gathered as part of a larger study (Staples, 1993) that examined attitudes, opinions and perceptions about consumer empowerment in the Massachusetts mental health system. Empowerment was defined as: a process by which power is developed, facilitated or sanctioned in order that subordinated individuals and groups can increase resources, strengthen self-images and build capacities to act on their own behalf in psychological, socio-cultural, political or economic domains. The study explored the potential of consumer self-advocacy organizations as developmental instrumentalities of empowerment. It also assessed the capacity of provider professionals and the mental health bureaucracy to facilitate and sanction consumer empowerment.

Interviews were conducted with 21 activists from a chapter of M-POWER, a member-run consumer self-advocacy organization. Gaining access to M-POWER members was not especially difficult due to the author's personal history with the organization, including membership and an active role on the original Empowerment Sponsoring Committee (1986-1990) which spawned the organization. This committee was composed of a mixture of mental health consumers, providers and community organizers. It raised the initial money, hired the first staff and oversaw the beginning organizing drives, disbanding in 1990 when M-POWER officially was founded as an organization totally comprised of and controlled by consumers. The relationship has continued while I have served as an occasional trainer, consultant and supporter.

I conducted one-hour interviews with each of the 21 respondents. Questions explored whether and, if so, how participation in a member-run consumer self-advocacy organization had affected their lives. Both individual and collective levels of empowerment were examined. Common themes in the empowerment literature were investigated, including the growth of self-confidence and self-esteem, increased skills and self-efficacy, the development of critical consciousness, the politicization of anger, organizational ownership, experience in collective action, and the development of organizational clout. The attitudes and perceptions of M-POWER members shed light on a member-run consumer self-advocacy organization's capacity to function as a developmental instrumentality of empowerment.

The role of provider staff as facilitating actors in the empowerment process and the effectiveness of the mental health bureaucracy as a sanctioning instrumentality were examined through a combination of the consumer interviews and open-ended questions on a survey. As part of the larger study, the survey compared and contrasted attitudes, perceptions and opinions about consumer empowerment among four groups—organized consumers (21 respondents), unaffiliated consumers (23), department of mental health case managers (23) and provider staff from private contracted agencies (29). The survey included 35 statements measured by a Likert Scale. Those data are not reported here. However, optional open-ended questions explored barriers to and changes necessary for increasing consumer empowerment, especially regarding provider staff and the mental health bureaucracy. These data do inform the analysis that follows.

The next three sections suggest how greater consumer empowerment can be developed, facilitated and sanctioned in the Massachusetts mental health system. Roles and responsibilities attendant to organized consumers, provider professionals and the Massachusetts Department of Mental Health are considered in turn. Limitations and barriers are identified. Recommendations for action to overcome this resistance are offered.

DEVELOPING CONSUMER EMPOWERMENT: CONSUMER ORGANIZING

Ownership

M-POWER, a member-run consumer self-advocacy organization, has local chapters in three Massachusetts cities, a paid staff of five and a $100,000 budget. Respondents to this study were volunteers recruited from one of the three chapters by staff or this researcher.

> The progress I've seen among the members of M-POWER in the last one-and-one-half to two years is just astounding. We've learned to chair meetings; we've learned to do different types of campaigns; we've learned to do workshops; we've learned public speaking. All kinds of things that none of us ever did before in our lives and probably never dreamed that we would ever do. We're finding skills that we didn't know we had. (Mary, M-POWER member)

The M-POWER members spoke eloquently about their sense of ownership of the organization. Other programs may allow for varying degrees of input and consumer participation, but the experience in this grassroots membership organization seems to be qualitatively different. For this is their organization and they are in control:

> ... you're actually developing an organization, you're controlling it. It's not token responsibility; you really feel that. You know from the start that you're cherished and wanted.... for the first part, people who come into **M-POWER** don't think they can handle that kind of thing. Then they see their peers handling it and they see people honestly trying to convey to them that yes, you can handle it if you want to do that. It's all up to you. I think the control belongs to the consumer and they can really feel it. They're not just being *told* that they have the control. (Bob, M-POWER member)

> M-POWER gives the consumer a form in which to fix the system, not the system having an opportunity in which to fix the person.... It gives the consumers ... what was taken away in psychiatric hospitals ... most psychiatric settings, even the best psychiatric settings ... you're asked to strip yourself of your rights.... M-POWER reverses that role. (Edith, M-POWER member)

Meetings

Over the past several years, I was able to observe a number of M-POWER meetings. Individual members of the organization were coping with all manner of psychiatric problems. Yet, contrary to what one might expect based on societal stereotypes about mental patients, the meetings were productive, democratic and fun. Strategic options were considered and debated. Rational decisions consistently were made. Agendas were covered. Business was taken care of. And this all was accomplished within a highly participatory, non-hierarchical, organizational structure and meeting format. While disruptive behaviour occasionally occurred, the leaders and members consistently demonstrated an ability to manage such situations effectively, respectfully and sensitively. Members repeatedly attested to the empowering experience of attending these meetings:

> ... it's being able to sit at a meeting, an M-POWER meeting, with our peers, all of whom have a mental illness. But when

we're at an M-POWER meeting, you wouldn't know it. It's just like a meeting of any other group or organization. Like nobody acts crazy, y'know. We have camaraderie between us, like we socialize before the meetings, we conduct meetings with agendas. We go through that meeting just as well as any other group or organization, maybe better. We don't talk about that we're sick and poor. We talk about what we *can* do about improving the mental health system.... We feel the courage to try and it's like you would never know we were a bunch of people with mental illness ... we follow the agenda; we make decisions; we have discussions; we brainstorm. We come up with all kinds of ideas, and we narrow them down to what we want to do. And then we take votes of what we want our actions to be. And I think those meetings are very empowering. (Sarah, M-POWER member)

... that's had a real profound impact on me and has helped me to overcome tons of mentalism ... realizing that given the opportunity and the support and the time to talk and think things through, that a person that can't read and write can sit at the same board meeting that I can sit at, and deal with the same issues, and bring up points I hadn't considered. (Carol, M-POWER member)

I think people listen when we're in a group. It's kind of hard to tell a group of 50 people or more you're wrong. (Robyn, M-POWER member)

Individual Empowerment

Organizational activists described in rich detail how their sense of personal empowerment had grown. They spoke about increased self-confidence and transformations in their self-images. They reported the development of new skills and growing feelings of self-efficacy. And they recounted their heightened awareness of societal stigma, discrimination and oppression. Most members had begun to confront their own internalized stigma and were involved in a redefinition of negative stereotypes and characterizations. The growing critical consciousness of many activists had reframed and politicized their own anger as a healthy emotion which could be channelled into constructive action:

M-POWER makes you take risks that you might not normally take, like standing at a podium and saying, "I'm a mental health consumer, and I'm angry." (Edith, M-POWER member)

I've felt the stigma of being mentally ill many times. M-POWER has helped me overcome that feeling. I feel now I'm a worthwhile person. I can contribute to the world and do something good.... I feel comfortable giving speeches and doing things for M-POWER. It's given me a cause that's helping myself personally but it's helping other people too. (Sarah, M-POWER member)

It's made me more aware of what my rights as a client are. It's really given me some serious issues to think about as far as how clients are treated, how clients and professionals either work together or work against each other. And it's really just increased my whole awareness of mental health in general. (Joyce, M-POWER member)

... there definitely are people who are ... developing an awareness that the mental health system in some ways has been unhelpful to them if not abusive and oppressive. Other people have had that awareness right along but haven't felt safe expressing and now are developing a feeling of safety and are expressing that. (Alice, M-POWER member)

Collective Empowerment

These changes took place within the context of organizational participation. New skills were developed in a variety of organizational activities, including recruiting new members, researching issues, planning campaigns, developing strategies and tactics, chairing meetings, public speaking, engaging in direct action and negotiating with institutional officials. Members emphasized the importance of dialogue with other activists in the process of consciousness-raising. Discussions about societal stereotypes and the phenomenon of internalized stigma were commonplace both at regular meetings and in less formal gatherings. Experienced leaders described and modelled their own struggles to overcome internalized stigma:

I spoke at the rally last summer. I've done a couple of workshops; I've been on TV. And so I'm out now. My name is out. I don't care anymore; I'm proud. I'm not proud of the fact that I have a mental illness. I'm proud of the fact that I have one and I've survived, and I've done as well as I have. And I'm doing as well as I have in spite of it. And I think that's something to be proud of. (Mary, M-POWER member)

It's degrading to other people to oppress them in the way you've been oppressed ... in M-POWER I've always sort of wanted ... a certain solidarity among the membership where nobody is better than anyone else and no one is worse than anyone else.... being in M-POWER has ... made me want to eliminate the stigma, both internal and external. (David, M-POWER member)

When we did a rally in M-POWER, I couldn't go public then. But when I was asked to speak about what happened to me and talk to people, I went public. And I'm glad I did. And today if they have another rally, I'm going to speak at it. But that first thought, y'know, I live in (X city); how am I going to face people here. I was petrified to do that. (Robyn, M-POWER member)

The M-POWER organization clearly seemed to be providing a vehicle for united action leading to collective empowerment to alter the social situation of mental health consumers. Members had a strong sense of ownership and control over this, their own organization. Meetings and collective actions were experienced as empowering at both the individual and collective levels. There was widespread consensus that the organization was developing considerable political clout. In the words of one M-POWER member, the organization had become an "incubator of empowerment."

The data clearly indicated that M-POWER had functioned as a developmental instrumentality of empowerment. Organizational activists had undergone profound changes in consciousness, confidence, self-esteem and skills development — a counter socialization process reversing much of the damage done by the learned helplessness and internalized stigma attendant to socialization into the role of "mental patient." Other investigations have yielded similar findings with different populations (Hoffman, 1978; Mondros, 1981; Kieffer, 1984). The evidence supports the generalized conclusion that client self-advocacy organizations have the potential to foster personal and collective empowerment for mental health consumers. Thus, initiating, developing and supporting such organizations may be a viable means for increasing consumer empowerment in the mental health system.

Limits of Self-Advocacy Organizations

It is important to examine limitations of consumer self-advocacy organizations, for they can not remedy all the deficiencies in the mental health system. These are voluntary organizations; therefore consumers can choose not to join. Obviously, non-members will not derive the benefits of participation. Other clients may wish to be involved with such an organization only to discover that none exists close by. Indeed, this complaint was heard from some of the unaffiliated consumers who were surveyed. And given the costs of developing and staffing such groups, it is unlikely that all areas of Massachusetts will be "organized" in the near future. Clearly, other services such as social clubs, day treatment, clubhouse work programs and residential facilities can be expected to deal with more mental health consumers than will client self-advocacy organizations. A significant expansion of consumer empowerment also will require changes in these programs and the providers who staff them.

When consumers do become involved in member-run self-advocacy organizations, the empowerment generated also may be differential. First, they may participate to varying degrees and at disparate levels. Despite the non-hierarchical, open, democratic structure and style of M-POWER, some members are more involved than others. And while leadership functions and roles are rotated frequently, nevertheless there is a discernable, although permeable, core group of activists. Opportunities for personal growth and the development of new skills and capacities are more available for those who choose or are chosen to play leadership roles.

Second, consumer self-advocacy organizations may have more capacity to engender empowerment among individuals than at the collective level. The interviews did document members' perceptions about M-POWER's growing political clout and the organization currently is engaged in campaigns to develop a consumer bill of rights and to change DMH policy guidelines regarding informed consent. However, the most dramatic testimony from organizational activists described transformations in consciousness, personal growth, increased confidence and the development of new skills.

While the voice of organized consumers arguably is becoming stronger and more audible within the mental health system, basic needs resources for income, housing, health care, safety and employment are shrinking. This deterioration in material conditions is largely a product of almost two decades of social welfare cutbacks at the state and federal levels. Mental health consumers, like so many relatively powerless groups (e.g., welfare recipients, public housing tenants, racial minorities, low-wage workers, children and low-income women), have been unable to stem the tide. They have not taken successful collective action as a group organized "for itself" to alter economic and political relations of power at the macro level. Thus, while personal empowerment may be increasing and some measure of collective power may be developed within the mental health bureaucracy, these gains may be occurring within a larger context of growing disempowerment for mental health consumers as a group in American society.

Mental health consumers are impacted profoundly by economic conditions and social welfare policies at the state and national levels. Clearly, a relatively local consumer self-advocacy organization has limited capacity to alter power relations in these arenas. Translating individual and middle level collective empowerment into political clout at those levels is more complex than simply aggregating empowered individuals and local groups. While there is a growing mental health consumer movement across the United States, it has yet to generate the requisite collective empowerment to realize fundamental political and structural change. Both a strategy and a structure are needed. Until and unless both are developed, prospects for collective empowerment will be limited substantially.

Thus, locally based member-run client self-advocacy organizations may be necessary but not sufficient for increasing consumer empowerment in the mental health system. There are compelling reasons to foster the development and expansion of such organizations. But not everyone chooses or has the opportunity to join. Members participate unevenly and therefore experience empowerment differentially. The current capacity of these organizations to generate empowerment is limited. More is required from both provider staff and the DMH bureaucracy if consumer empowerment is to be broadened and deepened.

FACILITATING CONSUMER EMPOWERMENT: ROLES FOR HELPING PROFESSIONALS

"Too many mental health professionals believe that empowerment is something to be given rather than facilitating conditions by which the consumer can take control" (Provider in response to a question regarding barriers to increased consumer empowerment).

Over the past several decades a consumer rights movement has swept across the United States. The recipients of services have challenged the power and prerogatives of professional providers in virtually every field, including medicine, psychiatry, law, education and social work. Much of the conflict has focused on the traditional model of professionalism, characterized by elitism, distance, exclusivity, monopoly of knowledge and expertise, paternalism, lack of accountability to the public, and power differentials with clients. Self-help groups and consumer rights organizations have formed in reaction to a professional paradigm which increasingly has come under fire both for the quality and quantity of outcomes produced and for the process by which help is delivered.

Part of the process of overcoming internalized stigma, building self and collective esteem and developing critical consciousness is to turn the tables on the powerful. Qualities once perceived as deficits are redefined as strengths. Characteristics of the mighty are questioned and critically reinterpreted. Minuses become pluses and vice versa. Thus emerge phenomena such as "Black Pride" and "Gay Pride." Clients of services redefine themselves as "consumers of services" or "survivors of the mental health system." Previous "helpers" now may be viewed as "oppressors." Such polarization also may be essential to drive the process of change. A recognition of subtleties, exceptions and shades of gray often is achieved at the price of an "analysis paralysis." To paraphrase community organizer Saul Alinsky, people don't take bold, decisive action when they believe that they are 51% right. A high octane antithesis is required to fuel the engines of paradigmatic change.

However, an empowerment approach includes a constructive role for service providers. This paper seeks to contribute to the developing synthesis which will replace the traditional model of professional helping. That new paradigm takes full advantage of valuable contributions from professional knowledge and expertise, while eliminating the disempowering aspects intrinsic to the conventional provider-consumer relationship (Staples, 1997). "Helping as usual" no longer will suffice, but a remodelled role for professionals usually will be helpful.

What are the implications for provider staff in the mental health system? While many providers are supportive of increased consumer empowerment, remedial education and changed practices often will be necessary before they become effective facilitators of empowerment. Frequently, providers underestimate consumer capacity and overestimate the role of staff in the empowerment process. Such attitudes may be a product of the traditional model of professional-client relationships.

An empowerment approach necessitates changes. Empowerment is not something to be done to or for another. It entails action on behalf of oneself or with one's group to obtain and exercise greater control over one's own life. Thus mental health providers inherently are limited in their ability to increase consumer empowerment. However, the empowerment process can be facilitated by staff who establish relationships, provide access to resources, furnish opportunities, strengthen capacities and create sanctions which enable individuals and groups to develop greater personal and collective power.

Practice Principles

The empowerment literature, data from the study and my personal experience as a community organizer help generate a number of practice principles which providers can employ in order to facilitate consumer empowerment.

1. Establish working relationships with individuals and groups, based on collaboration, trust, and the sharing of power. Interactions should be characterized by genuineness, mutual respect, open communication, and informality (Gutiérrez, 1990; see also Cochran, 1990; Deegan, 1990; Fox, 1984; Hegar and Hunzeker, 1988; Pinderhughes, 1983; Rappaport, 1981; Rose and Black, 1985).

Professional training generally does not foster the creation of such relationships. Indeed, the classic concept of "professional distance" is dramatically opposed to this approach. The traditional model emphasizes professional expertise and control and has been fundamentally elitist in nature. Facilitating empowerment requires "helpers" to share their power, to decrease professional distance and to work in a more egalitarian alliance with their clients. Both the interviews and survey data from open-ended survey questions highlighted the failure of many providers to work with consumers in such a manner. Consumers and providers tended to agree that professional helpers are less likely to share power when it is viewed in "zero sum" terms as a finite and scarce resource. Under such circumstances there is a tendency to think competitively; the other's gain is seen as one's own loss. Power is regarded as something to be preserved and protected. A dynamic of "I can't be up if you're not down" prevails; status differentials are defended rather than deconstructed and dismantled. An empowerment paradigm reframes expanded consumer power as a "win-win" situation for professional helpers, making it more possible to establish working relationships with clients based on partnership and mutuality.

2. Help consumers become aware of the linkage between personal problems and institutional power relations. Facilitate consciousness-raising and critical analysis. Help consumers aggregate individual problems. Work toward collective solutions where appropriate (Chavez, 1990; Cochran, 1990; Cox, 1991; Freire, 1970, 1973; Gutiérrez, 1990; Kieffer, 1984; Rose and Black, 1985; Simon, 1990; Solomon, 1976; Staples, 1990).

Under the traditional mental health model, professionals usually offer help and services for individual clients with personal needs and problems. Typically, the client is the exclusive target of change; the focus of helping is at the individual level with an emphasis on internal indicators of empowerment such as self-esteem, feelings of self-efficacy and a sense of greater control over life. Such assistance is essential for mental health consumers and should not be trivialized. However, at times, facilitating both personal and collective empowerment will require providers to do more at the collective level and along external dimensions outside the minds and feelings of consumers. Individual problems obtaining basic needs resources for income, housing, education, transportation, employment and training often entail systemic solutions. Collective action may be necessary to produce these institutional changes. In such instances, consumers should be the torque of change not the target. Staff can play an important role helping clients raise consciousness and connect with consumer self-advocacy organizations. At the same time, they must be careful not to impose their agenda for social action.

3. Actively involve consumers in the change process and enable them to experience a sense of personal power within the helping relationship (Gutiérrez, 1990). Maximize opportunities for decision-making and taking action. Don't "do for" consumers if they can act on their own behalf, but model where appropriate (Cochran, 1990; Kieffer, 1984; Mathis, 1990; Pernell, 1985; Pinderhughes, 1983; Rappaport, 1981; Rose, 1990).

The classic model posits a professional expert (independent variable) ministering to a relatively passive client (dependent variable). An empowerment approach entails giving the consumer a very active voice and role in the helping process. The consumer's own actions are presumed to have a causal effect on her or him. Thus, the dependent ("the helped") also become independent variables ("helpers") for themselves. They move from objects to be acted upon to subjects (Freire, 1973) capable of acting in partnership with providers to produce changes at both individual and collective levels and along internal and external dimensions. Current teaching in the "helping professions" does stress a more active role for clients. And most providers accept this approach intellectually. But in practice, their first instinct often is to "do for" not to help clients "do more." Consumer interviews documented this tendency. More training is needed to close the gap between rhetoric and action.

4. Help consumers strengthen self-images, including: self-esteem, dignity, confidence, efficacy and sense of control (Barton, 1984; Chavez, 1990; Deegan, 1988; Fox, 1984; Hirayama and Hirayama, 1985; Kieffer, 1984; McDermott, 1989; Pinderhughes, 1983; Rappaport, 1981).

Feeling good about oneself is essential for developing the internal dimensions of individual empowerment. Providers can play a key role in facilitating such growth by building on consumer strengths (Dodd and Gutiérrez, 1990), rather than focusing exclusively on weaknesses. Under the classic "deficit model," the professional diagnoses the client's problems and employs expertise to ameliorate them. An empowerment approach does not ignore the consumer's difficulties and troubles but begins positively with a mutual recognition of assets and abilities. These competencies and capacities are valuable resources which are used extensively in the helping process. Consumers experience themselves as active, able and autonomous rather than passive, weak and dependent.

5. Work with consumers to develop new knowledge and skills. Challenge them so as to maximize opportunities for growth. Help them stretch without breaking (Cox, 1991; Gutiérrez, 1990; Hirayama and Hirayama, 1985; Kieffer, 1984; Pernell, 1985; Sherman and Wenocur, 1983).

Enhanced self-images are necessary but not sufficient for increased consumer empowerment. In order for people to take charge of their lives, they frequently need additional knowledge and skills. These concrete tools help consumers make real changes in their life situations. Thus, the external dimensions of empowerment are developed. The role of the professional is to provide both stimulus and support; challenges, choices and chances to grow. An adult education model seems most appropriate.

6. Help consumers achieve tangible instrumental results (material resources, access to programs and services, opportunities for personal advancement, institutional changes) and expressive benefits (social relationships, reduction of isolation, public and peer recognition, building community, group solidarity) (Gutiérrez, 1990; Hasenfeld, 1987; Hirayama and Cetingok,

1988; Mathis, 1990; Pinderhughes, 1983; Rose and Black, 1985; Staples, 1990).

Empowerment is more than a process. It transcends self-perceptions and can't be confined to the acquisition of knowledge, capacities and skills. "Have nots" need more than to "have a say" in decisions and processes which affect their lives. There must be a product dimension to empowerment which incorporates instrumental as well as expressive pay offs. Both the material conditions and qualitative aspects of one's life should improve as empowerment is developed. Staff must be more than providers of insights, esteem and enlightenment. The helping process product also should include substantive results and benefits.

Facilitating Techniques

Consistent with the above practice principles, a number of specific techniques can be employed by helping professionals. These methods and practices are well documented in the empowerment literature.

- Listen carefully to the consumer (Cochran, 1990; Shulman, 1984; Staples, 1990).
- Enable consumers to identify their own needs and to define problems (Deegan, 1990; Freire, 1970; Gutiérrez, 1990).
- Encourage consumers to express anger. Validate their concerns (Cox, 1991; Deegan, 1992; Kieffer, 1984).
- Identify and build upon existing strengths (Dodd and Gutiérrez, 1990). Respect what already has been learned. Remind consumers of past achievements. Help them recognize existing capacities (Cowger, 1994; Pinderhughes, 1983; Rappaport, 1981).
- Help raise consciousness about institutional power relations and the efficacy of collective action (Kieffer 1984; Moreau, 1990; Simon, 1990).
- Help consumers develop and strengthen critical thinking abilities (Burghardt, 1982; Freire, 1973; Mathis, 1990).
- Expose consumers to alternative paradigms, different ways of thinking about and understanding social reality (Chavez, 1990; Pernell, 1985; Rose and Black, 1985).
- Educate, provide and share information (Hegar, 1989; Nystrom, 1989; Weaver, 1982).
- Teach and develop skills, especially those for strategic analysis, planning and taking action (Biegel, 1984; Dodd and Gutiérrez, 1990; Hirayama and Hirayama, 1985).

- Create a safe environment for developing and strengthening skills and competencies. Be supportive and make it possible for consumers to experiment, practice and to make mistakes (Cox, 1991; Deegan, 1988; Pernell, 1985).
- Work with consumers to help reduce internalized stigma and mentalism that they may have developed as a result of life experiences in general society (Chamberlin, 1978; Deegan, 1992; Rose and Black, 1985).
- Help consumers develop goals and visions for change (Chavez, 1990; Fabricant, 1988; Fisher, 1984).
- Provide opportunities and encouragement for consumers to make informed choices (Coppola and Rivas, 1985; Hegar, 1989; Hirayama and Cetingok, 1988).
- Help consumers recognize, explore and create meaningful options for decisions and action including mutual aid, advocacy and collective strategies (Cochran, 1990; Fox, 1984; Pernell, 1985).
- Share expertise and opinions without imposing them, manipulating for agreement or creating deference (Hegar and Hunzeker, 1988; Rose, 1990; Solomon, 1976).
- Utilize the pedagogy of the question. Ask questions rather than telling consumers what to do (Burghardt, 1982; Freire, 1970; Simon, 1990).
- Help consumers think through the possible outcomes and consequences of potential decisions and actions (Chavez, 1990; Kieffer, 1984; Rose, 1990).
- Provide supports once decisions are made or actions are undertaken (Cochran, 1990; Pernell, 1985; Pinderhughes, 1983).
- Recognize, legitimate and help strengthen existing networks and natural support systems (Balgopal, 1988; Humm-Delgado and Delgado, 1986; Solomon, 1976).
- Refer consumers to advocacy, social action and self-help/mutual aid groups when possible, allowing them to decide if participation is appropriate (Cox, 1991; Pernell, 1985; Sherman and Wenocur, 1983).

Lip service is often paid to principles and techniques such as these. Indeed, significant numbers of providers already have changed their attitudes and practice in ways that are more consistent with these ideas. Others have attended training sessions and workshops which have featured an empowerment approach. However, an institutionalized change in the helping paradigm used by mental health staff will require greater depth and breadth of remedial education throughout the entire mental health system (Shera and Page, 1995).

SANCTIONING CONSUMER EMPOWERMENT: SYSTEMIC SUPPORT

The mental health system is based on a mentalist philosophy. Offering cosmetically improved programs, a few consumers on committees and minimal staff training is not enough if too much of the old mentalism is intact. The system can't be easily fixed. (David, M-POWER member)

How can the Massachusetts mental health bureaucracy operate so as to sanction greater consumer empowerment? Certainly, the willingness and ability of provider staff to facilitate consumer empowerment is linked to perceptions of their own power within the bureaucracy. Lack of power by staff is intertwined with anxiety and anger about cutbacks, fear of job loss, low morale, over-work and burnout. There is a widespread perception that field staff steadily are losing power within the mental health system due to budget cuts and managerial restructuring.

Large private insurance companies play a powerful but often hidden role. The Department of Mental Health (DMH) does not possess unilateral power, and its policies and practices often are dictated by corporate profit seeking in the market economy. Nevertheless, DMH management can evaluate the workload expectations, communication patterns, supervision models, decision-making processes and general working conditions for field staff. Improving the circumstances of provider staff is both an end in itself and a means to increasing consumer empowerment.

There also is a need for provider training and remedial education. It is important to recognize that the DMH already has done considerable good work in this area. However, more is needed. Training should be broad enough to include all regions in the state and all levels within the bureaucracy, deep enough to provide more substance and systematic enough to be consistent. The practice principles and techniques suggested herein should be incorporated into that educational material. Most important, organized consumers should be given a central role in the design and delivery of this training.

Increased consumer empowerment can be sanctioned by strengthening and enforcing individual client rights. Laws, regulations, policies and procedures should be structured to maximize consumer dignity, choices and decision-making opportunities. Enforcement must be vigorous in order to close the gap between rhetoric and reality. Both psychiatric hospitals and community programs should be evaluated to assess whether individual consumer rights are guaranteed and actually protected.

Consumer empowerment requires more than token participation in insignificant decisions. Yet, organized consumers frequently criticize DMH for this very practice. The experience of Bob, an M-POWER member, is instructive. DMH recently has begun a restructuring process and has reached out for consumer involvement. Bob has participated but feels that "DMH is not making a real sincere effort." He believes, "The department only wants feedback on what they've predetermined." In support of this view he cites a pattern of unrealistic deadlines, rushed meetings and poor scheduling for consumer input. In one instance, clients were presented a thick document set forth in highly technical language and asked for written responses and changes within three days. He argues, "There will be participation, but no one will know what they participated in. There's lots of motion, but things pretty much stay the same."

The actions of DMH in this process do not seem to match its rhetoric. Bob feels that he and other consumers have been given the message that their input is mere window dressing. Likewise, hiring a few more consumers for positions within the mental health system is not sufficient for expanding empowerment. More than a minimal transfer of some of the actors filling various roles is required. There must be a transformation in the very nature of those roles resulting in altered relations of power between consumers and providers (Miller, 1971). Such a fundamental change would entail the genuine sharing of power between the DMH and its consumers. This would be operationalized by maximizing the role of consumers in decision-making, fully involving them in designing and implementing programs and making all aspects of the mental health system accountable to them.

David, an M-POWER member, believes that the DMH is making a good faith effort to respond to consumers, "but they just don't get it." He contends that the department must recognize and deal with consumers as an organized group. Otherwise, he predicts a pattern of trivial participation, token hirings, co-opted consumer input and superficial changes. "They have to get out of our way as we empower ourselves."

Guidelines for Organizational Support

There also are programmatic and structural changes which the mental health system can implement to help make such empowerment more possible. The following recommendations offer guidelines for program planning, development, staffing, management, monitoring and evaluation.

1. Involve consumers directly and centrally in any needs/assets assessment process.

Too often, mental health professionals have decided what consumers' needs are and how they best can be met. Methods for involving consumers in the needs assessment process have been described extensively in the social work literature (Siegel, Attkisson and Cohn, 1974; Sallis and Henggeler, 1980; Marti-Costa and Serrano Garcia, 1983; Delgado, 1996). Mental health consumers should play a central role in research design, gathering data, analysis of findings and recommendations for action. The assets and resources which they bring to the table should be incorporated into this process.

2. Include consumers fully in program design and development.

Once unmet needs are determined, programs usually are planned and put in place. An empowerment approach requires that consumers be equal partners in this process. They are a source of knowledge and expertise about how services should be designed and delivered.

3. Name a majority of consumers to all program governing and advisory boards. Where possible, select representatives from organized groups.

When consumers comprise a small portion of a board's numbers, it is easy for them to be ignored, intimidated or otherwise marginalized. In order for them to be empowered, they must be a powerful voting block. Program accountability will be served best when the consumers of services constitute a majority on governance and advisory boards.

Token representation on such bodies can lead to empty-handed empowerment. Rather than recruiting consumers merely as a type (i.e., examples of a particular group), representatives of various client organizations should be chosen if possible. This will help yield consumer input that better embodies the larger group than that provided by isolated individuals. Indeed, atypical individuals often are chosen for this very fact and become the personification of tokenism in the sorry and cynical tradition of "Uncle Toms."

4. Incorporate mutual aid into programs whenever possible.

Mutual aid is consistent with the goals and methods of empowerment. It also is not mutually exclusive with an important role for professional helpers.

However, the traditional model of professionalism is antithetical to this concept. Currently, mutual aid is undervalued and underutilized in many, if not most, mental health programs. Adoption of this approach holds potential benefits for both the quality of services and cost effectiveness.

5. Develop programmatic capacities for advocacy—especially self-advocacy by consumers.

Programs should not be limited just to helping individual consumers. Systemic and institutional change is also necessary for empowerment to be realized. There are two levels. First, programs themselves should have clear grievance guidelines so that individual or multiple consumers can challenge particular policies, procedures and practices. Second, programs should be able and willing to involve consumers in advocacy efforts to change institutions and systems such as the department of public welfare, local housing authorities, employers, media outlets, transportation authorities, local police, other mental health agencies and the mental health system itself.

6. Give consumers a central role in the hiring and evaluation of staff.

Empowerment principles underscore that helping professionals should be responsive and responsible to the people whom they serve. However, this is an area where the mental health system's rhetoric exceeds reality. Often, the actual participation of consumers in these processes has been limited and sporadic. Specific procedures should be instituted so that the mental health system can "walk the walk" of empowerment rather than simply continuing to "talk the talk."

7. Actively recruit and train current or former consumers to become staff members where possible and appropriate.

Such individuals will have insights and a perspective gleaned from their own experience in the mental health system. Since they are coping with their own mental disability, they have the potential to become powerful and inspirational role models for other consumers. There are a number of successful examples of consumers who already have followed this path. More are needed. Explicit policies should be developed to make the selection and education of such individuals a priority.

8. Develop formal structures and processes for consumers to monitor and evaluate services.

All programs should be accountable to the consumers whom they serve. Whether through pre-existing boards or by special committees, structures should be in place to enable consumers to watch over and assess the services provided (Finn, 1994). Evaluation processes should encourage constructive criticism and provide safeguards from possible staff reprisals.

The mental health bureaucracy is the primary source of services for current and former psychiatric patients. It follows that any department of mental health will be a primary target of social action by organized consumers seeking to improve policies, programs, procedures and practices. Provider professionals who interact with consumers on a regular basis at times will be the objects of criticism and change efforts. While many mental health staff have discarded the most pernicious aspects of the traditional helping paradigm, others have not. As more consumers organize, they can be expected to press for more changes in the behaviour of helping professionals.

Overall, I am optimistic that consumer empowerment will continue to increase in the Massachusetts mental health system. While challenges and barriers exist for each, the consumers, providers and administrators met during the course of my investigation give reason to be hopeful. All three demonstrate the commitment and energy to move forward. With insurance companies wielding increased power as unseen players in the mental health system, it becomes more imperative for these three stakeholders to work together to foster consumer empowerment. Even though they have distinct and different interests, there also is much common ground. Clearly, there are significant roles and responsibilities for each as they develop, facilitate and sanction consumer empowerment.

REFERENCES

Balgopal, P. R. (1988). Social networks and Asian Indian families. In C. Jacobs and D. D. Bowles (Eds.), *Ethnicity and race: Critical concepts in social work*. Silver Spring, MD: NASW.

Barton, R. S. (1984). *Cognitive and developmental aspects of empowerment: An empirical comparison between citizen leaders and non-leaders*. Unpublished doctoral dissertation, University of Oregon.

Biegel, D. E. (1984). Help seeking and receiving in urban ethnic neighborhoods: Strategies for empowerment. In J. Rappaport and R. Hess (Eds.), *Studies in empowerment: Steps toward understanding and action* (pp. 119-143). New York: The Haworth Press.

Burghardt, S. (1982). *The other side of organizing*. Cambridge, MA: Schenkman.

Chamberlin, J. (1978) . *On our own*. New York: McGraw-Hill Book Company.

Chavez, M. (1990). Empowerment in practice. *Networking bulletin: Empowerment and Family Support*, 1(2), 1-2, 16-20.

Cochran, M. (1990). The transforming role. *Networking Bulletin: Empowerment and Family Support*, 1(3), 25.

Coppola, M. and R. Rivas. (1985). The task-action group technique: A case study of empowering the elderly. In M. Parenes (Ed.), *Innovations in social group work: Feedback from practice to theory* (pp. 133-147). New York: The Haworth Press.

Cowger, C. (1994). Assessing client strengths: Clinical assessment for client empowerment. *Social Work*, 39(3), 262-268.

Cox, E.O. (1991). The critical role of social action in empowerment oriented groups. *Social Work with Groups*, 14(3/4): 77-90.

Deegan, P. E. (1988). Recovery: The lived experience of rehabilitation. *Psychosocial Rehabilitation Journal*, 11(4), 11-19.

Deegan, P. E. (1990). Spirit breaking: When the helping professions hurt. *The Humanistic Psychologist*, 18(3): 301-313.

Deegan, P. E. (1992). The independent living movement and people with psychiatric disabilities: Taking back control over our own lives. *Psychosocial Rehabilitation Journal*, *15*(3), 3-19.

Delgado, M. (1996). Puerto Rican food establishments as social service organizations: Results of an asset assessment. *Journal of Community Practice*, 3(2): 57-77.

Dodd, P. and Gutiérrez, L. (1990). Preparing students for the future: A power perspective community practice. *Administration in Social Work*, 14(2), 63-78.

Fabricant, M. (1988). Empowering the homeless. *Social Policy*, (Spring), 49-55.

Finn, J. L. (1994). The promise of participatory research. *Journal of Progressive Human Services*, 5(2), 25-42.

Fisher, R. (1984). *Let the people decide: Neighborhood organizing in America*. Boston: C.K. Hall and Company.

Fox, J. (1984). Social work ethics and children: Protection vs. empowerment. *Children and Youth Services Review*, 6, 319-328.

Freire, P. (1970). *Pedagogy of the oppressed*. New York: The Seabury Press.

Freire, P. (1973). *Education for critical consciousness*. New York: Continuum.

Gutiérrez, L.M. (1990). Working with women of color: An empowerment perspective. *Social Work*, (March), 149-153.

Hasenfeld, Y. (1987). Power in social work practice. *Social Service Review*, 61(3), 469-483.

Hegar, R.L. and Hunzeker, J. M. (1988). Moving toward empowerment-based practice in public child welfare. *Social Work*, 33, 499-502.

Hegar, R. (1989). Empowerment-based practice with children. *Social Service Review*, 63, 372-383.

Hirayama, H. and Cetingok, M. (1988). Empowerment: A social work approach for Asian immigrants. *Social Casework*, (January), 41-47.

Hirayama, H. and Hirayama K. (1985). Empowerment through group participation: Process and goal. In M. Parenes (Ed.), *Innovations in social group work: Feedback from practice to theory* (pp. 119-131). New York: The Haworth Press.

Hoffman, C. (1978). Empowerment movements and mental health: Locus of control and commitment to the united farm workers. *Journal of Community Psychology*, 6(3), 216-221.

Humm-Delgado, D. and Delgado M. (1986). Gaining community entree to assess service needs of Hispanics. *Social Casework*, 67, 80-89.

Kieffer, C. H. (1984). Citizen empowerment: A developmental perspective. In J. Rappaport and R. Hess (Eds.), *Studies in empowerment: Steps toward understanding and action* (pp. 9-36). New York: The Haworth Press.

Marti-Costa, S. and Serrano Garcia, I. (1983). Needs assessment and community development: An ideological perspective. *Prevention in Human Services*, (Summer),75-88.

Mathis, T. P. (1990). *Toward an empowerment-oriented practice: Implications for family centered social work in the 1990s.* Invitational paper presented at Annual Conference of National Association of Social Workers, Boston.

McDermott, C. J. (1989). Empowering the elderly nursing home resident: The resident rights campaign. *Social Work*, (March), 155-157.

Miller, S. M. (1971). Three Ts of power. *New Society*, 16, 1208-1210.

Mondros, J. B. (1981). *A study in neighborhood organization: Issue resolution and empowerment.* Unpublished doctoral dissertation, University of Pennsylvania.

Moreau, M. (1990). Empowerment through advocacy and consciousness raising. *Journal of Sociology and Social Welfare*, 17, 53-67.

Nystrom, J. F. (1989). Empowerment model for delivery of social work services in public schools. *Social Work in Education*, 160-170.

Pernell, R. B. (1985). Empowerment and social group work In M. Parenes (Ed.), *Innovations in social group work: Feedback from practice to theory* (pp. 107-117). New York: The Haworth Press.

Pinderhughes, E. B. (1983). Empowerment for our clients and for ourselves. *Social Casework*, 64, 331-338.

Rappaport, J. (1981). In praise of paradox: A social policy of empowerment over prevention. *American Journal of Community Psychology*, 9, 1-25.

Rose, S. (1990). Advocacy/empowerment: An approach to clinical practice for social work. *Journal of Sociology and Social Welfare*, 17, 41-51.

Rose, S. and Black, B. (1985). *Advocacy and empowerment: Mental health care in the community.* Boston: Routledge and Kegan Paul.

Sallis, J. and Henggeler S. W. (1980). Needs assessment: A critical review. *Administration in Mental Health*, 7, 205-206.

Shera, W. and Page J. (1995). Creating more effective human service organizations through strategies of empowerment. *Administration in Social Work*, 19(4), 1-15.

Sherman, W. R. and Wenocur, S. (1983). Empowering public welfare workers through mutual support. *Social Work*, 28, 375-383.

Shulman, L. (1984). *The skills of helping: Individuals and groups* (2nd ed). Itasca, IL: F.E. Peacock.

Siegel, L. M., Attkinsson, C.C. and Cohn, A.H. (1974). Mental health needs assessment: Strategies and techniques. In W. A. Hargreaves, C. C. Attkisson, L. M. Siegel, M. H. McIntyre and J. E. Sorenson (Eds.), *Resource materials for community mental health program evaluation* (pp. 57-58). Rockville, MD: National Institute of Mental Health.

Simon, B. L. (1990). Rethinking empowerment. *Journal of Progressive Human Services*, 1(1), 27-39.

Solomon, B. B. (1976). *Black empowerment*. New York: Columbia University Press.

Staples, L. (1990). Powerful ideas about empowerment. *Administration in Social Work*, 14(2), 29-42.

Staples, L. (1993). *Consumer empowerment in the Massachusetts mental health system: A comparison of attitudes, perceptions, and opinions within and between consumer and provider groups*. Unpublished doctoral dissertation, Boston University Graduate School.

Staples, L. (1997). Toward an empowerment model of social work. *Den Sociale Hoiskole i Aarhus* (pp. 37-49). Danis School of Social Work: Aarhus, DK.

Weaver, D. R. (1982). Empowering treatment skills for helping black families. *Social Casework*, 63, 100-105.

Chapter 8

AN EMPOWERMENT PRACTICE MODEL
FOR LOW-INCOME WOMEN

Jean F. East
Graduate School of Social Work
University of Denver

This chapter presents a project that was designed based on empowerment theory. The three domains of empowerment practice, personal, inter-personal and political, are described as they have been conceptualized in a model specifically designed for women who receive welfare and are affected by welfare reform. Feminist theory is also incorporated in this model.

Empowerment is a process by which people—individuals, groups, communities and organizations—gain mastery over issues of concern to them (Rappaport, 1987). Empowerment is also described as a multi-level construct that includes processes at the individual or intra-personal, interpersonal and political or community level (Gutiérrez, 1990; Zimmerman, 1995). As Rappaport (1995) notes, "empowerment is a conceptually complex and highly nuanced idea," and while common definitions are emerging, we need to continue to build on "our research based understanding of empowerment as more than a general idea" (p.797).

Application models and research on empowerment interventions for low-income women, many of whom are women of colour, is a significant topic. The effects of racism, sexism and classism on this population can lead to powerlessness experienced in many dimensions of life (Gutiérrez, 1990). This paper addresses this topic based on the author's personal experience as the co-creator and researcher of a project designed for women receiving welfare assistance. First the project will be described, including its background and philosophy. This will be followed by a conceptualization of the theoretical components of feminist theory and a postmodern perspective as integrated into empowerment theory. Based on this theoretical framework for empowerment, the specific ways in which the three empowerment domains, personal, inter-personal and political, have been conceptualized as principles and services will then be described. Finally, the research model currently being developed will be explored and initial findings reported.

The presentation of this empowerment model is a work in progress and is written partly in a narrative form. Rappaport (1995) notes that "a narrative approach that links process to practice and attends to the voices of the people of interest" is an appropriate means to extend empowerment research and practice (p.795). My voice and the voices of other women who participate in this process with me will be woven throughout this story.

THE PROJECT MODEL

The empowerment model described in this paper is based on a project which began in 1995 in Denver, Colorado, known as Project WISE, A Women's Initiative for Service and Empowerment. This project is unique in that it was designed by myself and a colleague based specifically on empowerment constructs and models. The philosophy of the project suggests that in order for women with low incomes to attain a sense of empowerment and a healthy interdependence with their community, they must have opportunities to experience change at the personal, inter-personal and political levels.

The target population is women with low incomes, and specifically those receiving AFDC or TANF, Temporary Assistance to Needy Families, as of July, 1997. The ethnic background of the women is 19% African-American, 40% Anglo, 40% Hispanic and 1% Native American. The women range in age from 19 to 45; some have received welfare for less than two years, but most have received this aid over a period of four or more years.

It is our belief that women who do not have adequate economic resources are confronted daily with policies and programs that do not meet their needs. They are also caught up in attitudes of sexism that create conflicting views about women and their place in society. In working with women who receive low incomes, they tell us that in order to become more empowered, many supports are needed. In a welfare reform environment, where the word empowerment is frequently part of the rhetoric of change, this author has found that the strategies for attaining economic self-sufficiency, and therefore assumed empowerment, are often limited and not inclusive of the experiences and needs of women. Many of the traditional services provided to women in welfare self-sufficiency projects, such as education, training, job search skills and access to child care, are not enough. They do not address the need for a personal sense of self-sufficiency. It is our observation that, in addition to human capital skills, access to the resources of child care, medical benefits and transportation, the women also need opportunities to gain a sense of mastery over their personal environment and the issues that concern them. Therefore, in creating Project WISE we have used the three empowerment domains as the basis for the program. It is our belief that participation in any one of the services, which were developed to match the three domains, would enhance an individual's sense of empowerment and that participation in all three areas would broaden and strengthen the empowerment process and outcomes. This model is particularly relevant with the demands of the new welfare legislation, the Personal Responsibility and Work Opportunity Reconciliation Act of 1996. One potential effect of this legislation is to add tremendous stress to the lives of women with low incomes.

In the Project WISE model, personal empowerment is conceptualized in a strengths based and feminist model of individual counselling. Personal empowerment includes processes for developing self-awareness, self-acceptance and self-esteem, and cultural identity/spirituality. Inter-personal empowerment includes increased knowledge and skills in such areas as assertiveness, decision-making, maintaining a healthy system of social and emotional support and accessing resources. The service component associated with inter-personal empowerment is support and psycho-educational groups. Political empowerment occurs through taking action in a wider community context on one's own behalf and on the behalf of others. This process includes critical thinking and consciousness-raising, making a contribution through volunteer activities and, in linking with others, taking control of and making positive changes in aspects of one's external environment. This process occurs through a leadership development project and involvement in the community, particularly in local welfare rights organizations.

In its first three years of operation, Project WISE has seen 81 individuals for counselling (four or more sessions), 307 women have participated in groups, and 45 women have participated in leadership development and advocacy activities. Fifty women have participated in at least two of the above activities.

In addition to services provided as conceptualized above, Project WISE strives to see itself as both an empowering and an empowered organization. "Distinctions have been made between *empowering* organizations which facilitate confidence and competencies of individual members and *empowered* organizations which influence the environment or community (Florin and Wandersman, 1990, p.44-45). Zimmerman (1995) notes that grass-roots organizations have the potential to be both. The framework proposed by Maton and Salem (1995) describes the characteristics of empowering settings that Project WISE works to incorporate. These include (1) a philosophy and belief system that is inspiring, strengths based and works to focus individuals beyond themselves; (2) a role structure that is accessible; (3) leadership that is inspiring, talented, committed to both setting and members; and (4) a support system that provides a sense of community (Maton and Salem, 1995, p.631).

Project WISE also works to be empowered by involving both participants and staff in influencing the distribution of power and decision-making within the local community, particularly in relation to welfare reform. We are involved in local community efforts to design welfare reform programs and advocacy organizations that challenge many of the welfare reform assumptions.

EMPOWERMENT PRACTICE AND A FEMINIST POSTMODERN PERSPECTIVE

Empowerment practice, in the context of this article, is that which has been proposed by Cox and Parsons (1994), Gutiérrez (1990, 1991), Rappaport (1987, 1995), Zimmerman (1990, 1995) and Zimmerman and Rappaport (1988) and will not be further elaborated at this point. Empowerment practice theory as it has developed has also been and is enriched by the integration of feminist theory (Brinker-Jenkins and Hooyman,1986; Gutiérrez,1991). This integration may be particularly important if one is developing and providing interventions with women. In many ways the integration seems obvious, for the feminist perspective is well grounded in the empowerment of women. However, I have found that in other ways the integration is challenging. While feminist social workers like myself seem naturally drawn to the integration of empowerment and feminist theory, especially in the application with women, I find that many of the women participants in Project WISE express anti-women sentiments. It is not uncommon in the group settings to hear a woman say, "This is a new experience for me, because I don't like women, I don't trust them." In working with inner-city women who are struggling with survival, Baines (1997) wrote that she experienced the application of some feminist principles as often not effective. Specifically, the goal of an egalitarian relationship; using such strategies as de-mystifying the helping process and self-disclosure were not helpful. In Project WISE we have found these experiences useful; however, I am challenged to consider how a feminist empowerment perspective may not fit for low-income women. This raises questions for me of how class and culture interact with gender experiences and how we can account for these in our empowerment interventions.

Despite this challenge, the feminist empowerment model developed by Worell and Remer (1992), integrated with the empowerment perspectives developed in social work and community psychology literature, is particularly applicable in the Project WISE model. Worell and Remer (1992) conceptualize empowerment in two ways; first, as an individual process that assists a woman "in dealing with her life situations through achieving flexibility in problem-solution and developing a full range of interpersonal and life skills" (p.22). Second, empowerment encourages women to develop an understanding of the external conditions "that devalue and subordinate them as women or as members of minority groups" (p.22). In essence these two goals encompass the three empowerment domains noted earlier. Within these goals Worell and Remer identify specific intervention strategies. These include such components as sex-role analysis, power analysis, reframing, assertiveness training, bibliotherapy and consciousness-raising (p.100). Some of these strategies have also been identified as empowerment strategies, such as power analysis and consciousness-raising (Gutiérrez, 1991); others may be more unique to feminist counselling goals, such as bibliotherapy. The Worell and Remer model (1992) helps to concretize feminist interventions and goals within an empowerment framework.

The feminist postmodern perspective is recent to my own thought development and relatively new to social work (Gorman, 1993; Hartman, 1992; Pardeck, Murphy and Choi, 1994; Pozatek, 1994; Sands and Nuccio, 1992a, 1992b; Saulnier, 1996). And despite feminist ambivalence to postmodernism (Farganis, 1994), I believe a feminist postmodern perspective can lend some perspectives to an empowerment process for women and especially for women of colour. Personally, the postmodern perspective has developed my understanding of the significance of meaning and the way in which knowledge and meaning are socially constructed.

Feminist postmodernism blends postmodernism and feminism, incorporating key postmodern themes into already established feminist theory (Flax, 1990; Fraser and Nicholson, 1990). The feminist postmodern themes that are relevant to the context of empowerment of low income women include (a) the rejection of a single truth, replaced by multiple realities; (b) a recognition of the presence of power in the formation of knowledge; (c) the centring of marginalized voices; (d) an understanding that the self is socially constructed in the context of narratives created by society and the self; (e) an understanding "that construction of the 'other' entails relations of domination" (Mascia-Lees, Sharpe and Cohen, 1989, p.11); (f) validation of the nonrational; and (g) the personal is political (Best and Kellner, 1991; Brinker-Jenkins and Hooyman, 1986; Gergen, 1991). Feminist and postmodern theories take the special experiences of women and put that experience in the centre; only then can empowerment as a process or an outcome be overlaid.

A feminist postmodern perspective on the personal, inter-personal and political domains of empowerment reinforces the idea that empowerment for women is about self-definition and that the meanings of empowerment and the self-definition may vary greatly among individuals. This leads me to understand that the application of empowerment principles is not only an individualized process but always occurs in cultural context. For women in welfare reform projects there are many cultures they must negotiate and in which they live.

PROJECT WISE PRINCIPLES AND INTERVENTIONS FOR PERSONAL, INTER-PERSONAL AND POLITICAL EMPOWERMENT

Empowerment practice is context specific (Fawcett et al., 1995). Each of the three empowerment domains needs to be specifically modified and applied to women, and in this case women with low incomes and affected by the welfare systems and their reforms. This application is important not only because this group of women has been historically oppressed but women are defined by professionals in ways that make them susceptible to being disempowered by the helping process (Schnitzer, 1996). Today welfare recipients, most of whom are women with children, are maligned almost daily.

While I will describe principles and interventions for empowerment within the context of each of the three domains, it is our experience that the process of empowerment does not occur in such a linear fashion. Empowerment is a developmental process and each of the interventions cross over in many ways.

Personal Empowerment: Principles and Interventions

Build self-esteem. Self-esteem, while not ignored in empowerment theory, is often not included as a specific component although it is implied. I believe for women it needs to be considered. Self-esteem is defined as the evaluation individuals make of themselves and a judgment of their worth (Coopersmith, 1967; Rosenberg, 1965). Zimmerman (1995), in an analysis of constructs related to psychological empowerment, states that "self-esteem is expected to relate positively to personal empowerment" primarily on the intrapersonal domain (p.591). He concludes that self-esteem alone is not an adequate measure of empowerment. In conjunction with other measurements however, self-esteem seems particularly applicable to the population of low-income women. It has been identified as a common problem for women in general (Bernstein and Lenhart, 1993; Sanford and Donovan, 1984; Walker, 1990). "Most women, at least in Western cultures, do not have a sense of satisfaction in themselves" (Bernstein and Lenhart, 1993, p.71). Participants in Project WISE, when asked what keeps them from succeeding, often say they have no self-esteem. In a focus group at Project WISE women described what self-esteem meant to them. Self-esteem was often described as an internal feeling. "You find something inside yourself that can push you and get you started in a direction of feeling good," said one woman. "You feel centred," said another.

It is important when considering self-esteem as a component of empowerment for low-income women and women of colour to be particularly sensitive to its multiple conceptions and meanings. For example, a definition of self-esteem that promotes self-reliance may be contradictory to the importance women give to relationships. Self in relation theory purports that self-esteem for women "is related to the degree of emotional sharing, openness, and shared sense of understanding and regard" (Surrey, 1991, p.57). One woman in our focus group discussion on self-esteem said, "When we do things for others we are also doing something for ourselves." In a feminist postmodern perspective it is important to consider multiple meanings of self-esteem.

Increase self-efficacy. Self-efficacy, one's belief that one can "produce and regulate events in one's life" (Bandura, 1982, p.122) has been recognized as a centre-piece to personal empowerment (Gutiérrez, 1990). For women in welfare reform programs the components of self-efficacy that include ego strengthening, developing a sense of personal power, developing initiative and taking personal responsibility are particularly important (Gutiérrez, 1991, p.203). Self-efficacy builds on self-esteem but moves to the realization that one can have control over one's life and that actions will lead to intended results. It involves both an internal and external process. One Project WISE participant interviewed said to me, "Self-esteem is inside yourself but self-efficacy is outside." Self-efficacy for women in welfare reform projects is related to many issues: negotiating the welfare system, employment, success in educational endeavours, parenting and family and partner relationships are common themes where women seek a sense of control.

Build on strengths. Building on a person's strengths is a common theme in both empowerment and feminist theory and practice. One must begin the personal empowerment process by asking women to identify strengths. This might well include helping women appreciate female related values, traditional caretaking roles and means of survival. Sometimes we begin with identifying the strength it took to make an initial appointment for help.

Incorporate the importance of relationships in women's development and growth. The incorporation of self in relation theory in women's development and empowerment is an important component of personal empowerment. This theory purports that women develop through mutually empathic relationships and that "an important shift in emphasis from separation to relationship as a basis for self experience and development [is essential]." "Further, relationship is seen as the basic goal of development; that is, the deepening capacity for relationship and relational competence" (Surrey, 1991, p.53). Self in relation theory suggests that not only is the helping relationship critical to the change process but that it is important in the empowerment process to support women in the significance of the relationships in their lives.

Incorporate spirituality. Brinker-Jenkins and Hooyman (1986) include spirituality as a component of feminist practice that incorporates the whole person and validates the nonrational. Of course spirituality for women has multiple meanings. It has been our experience that it is a theme interwoven in the meaning-making process for women, and therefore part of their empowerment process as well. In Project WISE we begin the first group by asking women to identify one strength. Inevitably one or two women name God or faith. I have explored this further in terms of participants' meaning and their understanding of spirituality. The meanings given spirituality are sometimes religious, but more often they have to do with an inner peace and a sense of purpose. In addition we have found the use of symbol and ritual meaningful to Project WISE participants.

Counselling: a means for personal empowerment. Individual counselling is often not named in the literature as a specific empowerment intervention. In the Project WISE model however, it is an important component. In addition, recent studies have documented that women on welfare face a number of issues that may require counselling resources. These issues include domestic violence, a history of past physical and sexual abuse, depression and low self-esteem (Rapheal, 1996). While the counselling model is grounded philosophically in a feminist empowerment perspective, many theoretical approaches are used depending on the individual and the situation. Insight oriented approaches often are used for women who can name a repeating pattern in their lives that they want to change. Cognitive approaches are helpful in re-framing coping and survival strategies that may no longer work or in re-labelling what has been defined as a deficit. Reality and problem-solving approaches help with immediate issues that must be resolved.

When asked how counselling has been helpful to their personal change process women have reported many experiences. One woman captures a common theme, "I really thought nobody cared about my problems ... I quit hiding from my problems ... and I found new ways to understand and deal with them."

Inter-personal Empowerment: Principles and Interventions

Reduce self-blame and support collectivity. Blaming oneself for life circumstances and feeling alone with one's experience is common among Project WISE women. With other women, experiences are shared. Together these experiences can be discussed, normalized and analyzed. A common question we ask in groups is, "So why do think so many of you think this about yourselves?" This can lead to power and sex-role analysis.

Advocacy for resources. One component of the inter-personal domain is "one's understanding of the resources needed to achieve a desired goal, knowledge of how to acquire those resources, and skills for managing resources once they are obtained" (Zimmerman, 1995 p.589). Lord and Hutchinson (1993), in a study of 41 men and women who had experienced extreme powerlessness in their lives, found that access to resources and participation in community life reduced isolation and contributed to a sense of competence. For women who are working towards both economic and personal self-sufficiency, access to and the ability to advocate for necessary resources for themselves and their children are essential to success. Therefore, a goal of an empowerment intervention would be to increase access to and positive experience with resources in the local community. Women are often able to help each other in this respect. We support their teaching each other how to negotiate the many systems they face.

Support stress management. Belle (1988) has documented the stress in the lives of low-income women. The Stress and Families Project "found that on a checklist of 91 life events, Stress and Families respondents reported a mean of 14.1 events during the previous two years in which they had been the central figure. In contrast, community surveys report an average of one or two events" (Dill and Field, 1988, p.183-84). Belle (1990) has also done a comprehensive review of studies on women's mental health and poverty and identified the associations to depression and higher levels of stress. It is our experience that this is exacerbated by the welfare reform legislation of 1996, which puts more demands on women receiving assistance. Women report that at times their stress level seems intolerable. Teaching stress management strategies, relaxation techniques, assertiveness and how to establish boundaries are often a part of the support given to helping women manage stress in their lives.

Groups as a means for inter-personal empowerment. The use of support and psycho-educational groups is an important way to enhance inter-personal empowerment. As Gutiérrez (1990) notes, empowerment practice must essentially include the opportunities for group experiences. Project WISE groups are time-limited. A core curriculum, called a Path for Change, is used for the six-week empowerment group. Women identify their own concerns that they want help with and this is combined with structured exercises to facilitate discussions. We have found that for many women a group experience is new. Some structure, with enough flexibility to let the women control the group agenda, has been most effective.

Political/Community Empowerment Principles and Interventions

Centre women's experience and voices. As Belenky, Clinchy, Goldberger, Tarule (1986) and others have noted, for women the development of a voice is an essential part of the development of self (Gilligan,1982; Miller, 1976). In the study done by Belenky et al., they found that the most disadvantaged women, economically and educationally, fell into the category of silence, a place where they had "little confidence in their meaning-making and their meaning-sharing abilities" (p.34). In each of the empowerment domains, feminist empowerment practice centres women's voices. In the wider community context, an empowerment model must create opportunities for this to happen.

Consciousness-raising. Because women in poverty and women of colour "are at the bottom of our social hierarchy in terms of political power, social workers must look at ways to work toward the interpersonal and political levels of empowerment" (Gutiérrez, 1991, p.202). Feminist theory brings a very important concept to bear on this process—the personal is political. This concept understands that "our feelings about ourselves ... are shaped by political forces ... controlled by others. To change that situation, we must impose ourselves on historical processes and material conditions and, in doing so, expose as false the myths of our powerlessness and dependence " (Brinker-Jenkins and Hooyman, 1986, p.14). The consciousness-raising model used by Project WISE incorporates the reflection and action process (Freire, 1973, 1996). The influence of sex-role socialization, institutionalized sexism, racism, classism and other forms of oppression are probed as women discuss personal issues and experiences. The group facilitator takes the responsibility for asking probing questions to stimulate reflection on personal experiences. The facilitator may also share information as a way to increase power. Participants then help each other with an action plan.

Involvement in the community. An individual's empowerment includes "active engagement in one's community and an understanding of one's sociopolitical environment" (Zimmerman, 1995, p.582). The integration of women's voices and perspectives in the community and in the policy debates that directly affect their lives is an important component of the empowerment process. Participation in community forums where one can have the opportunity to give voice to one's experience or involvement in community voluntary organizations has been found to be an important component to the development of empowerment in the political/community domain (Kieffer, 1984; Presby, Wandersman, Florin, Rich and Chavis, 1990; Zimmerman and Rappaport, 1988).

Leadership Training and Development: A Means for Political Empowerment

There are three components to the leadership development aspect of Project WISE. First, using a key community organizing strategy, the one-to-one interview (Hanna and Robinson, 1994), women are asked questions specifically about their experience with the welfare system and their concerns regarding welfare reform policies. Women understand that the information from the interviews is used by the local welfare rights coalition in their work on welfare reform. The one-to-one interview is also used to invite women to participate in their community. They are encouraged to become involved in the welfare coalition and attend upcoming events. The one-to-one interview provides a means for women to give voice to their concerns and to see themselves as citizens of the community at large.

The second strategy is focus groups. Women are asked to participate in an evening with Project WISE. A meal is served for the women and their children. The women then spend a hour with a facilitator and are asked to respond to questions that help guide the development of programs. We are particularly interested in the meaning they give to experiences and concepts that are used to define programs (i.e., self-sufficiency or self-esteem) and to issues faced locally in the welfare reform environment.

The third strategy is leadership training retreats. These are an overnight experience for a group of 15-20 women. A group of 4-5 women are identified and volunteer to be the planning team for the retreat. They meet regularly and learn how to facilitate meetings, develop workshops and fund-raise. The retreat provides a group experience, which includes time for personal reflection, learning, skill building and planning for action.

RESEARCH STRATEGIES AND EMPOWERMENT OUTCOMES

The study of grass-roots community organizations is "a fruitful arena for empowerment research" (Florin and Wandersman, 1990, p.44) and empowerment measures that can be developed within specific contexts (Zimmerman, 1995). While the experience of women on welfare would be related to others, it is unique in terms of the institutional relationships and dependency that women face (Belle, 1990). Studies of low-income women and empowerment are limited. It is therefore important to understand from the perspective of women and in their voices the meanings of the empowerment principles and interventions. It is also important to develop and measure-specific empowerment outcomes for interventions with low-income women.

The research on Project WISE is an evolving process. The methodology being developed is both qualitative and quantitative. The research strategies have included participant self-evaluation and staff evaluation using goal attainment scales, in-depth interviews, focus groups, case studies/narratives and researcher reflexivity.

Philosophically, a participatory and empowerment research process is being used (Fetterman, 1996). This implies that the research process influences both the researcher and the participants and that the research itself is a part of a social action strategy. Throughout both the implementation and evaluation of this project, the women's voices are both its guidance and its strength (Gluck and Patai, 1991).

The research on Project WISE began by carefully documenting the intervention and setting up data collection and management systems. The project began in May, 1995, and this process continued through 1996. Focus groups were used both as a political empowerment strategy and to illicit from the women the meanings of empowerment and related concepts. Specifically concepts such as self-esteem, spirituality, culture and empowerment have been discussed. These activities of the first eighteen months helped further elaborate the components of the three empowerment domains for low-income women as described earlier. It was also from this process that outcomes of success for personal self-sufficiency and empowerment were clarified. These outcomes include: (1) an increase in self-esteem and self-efficacy; (2) problem-solving skills; (3) meeting personal goals including leaving abusive relationships, managing anger, completing educational goals; (4) accessing resources and developing support systems; (5) employment and no longer needing welfare assistance; and (6) a sense that one has a voice and role in the community at large.

Beginning in 1997, three outcomes were tracked: self-esteem, meeting personal goals and employment. The first two were measured using a goal attainment scale. Employment was tracked using administrative data.

The goal attainment scale is set up with seven common domains: motivation, stress management, relationships, self-esteem, sense of personal control, parenting and resource use. Participants also identify their own goals for change. Participants rate themselves and their counsellors rate them at the beginning of involvement with Project WISE and again at closing or at three-month intervals.

In 1997, 50 women were actively involved in Project WISE activities. Of those, 25 (50%) were involved in counselling only and 25 (50%) participated in more than one activity. Given the Project WISE model, of particular research interest is the difference in outcomes based on level of participation. At follow up in June, 1998, the 25 who had participated at more than one level of empowerment activities seemed to be doing better in terms of the outcomes identified. In the group that had greater participation in empowerment activities 14 (56%) were employed compared to 8 (32%) in the group participating in only one activity. The group with more participation also had a greater number of individuals with reported increased self-esteem, (80% compared to 40%) and an increased number had met personal goals (68% compared to 48%). No cause and effect conclusions can be drawn from these differences given that no control or equivalent group could be established and the groups may differ on key variables such as motivation. However, these initial findings are promising and further research needs to be developed.

In addition follow up interviews have been conducted for 1997 participants whenever possible. Based on data from the initial 12 interviews, participants described the meaning each service had to them and how the service component impacted their lives. Interviewees generally stated that counselling helped individuals deal with and face specific personal issues or histories. Groups were particularly helpful in reducing self-blame, reducing isolation and the "I'm the only one" thinking. Leadership development and community advocacy added to an individual's sense of belonging in the community and to their ability to have a voice and be heard. Interviewees noted that all activities helped increase self-esteem.

There have been several research challenges over the past three years. Originally standardized scales were going to be used. The difficulty with the use of these scales was that post tests are difficult to get completed due to participant mobility. Also, participant feedback on the instruments has been mixed. The validity of the goal attainment scale, which more directly relates to participants' lives, is not known. Qualitative data have provided richer understandings of the Project WISE experience for participants but are time-consuming and scheduling is a problem. These challenges will continue to be addressed with the help of participants.

SUMMARY

The model presented here is an attempt to take empowerment constructs and design an intervention for women involved in the welfare system and in welfare reform projects. It is based on an understanding that empowerment occurs in three domains—personal, inter-personal and political. It is also based on empowerment theory, influenced by feminist theory and a feminist postmodern perspective. This integration strengthens the application of empowerment concepts for women and women of colour. Not only are gender, class and race/ethnicity considered key factors in an empowerment process, but meaning and the meaning-making processes related to these are recognized as essential components.

My intimate involvement in the creation of this model has been both exciting and humbling. It has strengthened my commitment to empowerment practice as a means for supporting the development of women, particularly those most institutionally oppressed. While the measurement of empowerment outcomes will be important, I believe most essentially that we are creating a community narrative (Rappaport, 1995) that can hopefully affect individuals, policy and practice. At the same time I am humbled by the process. As I listen to the stories of the women, I wonder at my audacity to think empowerment interventions can correct the injustices of our society. While I believe Project WISE has positively affected the lives of individual women, and that our advocacy work influences our community's response to welfare reform, the stories of abuse, violence, discrimination and punitive government policy often distress me. I continue to be challenged.

REFERENCES

Baines, D. (1997). Feminist social work in the inner-city: The challenge of race, class, and gender. *Afflia*, 12(3), 297-317.

Bandura, A. (1982). Self-efficacy mechanism in human agency. *American Psychologist*, 37, 122-147.

Belenky, M., Clinchy, B., Goldberger, N. and Tarule, J.(1986). *Women's ways of knowing.* New York: Basic Books.

Belle, D. (Ed.). (1988). *Lives in stress: Women and depression.* Beverly Hills: Sage Publications.

Belle, D. (1990). Poverty and women's mental health. *American Psychologist*, 45, 385-389.

Bernstein, A. and Lenhart, S. (1993). *The psychodynamic treatment of women.* Washington, D.C.: American Pyschiatric Press, Inc.

Best, S. and Kellner, D. (1991). *Postmodern theory.* New York: The Guilford Press.

Brinker-Jenkins, M. and Hooyman, N. (1986). *Not for women only: Social work practice for a Feminist Future*. Silver Spring, MD: National Association of Social Workers.

Coopersmith, S. (1967). *The antecedents of self-esteem*. San Francisco: W. H. Freeman and Co.

Cox, E.O. and Parsons, R. J. (1994). *Empowerment oriented social work practice with the elderly*. Pacific Grove, CA: Brooks/Cole.

Dill, D. and Field, E. (1988). The challenge of coping. In D. Belle (Ed.), *Lives in stress* (pp.179-196). Beverly Hills: Sage Publications.

Farganis, S. (1994). Postmodernism and feminism. In D. Dickens and A. Fontana (Eds.), *Postmodernism in the social sciences* (pp. 101-126). New York: The Guilford Press.

Fawcett, S., Paine-Andrews, A., Francsico, V., Schultz, J., Richter, K., Lewis, R., Williams, E., Harris, K., Berkley, J., Fisher, J. and Lopez, C. (1995). Using empowerment theory in collaborative health partnerships for community health and development. *American Journal of Community Psychology*, 23(5), 677-697.

Fetterman, D. (1996). Empowerment evaluation: An introduction to theory and practice. In D. S. Fetterman and A. Wandersman (Eds.), *Empowerment evaluation: Knowledge and tools for self-assessment and accountability*. Thousand Oaks: Sage Publications.

Flax, J. (1990). Postmodernism and gender relations in feminist theory. In L. Nicholson (Ed.), *Feminism/postmodernism* (pp. 39-62). New York: Routledge.

Florin, P. and Wandersman, A. (1990). An introduction to citizen participation, voluntary organizations, and community development: Insights for empowerment through research. *American Journal of Community Psychology*, 18(1), 41-53.

Fraser, N. and Nicholson, L. (1990). Social criticism without Philosophy: An encounter between feminism and postmodernism. In L. Nicholson (Ed.), *Feminism/ postmodernism* (pp.19-38). New York: Routledge.

Freire, P. (1973). *Education for critical consciousness*. New York: Seabury.

Freire, P. (1996). *Pedagogy of hope*. New York: Continuum.

Foucault, M. (1991). Govermentality. In G. Burcell, C. Gorden and P. Miller (Eds.), *The Foucault effect: Studies in governmentality*. Chicago: University of Chicago Press.

Gergen, K. (1991). *The saturated self*. New York: Basic Books.

Gilligan, C. (1982). *In a different voice*. Cambridge, MA: Harvard University Press.

Gluck, S. and Patai, P.(1991). *Women's words, women's words, women's words*. London: Routledge.

Gorman, J. (1993). Postmodernism and the conduct of inquiry in social work. *Afflia*, 8(3), 247-264.

Gutiérrez, L. (1990). Working with women of color: An empowerment perspective. *Social Work*, 35(2), 149-153.

Gutiérrez, L. (1991). Empowering women of color. In M. Brinker-Jenkins, N. Hooyman and N. Gottlieb (Eds.), *Feminist social work practice in clinical settings*. Newbury Park: Sage Publications.

Hanna, M. and Robinson, B. (1994). *Strategies for community empowerment*. New York: Edwin Mellon Press.

Hartman, A. (1992). In search of subjugated knowledge. *Social Work*, 36(6), 483-484.

Kieffer, C. (1984). Citizen empowerment: A developmental perspective. *Prevention in Human Services*, 3, 9-36.

Lord, J. and Hutchinson, P. (1993). The process of empowerment: Implications for theory and practice. *Canadian Journal of Community Mental Health*, 12, 5-12.

Mascia-Lees, F., Sharpe, P. and Cohen, C. (1989). The postmodernist turn in anthropology: Cautions from a feminist perspective. *Signs: Journal for Women and Culture in Society*, 15(11), 7-33.

Maton, K. and Salem, D. A.(1995). Organizational characteristics of empowering community settings. *American Journal of Community Psychology*, 23, 631-656.

Miller, J. B. (1976). *Toward a new psychology of women*. Boston: Beacon Press.

Pardeck, J. Murphy, J. and Choi, J. (1994). Some implications of postmodernism for social work. *Social Work*, 39(4), 343-346.

Pozatek, E. (1994). The problem of certainty: Clinical social work in the postmodern era. *Social Work*, 39(4), 396-403.

Presby, J., Wandersman, A. Florin, P. Rich, R. and Chavis, D. (1990). Benefits, costs, incentive management and participation in voluntary organizations: A means to understanding and promoting empowerment. *American Journal of Community Psychology*, 18,117-150.

Rapheal, J. (1996). *Prisoners of abuse*. Chicago: Taylor Foundation and Institute.

Rappaport, J. (1987). Terms of empowerment/exemplars of prevention: Toward a theory for community psychology. *American Journal of Community Psychology*, 15, 121-148.

Rappaport, J. (1995). Empowerment meets narrative: Listening to stories and creating settings. *American Journal of Community Psychology*, 23, 795-807.

Rosenberg, M. (1965). *Society and the adolescent self-image*. Princeton, NJ: Princeton University Press.

Sands, R. and Nuccio, K. (1992a). Using postmodern feminist theory to deconstruct "fallacies" of poverty. *Afflia*, 7(4),26-48.

Sands, R. and Nuccio, K. (1992b). Postmodern feminist theory and social work. *Social Work*, 37(6), 489-494.

Sanford, L. and Donovan, M. (1984). *Women and self-esteem*. New York: Penguin Press.

Saulnier, C. (1996). *Feminist theories and social work approaches and applications*. New York: Haworth Press.

Schnitzer, P. (1996). "They don't come in!": Stories told, lessons taught about poor families in therapy. *American Orthopsychiatric Association, Inc.*, 66(4), 572-582.

Surrey, J. (1991). The self-in-relation: A theory of women's development. In J. Jordan et al. (Eds.), *Women's growth in connection* (pp. 51-66). New York: The Guilford Press.

Walker, M. (1990). *Women in therapy and counseling*. Philadelphia: Open University Press.

Worell, J. and Remer, P. (1992). *Feminist perspectives in therapy*. New York: John Wiley and Sons.

Zimmerman, M. (1990).Taking aim on empowerment research: On the distinction between individual and psychological conceptions. *American Journal of Community Psychology*, 18,169-177.

Zimmerman, M. (1995). Psychological empowerment: Issues and illustrations. *American Journal of Community Psychology*, 23, 581-599.

Zimmerman, M. and Rappaport, J. (1988). Citizen participation, perceived control, and psychological empowerment. *American Journal of Community Psychology*, 16, 725-750.

Chapter 9

SELF-DETERMINATION AND CONSUMER CONTROL: GUIDING PRINCIPLES IN THE EMPOWERMENT MODEL AS UTILIZED BY THE DISABILITY RIGHTS MOVEMENT

Richard L. Beaulaurier
School of Social Work, Florida International University
Samuel H. Taylor
School of Social Work, University of Southern California

During the 1970s and 1980s, groups of disabled consumers began to suggest new and fundamentally different alternatives to traditional models of practice. These alternatives were designed and advanced by people who belonged to and were influenced by the disability rights movement (Frieden, 1983; Lachat, 1988; Roberts, 1989). The central belief of the founders of this movement was that if a critical mass of disabled people could be empowered and their civil rights were formally recognized, then severely disabled people could live and work in local communities rather than in institutions (Roberts, 1989). New associations and organizations were formed to raise the levels of self and public awareness regarding the basic civil rights of disabled persons and to suggest the possibility of their integration into community life. Some of these groups focused on policy, legislative change and community organizing such as American Disabled for Access Power Today (ADAPT), the World Institute on Disability (WID), the American Coalition of Citizens with Disabilities (ACCD), Disabled in Action (DIA), etc., while others (the Center for Independent Living [CIL] in Berkeley, the Boston Center for Independent Living [BCIL], etc.) focused on advocacy as well as on efforts to obtain unavailable services in an effort to promote and facilitate community living by disabled people. In part the success of both of these types of organizations related to their ability to empower disabled people, many of whom had never before lived outside institutional or special residential care settings. In recent years, many of the policies developed and promulgated by these groups have become the guiding principles in laws such as the Americans with Disabilities Act (ADA), which was drafted to protect the rights of disabled people and to remove structural barriers hindering their integration into society.

THE DISABILITY RIGHTS MOVEMENT

The emphasis on civil rights exhibited by many of the disabilities oriented interest groups is partly due to a growing recognition that historically people with disabilities have been systematically persecuted, neglected and even coerced into isolation. Within the last century the United States and other nations[1] have incarcerated and in some noteworthy instances even sterilized many people with disabilities (Reilly and Philip, 1991; Wolfensberger, 1969). In some instances the proponents of such policies have been prominent members of the social work community of their time (Renz-Beaulaurier, 1994, p. 197). Despite recent legislative successes there is little doubt that many people with disabilities are still isolated and effectively segregated from mainstream society. Indeed, one purpose of the Americans with Disabilities Act, passed in 1990, was to help remedy this situation.

Intellectual and academic support for advancing the civil rights of people with disabilities began as early as the 1940s (Berkowitz, 1980a; Berkowitz, 1980b; Meyerson, 1990), but it was during the 1960s and 1970s that people with disabilities began to organize for political action (Roberts, 1989). A principal purpose was to be able to gain new opportunities for independent and self-determined lifestyles in the wider community. Toward this end, many disabled people joined new organizations and associations that aimed to empower and help them integrate into mainstream communities. Such organizations had a strong self-help ethos and were formed by consumers to benefit consumers (DeJong, 1981; Frieden, 1983; Lachat, 1988). In combination with other factors, the efforts of these groups were successful enough so that their conceptualizations of self-determination, consumer control and non-discrimination were included in a variety of laws, the most important of which are the Rehabilitation Act of 1973, its amendments (1978 and 1992) and the Americans with Disabilities Act of 1990. These acts contain mandates that promote the notion of inclusion of people with disabilities into mainstream American life to the maximum extent possible.

INDEPENDENT LIVING

The Rehabilitation Act of 1973 stipulated that disabled people were entitled to the same rights which protected women and racial minorities through a significant advance in terms of their general or overall civil rights status. This legislation did not fully address the particular barriers that went beyond attitudes and discrimination such as physical and structural barriers. Although strong arguments have been made that disabled people should be considered a somewhat unique oppressed minority (Hahn, 1984; Hahn, 1996) in that people with disabilities needed changes to the physical environment as well as to attitudes and social structures. As one of the founders of the disability rights movement put it: "Before the civil rights movement, black people had to go to the back of the bus to find seating. Many people with disabilities could not even get on the bus" (Roberts, 1989, p. 231).

Informal networks of people with disabilities formed in the 1960s. This was followed by the sometimes linked yet often parallel development of independent living centres that formed in the 1970s, run by people with disabilities (Lachat, 1988, p. 1). The Center for Independent Living (CIL) in Berkeley was the first such organization. Founded in 1972 by University of California students, and growing out of the student organization they had founded earlier, CIL provided services such as peer counselling, advocacy, van transportation, training in independent living skills, attendant care referral, health maintenance, housing referral, and wheelchair repair (DeJong, 1981, p. 12). CIL was founded as a self-help group that was largely controlled and managed by people who were themselves severely disabled. Other centres with similar organizational structures and purposes quickly followed in Boston and Houston. Using these first centres as a model, others sprang up throughout the United States. By 1981 there were 18 free-standing centres in California that were quite similar to on the original model in Berkeley (DeJong, 1981, p. 12). Richards and Smith (1990) have spotlighted the most noteworthy difference between traditional service providers and independent living centres:

> What makes independent living centers very different from these other organizations is that [independent living] centers have substantial involvement of people with disabilities making policy decisions and delivering services. Why this emphasis on control by people with disabilities? The basic idea behind independent living is that the ones who know best what services people with disabilities need in order to live independently are disabled people themselves.

While the array of services may vary from one program to another, most centres offer a core group which includes peer counselling, information and referral, independent living skills training and advocacy. Other common services are community education, equipment repair and home modifications (Richards and Smith, 1990). Since their inception, ILCs have stimulated the politicization of disabled persons and fostered a sense of community (Kailes, personal communication, 1990). In the process they have forged a model of empowerment practice for people with disabilities that is rooted in the principles of self-determination and consumer control.

EMPOWERING PEOPLE WITH DISABILITIES

Ed Roberts, one of the early founders of the disability rights movement and the first director of the CIL in Berkeley, observed that the disability rights movement was launched more in spite of rather than in conjunction with rehabilitation, medical and social services professionals; he is not alone in that perception and perspective (Berrol, 1979; DeJong, 1981; Kailes, 1988; Roberts, 1989; Zola, 1979). In many ways, the disability rights movement remains a self-help movement to this day (Richards and Smith, 1990; Zola, 1979). However, some authors envision and support the notion of participation and active roles for social workers and other professionals as educators, advocates, allies and even leaders, providing they are able to engage consumers in ways that are empowering rather than domineering (Berrol, 1979; Hahn, 1991; Varela, 1983). This approach to empowerment is fairly compatible with some of the current conceptions of empowerment (Bricker-Jenkins and Hooyman, 1986a; Gutiérrez, 1990; Mondros and Wilson, 1994; Solomon, 1976). However, the principle of consumer control in the disability rights and independent living movements suggests that the degree of collaborative decision-making found in some empowerment models may not be appropriate for this model (Gutiérrez, 1990, p. 151). As viewed from the disability rights perspective, professional practitioners do not so much "collaborate" as offer options and discuss outcomes; in actual decision-making, practitioners follow the consumers' lead. In this sense such philosophical positions closely resemble the pluralism and participation approach set forth by Grosser and Mondros (1985).[2]

The following sections of this paper serve as an initial effort to articulate a framework for empowerment practice largely based on the conceptions of self-determination and independent living which are central to the disability rights movement. This practice model includes five major areas of knowledge and skill: (1) facilitation of goal setting and solution attainment by the consumer—without the practitioner setting the goals; (2) developing consciousness-raising skills which seek to impart or enhance consumer awareness of the potent limitations that reside outside themselves—in the form of attitudinal and structural barriers in the environment; (3) community liaison skills and knowledge in order to facilitate the creation and maintenance of interorganizational and intercommunity channels of communication and linkage; (4) educational skills to enable consumers to prepare for and control their own transition from dependence to independence and from segregated living facilities to community based facilities; and (5) specific knowledge of the tasks and activities necessary to facilitate transitions from medical, rehabilitation and other structured living facilities to community based, mainstream living arrangements.

Goal Setting

Social workers, especially those in health settings who may encounter some of the more disabled people in the course of their professional duties, have sought to offer forms of help that aid in coping with an unaltered environment (Renz-Beaulaurier and Taylor, in press-b). Increasingly, however, disabled people and their advocates are insisting that programs and services focus even more effort on making changes in the environment to accommodate their impairments (Hahn, 1996; Kailes, 1988). Social workers hoping to empower their disabled clients need to be aware of their own attitudes regarding selection of targets, potential for change and needed outcomes in order to collaborate more effectively in formulating the broadest possible range of choices for their clients.

Self-determination and the Range of Choices

Disability rights authors place a high degree of emphasis on self-determination (Hahn, 1984; Kailes, 1988). At times such authors have expressed suspicion about social workers and other "helping professionals" whom they perceive as often predetermining and circumscribing their range of choices (Kailes, 1988; Mackelprang and Salsgiver, 1996; Zola, 1983).

What is needed, according to Berrol (1979), is for professionals to seek a greater range of services from which disabled consumers are able to make informed selections. In addition to the traditional rehabilitative services, professionals need to help identify and locate services that "...allow for upward mobility and access to the community at large" (Berrol, 1979, p. 457). Increasingly this perspective is being reflected in legislation such as the amendments to the Rehabilitation Act of 1992, which is the premier piece of legislation funding disability programs in the United States. The purpose of this act is "...to empower individuals with disabilities to maximize employment, economic self-sufficiency, independence, and inclusion and integration into society" (US Department of Education, 1992, Title I, Sec. 101).

Social workers need to be alert and sensitive so that they do not direct clients or steer them toward "preferred" treatment options, especially when those options do not offer any future possibility of living and working in mainstream community settings (Renz-Beaulaurier, 1997). Rather their role is to work to expand the range of viable and available options. As the following examples demonstrate, however, it is not uncommon for the range of choices to be unnecessarily circumscribed. Nor is it unusual for options which seem similar at first glance to be quite different in practice.

The Example of Attendant Care

Many impaired persons with limited strength, mobility or coordination find that they must spend hours on simple household and personal hygiene activities that then leave them physically exhausted. By contrast, many other disabled people have learned that having an attendant help them with such activities leaves them with the time and energy to pursue more rewarding activities. An acquaintance of the authors spent two years in rehabilitation learning to dress himself without assistance. During this time he was not informed by any rehabilitation professionals or social workers about other options for completing the task. After considerable time and effort he managed to gain marginal competence, but the process left him physically exhausted. Later he learned that he could hire an attendant from outside the normal rehabilitation channels. He and his attendant currently spend just minutes on activities such as dressing and preparing breakfast, thus enabling him to pursue other, more financially, personally and professionally rewarding activities (Paul K. Longmore, personal communication, spring 1992). Although the rehabilitation literature has at times considered receiving assistance from another individual to be suggestive of dependence on that individual, some disability rights authors have suggested that this is only the case when the attendant is not under the direct control of the consumer (DeJong, Batavia, and McKnew, 1992; DeJong and Wenker, 1983; Zola, 1983). Independent living centres keep lists of personal attendants. In accord with the principles of the independent living service model, disabled people are encouraged to hire, train and, if necessary, fire their own personal attendants.

An important consideration as both social workers and disabled people look at the range of service choices available is the degree of consumer control that can be exercised within each particular option. The essential question concerns whether the disabled person will continue to be able to make choices and exercise options once an initial selection has been made. In the prior example, the disabled person was able to exercise considerable ongoing control over the activities of his attendant by virtue of the fact that he hired her, trained her and paid her for her services (DeJong and Wenker, 1983).

Not all attendant care promotes self-determination. Increasingly, people with disabilities, as well as seniors and others with chronic health conditions, are being offered home-care options, which at face value seem quite similar to the "attendant care" model described above. However there are often sharp and distinct differences with regard to who controls the training, hiring, firing and activities of the attendants. The model of care which predominates in the home-care industry is one in which a nurse or other professional, or paraprofessional trained and supervised by the agency, is responsible for care (DeJong et al., 1992). In this model the disabled person may have very little control or influence on the services offered or provided and even less to say about who will provide them. Some authors argue that these approaches are neither as effective nor as empowering as the independent living centre model of attendant care when it comes to furthering the client's goals (DeJong et al., 1992; Haggstrom, 1995).

The Example of Rehabilitation Technology

Zola (1983) noted that many disabled people may choose to eschew complex and sophisticated technological interventions. He notes that such approaches may actually make people with disabilities more dependent on the array of professionals and technicians who are required to come to repair, service, maintain and adjust them. A friend of the authors found himself in such circumstances when he purchased a "conversion van" that was equipped with a hydraulic lift for his wheelchair. He discovered, to his chagrin, that the lift broke down rather frequently and that ordinary auto mechanics did not know how to service it. Each time the lift broke down he found himself stranded until a professional mechanic from the lift manufacturer could be dispatched. Eventually, our friend was able to find a car into which he could manually lift his wheelchair, obviating the need for a mechanical lift. While this required more effort, there was no fancy machinery to break down. Some manufacturers have begun to address this problem by making some of their vehicles and conversions simpler and less high-tech. To address consumers' needs for such vehicles, at least one German disability journal, *Leben und Weg*, actually reviews unmodified, production automobiles for their practicality and use by disabled persons.

The flip side of this problem, however, is that once people have "graduated" from a rehabilitation system, they may no longer be apprised of ongoing technological advances. Zola (1983) reported that many disabled consumers are prevented from gaining needed benefits from newly designed or advanced assistive devices simply because they are not aware of their existence. By way of example, several blind persons known to the authors use computers for writing and reading that are fitted with software and hardware that allow their computers to "talk." They continually encounter people with virtually identical situations who are still struggling along with less technologically sophisticated devices, such as audio tapes, mechanical brailers and ordinary typewriters. In such cases the benefits of recent computer technology more than compensate for maintenance and service problems.

Another example identified by Zola is in the area of materials technology. It is currently possible to make assistive devices such as canes and prostheses that are lighter and stronger then their predecessors. Such advances, however, are of little use unless consumers are aware of them (Zola, 1983). This suggests that social workers need to be aware of the benefits of technology, but they also need to become informed about potential costs, the degree to which disabled persons will be able to maintain and service the technology themselves and the extent to which new technologies also require an ongoing reliance on specialized professionals for repairs and maintenance.

Choices between Changing Disabled Individuals or Changing the Environment

One set of guidelines that social workers would be well advised to take into account when seeking to maximize the choices of clients are those set forth under the Americans with Disabilities Act (ADA). The principle behind "reasonable accommodation" is that the environment rather than the person should be modified whenever it is possible to do so without creating huge expenses or Herculean efforts. In the past, services to people with disabilities have tended to emphasize changing the individual (DeJong, 1981; Renz-Beaulaurier, 1997). The social work practitioner in working with a disabled client should note whether changes to the environment as well as to the client have been explored, considered or even suggested. If not, the social worker should seek to identify reasonably helpful accommodations that can be made in the home and work environments of clients. At work, as well as in many consumer related facilities such as transportation systems, service providers, shops and restaurants, "reasonable accommodation" is a matter of law under the ADA. While this is not always the case in residential facilities, such

Figure 1: Trade-Offs in Goal Setting: Equating Needs and Benefits

	High Consumer Control	**High Professional Control**
Level of Technology	Low-technology solutions are often easier and cheaper to maintain. The disability rights community is increasingly suspicious of high-tech solutions to problems which may in turn contribute to greater dependence.	Consumers who have not been in the "rehabilitation system" for some time may not be regularly informed or updated regarding technological advances in adaptive technology and apprised of the potential costs, limits and benefits of such advances.
Professional Helpers	Many people with disabilities prefer to maintain consumer controlled over helpers and attendants, where the disabled person is able to control the hiring, training and firing of the attendant, as well as determine the tasks that will be performed.	Disabled people may fear that professionals, attendants and home health aids will circumscribe rather than expand their range of choices, particularly where they are certified and controlled by an agency or health-care system.
Change Target	Recent directions in legislation support consider making changes in the environment to accommodate physical impairments at least equally important in comparison with the traditional approach of changing the individual.	Traditionally, service agencies, especially health and rehabilitation agencies, have sought to change individuals in ways that make them more able to adapt and navigate an unmodified environment.
Costs and Benefits	Many care options favoured by people in the disability rights movement, such as modifications in the physical environment, the hiring of an uncertified attendant or low-tech, are relatively inexpensive. However, advocacy efforts may be required before third party insurers or service agencies will pay for them.	Traditional approaches to service delivery which include long-term care, rehabilitation or high-tech assistive devices are at times more expensive than other approaches and place access to services and resource allocation under the control of certified or approved contract providers.

guidelines may still be helpful in determining what changes should, or can, be made to facilitate living in mainstream communities. Moreover, many independent living centres offer assistance either in modifying existing housing or finding other housing which has already been made accessible to people with disabilities (Richards and Smith, 1990; see also http://copwww.ci. phoenix.az.us/NONPRFIT/abil.html).

In some cases modifying the environment may even represent a cost savings over treatment options that seek to enhance certain areas of physical functioning of a disabled person. Renz-Beaulaurier (1997) reported the case of a disabled person who found his wheelchair so much easier and energy saving as a means to get around that he abandoned the use of crutches altogether. For the client who would prefer the wheelchair, this might well be a viable alternative to lengthy and expensive medical rehabilitation efforts. Renz-Beaulaurier and Taylor (in press-a) have argued that many third party payers, in an era of managed care, may not be particularly open to suggestions about an expanded range of treatment options, especially when they seem to be non-medical in nature. However, pressing and advocating for such options may be more welcome if they are couched in terms of potential long-term cost savings.

Consciousness-Raising

One of the roles of social workers is to help people with disabilities begin to recognize themselves as the definitive experts on their particular conditions. To be empowered they must come to see themselves not merely as recipients of continuing treatment but also as the persons best qualified to decided on its course. Zola (1979, p. 454) asserted that many problems encountered by disabled people simply cannot be understood by able-bodied persons simply because they have not lived with the impairment and stigma associated with having a disability. Disability rights authors explain that this level of disability consciousness may not be obvious even to people with disabilities, especially when they have been socialized to passively accept the wisdom of experts (DeJong, 1981). Roberts (1989, p. 238-239) argues that special efforts may be necessary to convince disabled people (and others) that even severely disabled people can "...live independent, productive lives with dignity and respect." The social worker's role can be very instrumental in helping people with disabilities become aware of their rights and assisting them in developing what Roberts calls a "can do" attitude (p. 239). Moreover, as people with disabilities become aware of their rights they are more likely to come to see themselves as deserving, rather than dependent on the largess of a sometimes indifferent society. As consciousness rises, disabled clients eventually begin to realize that they are not the "half-persons" they are stereotyped to be. They may discover that their state is in fact unique, and in many cases has unrecognized or even unappreciated values and aspects. In fact, a study by Weinberg (1988) reports that many of the people who have lived with their disabilities for a longer time find qualities of uniqueness in their identity as disabled people and would not wish to become able-bodied even if they were given the opportunity.

Another important element of consciousness-raising involves the discovery of others who have a similar problems. It is tempting to categorize disabled people by the type of disability or with others who have the same or similar functional impairments (e.g., cerebral palsy, spinal cord injury, post-polio, etc.). Indeed this is understandable because hospital wards, support groups and umbrella organizations such as the Multiple Sclerosis Foundation, Inc., the March of Dimes, etc., often limit their attention and focus toward relatively specialized areas of physical impairment. However, many disability rights activists are now taking the perspective that the most important problems facing disabled people have to do with stigma and discrimination. This minority group perspective is rapidly replacing the older functional limitations labelling process in legislation and policy-making (Hahn, 1996). Social workers must recognize that for many disabled people the physical and attitudinal barriers to employment, mobility and other life activities may be more persistently problematic than their impairments in and of themselves. Moreover, the discrimination, paternalistic attitudes and lack of physical accommodations faced by people with cerebral palsy, spinal cord injury, blindness and other disabilities may be very similar even though the physical nature of their impairments are often different. As a result, social workers need to help make people with disabilities aware of the ways in which the lack of physical and attitudinal accommodations can impact and effect all disabled people. This is an essential precursor for efforts to help them develop strategies for countervailing these barriers.

Finally, it is not merely the consciousness of disabled people that needs raising. Disability consciousness is not merely for disabled people any more than feminist consciousness is just for women (Bricker-Jenkins and Hooyman, 1986b). A critical examination of environmental interventions that are beneficial to disabled people suggests that such changes are also beneficial to non-disabled people. Examples are as replete as they are mundane. Anyone who has recently strolled with a baby carriage, biked or skated on the sidewalk or wheeled groceries in a cart for several blocks knows the value of curb cuts. Ramps and other alternatives to steps and stairs are beneficial to many non-disabled people in that they allow all manner of wheeled traffic—from lawyers pulling a box of legal briefs on a luggage cart to parents pushing baby carriages. Similarly, non-slip floors are not only beneficial to mobility impaired persons but to all the people who might otherwise have slipped and fallen on them. A traveller walking through any modern airport is likely to see an astounding variety of wheeled luggage. While this may not be a direct consequence of disability access policies, one cannot help but wonder if all this wheeled traffic would be practical without ubiquitous curb cuts, elevators and other environmental changes in airports which were required to become more user-friendly to disabled people—and also, therefore, to wheeled luggage.

In a less mundane sense, a world that is ready to accommodate disabled people will also be ready to receive those of us who are only "temporarily able-bodied" as we gradually become more functionally impaired over the course of our life spans. In disability rights circles, the term "temporarily able-bodied" or TAB is a slightly pejorative term used to describe non-disabled people. The term particularly connotes persons who do not acknowledge the possibility that they too could be (and perhaps even probably will be) disabled at some point in their lifetimes. Stereotypically, TABs see environmental accommodations for people with disabilities as benefiting others, often at their expense. An alternative view supported by the disability rights movement is to see environmental changes (both attitudinal and physical) as beneficial to most everyone, since virtually everyone will be disabled at some point in their lives or will have a close friend or loved one who is. Seen from this perspective, policies and physical structures which exclude disabled people are shortsighted since over the long term they tend to exclude more than just the minority of "currently" disabled people. Social workers need to begin to see encounters with such attitudes as opportunities to raise the consciousness of non-disabled people.

Community Liaison

As consciousness levels rise in many disabled clients, they may require contact with disability organizations and support groups which are indigenous to their community. Moreover, contact with disabled persons who are well integrated into their communities tends to raise consciousness and can begin to empower clients by offering them role models and the benefits of the wisdom gained by people who have "been there" (Saxton, 1983). This is similar to the process of finding natural supports which has been described by Pinderhuges. Writing from a traditional ethnic minority perspective, she encourages creating linkages with natural supports such as family, church groups and fraternal or social organizations (Pinderhuges, 1994, p. 23). The particular groups described by Pinderhuges do not exist in the same way in the "disability rights community." However, an increasing number of independent living centres, disability rights organizations and similar associations focus on such pan-disability issues as discrimination, civil rights and community integration. A partial indication of the extent to which this perspective has permeated the popular culture can be obtained by noting the number of such organizations that are listed on the world wide web (see for example: http://www.yahoo.com/Society_and_Culture/Disabilities/Organizations/).

Social workers need to augment their disabled clients' knowledge of community networks to facilitate such linkages, particularly within the disability community, in order to help clients avoid the historical isolation and disempowerment that has characterized this population. A range of vital and active community supports which can be readily accessed by social workers have been created by people with disabilities. These supports most often take the form of independent living centres which have been founded and administered for and by disabled people, advocacy organizations, newsletters and newspapers, world wide web pages and internet newsgroups. Social workers need to have awareness and an understanding of these functional communities of disabled people in order to be able to link their disabled clients to such important resources. Beyond awareness however, social workers need to have community liaison skills (Taylor, 1985) if they hope to create linkages between these organizations and their services, and the organizations in which they work.

Educational Skills

Attitudes and barriers

In order to educate, social workers must first be knowledgeable. From the discussion above it is clear that social workers engaging people with disabilities must be knowledgeable about the service communities and task environments in which they work. It is also clear that they will need to be well versed in the range of traditional and non-traditional approaches to treating the problems of disabled people. What is probably not as obvious is the need for social workers to be knowledgeable about the unique and cloaked nature of discrimination toward people with disabilities. Hahn (1996, p. 42) sums up this perspective by noting that, "Unlike the experience of many minorities, opposition to disability rights seldom has been marked by overt displays of bigotry or hostility." This can be problematic, Hahn continues, if it means ignoring "... patronizing attitudes [that] can be a more formidable barrier to the attainment of equal rights than blatant animosity."

Many disabled people may face subtle forms of conscious or unconscious bigotry which can result in hidden feelings of aversion, paternalism or even antipathy (Hahn, 1996; Yuker, 1988). Unfortunately, it is not uncommon for these attitudes to be manifest in the treatment services offered to people with disabilities. Paternalism can manifest through overprotectiveness, or as a circumscribing or curtailing of clients' decision-making powers "for their own good."

It is important to recognize that an important part of the ability to determine one's own fate is the ability to choose risky options. Zola (1983, pp. 351-353) notes that the laudable goal of protecting vulnerable people from harm may be achieved at the cost of growth and freedom. He goes so far to say that a life without the possibility of risk is not "real" in a world where "real" people are sometimes hurt or make unwise decisions.

Aversion to people with disabilities can have even more unpleasant consequences. During this century such antipathy often resulted in segregation or the loss of reproductive rights (Reilly, 1991; Renz-Beaulaurier, 1997; Wolfensberger, 1969). However, it is likely that these days social workers will encounter more subtle feelings and behaviours. For example, the assumption that people with disabilities are likely to feel more comfortable living or working with other disabled people may mask a deeper attitude; namely, that the person making such an assumption may feel uncomfortable living or working with people with disabilities.

Change tactics and techniques

Clearly, social workers' roles encompass educating disabled people, their families and their personal support systems about the difficulties they are likely to face as they deal with systems and communities that are not sensitive to their needs. Moreover this role may include enabling and thus empowering disabled people to develop competency in client advocacy, class advocacy and the tactics and techniques of community and social change. While an extensive description of these techniques is beyond the scope of this paper, advocacy practice with disabled people by social workers has recently been explored by (Renz-Beaulaurier and Taylor, in press-a) and discussed from a disability rights perspective by Kailes (1988).

Social workers will also need to develop skills and competencies that will allow them to work in, and in some cases create, program and organizational designs for service delivery that empower people with disabilities. The approach to human services program design and delivery which is probably most compatible with the consumer control and empowerment philosophy of the disability rights movement is that of Rapp and Portner (1992). This approach inverts the traditional organizational chart putting clients at the top. They write that "...the pinnacle of the chart is the client, and all organizational personnel are subservient" (pp. 277-278). Although this approach toward the design and implementation of responsive programs and services resembles the models of administration and organizational design favoured by the independent living community, there are some specific suggestions and features that are unique and worthy of attention. Beyond the professional literature written from a traditional human services perspective, social workers may want to explore the burgeoning literature concerning the management of independent living centres and services. A good starting place is Frieden (1983) and Crewe and Zola (1983, part 3).

Basic models for creating change in communities can be found in Taylor and Roberts (1985), Rothman (1995) and Weil (1995). Berrol (1979) has suggested that one of the most legitimate roles for non-disabled professionals is to educate groups and individuals in order to transfer the skills and knowledge necessary to create social changes. In as much as the practitioner must be careful not to dominate client's decision-making, even while assuming the role of expert, consultant or educator, Berrol's approach is consistent with the "pluralism and participation" approach to community social work developed by Grosser and Mondros (1985). In both Berrol's and Grosser's and Mondros's approaches the social worker facilitates accomplishing goals set by a client or client systems.

Conclusion: Empowerment Means Refocusing

Social workers must begin to re-focus their activities to begin the transition toward empowerment objectives: to maximize and expand the range of life choices of clients with disabilities, to assist and facilitate client decision-making with regard to life choices and to bolster and promote achievement of life choices. Social workers must be prepared to use their unique skills and their legitimate expertise to foster the ability of persons with disabilities to choose the their own goals, especially in light of their newly legitimated civil rights. In short, social workers must begin to move more collaboratively in the directions pioneered by people with disabilities, their movements and the associations and organizations they have formed to achieve those ends.

The framework outlined above should help social workers to assist people with disabilities to take a strengths perspective with their disabled clients which focuses not so much on the impairments or inabilities of disabled consumers, but rather on the social and physical barriers which must be removed in order to achieve greater integration into local communities. In this way the social worker helps disabled individuals to see their problems in relation to a non-adaptive and even dysfunctional environment, rather than exclusively as a problem residing in themselves.

Since independent living solutions result from thinking about how to change the environment rather than just focusing on the individual, social workers seeking to empower disabled consumer will need to have community organizing, client and community advocacy, and an understanding of bureaucracies as part of their practice repertoire in addition to their customary clinical skills. The discussion above also highlights, however, that how social workers engage disabled consumers may be as important as what skills or activities they employ. Empowerment of disabled individuals requires that consumers remain in control of the change process. The social worker's role is to facilitate collaboration and partnerships for the realization of goals and solutions, but not to set them for people with disabilities. In general, social workers will need to consider how to offer more help to individuals in exploring their range of choices. Not only are such goals consistent with the disability movement, they are in line with historic social work professional values that aim to foster the independence and self-determination of clients.

ENDNOTES

[1] For example, there has recently been a scandal in Scandinavia over the sterilization of young women viewed as mentally disabled.
[2] For an example of the differences between these empowerment approaches see Kailes (1988, p. 5).

REFERENCES

Berkowitz, E. D. (1980a). *Rehabilitation: The federal government's response to disability 1935-1954*. New York: Arno Press.
Berkowitz, E. D. (1980b). Strachan and the limits of the federal government. *International Review of History and Political Science*, 17(1), 65-81.
Berrol, S. (1979). Independent living programs: The role of the able-bodied professional. *Archives of Physical Medicine and Rehabilitation*, 60, 456-457.
Bricker-Jenkins, M. and Hooyman, N. R. (1986a). A feminist world view: Ideological themes from the feminist movement. In M. Bricker-Jenkins and N. R. Hooyman (Eds.), *Not for women only* (pp. 7-22). Silver Spring, MD: NASW.

Bricker-Jenkins, M. and Hooyman, N. R. (Eds.). (1986b). *Not for women only*. Silver Spring, MD: NASW.

Crewe, N. M. and Zola, I. K. (Eds.). (1983). *Independent living for physically disabled people*. San Francisco, CA: Jossey-Bass.

DeJong, G. (1981). *Environmental accessibility and independent living outcomes: Directions for disability policy and research*. East Lansing, MI: University Center for International Rehabilitation, Michigan State University.

DeJong, G., Batavia, A. I. and McKnew, L. B. (1992). The independent living model of personal assistance in national long term care policy. *Generations*, 16(1), 43-47.

DeJong, G. and Wenker, T. (1983). Attendant care. In N. M. Crewe and I. K. Zola (Eds.), *Independent living for physically disabled people* (pp. 157-170). San Francisco, CA: Jossey-Bass.

Frieden, L. (1983). Understanding alternative program models. In N. M. Crewe and I. K. Zola (Eds.), *Independent living for physically disabled people* (pp. 62-72). San Francisco, CA: Jossey-Bass.

Grosser, C. F. and Mondros, J. (1985). Pluralism and participation: The political action approach. In S. H. Taylor and R. W. Roberts (Eds.), *Theory and practice of community social work* (pp. 154-178). New York: Columbia University Press.

Gutiérrez, L. M. (1990). Working with women of color: An empowerment perspective. *Social Work*, 35(2), 149-161.

Haggstrom, W. C. (1995). For a democratic revolution: The grass-roots perspective. In J. E. Tropman, J. L. Erlich and J. Rothman (Eds.), *Tactics and techniques of community intervention* (3rd ed., pp. 134-142). Itasca, IL: F. E. Peacock.

Hahn, H. (1984). Reconceptualizing disability: A political science perspective. *Rehabilitation Literature*, 45.

Hahn, H. (1991). Alternative views of empowerment: Social services and civil rights. *Journal of Rehabilitation*, 57(4), [downloaded from WebLUIS on-line database].

Hahn, H. (1996). Antidiscrimination laws and social research on disability: The minority group perspective. *Behavioral Sciences and the Law*, 14(1), 41-59.

Kailes, J. I. (1988). *Putting advocacy rhetoric into practice: The role of the independent living center*. Houston, TX: Independent Living Research Utilization.

Lachat, M. A. (1988). *The independent living service model: Historical roots, core elements, and current practice*. Hampton, NH: Center for Resource Management.

Mackelprang, R. W. and Salsgiver, R. O. (1996). People with disabilities and social work: Historical and contemporary issues. *Social Work*, 41(1), 7-14.

Meyerson, L. (1990). The social psychology of physical disability: 1948 and 1988. In M. Nagler (Ed.), *Perspectives on disability* (pp. 13-23). Palo Alto, CA: Health Markets Research.

Mondros, J. B. and Wilson, S. M. (1994). *Organizing for power and empowerment*. New York: Columbia University Press.

Pinderhughes, E. (1994). Empowerment as an intervention goal: Early ideas. In L. Gutiérrez and P. Nurius (Eds.), *Education and research for empowerment practice* (pp. 17-30). Seattle, WA: Center for Policy and Practice Research.

Rapp, C. A. and Portner, J. (1992). *Social administration: A client-centered approach.* New York: Longman.

Reilly, M. D. and Philip R. (1991). *The surgical solution: A history of involuntary sterilization in the United States.* Baltimore, MD: Johns Hopkins University Press.

Renz-Beaulaurier, R. L. (1994). The role of choice in empowering people with disabilities: Reconceptualizing the role of social work practice in health and rehabilitation settings. In L. Gutiérrez and P. Nurius (Eds.), *Education and research for empowerment practice* (pp. 195-205). Seattle, WA: Center for Policy and Practice Research.

Renz-Beaulaurier, R. L. (1997). Empowering people with disabilities: The role of choice. In L. Gutiérrez, R. Parsons and E. Cox (Eds.), *Empowerment in social work practice: A sourcebook* (pp. 73-84). Pacific Grove, CA: Brooks/Cole.

Renz-Beaulaurier, R. L. and Taylor, S. H. (in press-a). *Challenges and inconsistencies in providing effective advocacy for disabled people in today's health services environment: An exploratory descriptive study.*

Renz-Beaulaurier, R. L. and Taylor, S. H. (in press-b). *Health social work practice with disabled people in the era of the Americans with Disabilities Act.*

Richards, L. and Smith, Q. (1990). *An orientation to independent living centers: A national technical assistance project for independent living.* Houston, TX: Texas Institute for Rehabilitation Research.

Roberts, E. V. (1989). A history of the independent living movement: A founder's perspective. In B. W. F. Heller, M. Louis and L. S. Zegens, (Eds.), *Psychosocial interventions with physically disabled persons* (pp. 231-244). New Brunswick, NJ: Rutgers University Press.

Rothman, J. (1995). Approaches to community intervention. In J. Rothman, J. L. Erlich and J. E. Tropman (Eds.), *Strategies of community intervention* (5th ed., pp. 26-63). Itasca, IL: F. E. Peacock.

Saxton, M. (1983). Peer counseling. In N. M. Crewe and I. K. Zola (Eds.), *Independent living for physically disabled people* (pp. 171-186). San Francisco, CA: Jossey-Bass.

Solomon, B. (1976). *Black empowerment: Social work in oppressed communities.* New York: Columbia University Press.

Taylor, S. H. (1985). Community work and social work: The community liaison approach. In S. H. Taylor and R. W. Roberts (Eds.), *Theory and practice of community social work* (pp. 179-214). New York: Columbia University Press.

Taylor, S. H. and Roberts, R. W. (Eds.). (1985). *Theory and practice of community social work.* New York: Columbia University Press.

US Department of Education. (1992). *Continuation application for grants under centers for independent living.* Washington, D.C.: US Department of Education, Office of Special Education and Rehabilitation Services.

Varela, R. A. (1983). Organizing disabled people for political action. In N. M. Crewe and I. K. Zola (Eds.), *Independent living for physically disabled people* (pp. 311-326). San Francisco, CA: Jossey-Bass.

Weil, M. (1995). Women, community and organizing. In J. E. Tropman, J. L. Erlich and J. Rothman (Eds.), *Tactics and techniques of community intervention* (3rd ed., pp. 118-133). Itasca, IL: F. E. Peacock.

Weinberg, N. (1988). Another perspective: Attitudes of people with disabilities. In H. E. Yucker (Ed.), *Attitudes toward people with disabilities* (pp. 141-153). New York: Springer.

Wolfensberger, W. (1969). The origin and nature of our institutional models. In R. B. Kugel and W. Wolfensberger (Eds.), *Changing patterns in residential services for the mentally retarded* (pp. 59-172). Washington, D.C.: President's Committee on Mental Retardation.

Yuker, H. E. (1988). *Attitudes toward persons with disabilities.* New York: Springer.

Zola, I. K. (1979). Helping one another: A speculative history of the self help movement. *Archives of Physical Medicine and Rehabilitation*, 60, 452-456.

Zola, I. K. (1983). Toward independent living: Goals and dilemmas. In N. M. Crewe and I. K. Zola (Eds.), *Independent living for physically disabled people* (pp. 344-356). San Francisco, CA: Jossey-Bass.

Chapter 10

NEVER TOO OLD: EMPOWERMENT—
THE CONCEPT AND PRACTICE IN WORK
WITH FRAIL ELDERLY

Enid Opal Cox
Graduate School of Social Work
University of Denver

The issues generated from empowerment intervention projects and research with elderly who are experiencing disability, loss of independence and/or the need for care to engage in activities of daily living and other supporting tasks are addressed in this chapter, as well as the related academic debate. The context of social work practice with frail elders will be discussed briefly as will the meaning of empowerment from a variety of perspectives. Challenges, issues and opportunities related to the development, implementation and funding of empowerment-oriented interventions with elders in key health and social services serving the elderly in the US will also be explored.

THE CONTEXT

Aging in society is a phenomena that presents new challenges never before faced by as large numbers of people. There are issues associated with an additional 15 to 20 years of life that one may have after the traditional life cycle activities have been completed (Moody, 1988, 1992), as well as issues faced historically by older adults such as workplace displacement and other forms of age discrimination. Current policy debate has also added stress to late life issues by depicting the elderly as an unworthy or at best an unproductive and therefore undeserving group for receipt of government funding (Lamm, 1997; Longman, 1988; Moody, 1992). This situation imposes two primary challenges to elderly who experience failing health and increased need for care: 1) how to cope with care needs and the stigma of being perceived of as needy; and 2) How does an elder find meaning and valued roles under these circumstances.

Thomas Cole (1992) calls our attention to a key factor related to the intergenerational equity discourse by observing that our struggle is deeply rooted in our culture's inability to provide convincing answers to deep existential questions like the quality of life in old age, the unity and integrity of the life cycle and the meaning of aging. He summarizes his critique of the current views of aging in our society asserting that: "In rebuilding a moral economy of an extended life course, we must not only attend to questions of justice within and between different stages of life, we must also forge a new sense of the meanings and purposes of the last half of life" (p. 237).

Another complicating factor in our effort to understand late life issues and the role of empowerment is the extreme challenge presented by disabilitating terminal illness that increasingly requires intensive care and/or Alzheimer's disease or other forms of dementia that severely inhibit the mental functioning of elderly individuals who experience these problems. Moody summarizes this challenge in his description of the ethical dilemmas of Alzheimer's disease, through a case example:

> ... as the disease progressed Murray's memory loss and confusion became progressively worse. The terror of the situation is that this patient still recognizes what is happening and foresees what lies in the future. This awareness of vulnerability casts its shadow over all his relationships and finally compromises what the patient takes to be his own dignity. (Moody, 1992, p. 132)

We are often challenged by health and social service providers to justify our efforts to expand empowerment-oriented practice when faced with these aspects of late life frailty.

On the other hand, research concerning elderly care-receivers and elderly patients demonstrates the strong capacity of this population to in fact participate in the self-care processes, cope with extremely difficult circumstances and continue to be a vital and contributing force as family members and community members (Cox and Dooley, 1996; Browne, 1995).

LATE LIFE CHALLENGES: DEFINING EMPOWERMENT

While considerable work has been done regarding the conceptualization of empowerment-oriented social work practice with the elderly and a growing literature is evident in other professional fields, empowerment has been used in a number of ways regarding "frail elders" and the related issues of health and social services designed to meet their needs. How do we understand the variety of approaches to empowerment in late life?

Empowerment is often used interchangeably with such terms as competence, autonomy, self-care, participation in health-care decision-making, social action and gaining resources. The following sections describe some of the differing notions of empowerment as they have been expressed by elderly who are experiencing late life frailty and a loss of independence, and those of selected service providers, academic educators and researchers.

PERCEPTIONS OF ELDERS

In two separate studies over 200 elderly individuals, who required a minimum of eight hours of care per week to accomplish activities of daily living, were interviewed in depth regarding their experience in coping with loss of independence, use of care-givers and other aspects of their situation. Sampling was purposive based on care-receiving status and cognitive ability to be interviewed. General findings of these studies have been reported elsewhere (Cox and Dooley, 1996; Cox, Parsons and Kimboko, 1988; and Cox, Dooley, Liston and Miller, 1998). None of the respondents had participated in empowerment-oriented intervention programs as described by Cox and Parsons (1994). However, the descriptions given by respondents regarding empowerment included an interesting and significant range of ideas which may help us. The following themes emerged regarding these elders' understanding of what it means to be empowered:

1. being able to take care of one's self
2. not being a burden to others—especially children
3. having resources such as income, appropriate housing and medical coverage
4. having friends and family members who care about them
5. having knowledge about services and programs and how to deal effectively with professionals
6. being able to be useful or give something of values to others
7. being able to change the environment including professional behaviours, service delivery problems including content, access, amount, etc.

Most of these elderly care-receivers were focused on a struggle to increase their ability in self-care. Empowerment meant having resources including money, housing, health care and personal support workers (willing helpers and providers of emotional support) that contributed to their independence. Another critical part was being useful and helping others, especially those who were providing help. Knowledge and ability to use formal services were also important.

Issues of community service and political aspects of personal empowerment per se were seldom mentioned by respondents (Cox and Dooley, 1996). In another set of interviews conducted with over 50 elderly who participated in empowerment-oriented intervention based on the Cox and Parson's model (1994), individual elders were asked to describe the process of empowerment post intervention. Here elders' responses often included descriptions of the importance of working with others in their efforts to meet their own needs, as well as in efforts to meet mutual needs and improve environmental conditions (Cox , 1988).

While research regarding the perceptions of empowerment among the elderly is limited, there is even less regarding the impact of empowerment-oriented interventions with elders. Limited preliminary work indicates that the consciousness-raising processes included in empowerment-oriented strategies increases awareness among participants of the potential meaning of empowerment for their lives personally and politically (Cox, 1988; McInnis-Dittrich, 1997).

In sum, elderly persons who are facing increased dependency have many different perceptions of empowerment. However, issues related to this concept are of increasing concern to many elders as challenges of late life threaten independence.

PERCEPTIONS OF AGING NETWORK SERVICE PROVIDERS

Empowerment has become a popular word among many professionals who work in aging, and it has even gained attention among a number of detractors. Few conferences in the past ten years have not included at least one session on empowerment. While definitions are not always offered in articles and reports describing empowerment efforts, it often easy to determine the implicit meaning from the authors' descriptive materials.

A recent survey was sent to 12 program administrators who had received funding under an empowerment initiative for special funds available for outreach through the Denver Regional Government's Area Agency on Aging. They were asked to provide their own definition of empowerment. Respondents were directors of health and social service programs including a visiting nurses service, transportation programs, senior centres and home health-care programs. Their definitions encompassed the following perceptions. Empowerment: is providing the right resources for people, i.e., effective referrals; has to do with social action; is self-care; is letting people have more say about the services they get; and is just a new buzz word. Two respondents had read about empowerment in the academic literature and had definitions similar to those of Zimmerman (1995) and/or Cox and Parsons (1994) that included some reference to various levels or dimensions of empowerment and to collective action and consciousness-raising.

ACADEMIC DEFINITIONS OF EMPOWERMENT AND THE FRAIL ELDER

The increasingly abundant academic discourse on empowerment has not focused in large degree on empowerment and the elderly or, more specifically, on the elders who are coping with increased dependence because of physical decline. A few social work researchers offered definitions of empowerment that are congruent with those of Zimmerman (1995), Rappaport (1995) and the Cornell Group (1989), which include, for example, the need for a critical understanding of one's environment and circumstances, participation with others in critical consciousness processes and action to change internal and external barriers to meeting the needs of individuals and groups (Mok and Mui, 1996; Browne, 1995; Cox and Parsons, 1994; Sotomayor, 1991). However, the large majority of work related to empowerment and aging when it is presented, does not clearly define the author's perception of empowerment or defines empowerment using related constructs such increasing autonomy, competence or sense of efficacy (Spitzer, Bar-Tal and Ziv, 1996; Delgado, 1996; Rakowski, 1998; Pujnamaki and Aschan, 1994; Malin and Teasdale, 1991; and Waters and Goodman, 1990).

Observing the importance of consciousness-raising as a part of the empowerment process, Joseph (1997) states:

> Beyond the recognition and respect for the current character and culture of frail elders, which form the basis of any empowerment work (starting where the people are), the requirement for a specific definition may be too limiting. There is after all a rich history in the liberation movements of the 20th century particularly the women's movement where the term "consciousness raising" was coined to describe the process by which women 'together' discovered the 'truth of their situation' in a safe space later deemed a 'consciousness

raising group.' In these groups emerged a collective process of learning and transformation.

Having rejected established theory and behavior that resulted in sexism and its attendant oppression, women struggled to educate themselves and the society about the pervasive inequality between genders and the myth of this being a 'natural' much less, a desirable state. Like these women, the elderly (many of whom are women) can begin to unmask the world them as they are encouraged to discuss experiences of all kinds, childhood, work, stereotypes of aging and disability (ageism), of body images etc. By sharing individual problems, members soon recognize the commonality of their 'aging' experience and the power-relations hidden in their personal and public lives.

Social workers and elders need to understand and deepen their use of models and approaches to consciousness raising and the 'personal is political' which can help elders to transform their perceptions of their lives, strengths, and capacity to change their world. (p. 2)

Other work on empowerment that offers valuable insight, though not specifically related to frail elders, includes empowerment efforts focused on disability (Gadacz, 1994). Gadacz describes empowerment issues in the context of disability, and the important role individuals living with disability can take in the disabled consumer's movement to change environmental conditions that discriminate against people on the basis of physical disability. A comprehensive model of empowerment interventions based on the importance of critical consciousness and collective action is described. Many aspects of the disability context overlap with the context of frail elders, but there are significant differences that require our focus on the meaning of disability in both settings separately. Breton's (1996) provocative analysis of issues related to competence promotion and empowerment, also not directed specifically to work with the elderly, directly addresses issues that are recurring among those struggling to expand empowerment-oriented interventions with elders. Specifically she notes "that entitlement should not be confused with empowerment" while "awareness and the exercise of the right to access resources is a necessary condition for empowerment it is not a sufficient one" (p. 32). This observation is clearly reflected as confusion of divergent perceptions among service providers noted above. She also stresses that empowerment requires not only a conscientization process that produces awareness but the right and responsibility to participate in creating resources, in influencing the nature and character of existing resources and in eliminating inappropriate or ineffective resources. When personal competence is isolated from the interpersonal, social and structural contexts, this does not satisfy the definition of empowerment.

In sum, key differences in perceptions of the meaning of empowerment are often related to: 1) whether the organizational and/or political/community dimensions are considered an integral part of empowerment, and 2) whether collective communication and action with others experiencing similar challenges are considered critical aspects of empowerment. These differing perceptions naturally guide the discourse concerning development of health and social service interventions targeting the frail elderly, and may well represent a consciousness-raising process in themselves.

ISSUES AND CHALLENGES IN THE DELIVERY OF EMPOWERMENT-ORIENTED SERVICES TO THE FRAIL ELDERLY

As reviewed above there is no consensus regarding what empowerment means and hence no agreement about the nature of empowerment-oriented services in the targeted population. The following discussion will in general refer to empowerment-oriented services as those services that seek to engage elders in the empowerment process in response to challenges they are facing. The empowerment process includes (1) a critical review of attitudes and beliefs about one's self and one's socio/political environment, (2) the validation of one's experience, (3) increased knowledge and skills for critical thinking and action, and (4) action taken for personal and political change (Gutiérrez, Parsons and Cox, 1998). Empowerment-oriented social work practice models often provide a description of empowerment interventions and outcomes using a systems analysis that includes personal, interpersonal, organizational and political/community level of consciousness and activity (Gutiérrez, Parsons and Cox, 1998; Cox and Parsons, 1994; and Lee, 1994). In practice, the interrelatedness of these levels or dimensions of empowerment is constantly reaffirmed.

FROM METHODS TO PRACTICE SITES

The effort to integrate empowerment-oriented methods into practice has met many barriers. The following is a brief discussion of factors that have been identified as having strong impact on this effort. This discussion is organized into two parts: a) current policy approaches, biomedicalization of aging, worker disempowerment; and b) factors related to the state-of-the-art in development, implementation and evaluation of empowerment-oriented interventions targeting the frail elderly.

Current Social Policy Directions

The current political climate is hostile to the development of new social services in almost any form. As the more conservative take leadership in government during a time of internationalization of the economy, they foster goals of reduced government and privatization of social welfare activity and enact cutbacks eliminating social work programs and departments. Cuts in programs and services for the elderly are further fuelled by the intergenerational equity debate as a form of policy analysis that blames the lack of resources for children, youth and other populations' needs on the over-utilization of public resources by the elderly (Lamm, 1997; Longman; 1987; Minkler, 1991). Several observers of aging policy suggest that the deservingness of the old is being seriously challenged by both conservative and liberal forces (Hudson, 1996).

This negative attention on the elderly has made programs and services for the aging less popular with many local foundation boards as well as federal, state and local government policy-makers.

Biomedicalization of Aging

Another aspect of the general health and human services arena that has a major impact on the field of aging has been the biomedicalization of aging. This has strong implications for the development of social work and psycho-social services on behalf of the elderly.

The biomedicalizaton of aging or the social construction of aging as a medical problem is elaborated by Estes and Binney (1991) as follows:

> The social construction of aging as a medical problem focuses on the disease of the elderly—their etiology, treatment, and management—from the perspective of the practice of medicine.... This means that the emphasis of the medical model with its emphasis on clinical phenomena take precedence over, and in many cases define the basic biological, social and behavioral processes and problems of the aging. (p. 18)
>
> This methodological individualism ... limits the degree to which larger social and environmental factors are

considered because the primary focus is on illness as an individual problem with individual causes and individual solutions (pp. 19).

This biomedical approach to intervention is clearly in opposition to empowerment-oriented interventions that seek to foster collectivity and consciousness raising with respect to the person in environment including the political/ economic system.

The reduction in social service dollars for services and programs for the elderly through public human service programs (Rosenzweig, 1995) and the shift of Older Americans Act resources from social service to health-care services have greatly reduced social service oriented sites for the development of social work interventions and placed most social work program development opportunities targeting the frail elder population in sites controlled by biomedical orientation. Nowhere is this mismatch of need and service model more evident than in the community based long-term care effort to provide appropriate services in the homes of frail elders using a medical model. Rosenweig (1995) describes the extent and limitations or services available through Medicare and Medicaid at the community level. Restraints (such as physician approval of service, requirements that the service recipient must be home bound and that social service, if provided, must be removed if nursing care is not required) illustrate barriers in a medical model addressing the extremely complex biopsychosocial issues of late life care needs.

The medical model is undergoing some degree of challenge especially from medical professionals committed to the importance of psycho-social aspects of health, to health prevention and to self-care or self-determination in patient services. However, health-oriented arenas remain a difficult base for the development of empowerment-oriented programs. In recent years, social work has increasingly lost its status and ability to control its function and methodological autonomy in most health-care settings (Rose, 1997; Holmes and Saleebey, 1993; Fabricant and Burghardt, 1992). Shrinking resources have aggravated the situation by increasing inter-professional competition, leaving little energy for the initiation of innovative social service models.

Worker Disempowerment

An overriding sense of powerlessness among many gerontological social workers has risen in response to decreasing governmental resources and privatization (introduction of the profit motive into more aspects of health and social services), coupled with increasing work loads, lower status and salaries (Fabricant and Burghardt, 1992). Riffe and Kondrat (1997) note:

> Within the past decade, increasing pressures have come to bear on the individual practitioner to treat mental health issues in a more cost effective manner ... some of these strategies have lead to a more integrated community system of care.... However, some of the policies regulate the relationship between the client and the social worker and the growth of the relationship between worker and client. (p. 42)

The regulation of the nature of services that has occurred in many health and social service programs limits the number of visits, specifies the content of the client worker exchange and reduces dramatically the types of assistance that can be given (Sabin, 1992; Riffe and Kondrat, 1997; Rose, 1997; Fabricant and Burghardt, 1992).

Results from a survey of 25 gerontological social workers in Colorado in 1996 and from focus groups of members of the Colorado Association of Gerontological Social Workers, found that participants had extreme difficulty finding positions in which traditional social work methods could be practiced and even fewer opportunities to incorporate empowerment-oriented interventions. Workers also identified the professional licensure process as a strong obstacle to the incorporation of empowerment-oriented practice and to other aspects of their work with frail elders. Social workers in Colorado are licensed as psychotherapists and the ethical regulations include restrictions on client worker relationships. Therefore, mutual work with clients in self-help efforts, transporting clients and other informal interactions can lead to disciplinary action. Several participants believed such restrictions were very detrimental to their professional autonomy and added stress to an already difficult situation.

In sum, the constraints of existing health and social services with respect to the development and incorporation of empowerment-oriented practice models are strong and comprehensive.

STATE OF THE ART CHALLENGES: EMPOWERMENT-ORIENTED INTERVENTIONS WITH FRAIL ELDERS

Despite lack of consensus regarding empowerment, limited resources to implement empowerment-oriented processes and other barriers to the comprehensive development of empowerment-oriented programs for the frail elderly, many efforts are being mounted. This section provides an overview of some of the successes and issues that have emerged: what has been tried, what works and what indicators for action elders have offered us.

Guidance from the Elders

Research that articulates the perspective of the elderly population who are in need of personal care including their concerns, ways of coping and their thoughts on empowerment in late life is limited. However, the work that does exist has provided critical insights for empowerment-oriented practitioners.

Recognition of the importance of autonomy and patient participation in community based long-term care and other health settings has increased over the past two decades (Lott, Blazey and West, 1992; Hennessy, 1989; Zawacki and Patterson, 1984; Haug, Wykle and Namazi, 1989). Case studies of patient control of their care have provided many individual examples of effectiveness. However few studies have recorded the perceptions and roles of elderly care-receivers in their care process. In a multicultural study of elders' perceptions of their loss of independence and care processes, Cox and Dooley (1996) report findings that suggest what empowerment interventions involving the frail elderly must address: beliefs and values regarding independence/dependence; the strategies elders use for self-care; communications with professional and personal care-givers; ways elders can assist care-givers and reposition themselves as valued family members; how social support networks in late life can be maintained; and what strategies can be used to maintain mental health and other meaningful activities (roles). Further study of the strengths and coping processes of elderly individuals who are providing answers to some of the questions raised above regarding the meaning of aging, and the creation of valued roles and activities in late life will be of great value to intervention development.

Small Group Interventions

Regardless of limited resources and few opportunities for ongoing programs, a series of small demonstrations described in the literature indicate that small group interventions based on an empowerment-oriented model have been very successful in improving the quality of life for elderly care-receivers. (McInnis-Dittrich, 1997; Mok and Mui, 1996; Cox and Parsons, 1996; Cox and Parsons, 1994; Cox, 1988). These group interventions have worked best in senior housing facilities, nursing homes and community based apartments or hotels where group participants have regular contact. Group meetings address issues such as safety, housing concerns and ways to change health-care delivery. Activities include education (consciousness-raising activities), self-help and social action. The potential for engaging frail elders in all aspects of the empowerment process has been demonstrated.

Currently, efforts are being developed to serve isolated elderly care-receivers. The challenges faced with this population include how to facilitate the collective nature of empowerment process while restricted to essentially one-to-one interventions. Workers engaged in this challenge are attempting to utilize tapes, phone networks and very limited group meetings (one or two) to overcome this obstacle.

Resource Issues

As noted, with the current climate of diminishing human services and resources, the initiation of empowerment programs is a difficult task. However, in order to increase the use of empowerment-oriented practice in services and programs serving the frail elderly, a number of strategies are in progress: 1) to advance an understanding of the concept of empowerment among service providers incorporating development of collectivity, consciousness-raising and action and reflection (Gutiérrez, Parsons and Cox, 1998); 2) work with locally based agencies and foundations to integrate empowerment-oriented interventions into existing services, such as visiting nurse services, senior centres, senior clinics and mental health programs serving the elderly and; 3) further demonstration and research to test the efficacy of empowerment program designs and interventions.

Pilot efforts to involve social service administrators in staff development for empowerment-oriented interventions have met with mixed response. Most of the 120 participants in a Denver area training endeavour expressed interest. However, focus and attention quickly moved to interventions that provided education and training for elder clients for self-care or interventions that emphasized elder clients having a voice in the services and programs they received. Only a few participants were enthusiastic about an empowerment process that supported elders involvement in influencing the decisions (especially on larger policy issues) that affected their lives. Resistance to political aspects of the empowerment process centred around two issues: the beliefs among providers that frail elders do not have the energy or capacity for such participation; and an awareness that the ideological climate of agencies and organizations in which they are employed would inhibit any work related to political change. The most difficult obstacle to the introduction of an empowerment-oriented philosophy into existing programs was the expressed concern by administrators about lack of staff time and other resources needed to initiate new programs or modify existing programs.

Programs that have been initiated in some agencies in the Denver metropolitan area suffer from two limitations: staff competency and ongoing commitment to the programs. Considerable success is evident in the incorporation of empowerment-oriented practices such as the addition of mechanisms for more participation of elders in decision-making in care planning, participation on decision-making teams and boards, stronger training of nursing home residents regarding their rights, increased health education programs and numerous other programs described as empowerment programs by their sponsors. But, few have developed and used a comprehensive empowerment process design. Many lack staff who have been trained in or participated in empowerment-oriented interventions, and few have administrative support for more comprehensive programs. Currently, a number of key agencies have agreed to sponsor one empowerment-oriented group to be supervised by the University of Denver Institute of Gerontology, which has empowerment expertise.

Research Agenda

The effort to further empowerment-oriented practice models through the use of research and demonstration projects has been limited by a number of factors. Preliminary efforts to gain funding from well-endowed sources such as the National Institute of Mental Health and the National Institute of Health (Aging) have generated three key areas of difficulty in meeting their research design requirements for funding.

One area of concern continues to be specificity in the intervention. Pilot projects with less rigorous research demands have used holistic intervention approaches that combined small group activity with one-to-one intervention and allowed a great deal of decision regarding the content and activities to group members. While these activities differ from group to group and individual to individual, the overall impact is to mobilize the group and their efforts together through the empowerment process. This degree of flexibility is difficult to measure and replicate by existing research methods.

The second issue is the lack of accepted measurement tools regarding empowerment in general and empowerment of frail elders specifically. Work in this area will be assisted by developments in mental health and other arenas.

Third is the complication in measurement because of deteriorating health conditions of many elderly and measurement of their health status in general. Not only do severe health factors effect feelings of efficacy and sense of empowerment but much work is yet to be done in establishing the specific role of empowerment in health and mental health status. Measurement of health status is not always an easy task. A specific example of this problem was recently demonstrated in a project that attempted to measure levels of self-efficacy, autonomy, empowerment and depression among elderly stroke survivors. The measurement of stroke-related disability could only be measured in terms of functional status because current medical knowledge does not allow for clear comparison of degree of severity of stroke (Cox and Miller, 1995).

FUTURE DIRECTIONS

The converging interests of self-care, autonomy, competency and empowerment advocates in practice with the frail elderly represent a growing enthusiasm about the potential of frail elders to create and fulfil important roles in their own care and in the well-being of their care-givers, other members of their support networks and their communities. This movement, in addition to the strong emphasis on cost-effectiveness in health-care provision and the increased visibility of the community based service vs. institutionalization in the long-term care debate, may provide the impetus for experimentation and change in health and mental health delivery systems that allows empowerment-oriented and other strengths based programs to be initiated.

There is also some compatibility between goals of cost efficiency and goals of empowerment. Ultimately, empowerment goals promote self-care, active participation of people in the issues that effect their lives and collective problem solving. Empowerment programs with the frail elderly most often have specific goals to increase knowledge and skills of individuals, their families as well as local communities in order to meet their own needs. Even though politically conscious constituencies may demand regulation of for-profit services and more government supported services, there remains some room for cooperative effort. Rose (1997) suggests that managed care modified into a system focused on health maintenance and health care rather than profit could offer the opportunity for social workers to have a strong role in the development of services. It is his contention that a program for "enrolled populations, paid through capitation, creates interesting opportunities unimaginable under indemnified fee-for-service regimens" (p.64). Community based care which is very compatible with empowerment-oriented service designs emerge.

Also, these programs are frequently conducted in multidisciplinary settings allowing for the potential collaboration and networking between health and social service professionals, an alliance that has powerful potential (Riffe and Kondrat, 1997).

In sum, there are some hopeful signs that turmoil in the existing systems may open opportunities for social workers who have become alienated and disempowered in today's settings to become instrumental in policy development and in the design of future delivery systems that will be empathetic to social work values and with empowerment-oriented practice. At the margin, workers can empower themselves in their everyday work if they plumb the depths of their practice to push towards the centre (Joseph, 1997). The common characteristics of the autonomy, competency and empowerment philosophies, as they are represented in a variety interventions, often result in unintended but highly positive overlap. Elderly who become better educated about medical conditions, drugs and intervention options may also become involved in broader self-help efforts such as for crime control and may begin to use the collective opportunities of educational groups, beginning the conscientiousization process so important to their ultimate empowerment. We start where we are.

Certainly social workers with an empowerment orientation can use such opportunities to help elders transform perceptions of their own lives and capacity to act. As elders unmask their world and challenge the stereotypes of aging, disability, body image and the myths of incapacity, they can rename their world based on self-determined strengths and limits in a process which galvanizes each one according to their needs, to work for life-affirming change, each as they can.

REFERENCES

Breton, M. (1996). Relating competence—promotion and empowerment. *Journal of Progressive Human Services*, 5(1), 27-44. H V (, 55] -

Browne, C. V. (1995). Empowerment in social work practice with older women. *Social Work*, 40(3), 358-364.

Cole, T. R. (1992). *The journey of life: A cultural history of aging in America.* New York, NY: Cambridge University Press.

Cornell Empowerment Group. (1989). Empowerment and family support. *Networking Bulletin* 1(1), 1-23.

Cox, E. O. (1988). Empowerment of the low income elderly through group work. *Social Work with Groups*, 11(3/4), 111-125.

Cox, E. O. and Dooley, A. (1996). Care-receivers' perceptions of their role in the care process. *Journal of Gerontological Social Work*, 26(1/2), 133-139.

Cox, E. O., Dooley, A., Liston, M. and Miller, M. (1998). Coping with stroke and rehabilitation interventions. *Topics in Stroke Rehabilitation*, 4(4), 76-88.

Cox, E. O. and Miller, M. M. (1995). *Coping with stroke: Perceptions of elderly who have experienced stroke and rehabilitation intervention.* Submitted to Spalding Rehabilitation Hospital.

Cox, E. O. and Parsons, R. J. (1994). *Empowerment-oriented social work practice with the elderly.* Pacific Grove, CA: Brooks/Cole Publishing Company.

Cox, E. O. and Parsons, R. J. (1996). Empowerment-oriented social work practice: Impact on late life relationships of women. In K. A. Roberto (Ed.), *Relationships between women in later life* (pp.129-143). New York, NY: The Hawarth Press, Inc.

Cox, E. O., Parsons, R. J. and Kimboko, P. J. (1988). Social services and intergenerational caregivers: Issues for social work. *Social Work*, 33(5), 430.

Delgado, M. (1996). Puerto Rican Elders and gerontological research: Avenues for empowerment and participation. *Activities, adaptation and aging*, 21(2), 77- 83.

Estes, C. L. and Binney, E. A. (1991). The biomedicalization of aging: Dangers and dilemmas. In M. Minkler and C. L. Estes (Eds.), *Critical perspectives on aging: The political and moral economy of growing old* (pp.117-134). Amityville, NY: Baywood Publishing Company, Inc.

Fabricant, M.B. and Burghardt, S. (1992). *The welfare state crisis and the transformation of social service work.* New York, NY: M. E. Sharpe, Inc.

Gadacz, R. R. (1994). *Rethinking disability: New structures, new relationships.* Alberta, Canada: The University of Alberta Press.

Gutiérrez, L. M., Parsons, R. J. and Cox, E. O. (1998). *Empowerment in social work practice: A sourcebook.* New York, NY: Brooks/Cole Publishing Company.

Hennessy, C. H. (1989). Autonomy and risk: The role of client wishes in community-based long-term care. *The Gerontologist*, 29(5), 633-639.

Haug, M. R., Wykle, M. L. and Namazi, K. H. (1989). Self-care among older adults. *Social Science Medicine*, 29(2), 171-183.

Holmes, G. E. and Saleebey, D. (1993). Empowerment, the medical model, and the politics of clienthood. *Journal of Progressive Human Services*, 4(1), 61-78.

Hudson, R. B. (1996). The changing face of aging politics. *The Gerontologist*, 36(1), 33-41.

Joseph, B. H. R. (1997). *Notes on empowerment and the elderly.* Unpublished.

Lamm, R. (1997). Death: Right or duty? *Cambridge Quarterly of Health Care*, 6(1), 111- 113.

Lee, J. A. B. (1994). *The empowerment approach to social work practice.* New York, NY: Columbia University Press.

Longman, P. (1987). *Born to pay: The new politics of aging in America.* Boston: Houghton Mifflin.

Lott, R. F., Blazey, M. E. and West, M. G. (1992). Patient participation in health care: An underused resource. *Nursing Clinics of North America*, 27(1), 61-76.

Malin, N. and Teasdale, K. (1991). Caring versus empowerment: Considerations for nursing practice. *Journal of Advanced Nursing*, 16, 657-662.

McInnis-Dittrich, K. (1997). An empowerment-oriented mental health intervention with elderly Appalachian women: The women's club. *Journal of Women and Aging*, 9(1/2), 91-105.

Minkler, M. (1991). "Generational equity" and the new victim blaming. In M. Minkler and C. L. Estes (Eds.), *Critical perspectives on aging: The political and moral economy of growing old* (pp.67-80). Amityville, NY: Baywood Publishing Company, Inc.

Mok, B. and Mui, A. (1996). Empowerment in residential care for the elders: The case of an aged home in Hong Kong. *Journal of Gerontological Social Work*, 27(1/2), 23-35.

Moody, H. R. (1988). *Abundance of life: Human development policies for an aging south*. New York: Columbia University Press.

Moody, H. R. (1992). *Ethics in an aging society*. Baltimore, MD: The Johns Hopkins University Press.

Perkins, D. D. and Zimmerman, M. A. (1995). Empowerment theory, research, and application. *American Journal of Community Psychology*, 23(5), 569-579.

Pujnamaki, R. and Aschan, H. (1994). Research note: Self-care and mastery among primary health care patients. *Social Science Medicine*, 39(5), 733-741.

Rakowski, W. (1998). Evaluating psychosocial interventions for promoting self-care behaviour among older adults. In M. G. Ory and G. H. De Frinse (Eds.), *Self-care in later life: Research, programs and policy issues* (pp. 85-117). New York: Springer Publishing Company.

Rappaport, J. (1995). Empowerment meets narrative: Listening to stories and creating settings. *American Journal of Community Psychology*, 23(5), 795-807.

Riffe, H. A., and Kondrat, M. E. (1997). Social worker alienation and disempowerment in a managed care setting. *Journal of Progressive Human Services*, 8(1), 41-55.

Rose, S. M. (1997). Considering managed care. *Journal of Progressive Human Services*, 8(1), 57-65.

Rosenzweig, E. P. (1995). Trends in home care entitlements and benefits. *Journal of Gerontological Social Work*, 24(3/4), 9-29.

Sabin, J. E. (1992). The therapeutic alliance in managed care mental health practice. *The Journal of Psychotherapy Practice and Research*, 1(1), 29-36.

Sharpe, P. A. (1995). Older women and health services: Moving from ageism toward empowerment. *Women and Health*, 22(3), 9-23.

Sotomayor, M. (Ed.). (1991). *Empowering Hispanic families: A critical issue for the '90s*. Milwaukee, WI: Family Service America.

Spitzer, A., Bar-Tal, Y. and Ziv, L. (1996). The moderating effect of age on self-care. *Western Journal of Nursing Research*, 18(2), 136-148.

Waters, E. B. and Goodman, J. (1990). *Empowering older adults: Practical Strategies for counselors*. San Francisco, CA: Jossey-Bass Publisher.

Zawacki, N. and Patterson, D. F. (1984). Putting the patient on the team: A teaching Strategy. *Journal of Nursing Education*, 23(8), 346-348.

Zimmerman, M. A. (1995). Psychological empowerment: Issues and illustrations. *American Journal of Community Psychology*, 23(5), 581-599.

Chapter 11

EMPOWERMENT IN FIRST NATIONS CHILD AND FAMILY SERVICES: A COMMUNITY BUILDING PROCESS

Brad McKenzie
Faculty of Social Work
University of Manitoba

Empowerment is a ubiquitous, but confusing concept in social work. On one hand, it captures in a single word both the essential mission of the profession and a preferred process for good social work practice. At the same time it has been used to describe such a broad range of goals and activities that it is in danger of losing its meaning. While the concept is most frequently used to reflect efforts to assist the disadvantaged in addressing problems associated with social and economic inequality, Mullender and Ward (1991) note that the principle of empowerment is also used by the political right to justify a reduction in state social services so that people will become more self-sufficient. More often the term is used to describe services that, while well intended, are not experienced as empowering by consumers. For these reasons it is important to critically review the key characteristics of empowering practice and the effects of efforts to implement services under the guise of empowerment in social work.

This chapter examines empowerment in child welfare practice. While general constraints to empowerment in this field are identified, most attention is devoted to First Nations child and family services.[1] Community controlled First Nations agencies have provided a full range of child welfare services to all reserves in the province of Manitoba since the mid 1980s, and this general model of service delivery is now widely established across Canada. A comprehensive evaluation of one First Nations child and family service agency in the province employing more than 80 staff and serving nine First Nations communities was completed in 1994. Over the past number of years this agency has provided a leadership role in First Nations child welfare across the country; in addition, it exhibits a number of characteristics which can be associated with an empowerment approach to practice. In August, 1997 a focus group discussion with supervisory and management staff in this agency was conducted to explore the theme of empowerment in more detail. Two general questions were posed. First, staff were asked to identify the nature and extent of changes in child welfare practice in their communities over the past ten years. As many of the staff had grown up in these communities, they were able to answer this question both as agency staff members and as long-term community residents. Second, staff were asked to identify both the constraints and opportunities which affected the development of an empowering approach to the provision of child and family services in their communities. Results from this group interview were used to supplement other forms of data collection employed in the study (see McKenzie, 1994) and as a way of validating the key themes which emerged in the analysis stage.

DEFINING EMPOWERMENT

A key issue is that of definition and the essential problem of attaching precise meaning to the concept of empowerment as it applies in social work. There are two reasons for the lack of clarity. First, empowerment is conceptually difficult to define because it is used to describe both the ends and means of social work practice (Staples, 1990); moreover, it is applied to different levels or dimensions of practice (Gutiérrez, GlenMaye and DeLois, 1995; Labonté, 1990). Second, the political correctness of the concept in the profession encourages social workers to define much of what social work does, including adhering to the general goal of client self-determination, as empowerment.

Despite these difficulties, empowerment remains an important concept in social work; thus it is important to clarify its essential aspects. Staples (1990, p. 29-30) defines empowerment as the process by which power is obtained as an individual or group moves from a condition of relative powerlessness to one of relative power. However, he also notes that the state of being empowered reflects the product or goal of the empowerment process, and that the relationship between these dimensions is often complex. Empowerment as both product and process has been defined as something that occurs at different levels. Thus, Staples argues that empowerment must be experienced in both the individual and social domain. Several authors (Pinderhughes, 1989; Rappaport, 1981; Gutiérrez, 1990) note its focus on developing skills for personal, interpersonal or social change, and Labonté (1990) defines a continuum of empowerment which includes personal empowerment, small group development, community organization, coalition advocacy and political action. The importance of nurturing empowerment practice among staff within the service organization has also received attention (Shera and Page, 1995; Gutiérrez, GlenMaye and DeLois, 1995). There is some debate about whether connections must be made between the different levels in order to realize goals associated with empowerment. A sequential process whereby one gains personal, collective and political power is suggested by some (Dodd and Gutiérrez, 1990; Labonté, 1990), but Callahan and Lumb (1995) caution that this may lead many to limit their focus to the personal level and more longstanding approaches to individual counselling. For this reason, several authors emphasize the importance of connections between the personal and the political as an essential and underlying feature of the empowerment process (Staples, 1990; Mullender and Ward, 1993; Labonté, 1990).

Four other aspects of empowerment are particularly important. First, it involves an emphasis on strengths and competencies (Rappaport, 1984; Pinderhughes, 1983; Simon, 1990; Gutiérrez, DeLois and GlenMaye, 1995; Weick, Rapp, Sullivan and Kisthardt, 1989). Second, it is connected to the capacity for self-action and the ability to achieve a greater measure of control over one's own life and destiny. In the social work context empowerment is inextricably linked to client participation and control in making their own decisions and taking action on their own behalf (Callahan and Lumb, 1995; Rappaport, 1984; Zimmerman and Rappaport, 1988; Simon, 1990). Indeed, Simon (1990) suggests that while social workers can assist in the empowerment process of their clients, they cannot perform this function for them. Empowerment, she argues, is a reflexive activity that can only be initiated and sustained by the subject who seeks power or self-determination. Although client empowerment is a central theme in social work there is widespread recognition of the enabling role played by social workers, and the connection between empowerment for workers and clients has received attention (Callahan and Lumb, 1995; Pinderhughes, 1983; Shera and Page, 1995). Finally, and perhaps most important, is the central focus of empowerment on addressing the powerlessness experienced by those who are in positions of dependency or vulnerability (Dodd and Gutiérrez, 1990). According to Callahan and Lumb (1995, p. 798), "the most important feature of empowerment is that it begins with an analysis of inequality and how it is maintained by the process of stigmatizing." The fundamental realignment of power, values and relationships that is implied creates a requirement for structural as well as individual changes; in addition, this premise supports the position that empowerment is being inappropriately used if it attempts to depict goals and processes which do not explicitly address the problem of inequality.

Based on this discussion, it is concluded that the general application of empowerment in social work practice has the following characteristics: a) it attempts to redress the problem of inequality and powerlessness and how these are maintained through stigmatization and structural arrangements in society; b) it reflects both a goal and a process of interaction which require skills emphasizing partnership with clients and a focus on strengths and competencies; c) empowerment occurs at different levels, including the personal, interpersonal and political, but the personal must be linked to the political in order to realize the full potential of empowerment; d) empowerment for clients, which is central to social work practice, can only be initiated and sustained by clients; and e) social workers can assist in this process but to do so it is important that they feel empowered both personally and through their employing service organizations.

BARRIERS TO EMPOWERMENT IN CHILD WELFARE

There has been some attention to empowerment within child welfare, but most often this has focused on youth in care (Gibson, 1993; Garfat, Craig and Joseph, 1989) or the promotion of family-centred practice (Cole, 1995). One exception is Callahan's and Lumb's (1995) report on a project which brought both clients and workers (primarily women) together to explore both powerlessness and empowerment as these were experienced by each group in their day-to-day lives. This self-directed project was focused on consciousness-raising about the contradictions between social control and helping and led to small, but concrete action steps which involved shared responsibility for knowledge building and implementation.

There are several characteristics about the current state of child welfare, particularly in relation to services to families, which complicate an empowerment agenda in this field. First, legislation and policies present a conflicting mandate between social control and the empowerment of families. This contradiction is reflected in the dual characteristics of legislation which embrace the principles of child protection and family support without sufficient recognition of the underlying conflicts and dilemmas which arise for all concerned: children, parents, social workers, policy-makers and the general community. Service philosophy may emphasize family support and preservation, yet the primary focus remains centred on child protection and related tasks such as risk investigation, assessment and placement related services. Crisis related intervention, operating from a more exclusive model of practice, where the emphasis is on the knowledge and skills of the expert operating within a hierarchical and authoritative service model, prevails, despite some efforts to alter this paradigm.

A second problem is resource constraints and an ideology which supports reduced funding and an emphasis on cost-containment. Most resources in child welfare are directed to crisis-oriented, reactive services, and there is limited attention to early intervention and responsive, supportive follow-up services. These trends are exacerbated by cutbacks in funding in child welfare; in addition, access to extra-agency helping services has become more difficult as social spending for these programs is reduced. These trends are supported by governments who encourage a return to the ideology of "blaming the victim," greater inequality through reduced spending on welfare and other income support programs, and the individualization of social problems such as child neglect and family violence. Child welfare, with its primary focus on child protection, is ill-equipped to address needs which arise because of structural inequalities and the loss of community and social supports.

Reflecting constraints imposed by government, society and agency mandate and structure, there is a tendency for staff to retreat from more inclusive approaches which stress collaborative work with families and social networks and focus on limited approaches to case management or specialized forms of practice such as risk assessment and abuse specific treatment. The issue is not whether these skills are important but whether they are appropriately located with a more comprehensive framework for practice that includes a commitment to empowerment at the personal, interpersonal and political level. In fact, inadequate attention is given either to an overarching normative framework for practice or to empowerment skills and approaches which must accompany child protection services. This trend is documented by Swift (1995) who uses discourse analysis of social worker responses to demonstrate how workers respond by subverting the social context of child neglect in favour of individualizing the problems of care-givers, who are primarily mothers. These responses, she argues, are shaped in part by the worker's social and organizational context where structural issues such as poverty, discrimination and inequality are either overlooked or minimized. While Swift's focus is on child welfare, it must also be recognized that the issues she raises may transcend practice within a variety of social work domains (Specht and Courtney, 1994; Holmes and Saleebey, 1993).

A fourth characteristic is the tendency to adopt single agenda, trendy solutions to very complex problems. For example, permanency planning, family preservation or community partnerships are viewed by some as solutions which can rescue a child welfare system which is costing too much and failing too many of the families and children it is designed to serve. While it is politically attractive to offer new approaches to complex problems, results seldom live up to expectations. The result is a disillusionment with new policies that are judged not on their merit but on seriously flawed expectations or a poorly conceived approach to implementation. In fact, most thoughtful proponents of new policies and programs emphasize both their limitations and the need for a comprehensive approach to intervention. For example, Pecora (1995, p. 109) notes that family based services are not a panacea and must be considered as just one part of a larger array of family services that must be provided. And Besharov and Baehler (1992) remind us that while reform efforts may focus initially on a specific area of child welfare practice, it must be recognized that each service represents one element of a broader system of highly interdependent components. Thus, empowerment-oriented services in child welfare, including family preservation and reunification, depend on high quality protection, foster care and treatment services, and we cannot make pre-emptive cuts to one component in order to fund new services without careful attention to the overall effects on service quality.

Finally there is limited attention in child welfare to more comprehensive approaches to evaluation, the requirement to consider a variety of different outcome measures from different perspectives and the need to give primacy to client-centred outcomes.

While these factors are generally applicable to the child welfare field, there are a number of special factors in Aboriginal communities which must be considered. First, Aboriginal children, families and communities have been subjected to policies and processes associated with colonization. Two key instruments of colonization have been residential schools (First Nations Health Commission, 1994) and the child welfare system (McKenzie and Hudson, 1985); both have separated children from their families, communities and culture, most often on a permanent or long-term basis. Family, community and cultural connections were denied, despite the importance attached to these within traditional Aboriginal teachings and practices. The devaluation of culture, language and other traditional practices over time has contributed to powerlessness and the internalization of dysfunctional patterns which are best understood as outcomes of oppression. While problems of poverty, sexual abuse and the alienation of youth are manifest, such observations minimize the resilience of Aboriginal people and communities and the strengths which do exist. Important transformational processes are emerging as communities regain control over their social and economic development, often with an approach that includes a revival of traditional values and customs. Two implications are particularly important in child and family services. One is the importance of jurisdictional control and the right of Aboriginal communities to attain policy as well as administrative control over the delivery of services to families and children. A second relates to the level of mistrust of child welfare policies and practices within Aboriginal communities. For most Aboriginal people, child welfare is a profoundly personal issue because most have experienced the loss of family members to a system historically unconcerned about the importance of cultural and family connections. While this mistrust may be reduced by the development of Aboriginally controlled services, the provision of services by Aboriginal staff and the evolution of culturally appropriate service models, it is not eliminated. It takes considerable time and effort for Aboriginal agencies to establish new, more inclusive working relationships with Aboriginal families and communities.

A second factor is cultural differences. While Aboriginal people do not embrace a single philosophy, significant differences between Aboriginal and non-Aboriginal peoples in world views, including cultural values and practices, are recognized (Hamilton and Sinclair, 1991). Of particular significance are the importance of traditional spirituality, cultural revival as a means to empowerment and a more holistic approach to services (see McKenzie and Morrissette, 1993). In child and family services this is reflected in the adoption of healing circles and ceremonies (Aboriginal Corrections Policy Unit, 1997), the medicine wheel as a guide to the development of intervention practices (Longclaws, 1994) and a service model which places great priority on family, community and cultural connections (McKenzie, 1994). This is consistent with the approach defined as family continuity (McFadden and Downs, 1995) where the emphasis is placed on practice first with the inner family circle, then with the extended family circle and finally on maintaining connections and links with the kinship network if placement outside the extended family network is required. A commitment to family continuity requires a comprehensive approach, including an emphasis on family preservation, placement within extended family networks or Aboriginal foster homes within Aboriginal communities wherever possible, family and community involvement in case planning, and family reunification if a child has been taken into care. A central issue is the approach to attachment and loss within Aboriginal communities. In the Aboriginal context, separation and loss most often have included ruptured attachments with family, community and culture; thus efforts are required to address attachment issues through the development of secure and trusting connections with extended family, culture and community as well as with primary care-givers. Because of the extent of community problems, including alcoholism and intergenerational patterns of sexual abuse, this is difficult, and agencies must focus on community building as well as services to children and families.

A third factor is the undeveloped nature of service responses in most communities. Child maltreatment, including sexual abuse, has replaced traditional patterns of family support for many families, and this intergenerational pattern, exacerbated by poverty and high employment, must be broken by models of intervention and healing designed for Aboriginal communities. However, most communities have limited access to specialized, culturally appropriate services for children and families. In these communities the task of community building for empowerment must be combined with a comprehensive service response to issues which often require immediate attention.

SUMMARY OF CASE STUDY

The evolution of First Nations child and family services in Manitoba has not been without controversy. Local political interference, serious management problems and the impact of services on women and children have been identified as problems in some cases (Gray-Withers, 1997; Teichroeb, 1997; Giesbrecht, 1992), and some services have been described as failing to meet community aspirations pertaining to prevention, local control and culturally appropriate service provision (McKenzie, 1997). However, these problems are not unique to First Nations agencies, and a recent review of Winnipeg Child and Family Services, the province's largest non-Aboriginal agency, concluded that its risk assessment procedures were inadequate, it was operating in a service information void without adequate attention to strategic planning, and that early intervention programs, as presently configured, were not cost-effective (Prairie Research Associates, Inc., 1997). In contrast, a comprehensive evaluation of the First Nations agency highlighted in this chapter concluded that it was providing high quality, culturally relevant services to the families and communities within its regional boundaries (McKenzie, 1994). Its innovative approach to service has been nationally recognized, and in 1998 the agency was selected as the winner of the Peter Drucker Award for Canadian Non-Profit Innovation. A brief summary of the service model and major accomplishments of the agency in this case study follow.

Values and Principles

Core agency values stress the importance of protecting children within families and communities, the right to community self-determination and the importance of culture and traditions. Four major philosophical principles are embraced: Aboriginal control, cultural relevancy, community based services and comprehensive, team-oriented services. Core values and principles, which emerged from a recognition of the historical effects of colonization and the conventional child welfare system on First Nations communities, are well integrated into the agency's service structure and planning process. For example, they are used to guide the planning process and as criteria in evaluating service effectiveness.

Aboriginal Control and Comprehensive, Community Based Services

The principle of Aboriginal control is reflected in a number of ways. Most staff are Aboriginal, and initial efforts at staff recruitment focus first on the local community. The agency is governed by a board of chiefs; as well each local community has a local child and family service committee which plays an important role in case management and service development, particularly in relation to prevention. At the case management level committees meet with local staff, often involving family members in the decision-making process where neglect or abuse has occurred. Such efforts serve both to empower families and community members in child and family services and to encourage the search for community based solutions to problems. Family group conferences were included in New Zealand's 1989 child welfare and juvenile justice legislation as a means of ensuring family participation in case management decisions (Fraser and Norton, 1996), but even in the absence of legislation similar practices have become common in many First Nations communities over the past decade. Community committees also have a key role in planning prevention initiatives for their communities. Once program plans for the year are approved, funds are allocated to local committees who manage these budgets and guide the development process for prevention in their communities in partnership with local staff.

The model of community based services adopted in these communities extends well beyond a recognition of the role played by local committees. While each community has locally based protection and prevention staff who are the primary service providers, they are part of a larger service delivery team which may include treatment staff, a supervisor, an abuse specialist and an alternate (foster) home worker. This community based team meets frequently to plan and coordinate local service provision and to provide mutual support to its members. A community oriented service approach (see Hadley, Dale and Sills, 1984) is adopted when new initiatives are being considered, and all new programs are preceded by a locally based needs assessment and planning phase.

Community building is advocated as a new approach to social work (Weil, 1996) and child welfare practice (Barter, 1997), but this agency has been engaged in these initiatives over the past number of years. For example, group programs for abuse victims have been developed in a number of communities, and a number of women from these programs have emerged to play leadership roles on these issues in their own communities and in a regional training capacity. A second example is an agency sponsored research project which employed participatory methods to develop First Nations child and family service standards based on community and cultural preferences (McKenzie, Seidl and Bone, 1995). It has also responded to community needs related to family violence and day care by developing initiatives in these areas. Community building is closely related to the principle of enhancing local democracy, and one of the more interesting initiatives is a regional planning workshop where staff and representatives from each community meet every two years in order to review agency programs and provide feedback on new initiatives which are required or being proposed.

Culturally Appropriate Services

Cultural relevancy in service provision is encouraged by Aboriginal staff, often from the local community, who bring an intimate knowledge of community values and knowledge to their work. There are consistent efforts to utilize elders as consultants, respect traditional ceremonies and practices and incorporate traditional practices as components of staff training and service development approaches. As well, there is a strong adherence to placement policies which utilize extended family members as the option of first choice, and every effort is made to utilize Aboriginal resources within the child's own community whenever possible. If placement occurs outside the community, the local worker remains actively involved in order to provide a community and extended family perspective to the case management process and to make family connections as appropriate. Culturally appropriate standards have been developed, notably in relation to foster care recruitment and training, and a range of placement resources within the agency has been developed, including therapeutic foster homes and a group home for adolescent sex offenders. In sharp contrast to the mid-1980s, almost all children requiring alternate care are placed in resources either within the local community or in resources operated by the agency.

Management Systems, Training and Team Oriented Services

The agency places a great deal of emphasis on team oriented services, and these teams have considerable autonomy in planning service responses and providing ongoing support to each other. Team building days are encouraged in the agency, and staff attribute professional and personal support from both team members and managers as key factors in sustaining a high level of staff morale and promoting client oriented services. Staff feedback on the buffering effects of social support is illustrated in the following examples. In one case, a new staff member who had worked at another agency described the difference in the following fashion:

> In the other agency I felt isolated, all alone with no one to confide in or no support. I just felt cut loose. The difference here is like night and day. I feel supported and valued and know I can turn to someone if I need to.

In another case the problem of interference from local political leaders was highlighted as a disempowering experience:

> Political intervention (our communities don't like the word interference) still happens and needs to be addressed. When it occurred with me I was able to get excellent support from management. This helped in dealing with a difficult and stressful situation.

The agency invests extensively in training and staff development, a factor also noted by staff as contributing to their empowerment and their ability to offer more effective client oriented services. Agency management was instrumental in promoting the development of a distance education B.S.W. program in the area, and a number of agency staff are enrolled in this program. Some financial support and time away from work for class attendance is provided. In addition, there has been an emphasis on ongoing staff development, including the provision of a supervisory training program based on the medicine wheel philosophy. Both training and support were identified as primary reasons for the low rate of staff turnover in this agency.

Agency management has a well-respected, progressive vision of services, and the stability of this leadership has helped to sustain a developmental approach to community services and programs. Three general characteristics are noteworthy. First, there is an emphasis on the needs of children as a first priority, and a related commitment to meeting these through connections with family, community and culture wherever possible. Thus, a holistic, wraparound service model which includes prevention, family support and community building emerges as a primary goal in agency services. Second, management systems are well developed and include careful attention to cost analysis as a component in an integrated model of strategic planning for the agency. An agency specific information system has been designed, and data from this and other sources are used not simply to monitor internal service processes but to identify new community and regional needs. Third, the approach to resource management is designed to maximize efficiency and flexibility in the use of funds. Three general strategies are apparent. Management has adopted a strong advocacy stance with federal and provincial levels of government to ensure some measure of funding adequacy. For example, it conducted its own study of special needs children served by the agency in a successful effort to increase funding levels for these children. It has also stressed financial accountability and efficiency within its own operations and reallocated resources as required to respond to new needs. Finally, it was successful in negotiating an adequate block funding arrangement for child maintenance expenditures with the federal government in 1992. This allowed the agency to utilize funds, normally available on a cost recovery basis for children in care, to provide a more innovative range of family support and treatment services. The flexibility afforded by this funding arrangement has enabled the development of a number of new service initiatives, including a team of treatment support workers. These staff have been able to provide a range of individual, group and community building services, particularly in relation to child sexual abuse in each community.

The agency's role as an innovator within First Nations child and family services is well recognized. It has developed a First Nations treatment foster home program with integrated training and support features, it has supported family preservation and reunification through direct financial support to families where necessary, and it has developed partnership agreements with the non-Aboriginal child welfare agency in Winnipeg to provide culturally appropriate services to community residents living off reserve. It has also played a leadership role on national issues, including an organizational role in the initiation of a First Nations Child Welfare League and the sponsorship of workshops on the subject of funding in First Nations child and family services.

Assessing Effectiveness from an Empowerment Perspective

The effectiveness of community based approaches to empowerment in First Nations child and family services is difficult to measure. However, Boyce (1993) suggests that empowerment criteria, including social justice, must be included in evaluation along with an examination of whether goals are achieved and efficiency expectations met. In relation to empowerment criteria, one needs to consider such things as whether the program altered power relations and inequalities between dominant and subordinate groups. In First Nations child and family services this may include questions about whether clients experience more control over their affairs, whether the community has more control and influence over child welfare services in an active participative way, whether groups within the community have more influence relative to the agency and chief and council, and whether the agency, including its staff, have been able to use its voice in dealing with government and the dominant child welfare system on a more equal footing.

Focus group feedback suggests that significant changes have occurred which reflect community empowerment goals. Community building by the agency has stressed work with women, often in a group context, and women from these groups have become advocates for family and child services at the community level. In some cases this has led to increased involvement in local politics. The agency has maintained an uncompromising stance on matters related to protecting children at risk, and this position is generally respected. Community participation and the demand to exercise more authority over decisions related to child and families has grown over the years, and in most cases this reflects a general concern for the well-being of children and families rather than a limited critique about how specific case decisions were made. The growth in community empowerment is positively regarded by staff, who suggest that the growing knowledge of rights and how to exercise these rights is apparent at the case level as well. One staff member provided the following example:

> I used to think that not having contested cases was a good thing. Now I know that is not necessarily so. When we take a child into care, I encourage all parents to consult a lawyer so that they can determine whether they wish to contest our assessment of the situation. This never used to happen in our community, and it was a function of the powerlessness parents felt when they dealt with the child welfare system.

Information is essential to the ability to exercise power, and this is communicated to families and community members through a variety of sources, including community presentations and print materials. However, the most important method is through the day-to-day communication by staff who are encouraged to share information about client rights, agency responsibilities and the opportunities that can be used to influence both the agency and other systems. While the agency frequently takes an advocacy stance on behalf of clients and communities, it encourages local leadership around new initiatives and tries to avoid taking control, even if this is requested. While this may mean waiting for a sustainable community initiative to emerge, this developmental approach is much more consistent with an empowerment approach to community practice.

Results from the evaluation of programs indicated that the flexibility of child maintenance funding had contributed to an increase in early intervention, support and treatment services for children and families, and positive outcomes were identified even in quite complex cases (McKenzie, 1994). There was a reduction in expenditures for out of home care between 1992 and 1994, but this was primarily attributed to reduced use of extra-community residential care. The 1994 study also demonstrated that children were generally placed with extended families or foster homes in their own communities. A modest reduction in the number of children in care was identified, and this has remained relatively stable since 1994. While this is of interest, changes in the number or rate of children in care is not a good indicator of service effectiveness because it is quite dependent on contextual circumstances related to risk. As First Nations communities with relatively high rates of sexual abuse move beyond denial, this may lead to an increase in the number of children placed in care. In this context, an increase in placement related services may reflect a community's beginning journey to health and wellness.

One of the most important findings from this study is the close connection between the empowerment of staff within this First Nations agency and the delivery of empowerment-oriented services to their communities. Staff interviewed both in 1994 and 1997 commented on the importance of training, support and the encouragement they received for self-growth. Education and training related to colonization, and the opportunities provided to explore Aboriginal culture and traditions both as a personal and a professional practice issue, were particularly appreciated. Some staff members noted that they, like their communities, had lost an understanding of their own cultural identity and the meaning associated with many traditional practices. While value is attached to this within the organization, the individual's right to make choices about how to utilize these in practice is also recognized, a position respected by staff in this agency.

DISCUSSION

The results from the agency case study summarized in this paper do not mean that the agency is without identifiable shortcomings or that an empowerment paradigm characterizes all services it provides. For example, new approaches in child protection might be expanded to include a form of culturally appropriate mediation where the use of the court process is minimized without sacrificing the rights of parents. As well, increased attention to culturally based service models at the community level and empowerment related client outcome measures in service evaluation may be possible.

However, there is evidence of considerable progress in meeting empowerment-oriented objectives for First Nations clients and communities served by the agency, and there is no question that the agency's services have made a positive difference to children and families. It is also abundantly clear that these changes would not have occurred in the absence of First Nations jurisdictional control over child and family services. The empowerment of staff working at the agency has been a key variable in achieving these outcomes, and they make efforts to include structural issues such as colonization and the effects of residential schools in the assessment of family circumstances. Effort is also made to apply a strengths-oriented approach to practice, and to work collaboratively with clients whenever possible.

Results from this study suggest a number of indicators of client or consumer empowerment in First Nations child and family services (see Figure 1). While many of these are anticipated from the general literature on empowerment, three general principles emerge from this research. One is the concept of voice. If empowerment is to redress problems of inequality it must enhance the rights of children and parents to make responsible choices, particularly in relation to decisions affecting their lives. In exercising one's rights, two general strategies are available: the ability to exit or leave one service in favour of another, and the ability to influence the nature of service individually or collectively through "voice" or interaction with the service provider (Hirshman, 1970). The ability to take one's business elsewhere is a market mechanism and is not applicable in this context. Thus, client empowerment in the social services, including child welfare, largely depends on the opportunities and the ability of consumers to express their preferences and have these considered. In the child welfare context, empowerment-oriented client services are dependent on strategies which recognize and effectively include the voices of children and families. A second principle is the emphasis on culturally appropriate services as a means to personal and collective empowerment. Culturally appropriate alternate care placements ensure an approach to attachment which recognizes the value of Aboriginal culture. In other ways, cultural revival, including language and ceremonies, is an antidote to colonization in that it affirms the identity of both the individual and the community from a strengths-oriented perspective. As well, cultural teachings (e.g., medicine wheel) and traditional practices (e.g., sweat lodge) enrich or become alternatives to conventional methods of intervention and are important aspects of the social work process with Aboriginal clients. Third, there is emphasis on a broader range of service responses to address needs from a more holistic perspective. In First Nations communities, child and family services agencies must play an active role in community work at the local level and provide leadership in developing an integrated, community based service response to a broad range of community needs such as child care and family violence.

Figure 1: Indicators of Consumer Empowerment in First Nations Child and Family Services

- Children's rights to safety, health and protection are not compromised.
- Children are aware of rights and can easily access supportive and protective services, including social workers, for help whether in or out of care.
- Individual and group programs for children are available within the community to respond to a variety of social, recreational and spiritual needs.
- Children have a voice and are involved whenever appropriate in decision-making regarding their needs and services.
- All efforts are made to support children in their own families prior to placement in alternate care as long as these efforts do not jeopardize their health or safety.
- Children demonstrate positive changes over time relative to developmental outcomes in physical, emotional, intellectual and spiritual domains.
- Children have positive, trusting relationships with their social workers.
- Parents and families can access a wide range of services to respond to their needs.

Indicators of community empowerment are shown in Figure 2. Community building is an important aspect of community empowerment, and mechanisms such as local child and family service committees can play a meaningful role in this process. While jurisdictional control over child and family service policy is essential, political interference in case-related issues must be minimized. Education and consciousness-raising about child and family service issues such as sexual abuse and the effects of residential schools are beginning steps to healing. Three outcome-oriented measures of community empowerment are suggested. These are the extent to which the community exercises a constructive influence concerning agency services and programs, the level of partnership arrangements between child and family services and other programs on community building initiatives, and the degree to which the community is proactive in dealing with issues such as abuse or the need for prevention.

A number of organizational and staff characteristics were associated with an increase in client and community empowerment in this case study (see

Figure 2: Indicators of Community Empowerment in First Nations Child and Family Services

- Political control of First Nations child and family services rests with First Nations communities, but there is no unwarranted political intervention in case management issues.
- There is increased evidence that the voices of women are acknowledged and involved in decisions regarding child and family services at the community level.
- Chiefs and councils demonstrate leadership in child and family service issues and support a variety of voluntary group and self-help initiatives for the well-being of children and families.
- The wider community has a voice and asserts increased levels of responsibility for the well-being of children and families, including the protection of children from abuse, provision of alternate placement for children within extended family and the community and a decision-making role relative to the delivery of child and family services.
- Effectively functioning local child and family service committees exist in each community which work in partnership with local workers in case management and community prevention.
- Community members, including elders and those most likely to be affected, are consulted on new community programs and take considerable responsibility in developing these initiatives.
- Child and family services works in partnership with the local community, including other agencies and services, on a community building agenda for children and families.
- Child and family services staff are actively involved as community participants, rather than experts, in a range of community activities.

figures 3 and 4). These are contrasted with characteristics typical of a more residual or crisis-oriented model of child welfare. The validity of these comparisons is strengthened by two observations. First, many of the empowerment-oriented characteristics identified in the case study are similar to those previously associated with empowerment-oriented organizations in the literature (Shera and Page, 1995; Gutiérrez, GlenMaye and DeLois, 1995; Dodd and Gutiérrez, 1990). As well, characteristics associated with the residual model have been identified in other child welfare agencies in the province, and both clients and communities served by such agencies exhibit lower levels of achievement on the empowerment indicators identified in figures 1 and 2.[2]

Several organizational characteristics were identified as contributing to empowerment. An adequate level of funding and the flexibility to be able to

Figure 3: Funding, Management Systems and Leadership in Child and Family Services

Residual Paradigm	Empowerment Paradigm
Funding	*Funding*
• Limited funding, oriented to protection	• Funding achieves level of adequacy to allow for prevention and support services as well as protection
• Child maintenance funding restricted to children in care	
• Carryover of funds not permitted	• Global funding for family and children to allow flexibility in responding to needs
	• Carryover of funds to allow longer term strategic planning
Management Systems	*Management Systems*
• Hierarchial model	• Participative, team-oriented model
• Crisis-oriented, reactive planning	• Viable strategic planning approach which involves community, staff and board
• Inadequate information related to needs and costs for planning	
• Inefficient use of technology	• Adequate information on individual and community needs, costs and service outcomes
• Narrow focus on service mandate related to protection	
	• Appropriate use of technology to assist in planning and management functions
	• Holistic, comprehensive approach to services
Leadership	*Leadership*
• Narrow or unclear mission and vision of services	• Well-developed vision of services which includes community and cultural values in mission statement and emerges from an analysis of the historical effects of colonization
• Mission and service goals absent or are not operationalized	
• Efficiency focused supervision	
• Case focused supervision which focuses on individual problems	• Mission and service goals guide service and are used to educate and develop consciousness
• Expert role encouraged	
• Top-down approach to planning and implementation	• Combines performance, efficiency criteria with personal concerns of staff in supervision
• Limited or narrow approach to evaluation	

• Cultural knowledge and traditional practices omitted or used in haphazard fashion • Limited attention to staff support and training; training restricted to certain kinds of staff • Poor communication between management and staff • Staff within the organization often overlooked in promotion or new job considerations • Community based staff may not be hired or may receive inadequate training and support to develop competencies • Agency has limited influence in field	• Focuses on strengths and combines individual with group, community, cultural and structural considerations • Collaborative work with clients encouraged whenever possible • Combined bottom-up/top-down approach to planning and implementation where agency engages with community and clients as active partner • Evaluation is an integrated component of planning and includes empowerment-oriented criteria • Promotes and integrates cultural knowledge and traditional practices, including the use of elders, in a respectful manner • Ensures a high priority on support, training and development for all staff in ways which recognize their personal and professional needs • Good methods of communication between management and staff

utilize funding for a more positive range of family and community support services are critical. These enable a more comprehensive service response and the shift from a purely protective service paradigm to one which incorporates empowerment-oriented prevention, support and treatment services. A progressive vision of services which emerges from a historical analysis of the impact of colonization on Aboriginal communities and the commitment of all staff and volunteers to this agency mission are important. The agency evaluated in this study returned frequently to its core values and an understanding of the historical role played by the child welfare system in their communities for direction in planning. As well, the agency's service mission had been supplemented by the development of public positions on such issues as domestic violence, which were used in community education and consciousness-raising. Emphasis on a participative, team-oriented management approach was valued, and the related leadership style in program development

Figure 4: Staff Characteristics in First Nations Child and Family Services

Residual Paradigm	*Empowerment Paradigm*
• Inconsistent commitment to agency mission and purposes • Limited attention to feedback and learning or focuses on specialized knowledge only • Assumes expert role • Individualizes problems • Focuses on own work almost exclusively; often feels isolated and unsupported • Limited approach to new skill development • May advocate for individual client • Often fails to work with groups where this might be possible • Limited approach to cultural learning and use in practice	• Strong commitment to agency mission based on empowerment • Openness to feedback and learning; builds consciousness about colonization, culture and community issues • Attempts to work collaboratively with clients • Emphasizes strengths; connects individual concerns to collective issues and responses whenever possible • Active team member who seeks and provides support • Challenges self by trying new approaches and developing new skills • Assumes advocacy and community oriented service stance • Seeks opportunities for group work and development of self-help skills among members • Integrates cultural learning as a means to own empowerment, and in work with clients

is best described as a combined top-down/bottom-up or partnership approach where active input and developmental support occurs from both directions. Supervisory and managerial support is a key variable in the empowerment paradigm; as well the emphasis on education and staff development is a priority, particularly in a First Nations context. Finally, the integration of cultural practices and traditions within the organization and opportunities to develop both personal and professional knowledge in this area were positively regarded.

The relationships established between staff and clients, and between staff and community residents, are key determinants of the extent to which empowerment-oriented objectives will be achieved. Children's needs and their right to protection from risk remain central, but training and education which stress a strengths-oriented approach is more likely to lead to a collaborative approach to working with clients. Although this is not always possible in child welfare, when these values are reinforced by agency goals and support systems the services provided are more likely to be transforming than simply remedial.

While these results support the importance of First Nations jurisdictional control over child and family services as a prerequisite to empowerment, such control provides no guarantee that empowerment-oriented outcomes will be realized for clients, communities or staff within these agencies. A more holistic framework for practice in First Nations child and family services is required, and four elements are suggested. First, an agency requires a well-integrated agency mission that emerges from an understanding of the effects of colonization and a commitment to healing the effects of this form of oppression through community building to promote prevention, local responsibility and self-help. Second, a service model that consistently priorizes the health and safety of children within a community based and culturally appropriate service approach is necessary. For example, new program initiatives in this agency emerge from a developmental process with the community, and alternate care for children places a priority on resources which are the least restrictive and as connected as possible to extended family, community and culture. Third, a leadership approach, which includes consistent attention to service planning and supervision, an advocacy agenda on behalf of the agency and support and training for staff, is critical. Finally, empowerment in First Nations child and family services is encouraged by a strengths-oriented approach by staff where attention is paid to the importance of cultural knowledge and traditional practices, consciousness-raising as an aspect of the helping process and a teamwork approach to service delivery.

ENDNOTES

[1] The term "child and family services" is preferred in these communities because too often the term "child welfare" has been associated primarily with child protection. Child and family services is intended to include a broader range of services for the well-being of children and families.

[2] Child welfare services are often characterized as too reactive or crisis oriented, and this criticism is used to describe Winnipeg Child and Family Services in a recent review (Prairie Research Associates, Inc., (1997). A more residually oriented approach is also identifiable in some First Nations agencies as demonstrated in the author's own research (McKenzie, 1997). Underfunding, a mandate too focused on protection and problems in planning and management systems were associated with the residual approach.

REFERENCES

Aboriginal Corrections Policy Unit. (1997). *The four circles of Hollow Water*. Ottawa: Supply and Services Canada.

Barter, K. (1997, June). *Building communities to reclaim children and families at risk*. Paper presented to Canadian Association of Schools of Social Work Annual Conference, St. John's, NF.

Besharov, D. and Baehler, K. (1992). Demonstration and evaluation strategies. *Children and Youth Services Review*, 14, 1-18.

Boyce, W. (1993). Evaluating participation in community programs: An empowerment paradigm. *Canadian Journal of Program Evaluation*, 8(1), 89-102.

Callahan, M. and Lumb, C. (1995). My cheque and my children: The long road to empowerment in child welfare. *Child Welfare*, 74(3), 795-819.

Cole, E. (1995). Becoming family centered: Child welfare's challenge. *Families in Society*, 76(3), 163-172.

Dodd, P. and Gutiérrez, L. (1990). Preparing students for the future: A power perspective on community practice. *Administration in Social Work*, 14(2), 63-78.

First Nations Health Commission. (1994). *Breaking the silence*. Ottawa: Assembly of First Nations.

Fraser, S. and Norton, J. (1996). Family group conferencing in New Zealand child protection work. In J. Hudson, A. Morris, G. Maxwell, and B. Galaway (Eds.), *Family group conferences: Perspectives on policy and practice* (pp. 37-64). Monsey, NY: Willow Free Press.

Garfat, T., Craig, I. and Joseph, C. (1989). Reflections on being in care: A demonstration of youth empowerment. *Child and Youth Care Quarterly*, 18(1), 5-16.

Gibson, C. (1993). Empowerment theory and practice with adolescents of color in the child welfare system. *Families in Society*, 74(7), 387-396.

Giesbrecht, B. (1992). *Report of the Fatality Inquiries Act respecting the death of Lester Norman Desjarlais*. Winnipeg: Queen's Printer.

Gray-Withers, D. (1997). Decentralized social services and self-government: Challenges for First Nations. In J. Pulkingham and G. Ternowetsky (Eds.), *Child and family policies: Struggles, strategies and options* (pp. 85-99). Halifax: Fernwood.

Gutiérrez, L. (1990). Working with women of color: An empowerment perspective. *Social Work*, 35, 149-154.

Gutiérrez, L., GlenMaye, L. and DeLois, K. (1995). The organizational context of empowerment practice: Implications for social work administration. *Social Work*, 40(2), 249-258.

Hadley, R., Dale, P. and Sills, P. (1984). *Decentralising social services: A model for change*. London: Bedford Square Press.

Hamilton, A. and Sinclair, C. (1991). *Volume 1: The justice system and Aboriginal people* (Report on the Aboriginal Justice Inquiry of Manitoba). Winnipeg: Queen's Printer.

Hirshman, A. (1970). *Exit voice and loyalty*. Cambridge, MA; Harvard University Press.

Holmes, G. and Saleebey, D. (1993). Empowerment, the medical model and the politics of clienthood. *Journal of Progressive Human Services*, 4(1), 61-78.

Labonté, R. (1990). Empowerment: Notes on professional and community dimensions. *Canadian Review of Social Policy*, 26, 64-75.

Longclaws, L. (1994). Social work and the medicine wheel framework. In B. Compton and B. Galaway (Eds.), *Social work processes* (5th ed.) (pp. 24-33). Pacific Grove, CA: Brooks/Cole.

McFadden, E. and Downs, S. (1995). Family continuity: The new paradigm in permanence planning. *Community Alternatives*, 7(1), 39-59.

McKenzie, B. (1994). *Evaluation of the pilot project on block funding for child maintenance: West Region Child and Family Services* (Final Report). Dauphin, MB: West Region Child and Family Services.

McKenzie, B. (1997). *Evaluation of Cree Nation Child and Family Caring Agency* (Final Report). Winnipeg: Faculty of Social Work, University of Manitoba.

McKenzie, B. and Hudson, P. (1985). Native children, child welfare and the colonization of Native people. In K. Levitt and B. Wharf (Ed.), *The challenge of child welfare* (pp. 125-141). Vancouver: University of British Columbia Press.

McKenzie, B. and Morrissette, L. (1993). Cultural empowerment and healing for Aboriginal youth in Winnipeg. In A. Mawhiney (Ed.), *Rebirth: Political, economic and social development in First Nations* (pp. 117-130). Toronto: Dundurn Press.

McKenzie, B., Seidl, E. and Bone, N. (1995). Child and family service standards in First Nations: An action research project. *Child Welfare*, 74(3), 633-653.

Mullender, A. and Ward, D. (1991). *Self-directed groupwork: Users taking action for empowerment*. London: Whiting and Birch.

Mullender, A. and Ward, D. (1993). The role of the consultant in self-directed group work: An approach to supporting social action in Britain. *Social Work with Groups*, 16(4), 57-79.

Pecora, P. (1995). Assessing the impact of family-based services. In J. Hudson and B. Galaway (Eds.), *Child welfare in Canada: Research and policy implications* (pp. 100-112). Toronto: Thompson Educational Publishing.

Pinderhughes, E. (1983). Empowerment for our clients and for ourselves. *Social Casework*, 64(6), 331-338.

Pinderhughes, E. (1989). *Understanding race, ethnicity and power: The key to efficacy in clinical practice*. New York: Free Press.

Prairie Research Associates Inc. (1997). *Operational review of Winnipeg Child and Family Services Agency, Volume 1* (Final Report). Winnipeg: Manitoba Family Services.

Rappaport, J. (1981). In praise of paradox: A social policy of empowerment over prevention. *American Journal of Community Psychology*, 9(1), 1-25.

Rappaport, J. (1984). Studies in empowerment: Introduction to the issue. *Prevention in Human Services*, 3, 1-7.

Shera, W. and Page, J. (1995). Creating more effective human service organizations through strategies of empowerment. *Administration in Social Work*, 19(4), 1-15.

Simon, B. (1990). Rethinking empowerment. *Journal of Progressive Human Services*, 1(1), 27-39.

Specht, H. and Courtney, M. (1994). *Unfaithful angels: How social work has abandoned its mission*. Toronto: Maxwell Macmillan Canada.

Staples, L. (1990). Powerful ideas about empowerment. *Administration in Social Work*, 14(1), 29-42.

Swift, K. (1995). *Manufacturing 'bad mothers': A critical perspective on child neglect*. Toronto: University of Toronto Press.

Teichroeb, R. (1997). *Flowers on my grave*. Toronto: HarperCollins.

Weick, A., Rapp, C., Sullivan, P. and Kisthardt, W. (1989). A strengths perspective for social work practice. *Social Work*, 34(4), 350-354.

Weil, M. (1996). Community building: Building community practice. *Social Work*, 41(5), 481-499.

Zimmerman, M. and Rappaport, J. (1988). Citizen participation, perceived control, and psychological empowerment. *Child and Youth Care Quarterly*, 18(1), 5-16.

Section 3

Critical Issues in
Empowerment Practice

Chapter 12

EMPOWERMENT PRACTICE IN A POST-EMPOWERMENT ERA

Margot Breton
Faculty of Social Work
University of Toronto

Three constructs, empowerment, competence and strengths, embody many of the changing or newer ways of practicing social work. The word newer is appropriate: the empowerment paradigm has been around for more than two decades—Barbara Solomon published *Black Empowerment: Social Work in Oppressed Communities* in 1976. Anthony Maluccio built a model around the concept of ecological competence in his book *Promoting Competence in Clients: A New/Old Approach to Social Work Practice* which appeared in 1981, the same year, Anne Weick published "Reframing the person-in-environment perspective," one in a series of articles which were a major influence on the development of the strengths perspective.

However, today's social, economic, political and cultural context is significantly different from the one which existed 20 years ago. One of the main characteristics of change in the political context is the brutal negative reaction to the empowerment of previously disempowered people and the consequent and often successful attempts to dismantle the policies, programs and services which empowerment had helped to bring about. At the same time, formerly disempowered minorities who have become empowered are no longer without a voice. This has produced changes in the relationships between the consumers and the providers of social services, the former demanding a greater say in the decisions regarding the services provided by the latter. Social workers and social work agencies are challenged to adapt to these changes just as they themselves feel disempowered by massive budgetary cuts, downsizing and elimination of jobs and services. *The Globe and Mail* (May 30, 1997) reported a survey of 382 social services in Toronto (Ontario) which together lost $19 million in mostly government funding while the workloads grew by 60 percent during the last year; 33 agencies closed in 1996 compared to 21 in 1995 and 7 a year earlier.

The economic context has been radically altered by globalization and international free trade. Unemployment and underemployment threaten the future of a whole generation of young people in the richest countries while slave-like working conditions for young people (children and young girls, mostly) have spread throughout the poorest countries. This global economy (among other factors) is spawning an ever-widening gap between rich and poor in many parts of the world (see, for example, the latest figures from Statistics Canada, in Mitchell, 1997; Chandler and Morin, 1996). People are not only discouraged by the inequality they clearly discern, they have become cynical about the willingness and/or the ability of anyone (politician, bureaucrat, professional) to do something about the situation. In addition to this cynicism, the bottom-line mentality which has been disseminated by neo-conservative economics has affected every part of the social welfare system. As Sacks suggests (1994, p. 100): "In this era of managed care and reduced funding many agencies have become *business welfare organizations* rather than *social welfare organizations*" (emphasis in original). For their part, clients who pay for services—and this is a growing trend: 39 percent of the 382 agencies referred to above implemented new user fees or raised existing ones in the past year— are now apt to demand value for the time and the money they invest in change or they commit to dealing with a particular problem or issue.

As for the socio-cultural context, many countries are experiencing a great upheaval in the norms and values held by citizens (young as well as older people, recent immigrants and long-time residents alike), producing a demand for changes in the ways everyone thinks about life and goes about living it. This in turn contributes to the uncertain climate for social workers who sometimes feel they are being asked to put aside their professional views (not to mention their personal ones) and wonder where all this change will be taking them and their profession.

Faced with this critical shift in the social, political, economic and cultural context, social workers seek to change (or are forced to change) their way of thinking about and going about their practice. Change, however, does not necessarily mean relinquishing empowerment-oriented practice based on competence and strength. It does mean adapting this practice to a post-empowerment context—a context in which maintaining a sense of competence becomes a prime focus for practitioners and service users alike. This paper is a beginning effort to develop a post-empowerment model. It uses an empowerment framework (Breton and Breton, 1997) to identify some elements of group work practice in a post-empowerment era.

The model assumes that groups are the instrument of choice for both the process and the goal of empowerment (Lee, 1997; Longres and McLeod, 1980). Empowerment requires transformations at personal and structural/political levels. It is not good enough to be aware that one has rights; one must also have a fair share of resources. As Rappaport (1981, p. 13) pointed out: "Having rights but no resources and no services is a cruel joke." So practitioners have the responsibility of choosing the best possible medium through which transformations can be effected at both levels. *The Social Work Dictionary*'s (Barker, 1991, p. 74) definition of empowerment as "the process of helping a group or community to achieve political influence or relevant legal authority," captures the requirements of both personal and political/structural transformations.

It is because groups provide a better opportunity of addressing the inseparability of private troubles and public issues that they are consistently chosen as the medium of consciousness-raising, a crucial component of the process of empowerment and of transformations at the personal level. It is because groups, through the strength-in-us mutual aid phenomenon, facilitate collective action and confrontation of environmental barriers to social justice that they are the best medium for attaining the goal of empowerment—a just share of resources—and thus effecting transformations at the structural/political level.

An individual citizen who, by virtue of her class status, is without the socio-economic-political resources through which she would have control over the factors that significantly affect her life is not like an academic who can acquire resources individually by applying for a research grant from a funding institution. An individual citizen cannot effect changes in the political system without the weight of others, be they loosely connected in a large group such as a social movement or closely connected in a small group (unless, of course, the citizen has the means of buying a politician, etc., in which instance she would not be without resources—she would not be disempowered—to begin with).

POST-EMPOWERMENT GROUP PRACTICE

The model proposed involves a series of six steps.

Step #1: Preparing for and Starting a Group

In the classic theory of group planning (Kurland, 1978), there are six major areas of concern: 1) identification of needs; 2) identification of purpose; 3) composition; 4) initial structure; 5) content; and 6) pre-group contact. All these areas are relevant to post-empowerment practice (PEP), but will be approached in a different way.

1. In classic theory, workers, potential members, agencies and other relevant or knowledgeable persons identify the potential members' needs. In PEP, as in empowerment-oriented practice, it is the potential members who identify their needs and/or concerns—this is part of acquiring a voice or of affirming it and of naming their world. It is crucial for people who have not been aware of their voice or who have a different voice that is unheard, unrecognized or unappreciated. And it is expected by people who consider themselves consumers choosing a service and trying to establish if this particular group and particular worker(s) will 'fill the bill.' Workers and agencies, for their part, identify a given population faced with a particular situation, whether of social marginalization, oppression or other.

2. As for purpose, the major concern in PEP is to provide potential members the opportunity to identify their own goals. Preparation for the group should no longer include, as it does in classic theory, establishing "the goals of potential group members as perceived by the workers" (Kurland, 1978, p. 177). However, workers and agencies still need to establish a "tentative conception of the group purpose" (Kurland, 1978, p. 177). Tentative does not mean confusing or unclear, it means provisional or exploratory; and groups and members avoid much grief when they heed Kurland's words.

3. The composition of voluntary groups can be done in a more or less democratic fashion. At one extreme, practitioners choose each member and only the chosen get invited to become members; at the other, the forthcoming group is publicized in one form or another, and interested individuals choose to join the group. It makes sense that in PEP the recruitment for groups be as democratic as possible—self-selection should be the norm. A clearly stated tentative purpose will facilitate the potential members' self-selection process. This process demands that practitioners trust would-be members, but it does not entail that they ignore their knowledge of the beneficial effects, in term of group functioning, of the law of optimal distance, which says that groups

function best when there is enough homogeneity to ensure stability and support and enough heterogeneity to ensure vitality and challenge. On the contrary, once a group is established, it will be the practitioner's task to see that the law is understood and respected in the sense that members and practitioner alike undertake to discover, valorize and capitalize on both the similarities and the differences between the individuals in the group. Understanding the law of optimal distance can also prevent members and practitioners from wrongly interpreting eventual group functioning problems, i.e., confusing essentially group composition problems (problems in the balance between homogeneity and heterogeneity) with other group functioning problems (e.g., problems in the decision-making process).

4. There has to be some initial structure; without some concrete arrangements no group can get going. However, in PEP the expectation is that opportunities will be provided for potential members to give their input regarding decisions about the initial structure.

5. As regards the group content, i.e., the means to reach the group's objectives, it is essential that practitioners preparing for group PEP think in terms of eventually eliciting and drawing on the members' actual and potential competence to reflect on their situation, draw the appropriate conclusions (with the help of other group members and of practitioners) and do something to change that situation. This competence can be assumed, at the stage of preparing for a group, but it has yet to be discovered in its specificity. In other words, practitioners cannot presume to know in advance the particular make-up of the individual members' competence, no more than they can presume to know in advance their particular needs, and they will have to invest time and energy in bringing to light the members' distinct competence.

This is an understanding of content different from one based primarily on the competence of practitioners who possess means (supportive, educative, therapeutic, etc. techniques, as well as intellectual, emotional, social and organizational resources) to help members attain a group's objectives. This understanding, essential to practice in the new social, economic, political and cultural context, takes nothing away from the competence of professional practitioners, nor from the importance of the skilled use of techniques and resources, it simply assumes that professionals do not have a monopoly on competence, skills and resources.

The assumption of competence existing outside of practitioners will also facilitate the discovery and use of competence within the community in which the groups are to be established. Preparing thus includes identifying the potential partners and/or natural helpers in that community who could support the group's objectives and the community resources that could sustain the members' competence. (Practitioners' and members' opinions of possible partners and resources may be different, however—preparing is not deciding in advance). Interorganizational collaboration of the kind described by Mulroy (1997) is one approach to building community based service networks that have the potential for long-term support (maintenance) of the members' competence. Social workers who, because of downsizing or restructuring, are required to work under professionals who have no social work training may have to contend with real or perceived pressures to discount their own professional competence. Adapting to a post-empowerment context requires that they not give in to these pressures while remaining open to learning from others.

In thinking about the means to reach the group's objectives, practitioners will ask themselves if they are ready to engage in social or collective action and if they will have the support of their institution or face severe obstacles. It is better to take the time to ensure a margin of backing than to start something one cannot bring to fruition.

6. Finally, the pre-group contact will take into account that many individuals who belong to marginalized populations have had bad experiences with and feel oppressed and shunted aside by the system in general and often by social services in particular. Therefore, practitioners have to expect the potential members' motivations to avoid failure, avert risks and maintain whatever control they have over their lives, including the power to say "no" to would-be helpers (Breton, 1985).

After this first step of preparing for and bringing people together in a group comes the second step, which involves conscientization and the acquisition or affirmation of a voice.

Step # 2: Conscientization and the Acquisition or Affirmation of a Voice

It is well known that the simple exchange of personal information is one of the most powerful mutual aid dynamics, dynamics that emerge from and are sustained by the strength of the individuals in the group and their competence to help one another. There are at least four necessary conditions, however, for the sharing of personal stories to lead to empowerment and to the maintenance of competence.

1. The stories are received with respect and accepted as representing reality as perceived by the members. These representations therefore constitute "legitimate knowledge" (Weick, 1992, p. 23). It is through the validation of their stories that members who have been without power, or have been marginalized, acquire or affirm their voice and learn to use it to "name [their] world" (Freire,

1993, p. 159). Without this authentic voice, they can only repeat what others tell them of themselves and their world. This implies that professionals abandon the banking notion of education (Freire, 1993), within which those who possess knowledge, the experts, deposit it in others, the passive recipients. Only when this notion is discarded can there be a real dialogue with members and a real sharing of expertise and of knowledge.

2. The stories and discussions which follow are taken as opportunities to substantiate the competence of members. The concept of ecological competence (Sundberg, Snowden and Reynolds,1978; Maluccio, 1981) wherein competence is "an attribute of the *transaction* between the person and the environment" that does not place "the burden of competence primarily on the person" (Maluccio, 1981, p. 7, emphasis in original), and thus makes it easier for people to change their view of themselves and of the world and to recognize their competence (see Breton, 1994). In a post-empowerment era, some stories will involve experiences of negative reaction to the empowerment of formerly disempowered groups (elimination of services, reduction in entitlements, loss of gender equality policies and programs, etc.) Conscientization will then take the form of reflecting on that reaction and its effects on the members' sense of competence.

3. The recognition of competence is used, by members who have never gone through a conscientization process, to confront their internal oppressor (Freire, 1993) and to contest their negative self-images and self-evaluations. For members who already have gone through this process and recognize their competence, the sharing of stories is an opportunity to reflect on how they use their competence and their positive self-images and self-evaluations. Have they really got rid of the internal oppressor, or, though they consider themselves empowered and no longer disenfranchised, are they still acting as though they were a disempowered minority instead of citizens who, in a democracy, win some fights and lose some? (Humour makes this confrontation work less painful).

4. The stories (the sharing of information) lead the members to identify the social, economic, political and cultural context common to their individual situations. Through reflecting on the public context of their private situation, members recognize or affirm their identity as political beings and realize or reconfirm their right, as citizens in a democracy, to participate on the social and political scene and be heard. Thus to the awareness of voice is added that of the right to use their voice not only to name their world but to attempt to change it in order to obtain a just share of resources and/or to maintain their competence. In a post-empowerment context, many previously silenced voices are competing to be heard and to obtain a share of shrinking resources. Winning

that competition—in essence shouting down less powerful voices—may be perceived as essential to maintaining a sense of competence. Groups need to address this dilemma and to recognize that the exercise of a right comes with responsibility; in this instance, the responsibility to take action and to use one's voice in a way that is respectful of other voices.

Step #3: Choosing, Evaluating and Taking Action

The process of conscientization and reflection, a process of politicization and liberation from the world of silence, creates a demand for change and leads to action to bring about that change. Thus in this third step, members first decide what type of action they want to take to make their voice heard. In helping the decision-making process along, practitioners once again have to trust members. Empowerment and the maintenance of competence involve self-advocacy (speaking for oneself), and the action chosen must follow from the members' own reflections on their situations. Actions that follow from the reflections/conclusions of others are not autonomous and responsible. This doesn't mean practitioners cannot propose options, but they must recognize the members' abilities to choose.

In the present socio-political context, it is not easy for members to decide what kind of action would best ensure that they maintain their sense of competence. Collective action such as fighting to regain lost programs and services or to obtain new resources may appear futile at first sight, while fighting simply to hold the line, to preserve the status-quo, is not liable to energize or fill people with enthusiasm.

Taking some action, however, is a *sine qua non* for maintaining a sense of competence. One approach to solving the problem is for members and practitioners to make the best possible use of the resources and the competence that exist in their community—a strategy which, in the present conjecture, social workers are pressured to adopt as a cost-saving one. This could mean connecting ex-members of various empowerment groups (previously established to pursue different objectives), thereby creating opportunities for an exchange of services, resources, wisdom, etc., and fostering the development of extra-group solidarity (Breton, 1990). That development could help to mitigate the adverse effects of the competition for scarce resources referred to above.

Having chosen an action, the members then evaluate the possible cost of the action—which might include the normal discouragement that follows a setback or failure, for action does not automatically imply success. This evaluation, incidentally, provides an opportunity to revisit the notion of success in light of the theory of ecological competence. (The multimillionaire entrepreneur who has amassed his or her fortune by despoiling the environment need not be perceived as a competent individual, and his or her wealth need not be seen as a sign of success). In evaluating costs, members consider the principle of least contest (Wood and Middleman, 1989). It directs them to start with less threatening actions, ones that provoke less resistance and provide a safer environment in which to learn to engage in various types of action. Practitioners who also may need to learn social action work should not hesitate to consult with organizations which specialize in advocacy.

Step #4: Radicalization

Radicalization refers to using the power of the group to provoke attention when the voice of members is not heard and their action brings no response. Not all groups, therefore, will have to take this step. However, after taking action (Step 3) all groups will assess the reactions to their action and/or demands, and members will reflect once more on their situation. Through this movement from reflection to action back to reflection, through this praxis, members acquire an increasingly critical consciousness of power versus their initial naive consciousness of the interconnectedness of issues (Freire, 1993). Increased critical consciousness leads to increased expectations to be heard and to have their requests attended to, hence the push to take radical action when expectations are dashed. Knowing the community and having consolidated alliances within it will prove useful in choosing and evaluating the cost of various radical actions.

In a post-empowerment era, it is politically risky to think in terms of radical actions—when services and programs are being cut all over the place, one does not want to do anything that might jeopardize one's own service or program, not to mention one's own job. There are, however, other risks if social workers fail to back up members in their quest to be heard and to have their demands responded to. One is that eventually social work's commitment to social justice—to an equitable distribution of social and economic resources—will become so weak that it will exist in theory only. (Social workers may keep their jobs but lose their soul.) Another is that organizations and individuals associated with other disciplines than social work will take the radical initiatives required. Social work may then become "irrelevant to the poor, the oppressed, the minorities and the marginalized" as Breton (1990, p. 25) argued will happen "if [its] actions do not reflect [its] concern for social justice". (Social workers could lose both their jobs and their soul).

Step #5: Focused Pressure

Once they have the attention of influential members of the community (politicians, bureaucrats, professionals, including social services representatives, business people, spokespersons for religious organizations, etc.), the members move to the next step and formulate precise demands either for legislation, for policies or for services. This will be easier if members, from the beginning of the group onward, have identified as precisely as possible what they want, what means they are ready to take to get what they want, what cost they are prepared to pay, etc. In a post-empowerment era the consumers of social work services may be expected to focus on pressuring social work organizations and social workers with demands to share more and more power (in effect provoking them to go through their own conscientization process). This development has already taken place in a number of agencies: empowered consumers sit on boards, they demand that social workers adapt services and programs to better suit their needs, etc. This welcome development adds to the considerable tensions experienced currently by social workers. Should agencies and workers listen only to the more vocal and more powerful consumers? If the empowered consumers do not use their voice in a constructive and democratic way but insist on negative criticisms or on looking after their own interests to the detriment of the interests of other consumers, will agencies and workers be able to address these issues without being labelled anti-something or close-minded?

These are new challenges for the profession, but it may be that the present crisis (stemming from changes in the political, socio-economic and cultural context) is an opportunity for the profession to transform and revitalize itself.

Step #6: Ensuring Ongoing Participation in the Life of the Community

The last step in empowerment as well as post-empowerment groups involves members finding their niche in the democratic structure of society, or to put it differently, consolidating their participation in the life of their community. This is no guarantee that the newly empowered will obtain everything they demand, nor should they expect to in a democracy. It means simply that their actions and demands have the same probability of success as those of any group in society that seeks its fair share of resources. A classic way for members of ensuring that their voices continue to be heard in the everyday life of their community is for them (or a few of them) to organize as permanent lobbies or to join other organizational systems that will watch over their interests (a homeless alliance as described by Sacks (1991), for example).

CONCLUSION

In the present post-empowerment context, when the democratic structure of a society is imperiled (which is what happens when public policies guarantee that the rich get richer and the poor get poorer), when the life of the community is endangered (which is what happens when many services and programs for ordinary as well as the most vulnerable citizens are dismantled), and when the newly empowered vie for a share of dwindling resources, one could argue that social workers have been handed an outstanding opportunity to apply their knowledge and exercise their professional skills, for they are positioned at the interface of individual and community. It is up to social workers to seize that opportunity and to put in practice what they believe in: that dynamic communities are essential to the development of competent individuals and families and to the maintenance of their competence. Empowerment and post-empowerment groups, building on the strengths and resources of persons and communities, are ideal vehicles to promote that development and to maintain that competence.

REFERENCES

Barker, R. L. (1991). *The social work dictionary* (2nd ed.). Silver Spring, MD: NASW Press.

Breton, M. (1985). Reaching and engaging people: Issues and practice principles. *Social Work with Groups*, 8(3), 7-21.

Breton, M. (1990). Learning from social group work traditions. *Social Work with Groups*, 13(3), 21-34.

Breton, M. (1994). Relating competence-promotion and empowerment. *Journal of Progressive Human Services*, 5(1), 27-44.

Breton, A. and Breton, M. (1997). Democracy and empowerment. In A. Breton, G. Galeotti, P. Salmon and R. Wintrobe (Eds.), *Understanding democracy. Economic and political perspectives* (pp. 176-196). New York: Cambridge University Press.

Chandler, C. and Morin, R. (1996, October 15). America's economic chasm: Gap between rich and poor grows wider. *International Herald Tribune*, p. 16.

Freire, P. (1993). *Pedagogy of the oppressed*. New York: The Continuum Publishing Company.

Toronto services cut back. (1997, May 30). *The Globe and Mail*, p. A6.

Kurland, R. (1978). Planning: The neglected component of group development. *Social Work with Groups*, 1(2), 173-178.

Lee, J. A. B. (1997). The empowerment group: The heart of the empowerment approach and an antidote to injustice. In J. Parry (Ed.), *From prevention to wellness through group work* (pp. 15-32). New York: Haworth.

Longres, J. F. and McLeod, E. (1980). Consciousness-raising and social work practice. *Social Casework: The Journal of Contemporary Social Work*, 61(5), 267-276.

Maluccio, A. N. (Ed.). (1981). *Promoting competence in clients: A new/old approach to social work practice*. New York: The Free Press.

Mitchell, A. (1997, May 13). Rich, poor wage gap widening. *The Globe and Mail*, p. A12.

Mulroy, E. A. (1997). Building a neighborhood network: Interorganizational collaboration to prevent child abuse and neglect, *Social Work*, 42(3), 255-264.

Rappaport, J. (1981). In praise of paradox: A social policy of empowerment over prevention. *American Journal of Community Psychology*, 9(1), 1-25.

Sacks, J. (1991). Action and reflection in work with a group of homeless people, *Social Work with Groups*, 14(3/4), 187-202.

Sacks, J. (1994). Book review of *Hard-pressed in the heartland*: The Hormel strike and the future of the labor movement. *Social Work with Groups*, 17(3), 97-101.

Solomon, B. B. (1976). *Black empowerment: Social work in oppressed communities*. New York: Columbia University Press.

Sundberg, N. D., Snowden, L. R. and Reynolds, W. M. (1978). Toward assessment of personal competence and incompetence in life situations. *Annual Review of Psychology*, 29, 179-211.

Weick, A. (1981). Reframing the person-in-environment perspective. *Social Work*, 26(2), 140-143.

Weick, A. (1992). Building a strengths perspective for social work. In D. Saleeby (Ed.), *The strengths perspective in social work practice* (pp. 18-26) New York: Longman.

Wood, G. and Middleman, R. (1989). *The structural approach to direct practice in social work*. New York: Columbia University Press.

Chapter 13

GROUP EMPOWERMENT: AN ELUSIVE GOAL

Alice Home
School of Social Work
University of Ottawa

Empowerment has become so popular in recent years that it is beginning to rival mutual aid as a focus of group work theory and practice interest. While this partly reflects increasing social work interest in this concept, it also shows growing recognition that groups have special potential to enhance empowerment. The historical traditions, practice models and principles of social group work make it particularly suitable for developing the personal mastery and participatory competence needed to fight oppression. However, there is little discussion in the literature of the difficulties which make group empowerment an elusive goal. This paper presents some theoretical perspectives and practice principles which inform empowerment-oriented group work, as well as identifying its promise and some pitfalls. The first section discusses the rationale, historical roots and practice principles of this type of work, while the second focuses on some issues and obstacles which make group empowerment challenging.

THE GROUP AS A CONTEXT FOR EMPOWERMENT

Empowerment is generally viewed as a process by which people gain mastery over factors that significantly affect their lives (Unger and Powell, 1990). While definitions vary, they share a focus on client strengths and feature goals combining personal change (stronger sense of self, increased competence) with enhanced political understanding and/or skills (Lee, 1994, Guittérez, 1990). Empowerment approaches are seen as an antidote to the compromised strengths, economic insecurity, limited access to information and/or training and lack of political experience which often beset oppressed populations (Lee, 1997).

While empowerment practice can take place in the individual, family or group context, the latter is seen as the "optimum medium" (Lee, 1997). Being in a group facilitates sharing oppressive experiences, which helps members break out of silence and isolation while reducing self-blame for situations beyond their control. Learning to distinguish between inappropriate self-blame and learned, self-defeating behaviours that contribute to oppression is a difficult, time-consuming task. As worker authority is diluted in the group setting, it can be easier for members to find the support and challenge needed to confront internalized aspects of powerlessness and oppression (Cox, 1991). Members who have identified and overcome these behaviours and attitudes can affirm others' right to examine structural components of their situation while acknowledging that personal change is not easy. Learning new skills such as mobilizing resources and self-assertion can also be facilitated in groups, if leaders and members are encouraged to share their expertise (Cox, 1991). Finally, taking action to bring about social change is both less intimidating and more effective in a group because of the "strength in numbers" phenomenon (Shulman, 1992).

ROOTS OF EMPOWERMENT-ORIENTED GROUP WORK

The characteristics of empowerment-oriented group work are rooted both in earlier social work models and in developments outside the profession. While empowerment theorists have only recently discovered the group's potential, early social group workers adopted an enabler role of helping members develop their competencies and power to participate. Involvement in group decision-making and social action was seen as an important vehicle for personal and social development (Shapiro,1991). Intermediate goals of strengthening autonomy and leadership were pursued through education, modelling and a gradually diminishing worker role (Home, 1996).

Early emphasis on participation and social action was diluted, however, by the rise of rehabilitative approaches to working with groups in the 1950s. Schwartz's notions of reciprocity and conceptualizations of groups as self-empowering, mutual aid systems (Lee,1997) eventually challenged the view that groups were primarily the context and means of treatment. The reciprocal model introduced themes of worker openness and shared authority, which were to be central to contemporary empowerment approaches. However, Schwartz's assumption of symbiotic independence between individual and society did not fit well with the experience of oppression, which reflects a breakdown in that relationship (Breton, 1989).

In contrast, structural and community work models recognized the powerless position of oppressed populations. The former examines societal components before placing a social problem within a person while focusing on what can be changed and on helping clients feel more powerful (Goldberg-Wood and Middleman, 1991). Although this model promotes grouping people in similar oppressive situations, it provides few specific guidelines as to how to use group process for empowerment. Early community work models provided a similar analysis as to why oppressed populations are denied access to resources and power. However, as personal change efforts were seen as deflecting energy from social action, individual needs were sometimes ignored. This lack of attention to the private sphere was parallelled by a neglect of process and developmental aspects of group life (Home, 1991). This can be a mistake because social action groups must develop the trust, cohesion and commitment needed to cope with external threats, co-option attempts and resistance from systems they are trying to change (Lewis, 1983).

Two influences outside social work provided some missing pieces to the group empowerment puzzle. The self-help movement reaffirmed that members are more than people in need (Shapiro, 1991), through their explicit recognition of the value of personal (vs. professional) expertise with a given social problem. This translated into member responsibility for organizing and leading meetings as well as for helping others. The second contribution of self-help groups was their pursuit of mixed personal and social change goals. These groups recognized members' need for support in coping with personal effects of a problem while engaging in social action to confront it (National Council on Welfare, 1973).

These themes were developed further by the women's movement, which chose to base its political analysis on concrete personal experiences. Feminists used consciousness-raising methods adapted from critical education to help women become aware of societal roots of their oppression while engaging in both personal and social action to challenge it (Home, 1991). It was essential to combine personal and social change:

> Confidence and strength in our own selves gives us the ability to fight for change and to cope with the problems and instability that go with the struggle. Only those who are taking responsibility for their own selves can create the enormous changes that are necessary in this society. Only a movement that understands the different strengths of women

and supports individual efforts to grow can succeed in challenging that society. (Bunch, 1975, p. 6)

This dual change focus was coupled with a belief that the small group should play a central role in fighting oppression on all fronts. Groups were formed for diverse purposes, ranging from therapy and assertion training through consciousness-raising to social action. All shared a concern for helping individual women while promoting critical social analysis and action, but the priority on one or the other varied with specific group goal (Home, 1988).

A final contribution to empowerment-oriented group work was the self-directed group approach, a blend of group and community work methods. While primarily directed at changing societal attitudes, policies and practices, these groups can also bring empowerment and growth on a personal level (Mullender and Ward, 1991). Unlike mainstream groups that build autonomy, participation and leadership gradually (Papell and Rothman, 1983), self-directed groups give members early control over all important planning decisions. Starting from an anti-oppressive value stance, this model emphasizes member control of problem definition, goal setting, consciousness-raising, selection of social action methods and evaluation of outcome (Mullender and Ward, 1991). Workers act in a peripheral facilitative capacity, and group structure is based on both open membership and an extended, open-ended time frame.

CHARACTERISTICS OF EMPOWERMENT GROUPS

Contemporary empowerment models are a unique blend of support/mutual aid, consciousness-raising and social action groups. They also incorporate some features of self-directed and feminist groups. They are based on anti-oppressive principles that it is unethical to "treat" oppressed people without helping them to confront their oppression (Lee, 1994). The latter can occur only if members are empowered, through a combination of personal work and consciousness-raising, to identify issues and reach for alternatives. These groups include empowerment not only as a theoretical base but also as the central organizing principle behind group goals, content and process (Lee, 1997). This means that empowerment groups are by definition multi-functional, with goals that include support, learning new skills and strengthening critical analysis (Cox, 1991; Lee, 1997). The foregoing implies a different view of the helping process, one which moves beyond mainstream traditions of sharing authority, facilitating mutual aid and enabling members to develop competencies and leadership (Shapiro, 1991; Lee, 1997). Empowerment groups add explicit goals of reflection, critical analysis and action against oppression. To reach these goals, groups and their members must take charge of their own empowerment.

These multi-faceted goals force workers to re-examine their professional roles as well as their relationship with members. In addition to adopting relevant mainstream roles in a flexible way, workers need to help members identify and obtain resources while developing skills in negotiation, political analysis, research and use of media (Home, 1991; Pernell, 1981). These skills are necessary if group members are to acquire the participatory competence required for effective social action (Keiffer, 1984). Relationships with members must be shifted to a more collegial model. This moves beyond mainstream formulations of shared authority to feminist and self-directed principles of developing the most egalitarian relationship possible, given real differences in power and experience (Cox,1991). It also means that within-group mutual aid and solidarity are not enough. These groups must be helped to develop alliances and partnerships with community groups and organizations (Breton, 1996). This expansion of members' networks beyond the group increases access to resources and provides opportunities to test new skills, both of which are necessary for the group to continue its work (Nosko and Breton, 1996).

SOME DILEMMAS OF EMPOWERMENT-ORIENTED GROUP WORK

Recent empowerment group models are theoretically consistent and their value base is attractive to practitioners. However, several dilemmas face workers interested in using groups to promote empowerment. This section will discuss two issues and illustrate them with practice examples. The first is the priority problem posed by combining goals, while the second is finding ways to share power and develop autonomy given contextual constraints on contemporary group practice.

Priority Issues: Individual vs. Group Empowerment

The first dilemma involves deciding whether the main priority in mixed goal groups is to be on fostering individual or group empowerment (Estes, 1991). Individual empowerment refers to the personal and interpersonal domains, with a focus on enhancing members' self-esteem, competencies, skills and critical awareness (Gutiérrez,1990; Zimmerman, 1995). Group empowerment involves taking action on the political and community fronts to change aspects of members' oppressive life situations (East, 1997). Individual and group empowerment are both seen as important, so there is little discussion of potential priority conflicts in the literature. Instead, attention is directed to how individual empowerment contributes to strengthening the group, which in turn enhances members' functioning (Gutiérrez, 1990).

It is true that priority issues rarely arise in those groups situated at one or other extreme of the individual-group empowerment continuum. Most groups of sexual abuse survivors, for example, help their members share experiences, develop coping strategies and reflect on societal roots of their oppression without undertaking collective action. Workers adopting a flexible role can facilitate social action activities, however, such as the production of a video by one such group that decided to challenge public silence about incest by making it more visible (Gagné, 1996). Similarly, groups whose goal is to bring about changes in laws, attitudes or policies can listen to and support individual members struggling with personal issues while remaining firmly focused on social change. Personal growth, satisfaction and increased self-esteem are seen as positive by-products rather than as goals of these groups (Lewis, 1991; Home, 1991).

In many combined goal groups, however, priority decisions are less clear-cut. One consciousness-raising group sought women interested in sharing and reflecting on their experiences, with a view to raising awareness and possibly taking action. Facilitators left decisions about goal priorities in members' hands to enhance group ownership without realising that members had joined for different reasons. The group empowered members to work on personal issues, reflect on life decisions and discover common oppressive experiences. Energized by new critical awareness, the group decided to organize a rally to challenge public attitudes regarding violence towards women. Succeeding in this social action increased members' self-esteem and participatory competence. There was a community empowerment effect as well, in that two women developed enough leadership to form new groups. However, the transition to a group empowerment focus had not been decided formally, and a few members who wanted to continue working on personal issues left before the group ended (Home, 1991). One might question whether group empowerment was achieved at the expense of individual empowerment of these members who were not yet ready for social action.

The empowerment literature acknowledges individual member's rights to decide on the extent and timing of their personal changes (Nosko and Breton, 1996). There is agreement also that groups must choose and pace their social change activities, though they may need some guidance if they take premature action, select overly ambitious change targets or procrastinate through low self-confidence or fear of failure (Home, 1991; Lewis, 1983). However, there is a fine line between providing this kind of consultative help and using worker power to influence decisions about including social action as a group goal.

There are two positions on this issue. The first holds that social action is essential to maintaining competence. This view sees increased confidence, skills and awareness as necessary but insufficient, as "empowerment comes from organised action on the socio-economic, cultural and political scenes" (Breton, 1991, p. 105). One reason for this stance is that helping people only to "take charge of their lives" can lend support to neo-conservative strategies designed to reduce dependency on public services. Another is that new awareness without action can leave members feeling overwhelmed and immobilized (Home, 1991). Finally, there appears to be an assumption that a self-directed group will inevitably choose social action (Mullender and Ward, 1991). While collective action may indeed be necessary, this belief can be incompatible with respect for the full implications of group self-determination.

A contrasting position on this dilemma is that contextual and cultural appropriateness should be the main criteria for determining the priority placed on individual or group empowerment (Zimmerman, 1995). This view holds that there can be no one route to empowerment, as ideological purity must be tempered by practical concerns. Specific goals are influenced not only by members' particular experience of oppression but also by agency context and cultural norms (Manning, 1997; Hirayama and Hirayama, 1997). For example, many women have been socialized to be dependent, while people who have been institutionalized live with a legacy of passivity and conformity. This means that expectations of early autonomy, leadership sharing and social action involvement may not be realistic in some populations and situations.

An example is a group of recently de-institutionalized psychiatric patients, brought together to form a mental health service consumers' group. The latter was not only a tool for developing members' competencies and changing their public image but also the only way to obtain secure funding. Although the choice to establish an official association meant meeting externally imposed deadlines, the workers hesitated to lead meetings, provide active direction or skill training through fear of impeding empowerment. However, just as bringing people together does not ensure mutual helping will occur (Shulman, 1992), grouping oppressed people is no guarantee of empowerment. Not surprisingly, the group floundered due to the mismatch between worker expectation and member competencies, resulting in discouragement and apathy for all. A contextual approach would have taken into account members' experiences as patients, which can lead to learned helplessness (Manning,1997). Individual empowerment goals of overcoming powerlessness, learning participation and leadership skills would have been prerequisite to any group empowerment goals.

The Pace of Empowerment

A closely related dilemma is how to translate principles of autonomy development and power sharing into practice. Once again, there are two positions on this issue. The first advocates a gradual approach, to allow members time to strengthen leadership and decision-making skills while the worker slowly withdraws to a more peripheral role (Papell and Rothman, 1983). A contrasting position is that only by exercising full power from the outset can group members overcome dependency (Mullender and Ward, 1991). The gradual approach helps to avoid unrealistic expectations of the type discussed in the previous example. However, it does carry the risk that the worker will not relinquish enough control to allow full development of indigenous leadership.

A case in point is a group of low-income women whose members were living with several types of oppression simultaneously. As East (1997) points out, low-income women are confronted daily with policies and programs that reflect the rhetoric of self-sufficiency attainment but fail to include strategies that reflect their experiences and needs. These women's paid work experience had been restricted by their sex-role socialization, while their employment opportunities had been undermined by economic restructuring (Cosse and Home, 1994). Mindful of how class and gender oppression can interact with powerful results (East, 1997), a graduate student decided to use her field placement to help these women develop a co-operative, with a view to fostering both social and economic empowerment.

This worker adopted a mainstream social goals approach, taking on initial leadership in deciding program content to give members time to develop confidence, identify competencies and research community resources. However, she blended in feminist principles of sharing her power and experiences as a woman while encouraging group members to reflect to reasons for their oppression. As members acquired more autonomy, the worker helped them learn new skills and increase decision-making competencies so they could choose a co-operative venture and arrange training. She withdrew to a peripheral role of supporting indigenous leadership, then remained available for telephone consultation after her placement ended to ease the group's transition to full autonomy.

Members made considerable empowerment gains. They felt more powerful, increased their confidence, competencies and awareness. However, group empowerment was less evident. The only training available in organizing co-operatives was offered in a mixed gender group led by a male leader. These women learned the hard way that their group had to be highly developed to resist outside pressure (Lewis, 1983) and that they needed extra time to prepare for full autonomy. Members' energies were co-opted into another venture, and their own co-operative was never formed (Cosse and Home, 1994).

Another example sheds further light on the difficulty of ensuring realistic pacing. A group formed to provide support for French-speaking adult adoptees searching for their biological parents had a secondary goal of stimulating reflection about members' shared situation, with a view to forming a self-help group (Rochon, 1994). Given the worker's and members' time commitments, only six bi-weekly meetings could be planned over a three-month period. The worker opted for a mainstream model that provided for an active initial role, both in planning program and in leading discussion. While this choice proved helpful in empowering individual members to continue their reflection and their searches, the short time-frame was not sufficient to allow for leadership transfer or autonomy development. Despite member interest in continuing to meet, the group did not become a permanent resource (Rochon, 1994).

Concluding Comments and Questions

These practice dilemmas show that while groups have enormous potential for empowerment, a number of issues are yet to be resolved. The meaning of group empowerment needs to be clarified in an effort to reach some agreement on whether collective action is always a necessary ingredient. Furthermore, the importance of achieving a successful social action outcome has to be weighed against process factors, such as learning leadership, negotiation or media skills. As the low-income women's group illustrates, an unsuccessful outcome may reflect insufficient time and limited community resources rather than low empowerment gains. On the other hand, the women's consciousness-raising group shows that obtaining a successful action outcome may not be empowering for all group members.

The individual-group empowerment issue is a complex one, to which there are no easy answers. There needs to be discussion and debate among scholars, workers and consumer groups on how to ensure groups make their own informed priority decisions without sacrificing the personal-political connection so essential to empowerment. Research is also needed to explore ways in which different groups deal with this difficult problem.

Another unresolved issue involves defining prerequisites for group empowerment in an era of increased social need and reduced social spending. Under pressure to produce the quick, concrete results needed to obtain or maintain funding, agencies often encourage workers to form groups yet fail to provide adequate preparation time, training or consultation (Home, 1996). In addition, many Canadian agencies emphasize short-term, goal-directed groups which leave little room for individual members to learn decision-making and leadership skills (Turcotte, 1996). An example is an agency under pressure to reduce by half the number of group sessions offered to sexual abuse survivors, even though these women clearly need time to overcome effects of long-term abuse before empowerment can occur.

These problems are worsened when members come from oppressed minorities, which have increased in terms of needs and numbers because of economic restructuring coupled with reductions in social spending. Denied access to preventive services, these people are understandably preoccupied by survival concerns by the time they are offered assistance (Home, 1996). For example, it is not easy to know how much energy to focus on securing adequate food and lodging for homeless group members and how much to concentrate on raising awareness (Thivierge, 1994). The latter cannot be ignored, however, as member interest in facing oppression is a key ingredient in successful empowerment (Lee,1994).

It seems clear that a competent, knowledgeable worker with a raised awareness and members interested in confronting their oppression (Lee, 1994) are necessary but insufficient conditions for group empowerment. Other requirements include either extensive experience and considerable autonomy on the part of some members, or an extended time-frame to permit development of needed individual and group competencies. In Canada, open-ended time-frames rarely are supported by social agencies, and there is little enthusiasm for social action groups, except in precariously funded alternative settings. Scholars and practitioners need to reflect on the impact of these constraints on contemporary group work, as well as on strategies to deal with them. Failure to act brings the risk that empowerment-oriented group work will be supplanted by approaches that deal only with the most obvious symptoms of complex social problems.

Despite the potential of groups to promote empowerment, it can be an elusive goal. Social spending cuts have resulted in the targeting of rare services primarily at the least autonomous populations. Moving through mutual helping and consciousness-raising to solidarity and action in collaboration with other oppressed groups takes many months, even when groups are relatively autonomous from the outset. Expecting empowerment while withholding the resources to develop it can lead to member and worker disillusionment and eventual disempowerment of both. It is essential to find ways to avoid this happening.

REFERENCES

Breton, M. (1989). Liberation theology, group work and the right of the oppressed populations to participate in the life of the community. *Social work with groups*, 12(3), 5-18.

Breton, M. (1991). Reflections on social action practice in France. In A. Vinik and M. Levin (Eds.), *Social action in group work* (pp. 91-107). New York: Haworth.

Breton, M. (1996). Plaidoyer contre les monopolisations professionnelles. *Intervention*, 102, 10-19.

Bunch, C. (1975), Self-definition and political survival. *Quest: A Feminist Quarterly*, 1, 2-6.

Cosse, P. and Home, A. (1994). Groupes de femmes : Outil de prise en charge collective. In Darveau-Fournier, L. and Renaud, C. (Eds.), *Actes du colloque Les journées Simone Paré 1992* (pp. 16-33). Québec : Université Laval.

Cox, O. (1991). The critical role of social action in empowerment-oriented groups. *Social Work with Groups* 14 (3-4), 77-90.

East. J. (1997). An empowerment model for low-income women, working paper, Faculty of Social Work, University of Toronto.

Estes, R. (1991). *Social development and social work with groups.* Paper presented at the 12th Symposium of the Association for the Advancement of Social Work with Groups.

Gagné, É. (1996). *Approche axée sur la compétence en intervention de groupe auprès de femmes survivantes d'abus sexuel.* Paper presented in Atlanta in November 1992 at the 14th Symposium of the Association for the Advancement of Social Work with Groups.

Goldberg-Wood, G. and Middleman, R. (1991). Advocacy and social action: Key elements in the structural approach to direct practice in social work. In A. Vinik and M. Levin (Eds.), *Social action in group work* (pp. 53-64). New York: Haworth.

Gutiérrez, L. (1990). Working with women of color: An empowerment perspective. *Social Work* 35, 149-155.

Hirayama. H. and Hirayama, K. (1997). Cross-cultural application of empowerment practice: A comparison between American and Japanese groups, working paper, Faculty of Social Work, University of Toronto.

Home, A. (1988). Les groupes de femmes : Outils de changement personnel et de développement. *Service Social*, 37(1-2), 61-85.

Home, A. (1991). Mobilizing women's strengths for social change: The group connection. In A. Vinik and M. Levin (Eds.), *Social action in group work* (pp. 153-173). New York: Haworth.

Home, A. (1996). Réussir l'intervention de groupe dans un contexte difficile : mission impossible? *Intervention* 102, 20-33.

Keiffer, C. (1984). Citizen empowerment: A developmental perspective. *Prevention in Human Services*, 2(2-3), 9-36.

Lee, J. (1994). *The empowerment approach to social work practice.* New York: Columbia.

Lee, J. (1997). The empowerment group: The heart of the empowerment approach and an antidote to injustice. In J. Parry (Ed.), *From prevention to wellness through group work* (pp 15-32). New York: Haworth.

Lewis, E. (1983). Le service social des groupes dans la vie communautaire. *Service social,* 32(102), 32-49.

Lewis, E. (1991). Social change and citizen action: A philosophical exploration for modern social group work. *Social Work with Groups,* 14(3-4), 23-34.

Manning, S. (1997). Building an empowerment model of practice through the voices of people with serious psychiatric disability. In *Empowerment practice in social work: Developing richer conceptual frameworks: Conference papers.* Toronto: University of Toronto.

Mullender, A. and Ward, D. (1991). *Self-directed group work.* London: Whiting and Birch.

National Council of Welfare. (1973). *Poor people's groups.* Ottawa.

Nosko, A. and Breton, M. (1996). *Group work with women who have experienced abuse: Applying a strengths, competence, empowerment model.* Paper presented at the 15th Symposium of the Association for the Advancement of Social Work with Groups, San Diego.

Papell, C. and Rochman, B. (1983). Le modèle du courant central du service social des groupes en parallèle avec la psychothérapie du groupe et l'approche de groupe structurée. *Service social* 32(1-2), 3-29.

Pernell, R. (1981). *Empowerment issues in social group work.* Paper presented at the 3rd AASWG Symposium, Hartford.

Rochon, J. (1994). *Partager et profiter de l'expérience des autres : un groupe pour adultes adoptés francophones.* Unpublished lecture notes. Ottawa : Université d'Ottawa, École de service social.

Shapiro, B. (1991). Social action, the group and society. In A. Vinik et M. Levin (Eds.), *Social action in group work* (pp. 7-34). New York: Haworth.

Shulman, L. (1992). *The skills of helping individuals and groups* (3rd Ed.). Itasco: Peacock.

Thivierge, F. (1994). Intervention de groupe auprès de la population itinérante de Montréal. *Service Social* 43(2), 147-157.

Turcotte, D. (1996) Quelques tendances de l'évolution récente des pratiques en service social des groupes. *Revue canadienne de service social* 13(1), 53-74.

Unger, D., and Powell, D. (1990). Families as nurturing systems: An introduction. *Prevention in Human Services* 9(1), 1-17.

Zimmerman, M. (1995). Psychological empowerment: Issues and illustrations. *American Journal of Community Psychology,* 23(5), 581-599.

Chapter 14

CROSS-CULTURAL APPLICATION OF EMPOWERMENT PRACTICE: A COMPARISON BETWEEN AMERICAN AND JAPANESE GROUPS

Hisashi Hirayama
College of Social Work
The University of Tennessee, Knoxville
Kasumi K. Hirayama
School of Social Work
The University of Connecticut

The purpose of this article is to examine the issues involved in a cross-cultural application of empowerment practice as it applies to group processes in Japanese society, which is culturally different from the US where this practice has been developed.

Some of our Japanese colleagues who have come to know American society and American social work are at times amused by America's interest in and emphasis on the importance of power in society and in interpersonal relationships. The fact is that empowerment is currently one of the most popular terms used by all kinds of people including politicians of all sides, corporate managers, labour union leaders, religious leaders, social workers and countless others. The term is commonly used to accentuate the importance of achieving upward mobility, personal advancement, self-assertion or self-sufficiency.

In Japanese, as in English, the term power, or *chikara*, has a variety of meanings, such as physical strength, energy, tenacity, effort or spiritual power, as well as authority, autocratic force, domination, control or oppression. In an ancient Japanese word, *tax* was also called *chikara*, or power, because it had a meaning of something produced by a collective power of the people (Kojien, 1991). Despite its variety of meanings, the term power in Japanese generally evokes more or less negative images in the listener's mind because the term is most frequently used in reference to *kenryoku*, or authoritative, dominating, autocratic forces that exert control over people and their life space. Thus, the term provokes such emotions as anxiety, fear, resistance and threat in the minds of hearers. However, the negative connotation placed on the term by the

Japanese does not mean that they are unaware of the existence or use of power in interpersonal relationships (Hirayama and Hirayama, 1995). But one difference between Americans and Japanese is that Americans, just as a noted existential psychoanalyst Rollo May (1972) has said, "confront, use, enjoy and struggle with power openly" (p.100). Japanese tend to avoid, deny and shun the open and visible use of power in daily living. If power is used, it is used covertly behind the scenes.

DISTINCTIVE CHARACTERISTICS OF AMERICAN SOCIETY

We think that Americans' open power consciousness and open power handling are attributed to several salient characteristics in American society. In contrast to Japanese society, American society is a multi-cultural, multi-ethnic and multi-racial society that emphasizes the importance of individuality and individualism and functions on a free-market ideology. People act in the belief that every citizen should have equal access to opportunities for self-fulfilment or the achievement of lifetime dreams. Competition, not cooperation, is a major ingredient for survival, achievement and success. How one uses one's power, control and influence to get ahead becomes a major concern among Americans who are preoccupied more with individual rights than with group solidarity. Autonomy, individual responsibility, self-identity and individual achievement become important goals for members of the society. Fostering a competitive spirit in the child is an important educational goal for many parents. Becoming independent and self-sufficient from an early age is always something to be encouraged, desired, practised and reinforced. A saying, "The Lord helps those who help themselves" is a well-accepted theme in American society. Individualism, not groupness, is a foundation of American ideology. Dependence or even interdependence is not regarded as a desirable quality in the American personality (Hirayama and Hirayama, 1986a).

DISTINCTIVE CHARACTERISTICS OF JAPANESE SOCIETY

In contrast to highly individualistic Americans, Japanese people cultivate a sense of group identity and solidarity, trying to derive their life satisfaction and security from their group affiliations. Their sense of self-esteem is more closely tied to the status and prestige of the groups they belong to, and their self-identity is more enmeshed with the group than is the Americans' (Hirayama and Hirayama, 1986a).

One significant difference in the Japanese group structure from that of American is a hierarchy. In Japan, the group structure in interpersonal relationships is arranged in a hierarchical order of respective position and status within the group to which one belongs. A noted Japanese sociologist Chie Nakane called Japanese society "vertical," in contrast to the more horizontally arranged society of America. Hierarchical relationships exist in most human relationships: parent-child, student-teacher, employer-employee, old-young, etc. Respective roles and functions of each position and status are generally well defined and prescribed. Such behaviours as attentive listening to opinions expressed by one's superiors, such as teacher or parent, or obeying commands by one's superiors is not only constantly reinforced but also rewarded by society.

In scanning the hierarchical structure and stratification of Japanese society, men as a group wield most power over other groups of people. Asians residing in Japan stay at the bottom. These power relationship are affected in turn by 1) one's role assignment within the reference group, 2) the role assignment of one's reference group within the larger society, and 3) the value or status attributed to these roles (Pinderhughes, 1995). For example, women in Japan, despite a law prohibiting gender discrimination in employment, continue to get the short end of the stick when seeking employment. In times of economic downturn, this problem is accentuated. On the job, women assume positions of less importance with considerably lower wages than their male counterparts, and most assume a subordinate or supportive role to men. Foreign permanent residents, particularly Asians, have very limited access to job opportunities and resources.

EMPOWERMENT PRACTICE

Over the past 20 years, empowerment practice has emerged as a major organizing theme in micro and macro social work practice in American social work. While many definitions are available, according to Browne (1995), empowerment has been defined as a process (Gutiérrez, 1990), an intervention (Parsons and Schram, 1989; Solomon, 1976), and a skill (Mandell and Schram, 1985) benefiting diverse client populations. The social work literature has suggested that empowerment is effective with such varied groups as oppressed ethnic and racial minorities (Solomon, 1976; Guitiérrez, 1995), immigrants and refugees (Hirayama and Cetingok, 1988), nursing home residents (McDermott, 1989), women of colour (Gutiérrez, 1990), homeless women (Lee, 1994), and elderly and older women (Browne, 1995; Kam, 1996). Furthermore, empowerment practice has been applied to work with families (Pinderhughes, 1983, 1995), groups (Pernell, 1986; Hirayama and Hirayama, 1986b; Lee, 1994; Berman-Rossi, 1992, Breton, 1992), and communities (Barr, 1995; Ejigiri, 1996; Lee, 1994;

Schuftan, 1996; Weil, 1996). Despite all that has been written, however, the definition of empowerment or empowerment practice remains ambiguous and vague (Barr, 1995; Browne, 1995; Schuftan, 1996). Browne (1995) stated that "what has been neglected is a critical analysis of empowerment's basic premises and underlying meanings and how the conceptualization of empowerment shapes interventions" (p.358). Also neglected has been an examination of the concept and practice of empowerment as it applies to a culture and a society different from those of the US, as most published articles have failed to pay sufficient attention to cultural and political contexts in which empowerment practice occurs.

DEFINITIONS OF POWER AND EMPOWERMENT

Webster's (1991) dictionary offers several definitions of power. But at least two of the definitions appear most relevant to social work. One is "the ability to do or act; capability of doing or accomplishing something," and the other is "the possession of control or command over others; authority; ascendancy."

The term "empower" is defined by Webster's (1991) as "to give power or authority to; to give ability to; enable; permit." This definition assumes the act of power being transferred to someone by someone else.

Review of the social work literature indicates that the concept of empowerment is defined variously and that there is no consensus what it really means. For example, Pernell (1986) defined it as the capacity to influence the forces which affect one's life space for one's own and others, benefit. Browne (1995) states that the concept of empowerment has been divided into three basic categories: as an intervention and product, a skill and a process. Solomon (1976), who advocated and popularized the term in the 1970s, defined it as an intervention and strategy. She asserted her position that as long as African Americans occupy a powerless position in American society, empowering the oppressed is the key to the achievement of African American autonomy, equality and self-affirmation. Pinderhughes (1995) stated that it is a process of "achieving reasonable control over one's destiny, learning to cope constructively with debilitating forces in society, and acquiring the competence to initiate change at the individual and systems levels. Thus intervention assumes a multilevel" (p.136). Saleebey (1996) defined the concept as "assisting individuals, families and communities in discovering and using the resources and tools within and around them" (p.298).

Cowger (1994) says, "Promoting empowerment means believing that people are capable of making their own choices and decisions. The role of the social worker in clinical practice is to nourish, encourage, assist, enable, support, stimulate, and unleash the strengths within people" (p.264).

Gutiérrez's (1990) work in empowerment with women of colour also viewed empowerment as a process but with a somewhat different focus. Her definition is one in which individual empowerment contributes to group empowerment and in which increases in group power enhance the functioning of individual members.

The absence of a clear definition, coupled with insufficient empirical evidence for effectiveness of empowerment practice, continues to pose serious challenges to social work theorists and practitioners who claim empowerment practice to be a viable practice approach. Furthermore, despite some claims that empowerment is an effective way to help the oppressed bring structural changes in the forces which oppress them, there is no hard evidence to support these claims at this juncture. Moreover, Breton (1992) argues that the social worker who represents a social agency which controls resources for the oppressed could not be a major force to liberate them from the oppressor and poverty. In her view, it is structurally not possible to achieve such a goal. If any change is achieved, it is not because of social work intervention but for other reasons such as changes in economic structure and redistribution of social resources. Thus, our contention is that it is more appropriate to consider empowerment practice in a modest and limited scope. It should be seen either as a process or a skill to be used by the social worker to achieve modest individual goals, such as increasing self-efficacy, self-assertiveness and autonomy, or group goals, such as increasing a sense of group solidarity, consciousness-raising and liberating oneself from subjugation to authority. Furthermore, if we are to use empowerment practice as a process or as a skill with modest and limited goals, despite some cultural differences we believe that it is possible to apply this practice approach to people in Japan or any other country of the world. The remainder of this paper discusses how this approach could be applied to groups in Japan.

EMPOWERMENT AS GOAL

If we define power as the ability to cause or prevent change, we can see that the influencing takes place within the boundaries of the various interacting systems such as people, groups, families, organizations and communities. This view of constantly transacting power among a variety of social units is important to any social worker who intends to use empowerment practice as a major process, be it his or her work with a family, a group, an organization or a community.

As we are group workers, we believe that small groups provide ideal conditions for group participants to experience, exercise and rehearse their power as they are provided with an opportunity for guided interpersonal interactions in group situations. After all, we consider a group as a microcosm of a given society, where all human interactions in a larger society are manifested and observed in a small group setting. Although empowerment practice may be applicable to a variety of people, we believe it is particularly meaningful when the concept is applied as a process as well as a goal of helping such relatively powerless groups of individuals as Asian minorities, the elderly, developmentally and physically challenged, mentally ill people and women who suffer from long- or short-term power shortage.

Gitterman (1979) conceptualizes people's needs and predicaments according to three interrelated problems in living: life transitions, environmental pressures and interpersonal processes. This framework for assessing people's particular needs in time and situation may also serve in understanding people's power. For example, persons who go through a life transition from middle age to old age must adapt to changes associated with the aging process such as reduction in energy, physical stamina and changes in their social position which are likely to result in reduction of income, health and functional abilities within social affiliation, status and relationships. Consequently, their exertion of influence diminishes greatly (Lowy, 1982). For instance, Japan's rapid transition to an aging society is creating a vast number of post-retirement men who experience a difficult life transition.

The specific goals of empowering people through groups vary from one type of group to another and are largely determined by the factors impinging on the nature of the organizing group: conditions of services, people's needs and desires and the agency's purpose and functions (Hirayama and Hirayama, 1986b).

For example, in a group organized for mentally ill patients, the group's aim would be helping members develop adaptive skills that enable them to cope more effectively with internal and external forces impinging upon their adaptive behaviours within the family, interpersonal and community systems. With this group, the worker must understand the fact that mentally ill people in Japanese society experience an enormous amount of stigma, discrimination and alienation, more than their counterparts in American society. Members participate in the group because they can share common concerns, experiences, needs and aims. Thus, empowering members in such a group has a dual focus: the individuals and the group as a whole. These are two inseparable entities, and the worker's attention should be directed to the point at which the two systems converge and interact with each other. It is important to empower not only individuals and a group as a whole but also families and significant others who equally share the pain of having a relative who suffers from a mental illness.

Nevertheless, goals for empowerment should be operationalized so that all group members and significant others understand, share and identify with the goals. Some goals for empowerment should be specific and skill related, such as learning to manage their internalized as well as externalized negative emotions of anger, resentment, guilt and hopelessness toward the self, family members, neighbours etc. Other goals should include learning to develop interpersonal skills for relationship, negotiation, compromise, assertion, confrontation and caring; learning to develop knowledge about the good use of community resources; and, most of all, learning to use and expand the external social support system by applying skills for pressure, negotiation, judgment and alliance. Thus, the initial goal for empowerment is to develop a system of mutual help within the group where participants can experience, learn and enhance their coping abilities, problem solving and social skills through a process of interpersonal transactions. In other words, the worker strives to make the group a reservoir of power resources where individual participants get as well as give help to each other.

EMPOWERMENT AS PROCESS

We will highlight a process of empowering members and the group as a whole, examining the unique characteristics of Japanese groups as well as identifying barriers confronting the group worker and members in the process of achieving the goals.

The literature in group work consistently tells us that the prerequisite for the development of group influence on the members is group cohesion, or the development of the feelings of group identity referred to as "we feelings." Without becoming a cohesive entity, there is little hope for any group to be influential to its members as well as other systems. Hartford (1972) states that group cohesion "creates norms of expected behavior, develops organization of the relationships between and among the members, it takes on meaning for the participants which has influence and control over them both within and outside of the group" (p.261).

A process of developing group cohesion in an empowerment group has been described by Gutiérrez (1995) as follows:

1. Group identification includes identifying areas of common experience and concern, a preference for one's own group culture and norms and

the development of feelings of shared fate; group membership becomes a central aspect of one's self-concept.

2. Group consciousness involves understanding the differential status and power of groups in society. For members of oppressed groups, this leads to feelings of relative deprivation, power discontent and a tendency to blame the system for problems related to group membership. This understanding can draw connections between personal problems and social structure.

3. Self-efficacy and collective efficacy refer to beliefs that one is capable of effecting desired changes in one's life. Gutiérrez's (1995) study with Latinos in the US suggested that group discussion and problem solving can contribute to the development of a Latino ethnic consciousness. Furthermore, an ethnic consciousness can affect one's thinking about specific problems and strategies for change. She concluded that "participants high in ethnic consciousness were more likely to attribute problems of Latinos to social and structural factors and to suggest collective solutions to individual problems" (p. 235).

We have observed some differences between Japanese and American groups in the process of achieving group cohesion. In a group of Americans, from the beginning, a great deal of exchange of member's personal experiences usually takes place, though their approaches to each other are cautious and tentative. In contrast, any observer of Japanese groups will be struck by members' orderliness, reservation, quietness and the absence of conversations among strangers. All members' attention is focused on the leader/worker who is expected to give directions to the members. However, whether in American or Japanese groups, the group worker's focal activity should be creating a group climate in which the members' ability to influence each other can be greatly enhanced. Mutual attraction based on shared experiences, needs and goals serves as the driving force for group cohesion. Our experiences with both American and Japanese groups tell us that, despite an initial appearance of a freer and more open exchange among the participants, perhaps because of the individuality of each participant, the American group usually requires a longer time than the Japanese group to develop cohesion. On the other hand, with Japanese groups, their initial acquiescent, cautious, polite, stiff and non-interactive behaviours will change quickly once they get a message from the worker/leader that it is all right for them to talk, debate and interact freely with other members in the group. Members' adherence to one of the important Japanese values, doing and working together in harmony with fellow human beings, seems to work in favour of the development of group cohesion, as the members strive to achieve goals for the benefit of all the participants.

Berman-Rossi (1992) states that development of the group as a whole is predicated upon the character of two internal group processes, that of member to authority and member to member. What is implied here is that unless the member to authority (represented by the group worker/leader) relationship can be resolved in group process, one can not expect the group to become an empowered, autonomous mutual aid group. In working with any type of Japanese group, the resolution of the relationship of member to authority is one of the most challenging issues facing the group worker and the members alike. As both worker and members have been accustomed to living in a society in which individual conformity to collective wills, subordination to authority and harmony with peers are a constantly reinforced norm, it is extremely difficult to break away from this type of interpersonal relationship.

Respect for authority or over-dependence on superiors is a deeply imbedded characteristic of the Japanese personality. For instance, Takeo Doi (1981), a scholar and psychiatrist, has introduced the concept of *amae*, a uniquely Japanese element in interpersonal relationships, to explain this characteristic. The Japanese term *amae* refers initially to the feelings that all normal infants at the breast harbour toward the mother—dependence, the desire to be passively loved, the unwillingness to be separated from the warm mother-child circle and cast into a world of objective "reality." Although *amae*, dependence and indulgence, is universally experienced by human beings, Doi (1981) believes that to the Japanese these feelings are somehow prolonged into and diffused throughout their adult life, so that they come to shape, to a far greater extent than in adults in the west, their whole attitude to other people and to reality.

Our contention is that unless the group can satisfactorily solve this issue of dependency on the authority figure, it is not easy to achieve the goals of empowerment, such as the development of autonomy, independent thinking, creativity and consciousness-raising. Resolution of the members' authority and power theme with the worker/leader is a key factor for the successful achievement of empowerment goals.

Social group work offers the concept of group development to explain the growth process groups experience over time. For example, Garland, Jones and Kolodney (1973) defined stages of group development as : 1) pre-affiliation, 2) power and control, 3) intimacy, 4) differentiation, and 5) separation. This is known as the life cycle model (Berman-Rossi, 1992). Just like a human life, in order for a group to mature it goes through varying developmental stages from a beginning stage to a termination stage. Just as a human being, a group (members) experiences pain, turbulence, joy and conflict in each stage of its development. Unless group members as a whole overcome inherent problems in each stage, the group can not be expected to reach its maturity. Within the life cycle model, stage 2 is known as power and control. This refers to power and control issues among members, i.e., status, ranking, the development of norms and role determination; included in this stage is the authority relationship between the worker and the members. The literature in group work informs us that members must reconcile the power and authority of the worker, in some kind of significant way, before they can fully develop their relationships with each other.

The group worker's strategies should be directed away from a dependent, paternalistic relationship between worker and members and directed towards a partnership relationship through which the group could be strengthened to increasingly command its own fate. This strategy itself would influence the resolution of the authority issue. The definition of the worker's role would become inextricably tied to understanding the group experience and the ways in which members contributed to each other. The concept of mutual aid holds the key to resolving the authority issue. Furthermore, the overall focus should be on the strengths of members rather than on their deficiencies or problems. In other words, members must be seen in the light of their capacities, talents, competencies, possibilities, visions, values and hopes (Saleebey, 1996). The strengths approach (Saleebey, 1996) calls for "an accounting of what people know and what they can do" and "requires composing a roster of resources existing within and around the individual, family, or community" (p.297). As members experience a new type of relationship with authority and power in the group process based on their strengths, they begin to develop collective consciousness, cohesion and group solidarity as well as heightened autonomy, self-identity, self-esteem, competence and self-efficiency. To this end, the worker enables members to develop, experience and utilize a variety of self-initiated and self-directed activities, such as arts and crafts, games, music, role-plays, journal and poetry writing, stress management exercise and sports, besides the usual talking-out approach in a group.

CONCLUSION

In borrowing some ideas from Zander's (1983) observations, first we will illustrate the differences by summarizing the qualities of Japanese groups and interpersonal relationships and by presenting the qualities of American interpersonal relationships and groups in comparison (Hirayama and Hirayama, 1986a).

Japan	United States
1. Unspoken mutual trust is more important than verbally agreed contract.	1. Verbally expressed contractual agreement is more important than nonverbal trust.
2. Group members work hard for the group, not for individuals.	2. People strive for their own success, not the group's success.
3. Meeting social obligations towards colleagues and superiors is most important.	3. Affirming and satisfying one's personal rights is most important.
4. Members cooperate with associates and help them.	4. Members strive to do better than their associates.
5. Persons in one's social environment bear responsibility for one's acts.	5. Individuals are solely responsible for their own behaviour.
6. Members should not embarrass or hurt others, even if they must conceal their feelings to do so.	6. Candidness or assertion about one's situation is most important, so it does not matter if frank comments hurt another's feelings.
7. Members' self-esteem and prestige are closely related to the group's image and prestige.	7. Members use the group as a context for the realization of their own goals and achievement.

In conclusion, in view of its particular cultural characteristics described above, an emphasis on groupness in Japan and an emphasis on individuality in the US, we submit that a group worker's primary focus in Japan should be on empowering members in group process to enhance their autonomy, individuality, self-affirmation and individual creativity by resolving worker-member (superior-subordinate) relationships while simultaneously gaining and using the collective power of the members for the benefit of both individual members and the group as a whole. Secondly, focus should be on strengthening members' connectedness and group solidarity with other social systems which have the same objectives. On the other hand, American group workers should primarily strive to empower members to enhance their connectedness to one another and to promote more interdependence by helping group members to relinquish some of their self-reliance and independence by subjugating themselves to the need of the group or the community as a whole.

REFERENCES

Barr, A. (1995). Empowering communities beyond fashionable rhetoric? Some reflections on Scottish experience. *Community Development Journal*, 30(2), 121-132.

Berman-Rossi, T. (1992). Empowering groups through understanding stages of group development. *Social Work with Groups*, 15(2/3), 239-256.

Breton, M. (1992). Liberation theology, group work, and the right of the poor and oppressed to participate in the life of the community. *Social Work with Groups*, 15(2/3), 257-270.

Browne, C. (1995). Empowerment in social work practice with older women. *Social Work*, 40(3), 358-364.

Cowger, C.D. (1994). Assessing client strengths: Clinical assessment for client empowerment. *Social Work*, 39(3), 262-269.

Doi, T. (1981). *The anatomy of dependence.* Tokyo: Kodansha International, 2nd edition.

Ejigiri, D. (1996). Race in housing and community empowerment: A critical examination. *Community Development Journal*, 31(1), 32-43.

Garland, J., Jones, H. and Kolodney, R. (1973). A model for stages of development in social work groups. In S. Bernstein (Ed.), *Explorations in group work: Essays in theory and practice.* Boston: Boston University School of Social Work.

Gitterman, A. (1979). Group work content in an integrated method curriculum. In S. Abels and P. Abels (Eds.), *Social work with groups* (pp. 66-81). Proceedings of Symposium.

Gutiérrez, L. (1990). Working with women of colour. *Social Work*, 35, 149-154.

Gutiérrez, E. L. (1995). Understanding the empowerment process: Does consciousness make a difference? *Social Work Research*, 19(4), 229-237.

Hartford, M. (1972). *Groups in social work.* New York: Columbia University Press.

Hirayama, H. and Cetingok, M. (1988). Empowerment: A social work approach for Asian immigrants and refugees. *Social Casework, The Journal of Contemporary Social Work*, 69(1), 41-47.

Hirayama, H. and Hirayama, K. (1986a). Individuality vs. group identity: A comparison between Japan and the United States. *Journal of International and Comparative Social Welfare*, II(1/2), 11-21.

Hirayama, H. and Hirayama, K. (1986b). Empowerment through group participation: Process and goal. In M. Parnes (Ed.), *Innovations in social group work: Feedback from practice to theory, selected proceedings of the 5th Symposium on Social Work with Groups* (pp. 119-131). New York: The Haworth Press.

Hirayama, H. and Hirayama, K. (1995). Use of the self in group work: Power and empowerment. In M. Feit et al. (Eds.), *Capturing the power of diversity, selected proceedings of the 13th Symposium of Social Work with Groups* (pp. 127-138). New York: The Haworth Press.

Kam, P. K. (1996). Empowering elderly people: A community work approach. *Community Development Journal*, 31(3), 230-240.

Kojien. (Ed.). (1991). *Nishimura, I.* Tokyo: Iwanami, 4th edition.

Lee, J. (1994). *The empowerment approach to social work practice.* New York: Columbia University Press.

Lowy, L. (1982). Social group work with vulnerable older persons: Theoretical perspective. *Social Work with Groups*, 5, 21-32.

Mandell, B. and Schram, B. (1985). *Human services: Introduction and intervention.* New York: John Wiley and Sons.

May, R. (1972). *Power and innocence.* New York: W. W. Norton.

McDermott, C. I. (1989). Empowering elderly nursing home residents: The resident's rights campaign. *Social Work*, 34, 155 -157.

Parsons, R. and Schram, B. (1989). Family mediation in elder caregiving decisions: An empowerment intervention. *Social Work*, 34, 122-126.

Pernell, R. (1986). Empowerment and social group. In M. Parnes (Ed.), *Innovations in social group work: Feedback from practice to theory, selected proceedings of the 5th Symposium of Social Work with Groups* (pp.107-118). New York: The Haworth Press.

Pinderhughes, E. (1983). Empowerment for our clients and for ourselves. *Social Casework*, 64, 331-338.

Pinderhughes, E. (1995). Empowering diverse populations: Family practice in the 21st century. *Families in Society*, 76(3), 131-146.

Saleebey, D. (1996). The strengths perspective in social work practice: Extensions and cautions. *Social Work*, 41(3), 296-305.

Schuftan, C. (1996). The community development dilemma: What is really empowering? *Community Development Journal*, 31(3), 260-264.

Solomon, B. (1976). *Black empowerment: Social work in oppressed communities.* New York: Columbia University Press.

Webster's ninth new collegiate dictionary. (1991). Springfield, MA: Merriam-Webster.

Weil, M. 0. (1996). Community building: Building community practice. *Social Work*, 41(5), 481-499.

Zander, A. (1983). The value of belonging to a group in Japan. *Small Group Behavior*, 14(11), 3-14.

Chapter 15

TOWARDS AN EMPOWERING SOCIAL WORK PRACTICE: LEARNING FROM SERVICE USERS AND THEIR MOVEMENTS

Peter Beresford
Department of Social Work
Brunel University, London

The focus of this discussion is empowerment and professional practice. As quickly becomes clear in social work and social care, empowerment goes far beyond professional practice. Some service users and their organizations reject the view that professional practice has any relevance to their empowerment. But professional practice is likely to continue to have a role to play in empowerment, for better or worse, and service users' organizations in the UK, North America and elsewhere are themselves increasingly becoming involved in both professional practice and service provision, as well as critiquing them. Most discussions about professional practice and empowerment have come from a professional perspective. This discussion is offered from a service user's perspective and aims to address both service provider and user discourses on empowerment. It is particularly concerned with the role of professional practice in empowerment; the nature of an empowering practice and the role of service users in it.

Empowerment is an inherently political idea in which issues of power, the ownership of power, inequalities of power and the acquisition and redistribution of power are central. This is highlighted by the competing concerns and agendas of people involved in social care as service providers and service users. It is therefore important to locate a discussion of empowerment and practice politically. The natural starting point for this, writing from a service user's perspective, is the movements of disabled people, survivors and others in receipt of social care services. Fiona Williams, the UK social policy academic, has commented on the way in which the disabled people's and social care service users' movements "have grasped the administrative categories (or subject positions) imposed upon them by policy makers, administrators and practitioners and translated these into political identities and new subjectivities" (Williams, 1996, p. 75).

It is these political identities and the movements associated with them that may offer the most helpful route to an understanding of empowerment and empowering practice from service users' perspectives. In order to do this, the present discussion focuses particularly on the UK psychiatric system survivors' movement in which the author is actively involved.

THE EMERGENCE OF THE MOVEMENTS

In recent years, movements of disabled people, psychiatric survivors, older people, people with learning difficulties and other groups of health and welfare services have emerged in the UK, North America, Europe and the Southern hemisphere. There are now local, regional, national, European and worldwide organizations democratically constituted and controlled by these groups. The UK umbrella organization of disabled people is the British Council of Disabled People (BCODP), which is a founder member of Disabled People's International. There are a number of national organizations of mental health service users in the UK, including the United Kingdom Advocacy Network, MINDLink, Survivors Speak Out, the Scottish Users Network, Afro-Caribbean Users' Forum and the Hearing Voices Network. These movements and organizations have grown in numbers, confidence and power since their origins in the 1970s.

There are differences as well as similarities between these movements. Some survivors include themselves as disabled, while others reject this identity because they see their experience and perceptions as different rather than as an impairment (McNamara, 1996; Plumb, 1994). There are also overlaps between people involved in the different movements. For example, some disabled people are also survivors and some survivors are disabled. There has also been a growing pattern of collaboration and joint activity between the two movements.

The movements have been much more than a reaction to welfare, but so far outside attention has mainly focused on the challenge they make to traditional public policy and ideology, particularly in health and welfare. The service system has also tended to conceive of them in its own terms as social care or service users' organizations and movements. This has been reinforced by the parallel shift to the market in welfare with a new emphasis on consumerism and the consumer and associated ideas of user involvement and user-centred services (Means and Smith, 1994). But the movements have generally not perceived themselves in this way. Instead one of their key objectives has been to transcend the conceptualization of their constituencies in narrow welfare terms.

They have conceived of themselves more broadly in political terms. Thus while they have important things to say about social care and welfare and have made a major impact on both, this arises from their broader political agendas and preoccupations. This is particularly true of the disabled people's movement, which of all these movements is perhaps the one which is most explicitly political (Campbell and Oliver, 1996; Oliver and Barnes, 1998). Its emphasis is on disabled people's civil rights and citizenship rather than welfare needs. The movements also represent a challenge to traditional politics and embody a new politics of their own. They have insights to offer about both old and new politics (Beresford, 1999). Colin Barnes, the disability researcher and activist, has described the UK disabled people's movement as "one of the most potentially potent political forces in contemporary British society" (Colin Barnes, foreword to Campbell and Oliver, 1996, p ix). The UK disabled people's and survivors' movements incorporate reformist as well as revolutionary politics. They are involved "in the formal political system ... and the promotion of other kinds of political activity" (Campbell and Oliver, 1996, p. 179).

NEW POLITICAL MOVEMENTS

The movements of disabled people and survivors are much more than collections of individuals, groups and organizations. Each has is own history, goals, values, culture, analysis and ways of doing things. As Jane Campbell of the British Council of Disabled People has said:

> Disabled people's organisations have clear objectives and their own philosophy. There is now a disabled people's culture and disability arts. The movement is multi-faceted. There is direct action campaigning on the street. There is letter writing and political work in parliament. There is intellectual work and arts. The movement involves all of these and people cross over. People who write the books are also on the picket line. This has given us a much fuller representation because we have a much more holistic approach and understanding. (Beresford and Campbell, 1994, p. 321)

The same is true of the psychiatric survivors' movement. In the 1960s and early 1970s, there were important challenges to the medicalization of distress, like anti-psychiatry, in which some mental health service users were involved. But these were relatively narrowly based, dominated by professionals and certainly not led by survivors themselves. In a short space of time, however, survivors have developed their own organizations, networks, knowledge and alternatives.

In the US, this is something which some survivors have done very much *On Our Own*, the title of a key text by Judi Chamberlin, one of the US movement's leaders (Chamberlin, 1988). In the UK, the movement grew with the involvement and help of allies and supporters who were not survivors themselves. One consequence of this was that the movement was more closely bound up with the service system and efforts to reform it. Louise Pembroke, then secretary of Survivors Speak Out, spoke of some of the dilemmas and contradictions that this posed:

> I want to make things better for people in the psychiatric system, but I also want to demolish it. There are dangers in collaboration, but there are positive things too, like patients' councils where we can at least help people gain their voice before leaving the bin. I feel one of the dangers with collaboration is that we can change the icing on the cake but we don't change the cake. To get separatist initiatives going we need money. We need to channel our energies more to fighting for that money. (quoted in Croft and Beresford, 1991, p. 72)

In the UK, there is now an increasing interest among survivors in developing their own alternatives. These include alternative ideas, theories, research, structures, therapies, knowledge, nutrition and media (Lindow, 1994; Read, 1996; Survivors Speak Out, 1996; Beresford and Wallcraft, 1997; Wallcraft, 1998). As Anne Plumb says, survivors see themselves variously as survivors of the psychiatric system, of social structures and institutions and of cultural practices and values (Plumb, 1994). Peter Campbell, a founding member of Survivors Speak Out, wrote:

> One great challenge for survivors is the establishment of our own identities. We are not only survivors of a mental health system that regularly fails to meet our wants and

needs. We are also survivors of social attitudes and practices that exclude us and discount our experience.... Survivors are not incompetent. Nor are we devoid of insight. Many of the problems we share with other disadvantaged minorities— unemployment, poverty, isolation—are the results of discrimination rather than incapacity.(Campbell, foreword to Bangay, Bidder and Porter, 1992, p. 6)

Members of the survivors and disabled people's movements make connections and identify with other movements like the women's, black people's, gay men's and lesbians' movements. They see themselves as sharing a number of key characteristics with them. They:

- "come out" about and take a pride in who they are and the validity of their experience and understanding;
- value their history and culture;
- experience social oppression; and
- frame their activities in political terms.

There has been some discussion among disabled commentators about whether the disabled people's movement is a liberation or new social movement (Campbell and Oliver, 1996, pp. 176-8) While there is no agreement about this, what is not in doubt among activist survivors and disabled people is that both have now established their own movements. The development of these movements clearly relates to the desire of survivors and disabled people to develop their own identities, collectivities and agendas as a basis for securing their own human and civil rights. But it also linked with their relation with existing politics and services and their inability to achieve their personal and collective objectives within them.

A POLITICS OF PARTICIPATION

The lives of survivors and disabled people have long been shaped and dominated by economic, social, cultural and political exclusion. They have both been kept apart in welfare institutions and service systems and restricted to the margins of society by discrimination, poverty and stigma. (Barnes, 1991; Read and Baker, 1996) This exclusion has defined their experience and identity. It helps explains the central priority which their movements give to participation. Participation is at the heart of both their objectives and their process. While neither movement claims to involve the mass of its constituency, both seek to involve members as fully as possible. There is a commitment to "mass action rather than elite action" (Shakespeare, 1993, p. 254); to participatory rather than representative democracy. "They are part of the underlying struggle for genuinely participatory democracy, social equality and justice" (Oliver, 1990, p. 13). Outside these movements, interest in direct democracy is currently focused on the role of new technology (Budge, 1996) and more consensual activities (Goodman, 1996). In the UK, there is also a new government-led interest in top-down initiatives for constitutional reform, democratization, devolution and subsidiarity. The survivors' and disabled people's movements instead stress bottom-up change based on self-advocacy; people acting and speaking on their own behalf. Great value is attached to each individual articulating their own experience, feelings and demands, challenging a long history of other people speaking for them. This commitment to participation has many expressions, such as those described below.

Inclusion

There has also been a concern to involve people on equal terms and to acknowledge diversity; for example, to include people who communicate differently: non-verbally, in deaf sign language, using braille and audio-tape and in minority ethnic languages. There is a strong sense in both the UK survivors' and disabled people's movements that the full and equal involvement of black people, women, older people and gay men and lesbians remains an objective rather than an achievement, but there is growing public debate and determination to make it possible (Morris, 1996a; Campbell and Oliver, 1996, pp. 132-8; Campbell, 1996, p. 223).

Self-organization

Another expression of the commitment of these movements to participation is their emphasis on the idea of self-organization. By this, survivors and disabled people mean establishing independent organizations and initiatives which they themselves control and which are democratically constituted. They have also developed different forms of action and organization. The disabled people's movement has pioneered new forms of direct action which are accessible to disabled people. These protests, demonstrations, boycotts and sit-downs have been effective and empowering and they have challenged stereotypes (Campbell and Oliver, 1996, pp. 152-6). Because survivors may have times when they feel vulnerable or stressed, their organizations have developed forms of working and collective action sympathetic to their participation; for example, providing quiet rooms and time-out at meetings, supporters for speakers and representatives; ground rules, safety and facilitation to help people who find being in groups or talking in public difficult; and running social as well as business meetings. Self-organization also extends to disabled people and survivors developing their own arts, culture, media, theories, knowledge and discussions.

Reuniting the Self and Society

This relates to a broader issue. The disabled people's and survivors' movements have recognized that support is a prerequisite for participation. There is a conscious linking of personal support and self-help with political change. Instead of seeing the two as polarized against each other, with mutual aid associated with the status quo and collective action with political change, as has often traditionally been the case, there is an appreciation that the two are inextricable. This connection is made in a variety ways. As Peter Campbell says:

> While user/survivor action is often significantly different from mainstream self-help work because of its concentration on social, structural and political change rather than individual change, every action group will spend energy and time supporting members through distress. Self-help principles lie close to the heart of most user/survivor enterprises. The public acceptance of the value of self-help, the valid therapeutic contribution of the non-expert, and the centrality of personal experience as a powerful tool for change have helped create a climate in which it is increasingly possible to tolerate and respect the positive activity of madpersons. (Campbell, 1996, p. 220-1)

This desire to reunite support and action has many expressions in the politics of these movements. It is reflected in their programs. In the disabled people's movement this is embodied in the concern to change both the individual disabled person's life and the broader society. The aim of the movement is "to promote change; to improve the quality of our lives and promote our full inclusion in society" (Campbell and Oliver, 1996, p. 22). At the core of this goal lies the idea of independent living. This turns on its head the political right's interpretation of independence as standing on your own two feet. Instead it means ensuring disabled people appropriate and adequate support and personal assistance to have the same rights, choices and opportunities as non-disabled people. It rejects the traditional welfare approach imposed on disabled people and survivors of restricting them to a separate segregating service system and demands instead a social and political structure which enables them to contribute and participate culturally and socially—in relationships and work. It was "the idea of independent living which gave a focus to the struggles of disabled people to organise themselves" (Oliver, 1996, p. 155). The concept "insists that biology is not destiny. Impairment does not necessarily create dependence and a poor quality of life, rather it is lack of control over the physical help needed which takes away people's independence" (Morris, 1996a, p. 10).

The movements explicitly and determinedly connect the personal and the political. They highlight both agency and structure; the psychological and the social. Thus while the disabled people's movement has emphasized the structural relations of disability, there is an increasing concern, particularly among disabled women, not to lose sight of personal impairment and the feelings, emotions and perceptions associated with it (Morris, 1996a, pp. 13-14; Crow, 1996).

Recently there has been some mainstream interest, as part of broader political realignments, in connecting politics and psychoanalysis. This is seen as offering a new route to understanding and reforming the interplay between personal and political forces (Samuels, 1993). Many survivors, however, have serious reservations about the so-called talking treatments, identifying their history of abuse, exclusion and Eurocentrism (Croft and Beresford, 1994). Their movement, however, offers an alternative route to reuniting the personal and political. As Peter Campbell says:

> For many of us, a central feature of our lives has been the way ... our perceptions, thoughts, ideas and feelings have been taken from us and possessed, processed, interpreted and described by others who have limited sympathy with who we are or who we might become.... The standard response to our distress sets us up beyond society and sets us at odds within ourselves. The challenge we face is to repossess our experience and to reclaim our dignity and value as citizens.... But we need not deny our distress to achieve acceptance. The boundaries of approved experience are narrow enough already. Through poetry and music, visual

arts, writing and action we must fight for a broader understanding, a re-evaluation of individual experience. (Campbell, foreword to Bangay, Bidder and Porter, 1992, p. 6)

Survivors have particular reasons to connect the personal and the political. Their experience is of psychiatry and broader social structures which devalue, reject and control their experience, emotions, perceptions and interior world. The medicalization of their madness and distress and the chemical and mechanical "treatments" they receive are frequently both physically and psychically destructive and sometimes lead to people's deaths. In the UK, distress is increasingly presented in dominant racialized images of dangerous, threatening people, particularly black young men, when the reality is a psychiatric system through which vulnerable women are particularly likely to pass and where people's rights are not just ignored, but routinely restricted, without adequate safeguards or accountability.

The disabled people's and survivors' movements are redefining and reclaiming their experience. The disabled people's movement has redefined disability (Hasler, 1993) and enabled disabled people to rethink themselves, (French, 1994) "transforming the individual and collective consciousness" of disabled people (Campbell and Oliver, 1996, p. 123). Survivors are increasingly challenging the medicalization of their distress and perceptions and rejecting psychiatry's preoccupation with causation and its denial of their feelings and legitimacy. They are beginning to rethink madness and distress. For example, hearing voices, which has long been treated as a defining sign and symptom of madness and mental illness, is now being reconceived in non-medical terms. Survivors and their allies are listening to, trying to make sense of and accepting voices (Romme and Esculer, 1993).

The survivors' movement is not only concerned with the particular situation of mental health service users but also with the broader impact of state, society and psychiatry on people's mental, emotional and spiritual well-being. It does not see madness and distress as confined to a deviant group, distinct from the rest of us, but as an inherent part of the human condition. Similarly, "the politics of disablement is about far more than disabled people" (Barnes, foreword, Campbell and Oliver, 1996, p. xii). Both movements are concerned with changing more than the position of a particular group in society. They challenge all forms of social oppression and the attacks state and society make on our bodies and our selves.

COMPETING EMPOWERMENT DISCOURSES

The concern of the survivors' and disabled people's movements in the personal and political, the psychological and the social and their interrelations, is reflected in the centrality of the idea of empowerment to them and their conceptualization of it to encompass the positive redistribution of both personal and political power. It is the idea of empowerment and the competing debates about it to which I want to turn next. As Clare Evans and Mike Fisher argue in chapter 19, empowerment in social work and social care has largely been defined by professionals. Because of this, it is important to examine both service provider and service user discussions of empowerment.

Many people involved in disabled people's, survivors' and service users' organizations use the term without explicit definition because they intuitively know what it means for them and there are shared meanings and understandings of it among them. For them it means challenging the disempowerment and discrimination they face, not being subject to service providers' arbitrary control, achieving their rights and being able to live their lives like other people. The idea grows out of both negative and positive experience. The definition of empowerment on which I am basing this discussion follows from this and is similar to that employed by Evans and Fisher:

> Making it possible for people to exercise power and have more control over their lives. That means having a greater voice in institutions, agencies and situations which affect them. It also means being able to share power or exercise power over someone else as well as them exercising it over you. (Beresford and Croft, 1993, p. 50)

Peter Campbell, a founding member of Survivors Speak Out, says: "What people are looking for with empowerment is a greater degree of control and say in what goes in in their lives; to have greater freedom and autonomy in services and much widely. It's an objective" (Campbell, 1994).

Different commentators from the movements identify different routes to empowerment. Mike Oliver argues that personal empowerment in the disabled people's movement has come from people's involvement in collective action (Oliver, 1996, pp.147-9). Terry Simpson, a survivor, on the other hand, has written about how his involvement in a support group empowered him to take action to change the mental health system (Simpson, 1996). But there is a shared emphasis on transforming people's lives and capacities. The aim of empowerment is liberation. Thus the emphasis in service users' discourse on empowerment is on people's lives and enhancing their rights, choices and opportunities. Their approach to empowerment is concerned with changing their position in society. It does not ignore issues of personal empowerment, but these are framed in terms of ensuring that people have the support, skills and personal resources they need for self-organization and participation to achieve broader change.

There has been an explosion of interest in the idea of empowerment in social work and social care in recent years (Braye and Preston-Shoot, 1995; Parsloe, 1996). The concept is now deeply ingrained in professional vocabulary, discussion and practice. Professional interest in the concept has developed in the UK in response to the new demands of the consumerist care market. It has offered social care professions facing uncertainty and insecurity new arguments for their own autonomy and consolidation by emphasizing the prior need for their empowerment if they are to empower service users (Stevenson and Parsloe, 1993). It is also now being embraced enthusiastically as providing a new paradigm for practice, giving it new vitality, legitimacy and credibility (Adams, 1996). Professional approaches to empowerment have been particularly concerned with personal empowerment; people taking increased responsibility for managing their lives, relationships and circumstances, to live in conformity with prevailing values and expectations and to change in accordance with professionally set goals and norms. Outside commentators have pointed to the regulatory as well as liberatory potential of such professional approaches to empowerment (Baistow, 1995).

While there are some links and overlaps between them, two competing discourses on empowerment emerge in social work and social services. These are the discourses of service users and service providers; one primarily concerned with liberation, the other more closely tied to the service system and professional objectives. The two discourses are different in form as well as focus and goals (Beresford and Croft, 1995). There are also significant differences in power and credibility between the two. The dominant discourse in social work continues to be the professional one. I have discussed elsewhere ways in which existing inequalities between the two discourses can be addressed and challenged. These include:

- the redistribution of resources, diverting more resources for analysis, dissemination, exchange and development to user-controlled initiatives;
- a new emphasis on constructive partnerships—between service provider and service user organizations;
- a changed approach to research, prioritizing emancipatory and user-controlled approaches to research;

- a twin-track approach to involvement and empowerment, based on supporting user-controlled initiatives for empowerment as well as professional agency-led ones;
- a greater emphasis on broadbased involvement, based on providing both access and support for participation to ensure fully inclusive involvement which challenges discrimination on the basis of age, race, class, gender, disability and sexual identity;
- highlighting the personal; prioritizing the personal concerns of service users to ensure their empowerment, rather than service system related issues, by humanizing schemes for participation and empowerment. (Beresford and Croft, 1995, pp. 68-71)

Disabled people's, survivors' and social care service users' organizations continue to be suspicious of professional claims and aspirations over empowerment. They have not only learned to be wary of the ambiguities of professional practice—its concern to regulate as well as to support—but they don't necessarily see it as having any role to play in their empowerment at all. There are, however, beginning to be some encouraging signs for the future. For example, helpful materials are beginning to be produced bringing together professional and service user perspectives (for example, Humphries, 1996; Ramcharan, Roberts, Grant and Borland, 1997).

REFOCUSING ON PRACTICE

There is also another development which may be helpful. This is the increasing focus on professional practice in service provider discussions of user involvement and empowerment, which interest in empowerment has encouraged. It is a development that may bring service provider and user agendas closer together.

Earlier I suggested that participation in social work and social services had primarily been constructed in terms of services as user involvement. In the UK, most of the state sponsored initiatives for involvement have been concerned with service users' participation in the planning and management of social services and health policy and provision. This has clearly been linked with the service system's own understandable interest in itself and broader concerns to improve its operation. However, research suggests that the gains from this for service users and their organizations have been limited (Bewley and Glendinning, 1994). It has involved great effort for very little change.

Fiona Williams has developed a typology which is helpful here. She distinguishes between three positions on difference and diversity in social welfare: the individualist, which has "emerged from the New Right's development of the mixed economy of welfare;" the managerialist, linked with the restructuring of health and social care; and the anti-discriminatory associated with the new social movements (Williams, 1996, p. 73). The first two positions, individualist and managerialist, reflect the concern with the individual's involvement in the service system. Disabled people's and service users' organizations, as we have seen, as part of new social movements, on the other hand, have been less concerned with the service system than with making direct changes in their members' lives. This reflects their understanding of and concern with participation in both personal and political terms. This has resulted in an increasing focus and emphasis among them on ensuring that service users have more say in and control over the individual support and practice which they receive.

This approach to involvement, which shows more signs of success than that tied to the organization and management of social services, links with two key concerns of the disabled people's, survivors' and other social care service users' movements. As we have seen, the first of these is their emphasis on the centrality of collective action as the basis for individual change. The second is their explicit linking of self-help and mutual support with working for political and social change.

The focus of the movements on people's lives, rather than the service system, means that they can avoid social services' own increasing preoccupation with organizational structure and managerialism. Their focus on both people's citizenship and their self-defined needs also offers the prospect, as Fiona Williams suggests, of combining "particularist interests with universalist values" (Williams, 1992, p. 216).

In the UK, the growing concern of the disabled people's and service users' movements on people's involvement in their individual and personal experience of social work and social services is reflected in two developments. Both have fundamental implications for the future of practice and professional discourse about empowerment. The first of these developments is the increasing focus that the movements are placing on increasing people's control and involvement in social services and social work practice. The second is the creation of direct payments schemes, embodied since 1996 in legislation. Research findings show that direct payments is a feasible, cost-effective policy option which is greatly preferred by service users who have been offered the choice (Oliver and Zarb, 1992; Morris, 1993).

Such schemes, pioneered by the disabled people's movement as a way of making possible independent living, have been interpreted in consumerist terms by UK government, which now permits some disabled people, including some survivors and some people with learning difficulties, as individual consumers to purchase services directly as they choose, instead of as previously with the UK community care reforms, with the local authority acting as purchaser and care managers acting as assessors. The disabled people's movement, however, has developed a model for direct payments which goes far beyond consumerism. It is based on self-definition of need rather than professional assessment and on disabled people's organizations providing support, expertise, training and independent information and advocacy to enable service users to set up and run their own schemes for independent living.

PROFESSIONAL PRACTICE AND EMPOWERMENT

At least three positions can be identified regarding the relation of professional practice and practitioners to people's empowerment. These can be summed up as:

- the primacy of professional practice in empowerment—service users need professionals to be empowered;
- service users' sole capacity to empower themselves: "only we can empower ourselves—power can't be given away; you can't empower us, but you should stop *disempowering* us;"
- the role of professional practice in supporting people to empower themselves; practitioners can offer support, skills and access to resources to support people's efforts to empower themselves.

The first of these positions is clearly associated with professional discourse on empowerment; the other two with service users' discourses. This discussion is most closely linked with the third position, but individuals and groups have various affiliations and these do not only depend on whether they come from a service provider or user perspective.

There are both objective and subjective components to empowerment. It is concerned with increasing the actual power people have and their personal capacity to use it. In social care, empowerment may help us to:

- regain control in a difficult time in our lives;
- reinforce our sense of self-worth;
- gain more power as members of a group facing oppression and discrimination;

- keep control of our lives when services intervene in them;
- gain power after being disempowered (for example, through being institutionalized or being infantilized as an adult);
- take greater control over our lives (in relation to others);
- have more control over institutions and agencies which affect our lives;
- safeguard our civil and human rights.

COMPONENTS OF EMPOWERING PRACTICE

Committing social care practice to empowerment demands much more than new language, mission statements and rationales for working. It requires fundamental changes in its governance, form, process and objectives. This includes prioritizing:

- user-led training and the systematic and the central involvement of service users in professional education and training (Beresford, 1994);
- service users' equal access and opportunities as social care practitioners (Beresford and Croft, 1993);
- user-led standard setting and definition of outcomes in practice (Harding and Beresford, 1996; Turner, 1997; Beresford, Croft, Evans and Harding, 1997; Turner, 1998);
- a participatory approach to care management, including self-definition of needs and design of support systems (Leader, 1995);
- user-led monitoring and evaluation of social care practice;
- user involvement in the registration and regulation of practitioners; and
- the central involvement of service users in the purchase of services/ support (Morris, 1996b).

A NEW APPROACH TO PRACTICE

The introduction of direct payments legislation in the UK has fundamental implications for the role and nature of social care practice and provision. The negative response to it of some local authority social services departments sadly in part reflects their recognition of the radical nature of this reform and their reluctance to accept it. The independent living schemes pioneered by disabled people's organizations have shown that it is possible to transform the role, relations and purpose of professional practice. They have redefined the meaning of skills, created new occupational roles and most important transcended traditional power relations in social care and social services. Now the service user is in control of the worker and the service she or he offers them rather than vice versa. The service user may employ the worker rather than being dependent upon them. The significance of this development cannot be overestimated in the continuing context reported by social care service users in the UK of being routinely disempowered by practitioners.

The discussions and developments emerging from UK disabled people's and service users' movements and organizations, of which direct payments/ independent living schemes are just one expression, highlight another crucial shift for practice if it is to be empowering. This is that it is a two-way rather than one-way process. Service users and their organizations challenge the professional assumption, which remains powerful and is still embodied in much professional training, even though it is certainly not internalized by all practitioners, that practitioners are equipped to help and care for others; that they are competent and complete to minister to service users who are 'vulnerable,' 'inadequate' and 'need' their 'help.' Not only does the experience of many service users suggest that this is not the case—that service providers have many limitations and inadequacies of their own, as we all do—but it also inevitably leads to unequal and unhelpful relationships between service providers and recipients based on assumptions of unequal abilities, understanding and judgments.

What is important instead and what is already evident as a hallmark of good practice is that the practitioner is open to learn and to gain skills and understanding from the experience, knowledge, views and ideas of service users. This takes place at individual, collective and structural levels; in individual practice and through the involvement of service users and their organizations in the broader construction of practice. Practice is based on two-way traffic between service providers and users. It is about the growth and development of practitioners, as well as service users, each learning from the other. While I am not suggesting that it is essential to have first-hand experience as a service user to be a practitioner, although this can certainly be helpful, such experience and understanding should be sought, valued and learned from. When learning from service users stops, is when we can expect practice to disempower, wither and die.

Such an approach to practice also gives a new meaning to the empowerment of practitioners. Instead of being based on workers having more status, power and resources, as some conventional commentators have suggested, their empowerment, like that of service users, is based on more equal relations rooted in trust, honesty, reliability and openness; qualities which service users prioritize in professional practice and highlight as empowering (Harding and

Beresford, 1996; Beresford and Trevillion, 1995). While we may have a long way to go before empowering practice is the rule rather than the exception, the efforts of service users, their organizations and progressive practitioners are now beginning to show us all the way.

REFERENCES

Adams, R. (1996). *Social work and empowerment*. Basingstoke: Macmillan.

Baistow, K. (1995). Liberation and regulation: Some paradoxes of empowerment. *Critical Social Policy*, 14 (3), 34-46.

Bangay, F., Bidder, J. and Porter, H. (Eds.). (1992). *Survivors' poetry: From dark to light*. London: Survivors' Press.

Barnes, C. (1991). *Disabled people in Britain and discrimination*. London: Hurst and Company.

Beresford, P. (1994). *Changing the culture, involving service users in social work education* (Paper 32.2). London: Central Council of Education and Training in Social Work.

Beresford, P. (1999). New movements, new politics: Making participation possible. In T. Jordan, and A. Lent (Eds.), *Storming the millennium: The new politics of change*. London: Lawrence and Wishart.

Beresford, P. and Campbell, J. (1994). Disabled people, service users, user involvement and representation. *Disability and Society*, 9(3), 315-325.

Beresford, P. and Croft, S. (1993). *Citizen involvement: A practical guide for change*. Basingstoke: Macmillan.

Beresford, P. and Croft, S. (1995).Whose empowerment? Equalising the competing discourses in community care. In R. Jacks (Ed.), *Empowerment in community care* (pp. 59-73). London: Chapman and Hall.

Beresford, P., Croft, S., Evans, C. and Harding, T. (1997). Quality in personal social services: The developing role of user involvement in the UK. In A. Evers, R. Haverinen, K. Leichsenring and G. Wistow (Eds.), *Developing quality in personal social services: Concepts, cases and comments* (pp. 63-80). Ashgate: Aldershot.

Beresford, P. and Trevillion, S. (1995). *Developing skills for community care: A collaborative approach*. Aldershot: Arena Ashgate.

Beresford, P. and Wallcraft, J. (1997). Psychiatric system survivors and emancipatory research: Issues, overlaps and differences. In C. Barnes and G. Mercer (Eds.), *Doing disability research* (pp. 67-87). Leeds: Disability Research Unit.

Bewley, C. and Glendinning, C. (1994). *Involving disabled people in community care planning*. York: Joseph Rowntree Foundation and Community Care magazine.

Braye, S. and Preston-Shoot, M. (1995). *Empowering practice in social care*. Buckingham: Open University Press.

Budge, I. (1996). *The new challenge of direct democracy*. Cambridge: Polity Press.

Campbell, P. (1994). *A survivor's perspective on mental health* (April 24, Lecture). Middlesex: West London Institute Social Work Department.

Campbell, P. (1996). The history of the user movement in the United Kingdom. In T. Heller, J. Reynolds, R. Gomm, R. Muston and S. Pattison, (Eds.), *Mental health matters*. Basingstoke: Macmillan.

Campbell, J. and Oliver, M. (1996). *Disability politics: Understanding our past, changing our future*. London: Routledge.

Chamberlin, J. (1988). *On our own: User controlled alternatives to the mental health system*. London: MIND.

Croft, S. and Beresford, P. (1991). User views, changes. *An International Journal of Psychology and Psychotherapy*, 9(1), 71-72.

Croft, S. and Beresford, P. (1994). User views, changes. *An International Journal of Psychology and Psychotherapy*, 12(3), 229-30.

Crow, L. (1996). Including all our lives: Renewing the social model of disability. In J. Morris (Ed.), *Encounters with strangers: Feminism and disability* (pp. 206-226). London: The Women's Press.

French, S. (Ed.). (1994). *On equal terms: Working with disabled people*. Oxford: Butterworth-Heinemann.

Goodman, S. (1996, November 18). City corporations challenged by people power as east enders seek a share in their future: Citizens of poor London boroughs are taking action to secure a contract on jobs. *Independent*, p. 8.

Harding, T. and Beresford, P. (Eds.). (1996). *The standards we expect: What service users and carers want from social services workers*. London: National Institute for Social Work.

Hasler, F. (1993). Developments in the disabled people's movement. In J. Swain, V. Finkelstein, S. French and M. Oliver (Eds.), *Disabling barriers—enabling environments*. London: Sage.

Humphries, B. (Ed.). (1996). *Critical perspectives on empowerment*. Birmingham: Venture Press.

Leader, A. (1995). *Direct power: A resource pack for people who want to develop their own care plans and support networks*. Brighton: The Community Support Network, Brixton Community Sanctuary.

Lindow, V. (1994). *Self-help alternatives to mental health services*. London: MIND.

McNamara, J. (1996). Out of order: Madness is a feminist and a disability issue. In J. Morris (Ed.), *Encounters with strangers: Feminism and disability* (pp.194-205). London: The Women's Press.

Means, R. and Smith, R. (Eds.). (1994). *Community care: Policy and practice*. Basingstoke: Macmillan.

Morris, J. (1993). *Independent lives: Community care and disabled people*, Basingstoke: Macmillan.

Morris, J. (Ed.). (1996a). *Encounters with strangers: Feminism and disability* (pp.194-205). London: The Women's Press.

Morris, J. (1996b). *Encouraging user involvement in commissioning: A resource for commissioners.* West Yorkshire: Department of Health, National Health Service Executive Community Care Branch.

Oliver, M. (1990). *The politics of disablement.* Basingstoke: Macmillan.

Oliver, M. (1996). *Understanding disability: From theory to practice.* Basingstoke: Macmillan.

Oliver, M. and Barnes, C. (1998). *Disabled people and social policy; From exclusion to inclusion.* London: Longman.

Oliver, M. and Zarb, G. (1992). *Personal assistance schemes in Greenwich: An evaluation.* London: Greenwich Association of Disabled People.

Parsloe, P. (Ed.). (1996). *Pathways to empowerment.* Birmingham: Venture Press.

Plumb, A. (1994). *Distress or disability?: A discussion document.* Manchester: Greater Manchester Coalition of Disabled People.

Ramcharan, P., Roberts, G., Grant, G. and Borland, J. (Eds.). (1997). *Empowerment in everyday life: Learning disability.* London: Jessica Kingsley.

Read, J. (1996). What we want from mental health services. In J. Read and J. Reynolds (Eds.), *Speaking our minds: An anthology of personal experiences of mental distress and its consequences.* Basingstoke: Macmillan.

Read, J. and Baker, S. (1996). *Not just sticks and stones.* London: MIND.

Romme, M. and Esculer, S. (Eds.). (1993). *Accepting voices.* London: MIND.

Samuels, A. (1993). *The political psyche.* London: Routledge.

Shakespeare, T. (1993). Disabled people's self-organisation: A new social movement? *Disability, Handicap and Society,* 8, 249-264.

Simpson, T. (1996). Beyond rage. In J. Read and J. Reynolds (Eds.). *Speaking our minds: An anthology of personal experiences of mental distress and its consequences* (pp. 233-4). Basingstoke: Macmillan.

Stevenson, O. and Parsloe, P. (1993). *Empowerment in community care.* York: Joseph Rowntree Foundation/Community Care magazine.

Survivors Speak Out. (1996, November 9). *Alternatives: Developing our own philosophy and responses.* Workshop discussion, Annual General Meeting. London.

Turner, M. (1997, May 29-June 8). Shaping up, community care. *Inside Supplement,* 8.

Turner, M. (1998). *Shaping our lives: Project report.* London: National Institute for Social Work.

Wallcraft, J. (1998). *Healing minds.* London: The Mental Health Foundation.

Williams, F. (1992). Somewhere over the rainbow: Universality and diversity in social policy. In N. Manning and R. Page (Eds.), *Social Policy Review,* 4, 200-219.

Williams, F. (1996). Postmodernism, feminism and the question of difference. In N. Parton (Ed.), *Social theory, social change and social work* (pp. 61-76). London: Routledge.

Chapter 16

SOCIAL WORK AND MULTICULTURAL ORGANIZATION DEVELOPMENT: TOWARD EMPOWERING AND EMPOWERED ORGANIZATIONS

Biren A. Nagda
Scott Harding
School of Social Work, University of Washington
Lynn Carol Holley
Graduate School of Social Work, University of Utah

Human services organizations in the United States are faced with the problems of a diminishing and shifting resource base and the challenges of increased demand for services (Adams and Perlmutter, 1995). Increasing racial/ethnic diversity, continuing social inequalities and a rise in other group-based tensions have posed special challenges for the social work profession (Gutiérrez, 1992; Strawn, 1994). Stigmatization of those on welfare serves to question and delegitimize the rights of excluded populations to government entitlements (Cox and Joseph, 1998).

The debate over welfare reform has largely ignored how drastic cuts in social services programs will create a dangerous climate for members of socially excluded groups living in or at risk of poverty, a disproportionate number of whom are women and children of colour. By ignoring basic economic realities and requiring poor women to take any available job, regardless of whether it pays enough to support a family or whether day care, transportation, health care and other services are available, welfare reform will likely contribute to a rise in poverty, hunger, homelessness and other costly social problems. Under such conditions, these families can logically be expected to turn to local human service agencies for assistance. In combination with the diminishing resources, these forces have the potential to result in the provision of fewer services for people who find themselves at greater risk for a diminished quality of life.

We wish to thank Richard Weatherley for his insightful comments on an earlier draft of this paper.

This "less for more" syndrome also has dramatic implications for human services organizations (HSOs). It fuels a survival instinct among HSOs that may result in competition over scarce resources and alignment with dominant cultural ideologies to secure funding, or a complete social neglect of people and issues. This set of circumstances has diverted organizational visions to survival strategies and/or led to a paucity of visions to meet the new challenges. The question arises: How can HSOs respond to these increasingly hostile and threatening environmental forces?

Emerging scholarship and practice in two areas hold promise in envisioning new forms of HSOs. Work in empowerment practice now recognizes the importance of organizations and agencies as a pivotal nexus for empowering staff and clients as well as being empowered to impact the greater socio-political environment (Perkins and Zimmerman, 1995). Converging with this thinking is work in multicultural organization development that is centrally concerned with organizational structures and responses to social injustices and promoting liberation (Chesler, 1994; Jackson and Holvino, 1988).

In this chapter, therefore, we aim to extend the thinking of empowerment practice and integrate the two emerging fronts: empowerment at the organizational level with an explicit focus on becoming multicultural. We first examine the history of the social work profession in the United States and its responses to social diversity and oppression. We present an ideal vision of multicultural human services organizations influenced by lessons from multicultural organization development, ethnic, empowerment-oriented and feminist social movement agencies and organizational empowerment. Next, we consider two case studies that examine the real nature of organizations operating in a climate of increasing social exclusion. One describes an organization focusing on social action; the other examines ethnic social services agencies. Analyses and discussion of the case studies vis-à-vis the ideal vision follow to discern the strategies of empowerment and the challenges and dilemmas that human services organizations encounter in attempting to meet the multiple goals of service provision and social inclusion through social justice.

DIVERSITY, OPPRESSION AND EMPOWERMENT IN SOCIAL WORK IN THE UNITED STATES

Empowerment is generally conceptualized as a way of increasing power in personal, interpersonal and political spheres (Gutiérrez, Parsons and Cox, 1998). Some scholars and practitioners see empowerment specifically as a way of confronting social injustices (Gutiérrez, 1989; Riger, 1984; Simon, 1994; Solomon,

1976). An emerging field within empowerment practice focuses on organizations. Zimmerman (in press) says: "Organizations that provide opportunities for people to gain control over their lives are empowering organizations. Organizations that successfully develop, influence policy decisions, or other effective alternatives for service provision are empowered organizations" (p. 19). This formulation of organizational empowerment helps distinguish two domains that HSOs impact: social services and social policy. In this section, therefore, we examine these two areas in more detail. We look historically at how the social work profession has addressed issues of diversity, oppression and empowerment in regards to social policy and practice.

SOCIAL POLICY

The history of social welfare policy in the United States is marked by a clear pattern of racism and discrimination against racial and ethnic minorities, much in the same way as the founding of the United States was based on the racist extermination of indigenous populations. By the colonial period, Native Americans and African Americans "were virtually defined as non-persons" by white society (Jansson, 1988, p. 28). Social welfare assistance was not extended to African Americans, most of whom were subjected to slavery, while a campaign of relocation and extermination continued against Native Americans. Because the most disadvantaged members of all social and ethnic groups were seen as a "moral and political threat to society" (Jansson, p. 40), their needs went largely unmet, giving birth to a legacy of institutional disinterest and neglect of the poor, especially racial minorities.

Opposition to compensatory strategies to assist people of colour turned, by the nineteenth century, into policies to "control, regulate and oppress racial minorities" (Jansson, 1988, pp. 51-52). A vicious racism emerged against those of Native American, Latino, Asian and African descent, who were perceived as less intelligent and capable than whites. Theories of genetic superiority gained favour, perhaps best demonstrated by the official government policy of manifest destiny that led to the virtual genocide against Native American peoples and the US acquisition of Mexican land through the Mexican-American war. Black slaves, the nation's largest minority group, were barred from receiving most poor law assistance, while free blacks "were simply denied assistance and forced to develop their own informal self-help mechanisms" (Trattner, 1989, p. 23). Following the Mexican-American war, state and federal governments endorsed policies that resulted in Mexicans living in what became the US southwest losing their lands to whites. Asian immigrants were denied US citizenship and experienced other racist policies (see Takaki, 1993).

Against this backdrop of racism many charity workers "stressed the individual-moral causes of poverty" (Trattner, 1989, p. 161; see also Abramovitz, 1996). There also emerged, however, a small but influential group of settlement house workers who led the struggle for racial justice. Although many settlement house workers ignored the needs of racial and ethnic minorities, some sought to improve housing and working conditions while leading efforts to eliminate racial prejudice and segregation. Many of these pioneering social workers were instrumental in the formation of the National Urban League and the National Association for the Advancement of Colored People (NAACP), two dominant welfare and civil rights organizations for blacks in the twentieth century.

Despite the organizing efforts of some social workers, welfare provision continued to be marked by discrimination, even during the massive expansion of social services in the 1930s known as the New Deal. Piven and Cloward (1993) note that despite the creation of new social welfare programs in response to rising disorder, many of the most needy, especially black Americans, received little public relief.

Unemployment and social security benefits were originally not extended to certain key occupations like domestic service and agriculture which employed large numbers of blacks and other people of colour (Abramovitz, 1996; Piven and Cloward, 1993; Leiby, 1978). The New Deal failed "to use its most important welfare legislation, social security, to increase blacks' economic security" (Katz, 1986, p. 244). Fearing federal interference on the "Negro question," Southern opposition to social security was intense. Local politicians successfully pressured the federal government not to penalize Southern states "whose administration of old-age assistance discriminated against blacks" (Katz, 1986, p. 254). As Ehrenreich (1985) aptly observes, the New Deal was "less than color blind."

Resistance by the victims of social inequality and racial discrimination continued, though largely outside of the formal structure of social work and the welfare state services. Pressure by African Americans, for example, led to the creation in 1941 of the Fair Employment Practices Commission, though racial segregation in employment was barely affected. Embarrassment on the world stage led the US to allow citizenship to immigrants from China, a US ally, during World War II. However, those of Japanese descent living on the West Coast were forced to move to internment camps. Rising black protest led to gradual political concessions to African Americans, such as the 1954 Supreme Court decision barring segregation in schools. Perhaps more importantly, the ruling was a symbol of the inevitable end of legal segregation and thus provided momentum to the civil rights movement.

The persistence of poverty and political powerlessness among blacks, Native Americans and other racial minorities helped fuel an intense period of protest, marked by demands for voting rights, education and job equality, and an end to segregation and racism (Ehrenreich, 1985). Yet despite landmark federal civil rights and voting rights legislation, and expanded welfare programs, many of the "Great Society" social policies of President Lyndon Johnson attacked formal patterns of racial discrimination, not segregation or economic inequality. As in the past, many communities of colour responded by creating a variety of forms of mutual aid and self-help.

Social policy over the past three decades has been marked by an emphasis on welfare reform and a shift from policies that target distressed (urban) areas. The focus on welfare reform can be seen as part of an increase in racial politics, as welfare programs (especially AFDC) in recent decades have been viewed as primarily benefiting racial minorities, in particular black Americans (even though most recipients are white). This group was a primary beneficiary of political action in the 1960s that resulted in a dramatic expansion of welfare benefits. The attack on welfare (under the guise of reform) is thus part of a larger assault on the social gains of the 1960s. It is an effort to reassert the primacy of the state and to reinforce the work ethic and discipline poor women with children.

SOCIAL WORK PRACTICE

Within the social work literature in the United States, three different approaches to working with people of colour are evident (Gutiérrez, 1992; Gutiérrez and Nagda, 1996). The ethnocentric approach, a traditional mode of practice, emphasizes client adaptation to dominant values, beliefs and behaviours. Such practice aimed to assimilate people of colour (and other immigrant groups) into the dominant social system by demeaning and degrading ethnic and culturally based values and lifestyles (Chau, 1991). Deculturation practices, such as the child welfare and boarding school experiences of Native American populations, (Horejsi, Craig and Pablo, 1992; Herring, 1989) are an example of this approach.

In the late 1960s and early 1970s, practice modalities changed from traditional monocultural, ethnocentric practice to ethnic sensitive practice. This approach stressed a sensitivity to the unique needs, values and choices of different racial/ethnic groups (Chau, 1991; Devore and Schlesinger, 1981). Ethnic sensitive social workers projected more feelings of tolerance, acceptance and support for clients of colour (Gutiérrez, 1992). Societal and professional changes influenced this change in practice. For example, the civil rights movement coupled with anti-racist organizing within and outside of the profession brought issues of racial justice and self-determination more to the forefront. At the professional level, this period marked the birth of separate professional organizations for African American and Chicano social workers who asserted that the National Association of Social Workers (NASW) was not meeting the needs of their group members (Iglehart and Becerra, 1995).

While there has been change in the individual approaches to practice with people of colour, little has been done to either build on the strengths of communities of colour or to affect the social conditions and challenges that these communities endure (McMahon and Allen-Meares, 1992). Other criticisms of ethnic sensitive practice include the equation of ethnicity to culture with the danger of stereotyping and typifying clients (Green, 1982; Jayasuriya, 1992; Longres, 1991); a prescription of practices that are more suited for working with refugees and new immigrants than with groups who have a longer history in the United States (Longres, 1981); and a lack of a social development agenda (Midgley, 1991).

More recent developments in social work, particularly the empowerment perspective, offer hope in confronting oppression and bringing about social change. This form of practice is motivated by a social justice goal through empowering processes of education, individual and social participation, involvement and action (Simon, 1994). As Nagda and Gutiérrez (1998) have noted: "Combining ethnic sensitive practice and an empowerment perspective leads to an *ethno-conscious approach* which celebrates the extant strengths and potential in communities of color. Its core concern is to actively involve individuals, groups, families, organizations and communities in confronting social injustices and power inequalities" (p. 5).

Given this historical backdrop, the challenge emerges for us to envision a context and a model where empowerment-oriented approaches to working with disenfranchised communities can mutually enhance the social service and social justice missions of social work. Social service organizations and agencies represent one critical context for change as they simultaneously interact with client systems, other organizations and other bodies of influence (e.g., funding and legislative bodies) (Gutiérrez, 1992). Such organizations would be committed to: (a) work with members of oppressed and disenfranchised groups to provide empowering and socially just services; and (b) impact the socio-political environment which influences the organizations and their clientele. We elaborate on such a vision below.

A VISION FOR MULTICULTURAL HUMAN SERVICES ORGANIZATIONS

The vision of a multicultural human service organization (MHSO) is informed by work in both empowerment practice and multicultural organization development (MCOD). As noted earlier, organizational empowerment involves being both empowering and empowered. HSOs can be empowering by providing a context for empowerment practice for both clients and workers. Participatory decision-making processes, shared responsibilities, a supportive climate and social activities are some ways of empowering staff and clients (Perkins and Zimmerman, 1995; Shera and Page, 1995; Simon, 1994; Zimmerman, in press). Organizations can themselves be empowered by being active and resourceful in the socio-political sphere (Gutiérrez and Lewis, forthcoming; Zimmerman, 1990). They successfully meet their goals and enhance effectiveness and are involved in "organizational networks, organizational growth and policy leverage" (Perkins and Zimmerman, 1995, p. 570).

Multicultural organization development (MCOD), an organizational transformation approach that embraces social diversity and social justice goals, helps formulate the potential for social service organizations for empowerment and social justice. A review of the MCOD literature reveals two dimensions as centrally important: (1) the level of representation and contributions of diverse social groups in the organizational culture, mission and products/services; (2) the extent of efforts to eliminate social injustices and oppression within the organization and in the community (Chesler, 1994; Cox, 1993; Jackson and Holvino, 1988; Katz, 1988; Nixon and Spearmon, 1991). "Multicultural" here means diversity inclusive of race, gender, ethnicity, sexual orientation, age, national origin, ability, social class and religion.

Drawing upon the MCOD literature, coupled with human services literature on ethnic (Jenkins, 1989), empowerment-driven ethno-conscious (Gutiérrez, 1992) and feminist social movement agencies (Hyde 1989, 1992; Riger, 1984), Nagda (1994) has articulated a vision of a MHSO. Recent scholarship on organizational empowerment in human services further contributes to this vision (Cox and Joseph, 1998; Gutiérrez, GlenMaye and DeLois, 1995; Shera and Page, 1995; Zimmerman, in press). Three broad propositions for MHSO, adapted and summarized from earlier work, are presented in Table 1 (see Gutiérrez and Nagda, 1996; Nagda, 1994; Nagda and Gutiérrez, 1998).

TWO CASE STUDIES

In this section we examine information from two case studies to better understand ways in which the three propositions outlined above may be applied

Table 1: Three Propositions for a Multicultural Human Service Organization (MHSO)

Proposition 1: A MHSO is dually focused on providing empowering services to its clientele and bringing about social change.
A MHSO's ideology, goals and actions are strategically aligned to create socially just conditions for its clients and society at large. It is committed to transformational politics to eliminate all forms of social oppression that disempower its clientele. It aims to provide services to a wide range of clients who have been socially, politically and economically excluded. These services are empowering at individual, interpersonal, organizational, community and political levels and build on client strengths and resources. Such services encompass educational, health care, skill building and enrichment, political activism and cultural activities across the life span. They may be provided in multiple settings (community, agency, client homes and schools) and use multiple practice methods (casework, group/family work, community organizing, action research, advocacy and social action among others) that are appropriate for the client context.

Proposition 2: A MHSO is a praxis-oriented, multicultural and learning organization that is in a dialectical relationship with its internal and external environments.
Within the organization, a MHSO aims to create workplace conditions that are consistent on its multicultural ideology and goals. It is committed to equitable and diverse social and cultural representation among its workforce, represented not only in numbers but also in the structures, norms, styles and values. It strives for the workplace to be an endeavour in multicultural learning and in supporting and challenging the growth of all its members. It recognizes the potential for conflict among its members as a result of identity based differences in social and political experiences, values, cultures and styles. It uses existing conflicts as learning opportunities for enhancing intergroup understanding, appreciation and synergy.

A MHSO scans and negotiates with external environments as necessary. It uses environmental threats and crises as opportunities to become a more multicultural and socially just organization. It realizes that times of change will create an organizational transition with stress, conflict, uncertainty and ambiguity. Although these conditions can enhance the transformational potential, there should be a consciousness of and concern for client and worker welfare. As a learning organization, the MHSO is continually reflective about its processes, structures, policies, practices and membership to create nurturing and sustaining communities within the organization, in client

---

communities and in the larger society. Workers are engaged in constant action and reflection about their practices — both internal and external — especially as they occur across social and cultural differences.

Proposition 3: A MHSO is embedded in a complex network of horizontal (client communities and other organizations) and vertical (professional, legislative and funding bodies) linkages.

At the most local level, the MHSO encourages and facilitates client collaboration and partnerships in organizational governance, program development, implementation and evaluation activities. It strives to build coalitions with other community groups and social movement organizations. It plays a strong role in encouraging, pressuring and facilitating the multiculturalization of other network and coalition members. It also plays an advocacy and brokering role for its clients with other community organizations.

With professional associations, it lobbies for accreditation, educational reform and development of a knowledge base for multicultural practice. With legislative bodies, it advocates clients' human and civil rights and pushes for legal and social policy reform that will create more fair and just policies and aid in bettering the life conditions of its clients and other oppressed groups. It seeks collaborative relationships with funding sources and advocates for funding that allows community agencies to develop relevant programs to meet clients' needs. It also advocates for funding agencies to include members of excluded groups in decision-making processes.

to real settings. The first setting is a social action coalition; the second is a group of ethnic agencies in a large city in the US northwest. The two case studies represent different foci: the former is an organization focused on state-wide community and political organizing, while the latter is a collection of individual social service agencies providing direct services to excluded communities. By examining these two case studies, we aimed to see how each could inform the other such that both the empowering and empowered thrusts of MHSO could be actualized. For each of the two studies, we first offer a brief description of the data, then discuss ways in which each proposition is demonstrated in each case. We discuss major overlapping themes that emerge from the analysis and then examine some of the challenges present as well as possible ways to address them.

Case Study 1: A Social Action Coalition

The California Homeless and Housing Coalition (CHHC) was created in late 1990 when two existing groups merged — the California Right to Housing

Campaign and the California Homeless Coalition. The coalition, a tax-exempt, non-profit organization, was formed to provide statewide leadership in working to end homelessness and promote the development and preservation of decent and permanently affordable housing in California. Over time, CHHC expanded its activities to include work on welfare and state budget issues. The alliance of homeless and housing groups under one umbrella created stronger statewide public education, organizing and advocacy activities.

Case Study 2: Ethnic Social Service Agencies[1]

Case study two consists of a purposive sample of 18 social service agencies which were created to meet the needs of communities of colour. Fifteen of these agencies were created to serve specific ethnic (e.g., Vietnamese, Ethiopian, Mexican) or racial (e.g., Asian American/Pacific Islanders, Latino) communities, while the other three served multiple racial groups. The sample was stratified by agencies' levels of stability and racial or ethnic group served, and one leader or former leader of each agency was interviewed. Leaders of agencies at the first two levels of stability (i.e., less-established and moderately established) were asked about their agencies' missions, services, structures, processes and capacity-building needs. Leaders of the most stable (or well-established) agencies indicated key factors that they believed led to their agencies' success and offered advice for the less and moderately established agencies.

We examine below the ways in which the two case studies illustrate the different propositions of MHSO.

Proposition 1: A MHSO is dually focused on providing empowering services to its clientele and bringing about social change.

Case Study 1

The California Homeless and Housing Coalition (CHHC) was an organization committed to social change in that it focused attention on the need to end homelessness by addressing the root causes of the lack of housing. It sought to provide decent affordable housing to all California residents in need; and to ensure that welfare reform addressed the needs of poor women, children and single men rather than penalizing poor people because of their social status. Specific projects of CHHC also sought to empower those who suffered social exclusion from mainstream society because of economic injustice — homeless people and those receiving public assistance.

Because its efforts were focused on political advocacy and public education, CHHC was not itself a direct provider of social services. However, the composition of this statewide coalition meant that its members (the board of directors, representatives on several ongoing projects, affiliated groups working with CHHC on advocacy activities) were themselves often engaged in efforts to provide empowering services to their clientele. This occurred most often with homeless service providers and homeless advocacy groups, welfare rights organizations and those working on supported housing issues.

Case Study 2

Consistent with this proposition, these ethnic agencies were created to provide services to racial or ethnic communities that have been socially, politically and economically excluded within our society. All agencies' missions included a focus on improving the circumstances of community members by strengthening individuals, families and/or the communities themselves.

The act of creating an ethnic agency attests to the founders' awareness that their community members face different problems than others. As one leader said: "We are cognizant of the fact that [our community members] have a more difficult problem in today's world. We want to assist them in meeting the challenges of today." Leaders of agencies serving immigrant and refugee communities noted that cultural (including language) factors resulted in disempowering circumstances for their community members. One leader pointed out that whether immigrants are from rural or urban areas in their country of origin, they "still don't know the American culture, don't know how to deal with the school system ... the work system .... They don't know the culture, they don't know the community, they don't know the resources .... They are uprooted from their [family and other support networks]."

The services provided by these ethnic agencies were empowering at the individual, interpersonal and community levels. For example, programs such as tutoring, homework assistance and mentoring allowed youth to continue in the formal education system and provided role models for success. Information and referral services, especially for new immigrants, ensured that individuals and families learned about available community resources. English as a second language (ESL) classes for adults were critical in empowering adults to become involved in their children's schools, to obtain better jobs and to become better equipped for negotiating their environments. Interpretation and mediation services assisted community members in communicating with other agencies and organizations and prevented further exclusion that could occur due to communication barriers.

In addition to empowering those individuals and families who were in need of social services, some agencies offered programs that encouraged involvement in, and thus reinforced, communities' cultures. For example, some agencies offered language classes for children to learn their native language; youth in one agency researched and presented speeches about their community's history and culture and were involved in community services activities. Other agencies sponsored classes, programs or community gatherings featuring their cultures' stories, dances, foods, festivals and histories.

Although these ethnic agencies were empowering for community members, and were empowered in that they developed and offered alternative services for community members, they did not focus on influencing social policies. One leader described his reasons for not wanting to combine a social action focus with his agency's mission to provide social services:

> I was absolutely opposed to [our agency] ... moving into [the same office with a politically active agency in our ethnic community] because I thought [the politically active agency] represented a political perspective that would narrow who the agency could serve. And I thought that I'd rather have it in a more neutral zone of [another ethnic social service agency] or a more independent zone of its own agency. But moving into an organization that was a grass-root organization, that ... had a very strong political agenda, would eliminate it as a resource for many folks who were not of similar political persuasion.

This view suggests that agencies with dual social services and social change goals may eliminate not only more conservative funding sources and individuals who might serve as staff, board members and other leaders but also a number of community members who otherwise might benefit from using the agencies' social services.

Proposition 2: A MHSO is a praxis-oriented, multicultural and learning organization that is in a dialectical relationship with its internal and external environments.

Case Study 1
CHHC's determination to achieve client and community empowerment extended to the 40-member board of directors, CHHC's primary decision-making body. The coalition strove to maintain a culturally and geographically diverse board who could represent the variety of constituencies concerned with homeless, housing, welfare and budget issues in California. A number of board

positions were reserved for people who were homeless or formerly homeless, public assistance recipients and consumers of mental health services.

Though numerically small, the organization made a commitment to hire staff who were reflective of California's cultural diversity. The CHHC workplace was also a setting of ongoing negotiation of both different individual work styles and norms, as well as the structure of staff responsibilities. Staff members, along with the board of directors, were encouraged to offer their own vision and ideas about programmatic and policy issues, to help develop different tactics and strategies for CHHC's social change activities. Differences and conflicts that emerged over the direction of CHHC policies were thus used as an opportunity to re-examine the organization's practices in relation to its stated programmatic goals.

Case Study 2

Relatively autonomous work units, as contrasted to a strong hierarchical organizational structure, are one way in which a MHSO can create an internal structure that is able to more quickly change to meet community needs. The leader of one social service agency described his agency's use of such work units:

> Each of the units … are separate entities unto themselves. We have a uniform financial management control, but we encourage a great part of the administrative decision-making to be at that lower level so that they operate autonomously....

> It encourages them to be very creative, to be … a better "listening post" out there as to what the needs and concerns are, and also react immediately.

> Beyond that, is to hire good employees and get behind them instead of being a barrier to their getting their work done. You need to be out there and be an advocate and find out what you can do to enhance their work and let them get on with what you hired them for.

Thus workers were empowered by their agencies supporting their initiatives, advocating for them and allowing them to do their work in a way that is enriching.

Another study participant discussed some possible difficulties in creating such an agency. This leader suggested that individuals who are strong enough to create agencies outside of the mainstream may have approaches that will interfere with such an empowering managerial style. As he stated,

> What you do is you get a lot of very committed and very strong-willed people coming together trying to put together organizations and many of those organizations were driven and they survived by these folks who were, you know, very strong personalities who were a little .... I wouldn't say dictatorial, but certainly [they] had a managerial style that was probably autocratic.

He recommends that such leaders may need to build their skills in managing an organization so that they are able to "let go" of the organization—to perceive the organization as "ours" rather than "mine."

At the level of client and community empowerment, and consistent with this proposition, racial/ethnic community representation among agencies' boards of directors, paid staff and volunteers was of primary importance to the agencies in this case study. Such representation sets the stage for community members to meet community-defined needs in a manner consistent with their cultures.

One leader described his agency's creative solution for ensuring that its board was comprised of his community's members and that board members had access to needed expertise that might not be available within their ethnic community. This agency is currently revising its leadership structure so that, while all members of the board of directors are ethnic community members, it is also developing a sub-board, which reports to the board of directors, that will allow the agency to formally include the "best business minds" who may not be ethnic community members.

Most of the staff and volunteers of these agencies were also ethnic community members. The leader of one agency, whose sole paid staff member and the majority of volunteers were ethnic community members, described the importance of ethnic group membership by explaining that the staff member must be able to:

> ... help the children to feel it's okay to be different, it's okay to look different, and it's okay to have a different culture than the American culture. So that individual needs to understand the culture and also be able to get it across to the children whether directly or indirectly.... So I guess the

person doesn't *have* to be [a member of my ethnic community], but the person has to be willing to know, to learn about the culture and be willing to share the culture and speak the language (italics indicate leader's emphasis).

This same emphasis on cultural knowledge was apparent when another leader who, when asked about his agency's volunteer qualifications, said that the only requirement was that they understand the community's culture. "The rest," he added, "we can work with."

Many agencies, faced with the lack of adequate financial resources, remained committed to providing needed services to their communities. They responded inadequate funding by recruiting large numbers of volunteers. These volunteers served in numerous roles, including mentors and tutors, language interpreters, performers at cultural events, outreach workers, counsellors, case managers and in administrative positions such as director, bookkeeper and clerk.

Proposition 3: A MHSO is embedded in a complex network of horizontal (client communities and other organizations) and vertical (professional, legislative and funding bodies) linkages.

Case Study 1

Aside from responding to ongoing state and federal policy issues and debates about homelessness, housing, welfare, budget issues, civil liberties and services, CHHC sought to organize its constituency so their voices were heard and their participation in the political process valued. Indeed, this commitment to include the socially excluded in the public policy-making process was embodied in the coalition's mission statement:

> CHHC believes that homeless and other low-income people must help lead and carry on the struggle to eliminate homelessness and ensure a decent standard of living for all. Without the participation and leadership of low-income people, problems and appropriate solutions cannot be adequately identified and we lose much of the strength needed to succeed.

This attempt to empower marginalized populations and the poor extended beyond words and into CHHC's actual work activities. The commitment to their clientele's direct participation in decision-making and shaping the organization's actual policies was most pronounced with the formation in 1993 of the California Homeless Network (CHN), a statewide coalition of homeless run and low-income-led organizations whose mission was to "involve and unify homeless and low-income people in California so our voices can be heard and impact social values, political policies and issues." CHN sought to build local and regional coalitions, organize, educate, network, advocate and engage in non-violent direct action in order to impact the state and federal budget process and address the economic and living conditions of homeless people.

Client involvement in organizational governance and program development, though often a slow and seemingly disorderly procedure, was critical to help ensure that the empowerment process did not skip those directly affected by social issues in favour of community involvement in setting key aspects of CHHC policy. Thus when CHN membership agreed in 1994 to stage a coordinated series of statewide takeovers of abandoned public housing in several California cities, the actions were carried out (with numerous arrests and significant media coverage) despite concern and some opposition among CHHC board members.

Similarly, CHHC worked at the grass roots level through the Fair Share Network to support and build the capacity of local community organizing projects on critical issues of income support for poor women and children receiving public assistance. Local chapters, most of which had significant involvement from welfare recipients, carried out autonomous local organizing activities while also helping to shape the more formal statewide advocacy and organizing efforts of the Fair Share Network. This dual strategy most visibly merged on the numerous occasions when low-income women came to the state capital, Sacramento, to testify before state lawmakers about welfare legislation and policy. Offering powerful and eloquent stories about life on the edge, these women were often more persuasive than their better dressed and educated allies and opponents.

With its membership in and association with other regional, state and national (professional) sources, CHHC sought to develop a knowledge base to educate the general population and thereby create a public climate that would facilitate its social change efforts. This, in turn, tied in directly to its legislative advocacy work, which sought to effect change on state and federal housing, homelessness and welfare reform issues.

Specifically, CHHC utilized its statewide network to promote policies that increased funding for vulnerable and socially excluded populations while also seeking to address the structural sources of social and economic injustice. To a great extent, the success of CHHC's advocacy work was reliant upon a statewide network of volunteers and affiliated professional organizations. As important, the statewide organization was highly dependent upon external funding sources — in particular, the network of state and national philanthropic foundations that supported social change efforts. However, because much of CHHC's activities were focused on social change (in the guise of political advocacy and public education), the number of funders willing to provide ongoing resources for these efforts was small. This reluctance among funders increased over time and eventually led to the demise of the organization in 1996. However, key projects of the organization remain active and were subsumed by CHHC's official political lobbying arm, Housing California.

Throughout its existence, CHHC was linked with numerous local and national organizations working on housing, homelessness and welfare issues. These networks were vital to the success of each individual organization; the relative strength of CHHC and other groups was magnified through these collaborative efforts. For example, while CHHC was often involved in political advocacy on federal issues that were largely decided in Washington, D.C., these activities were coordinated and carried out on a statewide level. Thus local and regional housing and homeless advocacy groups throughout California — some consisting of one paid or volunteer staffperson while others had several staff and large budgets — were linked to CHHC and often engaged in coordinated public education and legislative advocacy actions. The result of these joint activities was to bring a diverse group of organizations together in collective social change efforts, often accomplishing together what no single group could possibly achieve on its own. Coalition efforts, in conjunction with similar actions in other states, effectively created a national network of housing and homeless advocates working jointly on similar issues.

Case Study 2

The ethnic agencies were most likely to be linked to their constituencies through community representation on their boards of directors, through staff and volunteer involvement and through participation in community-wide events. One agency leader noted that their agency is viewed as an "in-city neutral territory area for a lot of [community members] when they have very sensitive meetings." He also stated,

> One of the ways we found to increase participation is to ask those [agency] programs to nominate people from their interest groups [e.g., youth programs, programs for the elderly] to sit on the board of directors so that they can have their advocate on the policy-making body of the organization.

And that helps then for them to go out and identify community members that are in a whole range of diverse different interest groups throughout the area that sort of then provide the support foundation of the ... local board memberships.

None of these agencies' boards, however, included clients or former clients. One leader spoke of the advantages and disadvantages of having such representation on boards of directors. He noted that the advantage of having only corporate-oriented board members is that their business expertise makes fundraising easier. He acknowledged, however, that such composition results in a wide gap between board members and clients: "A board that is not as informed as it could be with respect to what the services ought to be and ... therefore is more reliant on staff to inform it as to what's going on."

At least two leaders spoke at length about the importance of coalitions and other networks within their geographic communities and with national organizations. They emphasized forming coalitions with other groups that are marginalized from the mainstream. For example, one leader described the advantages of participation in the Minority Executive Directors Coalition (MEDC), a local coalition of agency directors of colour: "[This group] is a good place for networking, sitting down and discussing joint issues and collaborative efforts. He also noted the benefits of working with a group of "minority" community development corporations. Finally, he noted his agency's participation in a local public corporation within his ethnic community.

Another leader described her involvement in another cross-cultural alliance. When asked, "What are the benefits of such an alliance?" she responded :

I think mainstream agencies and systems have a belief in divide and conquer.... When you have a little pot [of money] and everybody's trying to fight over that pot, little agencies are like the baby scavengers at the edges. And as a little agency that's getting the droppings, you either have to come together in a group to have a defensive posture against a larger predator or you will just be stepped on....

[W]e may be strong in our communities as an agency, we may have significant impact in our communities, but the strength of just this little agency is not there unless you're all together.

[The] cross-cultural alliance that we belong to is wonderful. [Before, funders] had us arguing over moneys with each other ... and one of us would get more than the other and we would be angry at one another. So it kept us at bay with each other, let alone on the outskirts of mental health....

So in that sense we became a force ... not accepting certain things from the funding structure unless it was global for us as a group.

We never thought we had the capability of being able to stand together without somebody wedging in between [us] and causing this infighting to occur. And so since we've been doing it now for almost three years, we are a force to be reckoned with. And so when we called back to see [a city council member] or when...we wanted to meet with ... the mayor, [we did so]. I mean, we had movements that we hadn't had before. And so they had to do something with us, they had to pay attention.

While most of the social service agency leaders discussed the importance of collaboration with local coalitions or alliances, one leader also noted his agency's involvement in an ethnic organization that has regional and national foci. According to this study participant, such involvement provides the agency with "visibility and association with organizations [of his ethnic community] throughout the whole nation."

Finally, approximately one-third of the agencies, particularly those serving immigrant and refugee communities, served as advocates for community members by providing interpretation and/or mediation services between community members and other agencies. These agencies advocated for families with schools, courts and public welfare agencies. As described by one leader, "[W]e can assist them with the schools, where they maybe feel that the school either wouldn't understand them, or that the school is just not paying any attention to them, or we can maybe get in the door and they can't."

DISCUSSION

The vision of a MHSO presented above, and the subsequent case studies, helps deepen our understanding of the intersection of empowerment and multicultural organization development. The empowering and empowered dimensions of organizations that also embrace addressing needs of excluded and marginalized groups show both promise and challenge. Analyses of the case studies demonstrate that these organizations do indeed possess many, though not all, aspects of the proposed vision of MHSO (see Table 2 for a summary). Both focused on empowering excluded groups, a primary feature of MHSOs, and in fact were founded with that specific goal. In the first case study, CHHC emphasized empowering groups at the community and political levels, and it empowered individuals through its focus on grass roots organizing. Agencies in the second case study emphasized empowering individuals, families and communities by building on strengths.

In both cases, agencies demonstrated empowering aspects (as emphasized in Proposition 2) by including marginalized groups in the organization's leadership. The CHHC consciously included constituents in all aspects of their programs while the ethnic agencies incorporated communities' cultures into their programs. They, however, did not necessarily include clients in all aspects of program planning and implementation. Another empowering aspect was demonstrated by some of the ethnic agencies' concern for client welfare in times of budget crisis by their heavy use of volunteers to provide needed services when funding for paid staff was not available.

Agencies in both cases strongly and creatively illustrated the empowered dimension (Proposition 3) in their collaborations with other organizations. The CHHC considered collaboration with other social movement and politically focused organizations critical, while the ethnic agencies collaborated with other organizations within their ethnic communities and, in one case, with a coalition of leaders of other agencies providing social services to various oppressed communities. Both cases illustrated important advocacy and other brokerage functions, albeit in different capacities: CHHC by organizing constituents to testify before the legislature, and the ethnic agencies by intervening between individuals and families and various public and private organizations. Finally, both cases illustrated lobbying in some fashion with professional, legislative or funding organizations. CHHC sought to influence legislators, professional organizations and funding organizations, while ethnic agencies sought to influence funders to allocate more monies to agencies serving their own ethnic communities and, in one case, to multiple agencies serving oppressed communities.

While this analysis has pointed out ways in which these propositions can be implemented within HSOs, it also raises important questions and challenges in three primary areas: funding, legitimacy and maintaining empowering and empowered service and change missions. We examine these further.

Table 2: Summary of Case Studies vis-à-vis Three Propositions for MHSO

Proposition 1: A MHSO is dually focused on bringing about social change and providing empowering services to its clients.

Case Study 1	Case Study 2
• focus on affordable housing, addressing root causes of homelessness, including excluded groups in the policy process; focal population was those who were homeless and/or receiving public assistance • members often provided services that were empowering at the individual and interpersonal levels; grass roots organizing model was empowering at the individual level • public education was empowering at the community level • political advocacy was a primary focus	• focus on improving the circumstances of members of communities of colour • primary focus of most agencies was on empowering individuals and/or families • many agencies sponsored cultural events that were empowering at the community level • building on strengths was a stated goal of some agencies; most utilized other community members' skills, education and experiences in services provision

Proposition 2: A MHSO is a praxis-oriented, multicultural and learning organization that is in a dialectical relationship with its internal and external environments.

Case Study 1	Case Study 2
• culturally and geographically diverse board • consciously included members of excluded groups • diversity of staff representative of state population • negotiation of diversity of styles, visions and ideas to develop different social change strategies	• community representation among board, staff and volunteers • non-hierarchical structure of some agencies • consciously included ethnic community members and incorporated communities' cultures in agencies' programs

> **Proposition 3: A MHSO is embedded in a complex network of horizontal (client communities and other organizations) and vertical (professional, legislative and funding bodies) linkages.**

Case Study 1	*Case Study 2*
• organized constituents • facilitated formation of statewide homeless coalition • supported and built capacity of local community organization projects • arranged for constituents to testify to legislature • sought to influence state and federal issues • sought to influence professional organizations • sought funds for social change projects (lack of funds for such efforts eventually led to the organization's demise)	• some utilized former clients in services provision • some involved in coalition with other ethnic agency leaders • worked with other organizations within same ethnic/racial community at local, state and/or national levels • interpretation and mediation services • advocate for funding for programs to meet communities' needs • one agency advocated for funding for multiple excluded groups as part of a coalition

Funding. Despite its laudable missions, goals and programs, the domain of funding can make or break an agency. It appears that the funding issue for MHSOs is doubly complicated. On one level, the challenge is similar to other social service organizations faced with funding cutbacks, while on another level the challenge is unique as it brings to bear the agency's empowering and empowered missions. The questions we struggle with are: (1) How can an organization avoid changing its agenda in order to conform to the changing foci of funders? (2) How can organizations influence grantmakers so that they are willing to fund empowered and empowering organizations that serve excluded groups?

The case of CHHC is instructive in regard to the first question. After providing core financial support for homeless and housing public education and advocacy in the early 1990s, many key private funders began to withdraw from this type of grantmaking. Other key issues emerged (such as children and families) that drew increased interest from foundations and corporate philanthropists. For CHHC, the inability to change issues — which reflected an unwillingness to abandon its core philosophy and mission — resulted in a significant and rapid loss of long-term foundation funding. As a result, key staff were laid off and core activities waned due to a lack of resources. As private foundations will likely continue to change areas of interest together with greater scarcity in public funding, and with declining support for social change activities, organizations will be forced to focus more attention on developing self-sustaining revenue sources without abandoning their social change mission. Similarly, although creative in their ability to survive, ethnic social service agencies have experienced the stark reality of the political environment: funders continue to have the power to dictate who is served and the way in which services are offered.

Legitimacy. Funding provides a tangible financial resource that enables MHSOs to survive and grow. The success of MHSOs, however, is also dependent on legitimization resources that are not be necessarily tangible. Much of the MHSO work fosters, and is dependent on, agency-client, inter-agency and agency-funder/legislator relationships. Legitimization is a key component of these relationships. The case studies suggest ways in which legitimization within constituent communities, among other agencies and among the larger community can be obtained.

While social service agencies must seek legitimacy from multiple sources, the experience of the CHHC highlights one primary source: the coalition. To be an effective advocate for social change, local and regional agencies and organizations had to collaborate — to collectively endorse the concept of a statewide umbrella coalition as the most effective method for achieving a common agenda. While achieving legitimacy among allied organizations may have been the primary challenge, successful outcomes for CHHC also depended on the process of legitimization with funders and policy-makers. Because the coalition was often involved in public education and advocacy for stigmatized and excluded populations (homeless persons and welfare recipients), gaining legitimacy with elected officials and policy-makers posed a significant obstacle.

A clear challenge in this area, therefore, is the ability to garner support from different constituencies for multiple missions. Business and community leaders, as well as staff and clients, may or may not see the missions as complementary.

Social service and social change. One of the main thrusts of the vision of a social-justice-oriented MHSO is to foster the mutuality of providing empowering services and being empowered to impact social change that is wholly consistent with the dual mission of social work. It is clear from the case studies that the reality of such a joint mission is difficult and may be viewed by some as undesirable. All the social service agencies in the second case study were created to provide social services only, yet were responsive to the needs of communities of colour. Doing this in a way compatible with their cultures and languages may be viewed as radical in a societal context where assimilation has been the preferred way of incorporating groups into society. By providing support for group's cultures and a site for community building, these agencies are empowering at the individual, interpersonal and community levels, if not at the broader political level. Moreover, as one leader stated, there may be hesitation for an agency to be too closely linked with a strong social action agenda for fear of alienating community members.

Perhaps the most important question that emerges here is: Is it possible (or desirable) for one organization to meet each of the proposed characteristics of a MHSO? This raises the issue of a social service-social change mission contained within each agency versus looking at the ecological network of an agency.

ADDRESSING EMERGENT ISSUES AND CHALLENGES

The discussion thus far has highlighted ways in which the two case studies embody different aspects of MHSOs and outlined the issues and challenges raised. In this section, we propose strategies and approaches that may address the challenges. Overall, each of the strategies proposed deals with building internal and/or external organizational capacity. For example, to meet the funding challenges, agency staff need to learn how to speak the language of funders in order to be most persuasive (Toney, 1996). This suggests that social service organizations, no matter their size, should strive to build an internal capacity to engage in this level of advocacy. Further strategies could be developed whereby social change activities are incorporated into the social service programs funded by grantmakers. This can often require a MHSO to couch key activities in rhetoric that does not alienate more moderate funders so as to provide them with the political cover to support more progressive and radical activities. On a broader level, two different strategies could be used to build external capacity: (1) developing coalitions with other MHSOs to influence the existing grantmakers to change their funding priorities (as did the cross-cultural alliance described earlier); and (2) recruiting individuals with contacts in grantmaking communities to serve on boards of directors (as did the CHHC).

While we hold the view that social action is required to address structural inequalities that often require the need for social services, some individuals who use such services may hold different views of the origin of their problems. For this reason, they may avoid the very services that could empower them to work for changes that would benefit their communities. This reality suggests the need for MHSOs to involve members of excluded communities in education (consciousness-raising) efforts regarding the relationship of structural oppression, social exclusion and the need for social services. Gil (1998), in his discussion of social-change-oriented "radical" social work practice, notes how change at the individual level can lead to broader social change. He identifies the development of critical consciousness and the recognition of individuals' capacity to effect creative and productive alterations in social relations—to be social change agents—as key to this transformation. Such personal change is thus a springboard for more collective social and political action that seeks to reconstruct institutions and eliminate social injustice. In the absence of successful education efforts, many community members may prefer to seek services from agencies that focus solely on providing social services.

Finally, a coalition model, as exemplified by CHHC, provides an integrative way to address funding and legitimacy issues as well as the dilemmas of joint social service-social change missions. Mondros and Wilson (1994) refer to this type of coalition as an "organization of organizations." That is, while a social service agenda may operate at the most proximate interface with client systems, a social change agenda may be enacted through other mediating organizations, such as umbrella organizations and coalitions based on common interests (e.g., homelessness and affordable housing, increasing access to excluded communities and culturally responsive services). Given the present context and struggle to meet increased demand for services with limited resources, such diversification of agendas may indeed strengthen both missions rather than dilute one for the other. Working for social change within a larger coalition, for example, would help avoid the challenge of finding agency staff who are trained as both service providers and social change advocates. And at the risk of repetition, a primary challenge facing those interested in either a social change agenda or in providing culturally competent services to oppressed communities is finding a sufficient and consistent source of funding.

Furthermore, a coalition can serve the dual purpose of advocating with funders on behalf of service agencies while providing greater legitimacy to the separate agencies. An umbrella organization can also provide protection for agencies that are committed to providing empowering services but fear negative repercussions as they engage in social action activities. The fact that the CHHC assumed a primary leadership role on state and federal advocacy issues not only proved to be an effective model but it also allowed smaller local agencies to focus on service delivery. By appearing more moderate and client focused—they were not, at least at face value, engaging in social change activities — individual agencies could avoid many of the fundraising difficulties faced by CHHC and social justice groups. For example, many housing and homeless service providers were highly dependent upon government funding, a revenue source largely unavailable to social change organizations like CHHC (which never received any public funding). Social service agencies also had an easier time securing funding from private foundations if their activities were primarily service delivery.

CONCLUSION

It is worth remembering that the MCOD literature specifies the developmental nature of becoming more multicultural: a typology of organizations is represented as different points on a continuum from monocultural to multicultural (Jackson and Holvino, 1988). In designing change strategies for social service organizations striving to become more multicultural, two critical ingredients appear to be necessary: (1) a sense of agency safety (a lack of threat to survival) through strong legitimating forces both within the focal community and outside (i.e., access to funding); and (2) a commitment from agency and community leaders that an empowering and empowered social change agenda is necessary for improving the conditions that affect both the community and the agency.

Perhaps the true challenge of a joint empowering-empowered organization is the need to consider the multiple ways in which these agendas are enacted. In the current context of increasing hostility, we contend that "business as usual" may not be an available strategy and that newer ways of doing our work are imperative. On one level, the study of ethnic agencies conveys a sense of empowering social service provision as of primary importance. On another level, the study of the social action coalition provides an organizing strategy that can complement other agencies' focus on social services. It is also clear that empowerment and social change occur in many ways; in the case of ethnic agencies, for example, access to and provision of social services may indeed be part of a social change process. It appears that an empowerment-oriented practice, when combined with culturally responsive services, offers potential for incorporating more social change elements in the organizational mission and practice. One issue remains clear: there is a need for educating service providers, recipients and funders on the mutuality, not the opposition, of social services and social change.

ENDNOTE

[1] These were part of a larger study focusing on the structures, processes, strengths and needs of less-established agencies started by and for particular communities of colour in a large city in the US northwest.

REFERENCES

Abramovitz, M. (1996). *Regulating the lives of women: Social welfare policy from colonial times to the present* (revised ed.). Boston: South End Press.

Adams, C. T. and Perlmutter, F. D. (1995). Leadership in hard times: Are nonprofits well-served? *Nonprofit and Voluntary Sector Quarterly*, 24(3), 253-262.

California Homeless and Housing Coalition (1990). *Mission statement.* Sacramento, CA.

Chau, K. (1991). Social work with ethnic minorities: Practice issues and potentials. *Journal of Multicultural Social Work*, 1(1), 23-39.

Chesler, M. (1994). Organizational development is not the same as multicultural organization development. In E. Y. Cross, J. H. Katz, F. A. Miller and E. H. Seashore (Eds.), *The promise of diversity* (pp. 240-251). Burr Ridge, IL: Irwin.

Cox, E. O. and Joseph, B. H. R. (1998). Social service delivery and empowerment: The administrator's role. In L. M. Gutiérrez, R. J. Parsons and E. O. Cox (Eds.), *Empowerment in social work practice: A sourcebook* (pp. 167-186). Pacific Grove, CA: Brooks/Cole.

Cox, T. (1993). *Cultural diversity in organizations: Theory, research and practice*. San Francisco, CA: Berrett-Koehler.

Devore, W., and Schlesinger, E. D. (1981). *Ethnic-sensitive social work practice*. St. Louis, MO: C. V. Mosby Co.

Ehrenreich, J. H. (1985). *The altruistic imagination: A history of social work and social policy in the United States*. Ithaca, NY: Cornell University Press.

Gil, D. (1998). *Confronting injustice and oppression: Concepts and strategies for social workers*. New York: Columbia University Press.

Green, J. W. (1982). *Cultural awareness in the human services*. Englewood Cliffs, NJ: Prentice-Hall.

Gutiérrez, L. M. (1989). *Ethnic consciousness, consciousness raising and the empowerment process of Latinos*. Unpublished doctoral dissertation, University of Michigan, School of Social Work, Ann Arbor, Michigan.

Gutiérrez, L. M. (1992). Empowering clients in the twenty-first century: The role of human service organizations. In Y. Hasenfeld (Ed.), *Human services as complex organizations* (pp. 320-338). Newbury Park, CA: Sage.

Gutiérrez, L., GlenMaye, L. and DeLois, K. A. (1995). The organizational context of empowerment practice: Implications for social work administration. *Social Work*, 40(2), 249-258.

Gutiérrez, L. M. and Lewis, E. (in press). *Empowering women of color*. New York: Columbia University Press.

Gutiérrez, L. M. and Nagda, B. A. (1996). The multicultural imperative in human service organizations: Issues for the 21st century. In C. A. McNeece and P. Raffoul (Eds.), *Future issues for social work practice*. Needham Heights, MA: Allyn and Bacon.

Gutiérrez, L. M., Parsons, R. J. and Cox, E. O. (Eds.). (1998). *Empowerment in social work practice: A sourcebook*. Pacific Grove, CA: Brooks/Cole.

Herring, R. D. (1989). The American Native family: Dissolution by coercion. *Journal of Multicultural Counseling and Development*, 17(1), 4-13.

Horejsi, C., Craig, B. H. and Pablo, J. (1992). Reactions by Native American parents to child protection agencies: Cultural and community factors. *Child Welfare*, 71(4), 329-342.

Hyde, C. (1992). The ideational system of social movement agencies: An examination of feminist health centers. In Y. Hasenfeld (Ed.), *Human services as complex organizations* (pp. 121-144). Newbury Park, CA: Sage.

Hyde, C. (1989). A feminist model for macro-practice: Promises and problems. *Administration in Social Work*, 13(3/4), 145-181.

Iglehart, A. P. and Becerra, R. M. (1995). *Social services and the ethnic community*. Needham Heights, MA: Allyn and Bacon.

Jackson, B. W. and Holvino, E. (1988). *Multicultural organizational development* (PCMA Working Paper Series #11). Ann Arbor: University of Michigan, Program on Conflict Management Alternatives.

Jansson, B. (1988). *The reluctant welfare state: A history of American social welfare policies*. Belmont, CA: Wadsworth Publishing.

Jayasuriya, L. (1992). The problematic of culture and identity in social functioning. *Journal of Multicultural Social Work*, 2(4), 37-58.

Jenkins, S. (1989). The ethnic agency defined. In D. Burgest (Ed.), *Social work practice with minorities* (pp. 76-90). Metuchen, NJ: Scarecrow Press.

Jenkins, S. (1983). Children who are newcomers: Social service needs. *Journal of Children in Contemporary Society*, 15(3) 39-47.

Katz, J. H. (1988). *Facing the challenge of diversity and multiculturalism* (PCMA Working Paper Series #13). Ann Arbor: University of Michigan, Program on Conflict Management Alternatives.

Katz, M. (1986). *In the shadow of the poorhouse: A social history of welfare in America*. New York: Columbia University Press.

Leiby, J. (1978). *A history of welfare and social work in the United States*. New York: Columbia University Press.

Longres, J. F. (1991). Toward a status model of ethnic sensitive practice. *Journal of Multicultural Social Work*, 1(1), 41-56.

McMahon, A. and Allen-Meares, P. (1992). Is social work racist? A content analysis of the recent literature. *Social Work*, 37(6), 533-539.

Midgley, J. (1991). Social development and multicultural social work. *Journal of Multicultural Social Work*, 1(1), 85-100.

Mondros, J. B. and Wilson, S. (1994). *Organizing for power and empowerment*. New York: Columbia University Press.

Nagda, B. A. (1994). *Toward a vision of a multicultural human service organization: A confluence of ideologies, missions, goals and praxis*. Unpublished preliminary examination paper, University of Michigan, School of Social Work, Ann Arbor, MI.

Nagda, B. A. and Gutiérrez, L. M. (1998). *A praxis and research agenda for multicultural human services organizations.* Unpublished manuscript. University of Washington, Seattle, WA.

Nixon, R. and Spearmon, M. (1991). Building a pluralistic workplace. In R. L. Edwards and J. Yankey (Eds.), *Skills for effective human services management* (pp. 155-170). Silver Springs, MD: NASW Press.

Perkins, D. D. and Zimmerman, M. A. (1995). Empowerment theory, research and application. *American Journal of Community Psychology*, 23(5), 569-579.

Piven, F. F. and Cloward, R. (1993). *Regulating the poor: The functions of public welfare.* New York: Pantheon.

Riger, S. (1984). Vehicles for empowerment: The case of feminist movement organizations. *Prevention in Human Services*, 3(2/3), 99-117.

Shera, W. and Page, J. (1995). Creating more effective human service organizations through strategies of empowerment. *Administration in Social Work*, 19(4), 1-15.

Simon, B. L. (1994). *The empowerment tradition in American social work.* New York: Columbia University Press.

Solomon, B. (1976). *Black empowerment.* New York: Columbia University Press.

Strawn, C. (1994). Beyond the buzz word: Empowerment in community outreach and education. *Journal of Applied Behavioral Sciences*, 30(2), 159-174.

Takaki, R. (1993). *A different mirror: A history of multicultural America.* Boston: Little, Brown and Company.

Toney, M. (1996). Power concedes nothing without a demand: Building multiracial organizations with direct action. In J. Anner (Ed.), *Beyond identity politics.* Boston: South End Press.

Trattner, W. (1989). *From poor law to welfare state: A history of social welfare in America.* New York: The Free Press.

Zimmerman, M. A. (in press). Empowerment theory: Psychological, organizational and community levels of analysis. In J. Rappaport and E. Seidman (Eds.), *Handbook of community psychology.* NY: Plenum Press

Zimmerman, M. A. (1990). Taking aim on empowerment research: On the distinction between individual and psychological conception. *American Journal of Community Psychology*, 18(1), 169-177.

Chapter 17

THE ROLE OF SPIRITUALITY IN EMPOWERMENT PRACTICE

Larry Ortiz
Social Work Program
West Chester University of Pennsylvania
Glenn Smith
Christian Direction, Montreal

In a global perspective, empowerment practices are deeply influenced by the context within which they are practised. Historically, and contemporarily, spirituality is seen as an essential aspect of these practices. Although this is quite a foreign idea in much of North American research and theory on empowerment, there is an increasing body of literature and praxis in the two-thirds of the world that supports this observation.

The reasons for the silence about the integration of spirituality and empowerment based social intervention in the North Atlantic or other "developed" countries are not exactly clear, but they are no doubt ideologically based. For this separation, there are three possible explanations offered: historical antagonism between institutional religion and the helping professions, the secularization of modern society, and the influence of Cartesian philosophy in the social science. One, most professional social workers engaged in empowerment practice do not view institutional religion as friendly or a support system in progressive efforts directed toward changing the situation of the oppressed and disenfranchised. At best, formal religion in North America has taken a passive or hands-off approach to the needs of the poor and the social and economically marginalized. At worst, it has joined forces with conservative politics and campaigned to blame the poor for all kinds of social ills and to legislate controls over the lives of the marginalized through excessive regulation and a mean-spirited orientation. This behaviour is indefensible, and in all cases an inaccurate reading or interpretation of the spiritual beliefs that serve as the basis for religion, the Christian faith in particular. However, there is also a fallacy at work on part of those advocating on behalf of the marginalized that identifies spirituality as the same as institutional religion. Through omission they often overlook the importance of faith and spirituality in social action. Such an assumption, we believe, is short-sighted and is akin to throwing out the baby with the bathwater. Although spirituality and religion inform each other, religion is not necessarily spiritual, and to equate them as one in the same is to ignore the useful power of transcendence that may negate the destructive role of a rigid social code. Further, many poor and undeserved rely on faith systems to sustain them during a difficult and trying life, and for many it serves as a form of primary prevention. This transcendent force is very important and needs to be recognized, embraced and utilized as a strength in the lives of the marginalized in empowerment efforts. The authors are aware of and chagrined by the role institutional religion has played in political alignments that have coalesced to disenfranchise the poor and marginalized. But, spirituality is, on another dimension, another issue and should be viewed with its own integrity.

Two, the ongoing (process of) secularization of Western culture has been the source for the decline of the social significance of faith in many professional domains over the past several decades. This marginalization of faith is understood as the process by which traditional religious beliefs and values have declined in importance for both large groups of people and society as a whole as a means of integrating and legitimating everyday life in modern society. This phenomenon has unquestionably affected the social sciences through the omission of faith and spirituality in social science equations.

Three, spirituality has been viewed by many practitioners as appealing to transcendence while ignoring the temporal plight of the marginalized and the most vulnerable of society. Social scientists of all sorts become suspicious at this point because transcendence does not fit easily into social science methodology. Spirituality is hard to measure. Consequently, models of empowerment, which are based on social science theories and paradigms, ignore or dismiss spirituality and/or religion. The sentiment toward the transcendent is akin to Marx's reported position that religion is the opiate of the masses. Although there is an element of truth to this notion, and historically the Christian church in particular has mastered the process of anesthetizing the pain of abuse and poverty with a promise of a sweeter by and by, the essence of the power of spirituality in day-to-day life has been ignored. To dismiss this meaningful force in the lives of the marginalized as quaint and unenlightened is in effect arrogant and antithetical to empowerment principles.

Yet, the patterns of antagonism, secularization and rationality are not prevalent in all societies in which serious development and empowerment is practised. So in these places, what can be learned from those integrating spirituality and empowerment practices? Learning from this level of integration requires social workers and other social practitioners to question the fundamental presuppositions of their own world views and theories. The increasing cultural interest in spirituality means, among other issues, those ignoring the importance of spirituality could well be marginalized for ignoring what other societies are seeing as crucial to renewal. In our perspective recognizing spirituality is a welcome interest and one that can contribute to the holistic social transformation of the context. This paper will examine this postulate by defining spirituality, identifying models of spiritually based empowerment practices, along with providing specific examples, and in the final section identify integral contributions spirituality and even institutional religion can make to empowerment practice and praxis.

SPIRITUALITY DEFINED

Although we reflect and work out of a Protestant world and life view that has clear implications on how we understand and pursue spirituality within our own contexts and vocations, we understand that the term has both global and very elastic definitions. Within our own traditions, there is no common definition of the term, nor need there be. Nevertheless, we do need to understand each other. For that reason alone we understand the quest for the spiritual to be the process of pursuing a deep relationship with the transcendent. Lane (1984) defines it as, "a particular style of approach to union with God" (p. 2). Interestingly, in the larger Christian tradition, one usually looks at the motifs of spirituality rather than at a strictly theological reflection to learn on the subject (Smith, 1989).

With humility, therefore, the authors advance a definition of spirituality that is in part a content analysis of its usage in the social work literature. The common themes of interconnectedness between self, others and sense of ultimacy as well as the individual's need for generativity and inner meaning are consistent throughout the literature (Joseph, 1987; Canda, 1990; Derezotes, 1995; Bergren-Thomas, 1995). Researchers define spirituality and its manifestations in various ways, but these themes serve as a definition for spirituality that covers a spectrum of its usage.

Religion and religiosity are frequently operationalized as the pursuit of spirituality through activities such as ritual prayer, lighting candles, meditation, reading holy scriptures and abiding by a code within the context of a social institution. Religion provides a plausibility structure for spiritual beliefs. We agree with Peter Berger (1992) when he states, "[O]ne can say that religion is particularly in need of it [plausibility structure] because of the extraordinary and (for most people) meta-empirical character of its affirmations" (p. 172). It is, therefore, impossible to separate spirituality from religion and vice versa. However, in the lives of people the balance between the two is not always obvious, for in some there may be religion devoid of spirituality while in others religiosity is avoided, but there is nonetheless a deep spiritual commitment. One thing that does become clear is how one's world view is shaped by religion and spirituality.

As human beings, we understand that we live out of a basic set of beliefs, core values or ideas which inform and guide our actions. We act in the world around us in terms of a world view with which we make sense of life and direct how we live. One's spiritual beliefs are an integral dimension of a world view.

We would disagree with those who view public reflection as spiritually or ideologically neutral and private. This spirituality or religion or ideology is the ultimate commitment that provides personal and communal direction to life. It is what is of ultimate importance to a person, community, group or institution. It informs world views that are foundational to any political plan or, for that matter, any human enterprise in the public arena.

We maintain the position, however, that a distinction must be made between spirituality and religion. Earlier, we criticized social workers' failure to recognize this difference as a reason for overlooking the value of spirituality in the lives of their constituents. The value in distinguishing these concepts is a clearer understanding of how the existential qualities of spirituality, distinct from religion, and religion as a behavioural guide are both integrated into everyday life and give meaning to experiences, shape the world view and provide a kaleidoscope perspective for the future (Ortiz and Langer, 1997).

Clearly, one of the major problems in the literature and a popular misconception is the differentiation of the terms spirituality and religion. The failure to articulate clearly and operationalize the differences in the use of these terms creates a murkiness and confounding of concepts that leads to confusion and misconception. Although we recognize the relationship between these concepts, we also advocate for more precise usage of the terms, so that the utility and power of each concept might be better utilized in the lives of the socially marginalized and disenfranchised.

EXAMPLES OF SPIRITUALITY AND EMPOWERMENT PRACTICE

In this paper, empowerment is primarily referred to in the group sense. Essentially, it refers to a planned effort to enhance the power of devalued groups in society who have been politically and economically disenfranchised, discriminated against personally and institutionally, systematically alienated and, in general, lacking social power (Solomon, 1976; Maton and Wells, 1995). The goal of group empowerment is to positively affect the social conditions of the disempowered to the point of creating opportunities for them to define their plight contextually, develop plans and strategy for change and mobilize to that end. This process includes, in part, the following: "(1) a belief system that inspires growth, is strengths based, and is focused beyond the self; (2) an opportunity role structure that is pervasive, highly accessible, and multifunctional; (3) a support system that is encompassing, peer based and provides a sense of community; and (4) leadership that is inspiring, talented, shared and committed to both setting and members" (Maton and Wells, 1995, p. 184).

We want to provide several examples of spirituality in empowerment practices. Some examples are from social or political movements and others are vignettes of smaller scale locational endeavours.

In the examples we present two models of social change that are spiritually and (intentionally) theologically based principles for "the purpose of reflection and action upon the world so as to transform it" (Freire, 1972, p. 28). Following these paradigms are specific activities from various regions that demonstrate the successful integration of spirituality and empowerment practice.

THE SOUTH AFRICAN EXPERIENCE

The racial tension this country suffered for nearly 200 years is religiously based. Before apartheid became the official policy of the regime in 1949, it was first the doctrine of the Afrikaners' Christian Reformed Church. This was subsequently denounced as heresy by other reformed traditions in that country and by all Christian traditions across the globe. What is interesting is the spiritually based empowerment models that emerged within the Christian churches to combat this discrimination/heresy. History has now shown the incredible place that the church played in the emancipation of South Africa through people like Desmond Tutu, Michael Cassidy and Allan Boesak and structures like the Anglican Church of South Africa and African Enterprise.

The South African practitioner, John W. De Gruchy (1986), has contributed a significant reflection within his context on the subject of ministry as the task of the whole people of God which he defines as, "a common commitment, a common vision and a common sharing in the witness to the kingdom of God. The contextuality of the ordained ministry requires that this commonality become concrete in particular places in relation to the needs and struggles of the People of God" (DeGruchy, 1986, p. 34).

For De Gruchy this means, for example, that a pastor in a black church must focus on the struggle for human dignity, the empowerment of people, the affirmation of freedom in Jesus Christ and on faith as a resource for overcoming crisis. The white pastor on the other hand will focus on the way the gospel addresses fear, racism and commitment to sharing in the struggles of social justice. To do this the author states his vision to fulfil the vocation of the ministry, the pastor has to be a practical theologian who can discern the meaning of the gospel within the particular context of his or her ministry (DeGruchy, p. 40). In the final chapter of this work, De Gruchy explains how the pastor as practical theologian would do this in the South African context. It is here that we have a model of a hermeneutic that takes spirituality and social intervention seriously. He speaks of a "pastoral-hermeneutical circle" that maintains four moments. This contributes to the theological formation of the people of God which is "a dynamic process in which the ministry of the word of God, witness-praxis, theological reflection and an understanding of the historical context interact" (DeGruchy, 1986, p. 145).

To grasp the author's description of the process fully, one needs to understand the four moments he described earlier in his book. They are insertion-social, analysis-theological, reflection-pastoral and planning. The first moment describes the initial experiences of the congregation. In South Africa this might include, for example, the implications of a funeral of a church member shot dead by the state police. The second moment examines the reasons for those experiences. It is the attempt to interpret this *kairos*. Theological reflection, the third moment, is the spiritual analysis of the situation. The final moment is when "the pastor as practical theologian becomes an enabler of prophetic words and deeds within the congregation" (DeGruchy, 1986, p. 89). This whole process, for De Gruchy, is a spiral in which the witness and action of the church are the praxis.

This model has much to offer a contextualized social empowerment that seriously integrates spirituality. Unfortunately, it is highly clerical. Even with the author's disclaimers, one leaves the text with the distinct impression that only the ordained minister can engage in the process. But it is important to see how a holistic hermeneutic drives the empowerment in a context where religion promoted the marginalization of significant numbers of the population.

LIBERATION THEOLOGY: THE CASE OF HAITI

Perhaps we are more familiar with the model that has emerged from liberation theology in Latin America. In reality one must speak about liberation theologies because of the plurality of approaches that exist on the continent. For our purposes here we will look at the integration we are discussing in this paper with the praxis of liberation in Haiti. Although this reflection is the least developed of any country in Latin America, it is the only nation in the world that actually elected a person with such a political option to the presidency of the country.[1]

To grasp the complexity of the situation in Haiti, three socio-demographic realities need to be grasped. For the past three decades, the average annual rate of growth in the agricultural sector (which employs 74 percent of the country) has been stagnant and in the turbulent decade since the overthrow of the Duvalier regime in 1986, chaos has reigned, even in the ability of the World Bank to report verifiable figures. Second, every social indicator now places this nation as unquestionably the poorest in the Western hemisphere; Haiti is referred to in Canada as part of the Fourth World. Finally, in country migration and emigration makes all census figures highly suspect.

To understand the world view of Haitians, it is critical to grasp how superstition, fatalism, paternalism, population explosion, illiteracy, malnutrition and AIDS are affecting these people. As Hubron (1972) described in *Dieu dans le Vaudou Haitien*, voodoo runs through the nation's total economic and social framework. Understanding the world view is impossible if one does not understand the dialectic that goes on between the poor taxed by superstitions and voodoo practices of the dominant classes that use this belief system to give meaning to life yet control them. Everything from "spells" on the tap-tap (taxi) to protect it to participation in the national lottery (three per day) provide a lens on living.

All these factors surface in the Haitian urban context. More than 55 percent of urban dwellers live in absolute poverty. The causes are extensive unemployment and underemployment—90 percent of the urban population earns less than $150 per annum and only 20 percent receive the official daily $3 wage. Other causes are inadequate and unaffordable housing and a municipal infrastructure—only 21 percent of city dwellers have access to sewers and drinking water. Automobile emissions, open waste and the persistent use of charcoal continue to make ecological concerns a preoccupation of non-governmental agencies involved in transformative community development in cities.

Prior to all ... seeing, judging and acting (Boff, 1987),[2] liberation theology requires a lived commitment with the poor. This is deeply presuppositional within the reflection and surfaces constantly in the works of Latin American writers. In Haiti, it is estimated today that there are more than 3000 TKLs,[3] including 10-50 people across the country that represent the base communities within Roman Catholic parishes. Furthermore, better than 35 percent of the population is registered in Protestant congregations that take a different structural approach yet remain active in social life in this distressed country. This principle motivates much empowerment praxis. The Brazilian bishop, Dom Helder Camara's thoughts on praxis are summed in his statement, "[T]he first great discovery we made was that people who don't know how to read or write still know how to think" (Skudlarek, 1987, p. 131).

Liberation theology is practised through the instruments of a social-analytical reflection of the situation, a Biblical reflection concerning the poor and a practical mediation discovering the steps to implement a plan of action to overcome oppression. In the first mediation, the community reflects on the lived situation of the poor in their context (Schrieter, 1985, p. 13). It is at this juncture that theology becomes political and the involvement is "an urgent invitation to take sides with the abandoned and oppressed" (Boff, 1987, p. 161). The second mediation engages the community in the hermeneutical circle in which the Biblical text retains the primacy of value in a "tense, critical indeed dramatic relationship ... which rules the rhythm of the dialectical movement" (Boff, 1987, p. 135). The practical mediation, dictated by the previously praxis-mediated analysis, forces the community to ask the tough questions about the nature of the engagement, the social position to be undertaken and how to bring the second mediation to bear on the context.

Gustave Gutiérrez has shaped much of liberation reflection across the continent and especially in Haiti through the writings and work of Geoffrey Midi and Jules Casseus. We see how empowerment and spirituality intersect when he writes:

> [W]hen we assert that man [woman] fulfills him[her]self by continuing the work of creation by means of his[her] labor, we are saying that [s]he places[her] himself, by this very fact within an all-embracing salvific process. To work to transform this world is to become a man[woman] and to build the human community; it is to save. Likewise, to struggle against misery and exploitation and to build a just society is to be part of the saving action .... Any theological reflection on human work and societal praxis ought to be rooted in this fundamental affirmation. (Gutiérrez, 1973, p. 159-60)

THE AFRICAN AMERICAN CHURCH

The African American church has long been regarded as the backbone of the black community. It has been more than a place of worship, it has also served as a source of social and material support, social service centre, social control and activism. For many in the community it has served to provide them models, opportunities and a source of personal and group empowerment. When their white Christian counterparts neglected to take a stand against slavery, racism, discrimination and the poverty that disproportionately affected African

Americans, the African American church stood for justice through social change. The development of a separate institution, the black church "was necessary to ensure a sense of community, control over decision making, accumulation of wealth and property, black leadership, and an institutional basis to influence and challenge the dominant social and economic and political order" (Maton and Wells, 1995, p. 185). The history of the civil rights movement that had widespread implications for many different oppressed and disenfranchised peoples in the US was spoken from the pulpits, sung from the choir lofts and written on the walls of African American churches. The result was a political movement that brought in constitutional changes, anti-discrimination laws and an ethos of inclusiveness in America.

However, the African American church has lost part of its central role in the community. Several factors have contributed to this change: the decline in the African American male population; repression of females because of an inflexible authoritarian male model (Tapia, 1996); imitation of the excesses of the white church resulting in a progressive detachment from the poor and downtrodden; and a failure to retool its historical message to respond to new social problems. One of the most obvious indications of its loss of power in the African American community is the decline in attendance. Whereas "a generation ago 80 percent of blacks went to church. Today that figure is 40 per cent" (Tapia, 1996, p. 27).

However, some African American churches have turned to economic empowerment to meet the needs of their parishioners and establish a new level of relevance. Several efforts noted by Tapia (1996) include setting up schools, insurance companies, building housing, automobile refurbishing and retailing, credit unions and economic development corporations.

FEMINIST COMMUNITIES

Feminists spiritual support groups combine therapy, group work, spirituality and ritual to empower women individually and as a group. Characteristics of feminist spirituality are rooted in women's experiences "placing women at the center, reverencing the earth and all creation, valuing women's body and bodily functions, seeking an interconnectedness with all living things and placing an emphasis on ritual" (Neu, 1995, p. 189). These groups have multiple functions, on one end of the continuum they give women a sense of healing and personal power to celebrate their identity. On the other hand they create a context for women to create their own spirituality amid a patriarchal culture, while recognizing "the oppression of women, especially poor women and women of diverse racial and ethnic backgrounds, and their dependent children. They seek to change social structures and personal attitudes to stop oppression" (Neu, 1995, p. 191). Through feminist spiritual support groups women have experienced healing from the pain associated with past violence, release from the trauma associated with the profundity of making life decisions and affirmation in establishing life defining issues.

Some women believe that the formula for women's wholeness is the integration of political feminism with feminist spirituality. Although this notion is highly controversial and the source of some schism within the feminist movement, some women believe that mutual respect of the political and spiritual is warranted. Budapest believes that if blessings and rituals were done at political meetings, women would have a focus that is a blend of intellectual, emotional and spiritual power (Budapest and Downey, 1995).

CHRISTIAN BASED COMMUNITIES: THE SAN ANTONIO, TEXAS EXPERIENCE

Employing much of the theory and techniques of liberation theology as practised in Latin America, an attempt was made to adapt the praxis and concientization model to an American population living in a barrio and recently thrown out of work by the Levi Strauss Company that had relocated to Mexico. Representatives from Mennonite and Presbyterian congregations organized a small group of displaced workers around the common issues of their spirituality and loss of work. Using the praxis of collaboration as a model for community governance, the endeavour focused on raising the level of consciousness of its members regarding their plight, contextualizing their collective experiences, visualizing opportunities for themselves and taking action. The result has been a thriving supportive community that has supported its members in pursuing trades, college education and the opening of a collectively owned restaurant.

INTEGRAL ASPECTS OF SPIRITUALITY IN EMPOWERMENT PRACTICE

Spirituality and empowerment practice are companions and not forces working alone or opposite each other. We consider four factors in making the assumption of the compatibility of empowerment and spirituality. One, as discussed earlier, it is common that many disenfranchised people have a spiritual belief system with which they identify and in some cases are deeply committed to it. Although this belief system, be it either religious or spiritual, may have been used to reinforce the powerlessness of the group, it nevertheless is unrealistic to expect people to give it up to believe in a new untested political "religion." Instead, with informed contextualization and a rereading of the sacred texts it is very likely that an empowering theme may emerge, one that provides a conscientization of group members and inspires them to move toward social change. The reframing of these central belief systems into an empowerment dialectic helps the disempowered gain knowledge, strength and motivation to identify their needs, clearly define their plight, plan for social changes and mobilize themselves to create solutions to their problem of powerlessness.

Two, on a related point, disempowered people often need a purpose that transcends their mere existence as a rationale for moving beyond their present social position. It is not uncommon for the disempowered to possess poor self-esteem and fatalistic views of life. However, spiritual purposes, emerging from belief and faith systems, often serve as an important source of power that positively affects self-perceptions and replaces fatalism with possibilities. In the face of despair, spirituality is often the inspiration for taking risks to pursue change, both personal and social. There are many examples of personal and group empowerment activities that have occurred because people realized their god did not will their disenfranchised condition, nor was pleased with it.

Three, empowerment practice requires a sense of soulfulness (Moore, 1995) created in a caring, supportive and empathetic community that enables the person/group to believe in themselves, prepare for change, move out and risk all while creating a new order through social change. This soulfulness is inherently spiritual because it requires a sense of connection and relation with others that transcends mere empathy and reflects the deepest levels of understanding and belief in another person, while providing a supportive community that will counsel and console during the time of change and transition.

Four organized, religiously motivated endeavours can provide tangible support in the following manner "by instilling a mobilizing vision and critical awareness anchored in socially conscious religious principles; providing meaningful roles and action in the context of religious community; providing an array of spiritual, economic and human support resources, providing spiritually inspired leadership" (Maton and Wells, 1995, p. 185) and an opportunity to develop leadership and other organizing skills.

SUMMARY AND CONCLUSION

The absence of spiritual integration in much social empowerment today has deep historical roots that manifest themselves in the three reasons we identified earlier: political-religious antagonism, the secularization of society and the Cartesian influence in the social sciences.

Throughout much of history, most human beings found themselves in a lifelong, single, very uniform cultural context. Today, in Canada and the United States, we constantly encounter people of different cultures, religious beliefs and various lifestyles through technology such as television and the Internet, the economy, as well as by rapid transportation that takes us to other places in a matter of hours and maintains communication that unifies the globe. The suggestion now is that this plurality of beliefs is justified in intellectual, cultural and religious life. Therefore, interventions with individuals and groups need to consider the proper social-cultural-spiritual context.

The poor and the marginalized are teaching us that community transformation has everything to do with being spirit people. Empowerment requires following the lead of those who own the problem, understand their context, plan for social change and mobilize as a group for change. Maybe our modern practices and theories need to catch up.

Lessons from the international and marginalized North American communities provide social workers engaged in empowerment practice with some important thoughts and possibilities for integrating spirituality in empowerment practice. These integrative possibilities may range from celebrating the spiritual in everyday life to formal inclusion of spiritually based rituals, beliefs or behaviours in the empowerment process. For example, on one hand it is apparent that social workers should not dismiss the power of the spiritual in the lives of people and groups. It is a force that needs to be understood, embraced and utilized because it is quintessentially starting where the client is. On the other hand, inclusion of faith-based organizations and churches or other formal processes should be considered. Collaborating with these groups may or may not prove to be fruitful. However, one never knows until an attempt is made. But, an oppositional relationship with religious groups, of which the disempowered are members, is not likely to advance the overall goals of empowerment. These members most probably will be unwilling to choose a new and unproven religion over one known and proven. Social workers must find ways to work together with religious organizations that also serve the under-represented, if not to at least peacefully coexist.

ENDNOTES

[1] For an overview of liberation theology in the Haitian context see, Gedefroy Midy, Jalons pour une theologie haitienne liberatrice en dialogue avec G. Gutiérrez et J.L. Segundo. Unpublished doctoral thesis. Universite de Montreal. 1977; Jules Casseus, Haiti: Quelle Eglise, Quelle Liberation (Limbe: P.U.C.N.H., 1992).

[2] These three participles (often functioning as well as gerunds) summarize the three meditations of liberation practice.

[3] This is the Creole expression for the *"petites commaunates locales"* that are the small groups popularized in Brazil by liberation theology in that country.

REFERENCES

Berger, P. (1992). *A far glory*. Toronto: Macmillian.

Bergren-Thomas, G. (1995). Spiritual need or spiritual journey. *Journal of Gerontological Nursing*, 21, 5-9.

Boff, C. (1987) *Theology and praxis*. Maryknoll NY: Orbis.

Budapest, Z. and Downey, K. (1995) Spiritual dandelions. *Women and Therapy*, 17(½), 97-102.

Canda, E. (1990). Afterward: Spirituality reexamined. *Spirituality and Social Work Communicator*, 1(1), 13-14.

De Gruchy, J. W. (1986). *Theology and ministry in context and crisis*. Grand Rapids: Eerdmans.

Derezotes, D. (1995). Spirituality and religiosity: Neglected factors in social work practice. *Arete*, 20(1), 1-15.

Freire, P. (1972). *Pedagogy of the oppressed*. Maryknoll, NY: Orbis.

Gutiérrez, G. (1973). *Theology of liberation*. Maryknoll, NY: Orbis.

Hubron, L. (1972). *Dieu dans le vaudin Haitien*. Paris: Payot.

Joseph, V. (1987). The religious and spiritual aspects of clinical practice: A neglected dimension of social work. *Social Thought*, 39(2), 12-23.

Lane, G. (1984). *Christian spirituality: An historical sketch*. Chicago: Loyola University Press.

Maton, K.I. and Wells, J. (1995). Religion as a community resource for well-being: Prevention, healing, and empowerment pathways. *Journal of Social Change*, 51(2), 177-192.

Moore, T. (1995). *Soulmates*. New York: Harper.

Neu, D. (1995). Women's empowerment through feminist rituals. *Women and Therapy*, 16(2/3) 185-200.

Ortiz, L. and Langer, N. (1997). *Spiritual well being and aging*. (Unpublished manuscript).

Schrieter, R. (1985). *Constructing local theologies*. Maryknoll, NY: Orbis.

Skudlarek, W. (1987). A most transparent life: An interview with Dom Helder Camara. *Sojourners*, 19.

Smith, G. (1989). *Essential spirituality*. Nashville: Thomas Nelson Publishing.

Solomon, B. (1976) *Black empowerment*. New York: Columbia University Press.

Tapia, A. (1996). Soul searching: How is the black church responding to the urban crisis? *Christianity Today*, 40(3), 26-33.

Chapter 18

EMPOWERMENT THROUGH ORGANIZED RELIGION

Ram A. Cnaan
Program for the Study of Organized Religion and Social Work
School of Social Work
University of Pennsylvania

Barbara Solomon (1976) first introduced the concept of empowerment into social work in her book *Black Empowerment*. She saw the process of empowerment as a means of increasing the personal, interpersonal, political and economic power so that people could take action to improve their life situations. As her ideas took hold, social work professionals began to make the case for empowerment as the best means of assisting the needy and the disfranchised. Although social work scholars have yet to agree on a single definition of empowerment, there is general consensus that the term implies a dual commitment by the profession to: 1) assist clients in solving problems of immediate concern and 2) assist individuals and groups in asserting their needs and bringing about change in social systems and power relationships. Before discussing the role of organized religion in empowerment, it is appropriate to consider how the literature has defined and addressed issues of empowerment.

The literature provides several definitions of empowerment. Parsloe (1996) described empowerment as "users of social services having greater control over the services they receive" (p. xvii). Rappaport (1987) defined empowerment

The work on this chapter was supported by a generous grant from the Lilly Endowment to study the role of local religious congregations in the provision of social and community services. The author wishes to thank Stephanie Boddie and Eileen Lynch for helpful comments and editorial assistance. The chapter is dedicated to my friend and colleague Antonin Wagner, who marched the course of priesthood to social work and symbolizes the beauty in both.

as a process or mechanism "by which people, organizations, and community gain mastery over their affairs, and involve themselves in the democratic processes of their community and their employing institutions"(p. 122). To Osborne and Gaebler (1992), empowerment meant that the locus of control shifts from the agency to the community. Cohen and Austin (1997) offered a broader interpretation, noting that "despite its widespread acceptance, the concept of empowerment has been applied almost exclusively to the relationship between professional social workers and their clients"(p. 37) and suggested that empowerment be extended to service providers as well. They also pointed out that empowerment is not limited to help/service relationships but is relevant to all aspects of social life. This perspective agrees with that of Saleebey (1992) who wrote that empowerment "requires a deep belief in the necessity of democracy and the contingent capacity of people to participate in the decisions and actions that define their world" (p. 8).

Underlying these definitions is the assumption of an imbalance in power relationships in society. Empowerment helps rectify this imbalance by providing the weak with the means to counteract the oppression that can stem from power relationships, whether they be that of helper/client, rich or poor or of government. The goal of empowerment in all instances is to have individuals assert their preferences, assume an active role in the change process and have control over their environment. The literature cites a number of different means to achieve this goal yet totally neglects the role of the religious community in empowering people. I propose to reverse this trend by demonstrating the important, but unheralded, role of religious organizations in the human quest for empowerment.

In this chapter, I first discuss relationships between the powerful and the powerless as well as the tenets common to organized religion in America that call for support and equality for the oppressed. I then present examples of ways in which organized religion has helped empower populations that have been identified by social work as in need of assistance. Finally, I suggest that cooperation between organized religion and social work may significantly advance the cause of empowerment.

POWER AND POWERLESSNESS

Gaventa (1980) raised the issue of why non-elites fail to challenge the domination of elites in certain social relationships. He called this type of situation "quiescence." Logically, people should resist being dominated and exploited by others. Yet, if it is assumed that the elite elicit the cooperation of the non-elite by a process of bargaining in a mutually agreed upon field such as public hearings or negotiations, then non-elites may be unaware of either their right to refuse cooperation or the long-term effects of the power relationship. Robert Dahl (1961), in an attempt to solve this paradox, claimed that people have different interests. He distinguished between the *homo politicus*, the social activist who is involved in planning and decision-making, and the *homo civicus*, the non-activist who is involved in work, family, leisure and personal matters and rarely, if ever, in social issues. As many social workers can attest, this model reflects empowerment in our society. On the one hand, we have the middle and upper classes who are seldom the victims of powerlessness. On the other, we have the disadvantaged whose low income, job insecurity, poor housing conditions and low-level education are significantly associated with political apathy, minimal civic participation, alienation and passivity. Thus, the role of the so-called *homo civicus* for many disadvantaged people is not due to choice but to circumstances over which they have no control.

What Dahl and many others have failed to see is that gaining power is a dynamic process and keeping power is a means of perpetuating the powerlessness of others. Once certain groups or individuals gain control, their interests lie in maintaining the power relationship. One way to maintain the status quo is to create complex and intimidating procedural mechanisms that forestall any action or grievances on the part of the powerless. Faced with these formidable barriers, those seeking redress of power imbalances are likely to give up long before the process can gain momentum and lead to mobilization for change.

Existing power relationships that benefit the elite can also be maintained by keeping social processes that make any challenge to the status quo a threat to established norms. This implicit social pressure immediately puts the individual or group with a grievance at a severe disadvantage. Under the aegis of established norms, sanctions, rewards, political structures, due processes and laws created by those in power, the weaker segment of society lives almost normally with the power imbalance or is, at least, unwilling to rock the boat (Solomon, 1976). For example, shouts and threat in a formal meeting are viewed as unprofessional and unacceptable. Those who would challenge the power imbalance are viewed as un-American and too liberal even by those who are its victims. When the powerless attempt to revolt or change the power balance, they are almost always defeated, and their defeat becomes a lesson to others that attempts to overturn power relationship are costly and futile. Evans (1992) noted that powerlessness sets in motion a cycle of self-reinforcing defeats, also known as "learned helplessness." This is why Gaventa (1980) concluded that "A sense of powerlessness may manifest itself as extensive fatalism, self-deprecation, or undue apathy about one's situation" (p. 17). Gaventa further noted that:

> Continual defeat gives rise not only to the conscious deferral of action but also to a sense of defeat, or a sense of powerlessness, that may affect the consciousness of potential challengers about grievances, strategies, or possibilities for change. Participation denied over time may lead to acceptance of the role of non-participation, as well as to a failure to develop the political resources—skills, organization, consciousness—of political action. (p. 255)

How then can power imbalances be rectified? How can people raised in an environment that stresses obedience and conformity change their way of thinking and become actively empowered? Scholars have argued that one way to bring about change is through the involvement of people who know the importance of political participation in the political process. However, as Pateman (1970) noted, political learning and awareness are dependent, to certain degree, on political participation. Those who have had the opportunity to engage in a political process in at least one area are more likely to use the skills they have acquired in other political contexts. However, those who are denied participation, even if they are politically conscious, are unable to actively engage in any political activity. Salamon and Van Evera (1973), for example, found that lack of political participation and low voting rates among African Americans in the South were due more to fear of the local power elite than to political apathy. This showed that some patterns in power relationships are due to obvious fear of repercussions if and when resistance or "unaccepted" and "un-normative" behaviour is expressed. In this chapter, we will observe how organized religion can and did challenge such power relationships.

EMPOWERMENT AND ORGANIZED RELIGION

The major monotheistic religions in the United States share in common the belief that all human beings are created by God and equal in God's sight. This is the case even though in other parts of the world some religious groups believe in human dignity and worth for believers only. This belief in equality is expressed in religious tenets that call for equal and respectful treatment of all—poor and rich, young and old, man and woman, black and white—without exception. Yet one of the many contradictions between religious teaching and daily life is that many professedly religious people consider themselves superior to others. Nevertheless, the emphasis on the equality of all God's people by the religious community gives the concept of empowerment a powerful moral and ethical underpinning.

Unfortunately, the role of organized religion in individual and group empowerment has been widely overlooked and undervalued. As Warner (1993) pointed out, congregations socialize members from a young age to recognize that they are not the victims of circumstances and that they can solve personal and collective problems. Warner further noted that ethic groups in America have historically used organized religion as a means of creating a sense of community, sharing the adaptation experience and assisting one another financially and emotionally. This same scenario is being played out today among many Southeast Asian immigrants to the United States. Many who are neither Christians nor religious have become active church members because the church represents a base of support and communal life that goes beyond religious beliefs. This is true for many other groups in America. Haddad and Lummis (1987) and Chazanov (1991) found that among Sunni Moslems, the Imam, traditionally a member elected as prayer leader, has became a de facto community leader. The Imam represents his people in public forums (such as an ecumenical coalitions or vis-à-vis city hall) and also conducts marriages and funerals, visits the sick and counsels families. As with the case of Asian churches, mosques in the United States have become centres for education, social services, social activities and cultural events as well as religious worship. These roles are unique to America and stem from the fact that the nation's churches and mosques serve as a source of mutual support and a power base for people who share the same ethnic, socio-economic and religious heritage.

As noted earlier, Rappaport (1987) defined empowerment as conveying both a sense or feeling of personal control or influence and actual influence of both individuals and groups. In line with this definition, Strader and his colleagues (1997) reported that church volunteers who participated in a program of church based drug abuse prevention reported significantly higher levels of empowerment after the project than before the project. Their findings indicate that individuals who learn participation skills through church work are able to apply their knowledge and skills to other social arenas and demonstrate involvement in local power relationships. Brady, Verba and Schlozman (1995), in a major national study, also found that religious organizations are key teachers of political and civic skills. They defined these skills in terms of concrete activities such as letter-writing, participating in decision-making meetings, planning and chairing meetings and giving presentations or speeches in public forums. These activities represent the most rudimentary skills needed to transform and change power relationships. When the authors asked respondents where they had gained these skills, a significant number cited their church work. The authors concluded that church members who learn how to write letters in support of religious activities, collect money for a social ministry or organize weekly bible study groups can use those same skills to participate in political life. It is interesting to note that Brady, Verba and Schlozman (1995) considered their findings so surprising that they rechecked their survey data.

In the following section I would like to demonstrate how religious groups, institutions and theologies have helped people gain control over their lives and show that religion can be a key force in the quest for empowerment. The six examples are: African Americans, a Philadelphia based Hispanic community, women, gay and lesbian people, religious based coalitions and the contribution of liberation theology. Each one serves as an interesting case in and of itself, yet combined they weave the tapestry of religious contribution to human empowerment.

EMPOWERMENT OF THE AFRICAN AMERICAN COMMUNITY THROUGH ORGANIZED RELIGION

Historically, the black church was the only place where the African American community could gather for mutual aid and support. This was particularly true in the years prior to the Civil War when African Americans were held as slaves and forbidden any education. White churches of the day would not accept them because their members considered slavery to be acceptable and blacks to be inferior. For these oppressed people, the black church became a refuge where they could learn to read and write and develop a sense of community. Thom Moore (1991) described the activities of black church members:

What followed for them was among the earliest empowering activities of the slaves. They began organizing their own worship services. After a day's work or on Sunday evenings, at a prearranged time they would meet in a slave's home for an evening of singing, preaching, telling of Bible stories, and praying. At other times they would meet in open fields, which became known as "hush harbors," where they could be relatively safe from detection. (p. 153)

According to Raboteau (1978), the black church was the place where slaves gained experienced communal support, developed a sense of group and gained spiritual sustenance. Even today, as Sarfoh (1986) noted, the black church remains the only institution that seeks to foster a sense of personal identity as well as group unity and solidarity among ghetto residents.

W. E. B. DuBois (as discussed in Manning, 1985) attacked all Christian denominations not only for their support of slavery in the past but also for their indifference to racial segregation and discrimination in his own time. Nevertheless, he considered the black church of his day to be the social centre for the African American community and black clergy to be politically radical in the ante-bellum tradition of slave preacher and rebel Nat Turner, the most distinctive expression of the African American character. DuBois (1903) also wanted this because their congregations viewed their clergy as community leaders. And rightly so. The black clergy generally were better educated. They offered hope and were genuinely concerned with people's lives and struggles. Most important, these clergy were neither selected by nor dependent upon the powerful white elite.

According to Bear and Singer (1992), the black church is more than a place of worship. It is a multi-functional institution that has developed many communal institutions for African Americans such as schools, credit unions, banks, insurance companies and low-income housing projects, some of which are discussed below. Equally important, black churches and mosques are the hub of political training and political participation. Lincoln and Mamiya (1990), in a survey of black clergy, found that 92 percent advocated church involvement in social and political issues. According to Caldwell, Greene and Billingsley (1992), the social and political involvement of clergy in black churches is both significant and expected. This is important for empowerment because, as the literature notes, many in the African American community are unaware of or uninformed about political news and issues. Reese and Brown (1995), for example, reported that members of black churches are likely to hear two messages from the pulpit. One message stresses civil awareness, which leads to a heightened sense of racial identity. The other message stresses political activity, which leads to a clearer perception of the power imbalance among groups. As I discussed previously, both identity and the perception of a power imbalance are crucial to the evolution of empowerment.

The institution that is most influential in making African Americans politically aware is the black church. A national survey by the Pew Research Center for the People and the Press (1996), for example, found that black church members were much more likely to have heard from their ministers about health care reform (62 percent) than were white church members (19 percent), while the same percentage of black and white church members (73 percent) reported hearing about prayer in schools. In other words, the black church is active, both theologically and politically, in issues relevant to the quality of life of African Americans. In a comparative study of white and black congregations, Chaves and Higgins (1992) found "compelling evidence that black congregations are more likely to be involved than white congregations in *certain kinds* [emphasis in original] of traditionally non-religious activities: civil rights activities and those activities that are directed at disprivileged segments of their local communities." They also found that "this race effect is not explainable by the organizational or environmental variables available" (p. 438). As such, political education and empowerment are by-products of religion. People come to attend religious services and, in the process, become more politically aware and more prepared for political participation (Wilcox and Gomez, 1990). Wilcox and Gomez also found that regular church attendance and participation in church organizations and clubs increased political participation by African Americans.

Further evidence of empowerment by organized religion can be found in the civil rights movement. Black churches provided the social base that helped make the movement possible and served as the training ground for many of its leaders. Jesse Jackson, for example, said "the church was like my laboratory, my first actual public stage, where I began to develop and practice my speaking powers" (quoted in Frady, 1996, p. 59). Dr. Martin Luther King, Jr. was another example of the outstanding leaders produced by the black church (Battle, 1988). These churches did more than train leaders; they served as the local suppliers and headquarters of the civil rights movement. As Aldon Morris (1984) observed:

> Churches provided the [civil rights] movement with an organized mass base; a leadership of clergymen largely economically independent of the larger white society and skilled in the art of managing people and resources; an institutionalized financial base through which protest was financed; and meeting places where the masses planned tactics and strategies and collectively committed themselves to the struggle. (p. 4)

Following the civil rights movement, African American congregations became active in urban renewal, black business enterprises, economic redevelopment and housing projects. DePriest and Jones (1997) noted that Christian capitalism encourages African Americans to pool their dollars and invest in one another's enterprises and local communities. African American clergy encouraged their members to support black-owned businesses as a means of creating financially viable and stable communities. This model is in contradiction to that of white businesses whose support for the community is generally limited to charitable donations or services such as soup kitchens. These types of support, although they may help meet community needs, have no effect on rectifying the power imbalance.

Another important religious force in the African American community is the Nation of Islam. Under the leadership of Elijah Muhammad and the influence of Malcolm X, the Nation of Islam is credited with transforming the self-perception of African Americans. Feelings of inferiority to white people gave way to a new spirit of racial identity evoked in terms such as "black power," "black pride," "black consciousness" and perhaps most important, "black is beautiful." This approach is known as "reverse superiority." The fact that these messages were endorsed by religious authority empowered African Americans who, for generations, had seen themselves as powerless in white America and now experienced a sense of pride and self-importance. This change in perception invigorated and strengthened the civil rights movement and energized a generation of young African Americans (Battle, 1988; Lincoln and Mamiya, 1993). Battle (1988) noted that although the Islamic movement in the United States had its origins in racism, the Nation of Islam taught its members to focus on education and economic development. The Nation of Islam, especially under Elijah Muhammad's leadership, purchased numerous businesses and used them to train African Americans as employees and potential owners.

Currently, black churches have been expanding their efforts and advocacy in new directions. Tapia (1996) noted: "There is a rising class of black churches that are energizing whole communities through economic empowerment projects, effective work at getting kids off drugs, keeping them out of jail, and sending them to college" (p. 27). Black churches, more than any other group of churches, are also involved in acquiring properties in their communities and/or building new ones. DePriest and Jones (1997) highlighted a few such cases. Wheat Street Church in Atlanta, Georgia, for example, owns real estate valued at $33 million. The holdings include a senior citizens home and a low-income family development. Although both were built with public money, the church initiated the projects and, through its subsidiary nonprofit organization, has revitalized the community and provided local people with jobs and sense of pride. The congregation also has a credit union with approximately 1000 members and more than one million dollars in assets. This credit union, an institution common to many black churches, provides financial help to people who often are refused loans by commercial banks (a form of maintaining power by the elite). The empowerment offered by a credit union is attested to by a member who said "You become an owner and share in the proceeds through interest dividends" (DePriest and Jones, 1997, p. 196). This is but one example of how proactive African American congregations build an economic infrastructure in their community that provides employment opportunities, services and sense of ownership as well as social and economic skills for African Americans. Without the church, it is likely that their only contacts with the financial system would be as victims or servers at the lowest end of the spectrum.

Similar success stories of economic development in dilapidated urban areas have been reported for Hartford Memorial Baptist Church in Detroit, Allen African Methodist Episcopal church in Los Angeles and St. Edwards in Chicago (Stodghill, 1996). A story less often told is that of economic empowerment in rural America. Gite (1993) reported the case of Mendenhall Bible Church in Mississippi. Established in the 1970s, this nondenominational church, which has only 125 members, purchased a long-abandoned school building and remodelled it with the help of 200 volunteers from Aurora, Illinois. The building, now a business complex, houses a health clinic, law office, thrift shop, elementary school and recreation centre. The 200-member Greater Christ Temple Church in Meridian, Mississippi is another case in point. The church, whose members were near or at the poverty level, now owns three restaurants, a bakery, an auto repair shop and 4000 acres of farm land with 700 head of cattle and two meat-processing plants. The holdings of the church are under the auspices of its nonprofit corporation REACH Inc. (Research Education and Community Hope). According to Gite, Greater Christ Temple Church enabled its 200 members to get off welfare by pooling their resources.

EMPOWERMENT OF AN HISPANIC COMMUNITY THROUGH ORGANIZED RELIGION: A CASE STUDY

Our discussion to this point has centred on the role of organized religion in empowering African Americans, but I wish to stress that many other minority groups in America have been and continue to be empowered through organized religion. Jews in America, for example, formed many mutual help associations, free loan societies and other religious based mechanisms of support and enhancement that made their transition into mainstream society easier and faster (Tenenbaum, 1993). Due to space limitations, however, we have confined our discussion to one case study: Nueva Esperanza, a religious based nonprofit organization in Philadelphia serving the Hispanic community.

Nueva Esperanza, the idea of the Reverend Luis Cortes, is one of the few ecumenical grass roots Hispanic agencies in Pennsylvania (Blake, 1991).

Reverend Cortes first came to Philadelphia from New York in the early 1980s as a theology professor at Eastern Baptist Theological Seminary. Deeply disturbed by the fragmentation, under-representation and political weakness of Philadelphia's Hispanic community, he pushed for the formation of the Hispanic Clergy of Philadelphia and Vicinity, an ecumenical coalition. The coalition, in turn, formed Nueva Esperanza which means "new hope."

Through Nueva Esperanza, religious leaders working with the local Hispanic community have made enormous strides. They have built five housing units for senior citizen housing in North Philadelphia. They also developed Villa Esperanza, a home ownership project consisting of 14 three-bedroom townhouses project and another 21-unit housing development. Local residents, mostly Hispanic, were hired to work on both development projects. These housing projects have enabled people with very low income to obtain a $100,000 house for $35,000 with mortgage payments of only $300 a month. The goal of Nueva Esperanza is to empower people as residents, as home-owners and as employees in local businesses hired to carry out the job. In collaboration with a local businessman, they have also developed a full-service community laundromat (La Lavanderia del Pueblo) which handles 2500 loads of wash daily. La Lavanderia also serves as a community centre with a small library and classrooms for GED classes and bible study. In addition, Nueva Esperanza runs an afternoon tutorial program for children.

In 1997, Nueva Esperanza received a $656,000 grant from the Commonwealth of Pennsylvania to expand its job-training program. The fact that such a large grant was awarded to a religious affiliated organization indicates that organized religion is currently the main representative and advocate for the Hispanic community in Philadelphia. It should be emphasized that the grant award and the need to work closely with city officials have in no way diminished the advocacy role of the Hispanic Clergy of Philadelphia and Vicinity. They helped organize the campaign to prevent riverboat gambling in Philadelphia, which had the support of the mayor, and they advocated for increased representation and recognition of Hispanics on Philadelphia's police force. The successful lobbying by the Hispanic church leaders resulted in positive results in both instances.

In 1994, the City of Philadelphia, in collaboration with Camden, NJ, applied to the federal government for empowerment zone status and funding. Even before the federal government had made any decision, fierce competition erupted among many neighbourhoods in the city as to which one should be awarded the status and the money. The Hispanic Clergy of Philadelphia and Vicinity, Nueva Esperanza and Reverend Cortes fought hard and publicly to have American Street, where most Latino people reside, included in the empowerment zone. Finally, in 1995, Mayor Ed Rendell allocated $29 million of Philadelphia's share of the $79 million in empowerment-zone funding to American Street (Twyman, 1995). Despite the allocation, Reverend Cortes, Nueva Esperanza and the Hispanic Clergy of Philadelphia and Vicinity have remained at odds with city hall as to what businesses would be approved in American Street. The mayor's office, for example, has suggested locating a beer distribution centre on an empty lot, while Nueva Esperanza has pushed for a commercial centre that would house a Taco Bell, Pep Boys and classrooms. The stalemate is yet one more indication that organized religion is the sole voice speaking out for Hispanics in Philadelphia. And it is due to the efforts of organized religion that the social, political and economic rights of Hispanic people are currently being protected and advanced.

EMPOWERMENT OF WOMEN THROUGH ORGANIZED RELIGION

It is no surprise to most people that the more a modern American woman is identified with feminism, the less she is identified with organized religion (Wuthnow, 1988). This view, however, is mitigated by the influence of the extreme religious right and ignores the historical contribution of organized religions, whether intended or not, to promote the rights and equality of women.

For many generations, organized religion had provided women with the opportunity to assert themselves and work for the public good outside the home. During the nineteenth and early twentieth centuries, for example, more than half of all missionaries were women (Xi, 1997). Missionary careers enabled women to train for professions such as medicine, nursing and teaching, and some, such as Pearl Buck, the author who wrote of China and its people, became nationally and internationally known for their work in the mission fields.

Spurred on by the example of women missionaries, other women began to form moral reform organizations. These organizations provided many women with their first opportunity to act outside the realm of home and community (Breton, 1989). As Carol Smith-Rosenberg (1985) noted: "Using religion to develop extra-domestic roles, [women] created powerful local and national single-sex organizations expressive of women's particular angers, anxieties, and demands" (p. 142). Prior to 1835, all women's associations were allied with churches (Cott, 1977). These were primarily educational groups, prayer groups, auxiliaries and benevolent societies. The fact that churches supported organizations whose leaders and members were women is remarkable considering the social inequality of women at this time. By the end of the Civil War, these church based women's organizations had begun to assert themselves as autonomous entities, and women began to gain a public voice outside the church.

Organized religion has also produced many organizations that worked with female victims of violence or sexual harassment in a non-patronizing manner. One example is the settlement houses of the Salvation Army. Magnuson (1977) reported that the staff in "Army homes" never referred to the women as "fallen women" or "cases," but rather as "sisters," "our girls" or "sisters who have stumbled." Similarly, among Catholics, devotion to St. Jude caused women to feel "empowered in new ways. They broke off relationships with 'mean' boyfriends [and] rejected unwanted medical treatments" (Orsi, 1991, p. 159).

An example of a church affiliated project to empower women in Gilpin Court, an inner-city neighbourhood in Richmond, Virginia, was reported by Amy Sherman (1996). Victory Christian Fellowship developed a program to get the women off welfare and out of the projects with the help of a ministry called STEP (Strategies to Elevate People). STEP has an academy where Gilpin Court residents can study and complete their GED or transfer into a community college. The program is offered at times convenient for the women and provides each of the 50 participants with a "Family Sharing Team." Each team is composed of three to six white suburban women who provide emotional, spiritual and often practical support to program participants, many of whom are trying to raise children while trying to advance their education and job opportunities. The program, which seeks to empower women on welfare, represents a collaborative effort by an inner-city church and suburban ministries.

Membership in a religious congregation has helped women assimilate and adapt to a new society even though they may not fully adhere to its religious tenets. Winland (1994), for example, reported on a group of Laotian Hmong refugee women in Ontario, Canada, who became Mennonites. The Mennonite church provided these women with a sense of empowerment over their new environment while respecting their social practices and values as Hmongs.

In recent years, the struggle for gender equality has permeated the sphere of organized religion. Although women are more religious than men (Wuthnow, 1988), historically they have been denied access to formal positions of religious leadership, particularly clerical ones (Baer, 1993). According to Ozorak (1996), the reason for this inequality is that most religions in the past did not advocate equality between genders. Ozorak found that women, despite their lower status in official church circles, are able to empower themselves through contacts and collaboration with those of higher status.

Recently, a growing number of denominations have begun to ordain women and appoint them to leadership positions. These include many mainstream Protestant and Jewish (except Orthodox Judaism) denominations. Wallace (1992), who reported on a group of Roman Catholic women who served as pastors in small unstaffed churches, noted these women felt spiritually empowered due to their acceptance and recognition by parishioners. In contrast to male priests, the women pastors knew each parishioner personally, encouraged them to become involved in parish life and tended to empower members to take ownership of their parish. While more conservative and evangelical denominations do not accept women as religious leaders, it is likely that the trend to more female clergy will continue, as church attendance by women is much higher than that by men. Lehman (1985), however, believed that women pastors have little chance of being accepted in large wealthy congregations or of being promoted to high ecclesiastical positions. But the road has already been paved, and the growing presence of women clergy in many churches will doubtless influence young women in the future.

Empowerment of women through organized religion is also taking place on an international scale. De Sousa (1995), for example, described a church sponsored program in which poor Brazilian women, in three groups of twenty-five each, received training in health and sexuality issues. The women, in turn, were expected to teach others. The author noted that the program was successful. The women were empowered psychologically, cognitively and physically, as indicated by their increased positive self-perception, extensive community health work, a campaign for change and broader knowledge regarding sexuality. This type of program obviously could have operated successfully elsewhere, but the fact that the program was operated in Brazil under the auspices and support of both Catholic and Methodist churches made it culturally acceptable to the women and those in their social network.

EMPOWERMENT OF THE GAY COMMUNITY THROUGH ORGANIZED RELIGION

Empowerment of the gay community first began under religious auspices when Troy Perry established the Metropolitan Community Church in Chicago in the early 1970s. The church fast became a centre where gay people could, for the first time, express themselves publicly. Perry founded the church for two reasons. One was to organize the gay community; the other was to actualize his pentecostal-inspired belief that he was created gay by a benevolent personal God (Perry, 1972). Gay people today can find many organizations in which they can express their own sexual identity, but for the times, Perry's church was considered revolutionary.

Perry's work has lead to a national denomination for gay, lesbians and bi-sexual people called the Universal Fellowship of Metropolitan Community

Churches. The new denomination, which has 22,000 members, is based on an orthodox Trinitarian theology with overtones of pentecostalism (Warner, 1989). The public opposition of many evangelical and conservative denominations to gay behaviour and gay rights should not detract from our appreciation of the church structure that allowed gay people their first public and open organization. As Dennis Altman (1982) noted: "In many places, the church is the only form of the gay movement that exists" (p. 123).

The United States is not the only country in which gay people have found support and power in organized religion. Sweet (1995) reported that, in 1982, groups of gay people began to affiliate themselves with Protestant churches in the former (East) German Democratic Republic. These congregants have become a fast-growing nucleus of the gay emancipation movement. Although infiltrated by the Stasi (secret police), the growth of the gay community within the German church was so rapid that the state eventually embarked on a program to integrate gay people into the socialist society. What is of relevance here is that the East German Protestant churches, although under total state control, were the first institutions that enabled gay people to organize and work together.

The rise of gay religious institutions in the post-Stonewall era has accelerated the process of gay empowerment in organized religion. Gay congregants have begun to press for greater tolerance within mainstream religious denominations, thereby counterbalancing the increased influence of the religious right. Gay houses of worship have also filled a variety of religious, political and social needs within the gay community. Shokeid (1995), for example, conducted an ethnographic study of Congregation Beth Simchat Torah (CBST), a gay synagogue founded in 1973 in New York's Greenwich Village. The synagogue has over a thousand members and recently hired its first ordained rabbi. Membership in CBST has enabled gay Jews to gain a sense of personal and collective identity in a world that regards them as anathema. CBST has affirmed the full personhood of its members through a process of continual negotiation designed to ensure that synagogue practices reflect both Jewish and gay values.

Gay empowerment through organized religions is not limited to the right to be ordained (in some denominations) or form a new denomination. In her study of congregations in changing communities, Ammerman (1997) found that members of congregations which included gay people were more likely to be active in their support for gay rights. One example cited by Ammerman is that of St. Matthew's Catholic Parish in Long Beach, California. In 1986, Cardinal Mahoney had asked parishes in his diocese to establish formal programs to meet the needs of their gay members. These programs were related to, but not limited to, the rise of the AIDS epidemic. St. Matthew's responded by sponsoring a Mass of healing for people with AIDS. This initial program step led to the formation of Comunidad, a group of gay people who met monthly. These individuals eventually joined the church and became members of the parish. "Comunidad members are quick to point out that they are integrated into all areas of parish life as lectors, altar servers, Eucharistic ministers, choir members, song leaders, and members of other parish committees, especially the Peace and Justice Committees" (Ammerman, 1997, p. 167). In this case, gay Catholics not only fully participated in parish life but also received the support of the parish for their social action organization Comunidad. An interesting issue raised in Ammerman's study is why the parish is so hospitable to people whose sexual preference is at odds with traditional Catholicism. A possible explanation offered by the author is that "They may not understand why some people are homosexual, but they are convinced that if God made them that way, they should be treated with respect every part of creation is due" (Ammerman, 1997, p. 171).

Another congregation that opened membership to gay people is the First Congregational Church in Long Beach, California. The church is part of the United Church of Christ, a denomination that has formally designated several of its congregations as "open and affirming." According to Ammerman, this is a "designation for congregations who not only are open to lesbians and gays, but affirm them by supporting them for leadership positions and taking their concerns seriously as congregational issues" (p. 175). The United Church of God not only permits the ordination of gay people but also encourages congregations to employ gay ministers, although this decision is left to the discretion of the local congregation. The level of inclusion and support for gays evident in open and affirming congregations exceeds that of many secular social groups and organizations. The entire congregation, for example, will participate in campaigns and programs relevant to its gay members. Ammerman described the sense of total inclusion in the congregation as follows: "Gay and lesbian persons ... find here a home, a reconnection with church traditions they thought lost, a place that acknowledges their spiritual longing *and* accepts them for who they are. As well, parents of gay and lesbian children find here a place where they can talk about their children's lives (and deaths) without censorship" (p. 181). It should be made clear that no one in the congregation wants the place to become a "gay church." Members are happy with the present mix that makes this and similar congregations one of the very few arenas where gay people can come and celebrate their differences while being fully accepted by traditional society. The only other alternatives are gay bars and bath houses where the primary purpose is dating and sex.

At a time when the armed forces and many public organizations adhere to a policy of "don't ask, don't tell," a growing number of religious organizations, denominations and congregations are opening their doors to gay people, supporting them as individuals and assisting in their cause. While the gay lifestyle is vehemently criticized by some religious extremists (both individuals and organizations) who argue that religion and homosexuality are incompatible, the reality is that the gay community is finding empowerment in organized religion. Congregations across the nation are providing arenas where gay people can assert themselves without fear of sanction, where they are respected for who they are and where social action on their behalf is supported.

Even among evangelical groups, gay men and women are beginning to come to terms with their sexual identity. Thumma (1991) described one such group called Good News in Atlanta, Georgia. Following a long process of redefining themselves, members of the group managed to resolve the dissonance between their extreme religious beliefs and their homosexual lifestyle. Yet, as Clark, Brown and Hochstein (1989) reminded us, organized religion and especially the Judaeo-Christian tradition have historically kindled homophobic feelings on the part of their followers, thereby fostering anti-gay oppression.

EMPOWERMENT OF RELIGIOUS COALITIONS

The Industrial Area Foundations (IAF), which has its roots in organized religion, is a powerful catalyst for the social and economic empowerment of poor neighbourhoods. The IAF grew from the work of Saul Alinsky in Chicago. Alinsky, considered by many to be the father of community organization, carried out his work under the auspices of the Catholic church (Horwitt, 1989). The Alinsky model, which the IAF follows, calls for church based organizing. Under this model, the IAF provides professional organizers, while local churches provide institutional bases, linkages, members and moral support. This linkage of the church with community action helps to empower people and involve them in the process of social and economic change (Boyte, 1984).

In addition to the aforementioned church contribution to the civil rights movement, we should also acknowledge that the movement challenging US immigration policies toward central American refugees was rooted in religious groups (Wiltfang and McAdam, 1991). Many congregations sponsored refugees and helped them relocate, often in defiance of official government policy. On the labour front, Dwight Billings (1990) asserted that only organized religion helped Appalachian miners achieve solidarity against mine owners. Referring to "religion as opposition," he noted that "the repetition of collective symbols and their ritualized expression in sermons, prayers, and group singing helped to sustain miners' commitment to the sacred cause of unionism and solidarity" (p. 20).

Many members of congregations live in the same neighbourhood as their church. These local members often form residents' groups similar to secular neighbourhood associations. In a study of citizen organizations in a midwestern city, Speer, Hughey, Gensheimer and Adams-Leavitt (1995) found that church based organizations were more likely to be more intimate and less controlling than other organizations and that their members were more likely to feel empowered.

EMPOWERMENT OF THE OPPRESSED THROUGH LIBERATION THEOLOGY

Liberation theology is a form of political reform that originated in and embodies religious tenets, especially those of the Catholic church. Liberation theology, unlike other theologies learned and speculated upon in seminaries and universities, is a social movement whose purpose is to bring about radical social, economic and political change (Smith, 1993). The movement, which originated in Latin America and Brazil, is most often associated with Central and South America. Liberation theology was directly influenced by the work of the Second Vatican Council held in the 1960s. Council members issued an official Vatican document that, for the first time, placed social issues on a equal footing with religious issues. This socially oriented doctrine brought about major revisions in Catholic theology and was responsible for the rise of Catholic social activism (Ryle, 1989; Scherer-Warren, 1990). The cause of liberation theology received further impetus when Pope John Paul II issued *Populorum Progressio*, an encyclical specifically directed to Latin America and the issue of social justice for a society long exploited economically and politically. The Vatican's calls for action and involvement were received with rapt attention on the part of many concerned Catholic theologians in Latin America.

Scherer-Warren (1990) summarized the goals of liberation theology as follows:

> In the material sense, the Church must work for liberation from several forms of oppression: economic (classes and foreign exploitation), political (both internal and external), racial, ethnic, sexual, age and so on. In the spiritual sense, it aims to liberate people from alienation, false consciousness, lack of courage and encourages self-determination. It aims to recuperate the loss of dignity of the human person, and transform the oppressed into agents of their own history, supported by their faith in God. (p. 17)

Larrea (1994) identified three key tenets of liberation theology: (1) the historical liberation of people, classes, races and cultures that are economically, politically and socially oppressed; (2) an understanding of the ethical implications of an anthropological approach (helping by outsiders); and (3) a theological tenet that accepts total liberation as redemption from sin. Regarding the second tenet, Breton (1992) noted that social workers should use the same resources available to the poor and oppressed, including their support systems, in their efforts to bring individuals and groups together into larger communities. The idea behind liberation theology is not to have outside helpers study people's needs and offer solutions; the idea is have these helpers live with the oppressed people, allow the people to learn about their situation by themselves, form plans of action and carry them out on their own in a nonviolent way. By forming a group of people who are each close to a small number of people and also to the larger community of people who suffer from the same problem, the members' sphere of influence is increased beyond their own group and a greater cooperation is achieved. It is interesting to contrast these tenets of liberation theology with the way empowerment is conceptualized in social work literature. Simon (1990), for example, suggested that empowerment decreases feelings of alienation from the dominant culture, helps individuals to develop the capacity for collective action and leads to the development of a sense of community and a sense of responsibility for and ability to resolve problems. The similarities in the approaches of social work and liberation theology to empowerment are indeed striking.

Pena (1994) reported that only the Catholic clergy were able to get different protest groups in Peru to cooperate with one another. By preaching liberation theology from the pulpit and in small group sessions, Catholic priests and sisters presented the idea of protest as acceptable to God and hence justified as a means to a better Christian life and the advancement of justice on earth. Smith (1991) noted that this theology was disseminated through thousands of base Christian communities (*Comunidades Eclesais de Base*, BEC). This method is clearly not limited to Peru and represents liberation theology praxis in Central and Southern America. Boff (1985) described BEC as groups of 15 to 20 families that meet a few times a week to hear the word of God and share their problems through the inspiration of the Gospels. A pastoral staff, consisting of priests, sisters and laity trained by a small number of itinerant liberation theologists at risk of torture, imprisonment, exile and death for their activities work together to keep the movement going.

Young (1980) reported that a movement based on liberation theology principles began in Brazil in the early 1950s. Although it preceded the Second Vatican Council it serves as the foundational basis for the movement, which was in the 1960s. The movement started in a local Catholic church and soon spread throughout Brazil via church related groups and teaching. The success of the movement led to concessions by the ruling party, but it was brutally suppressed following the 1964 *coup d'etat*. Since then, members of the movement have adopted more subtle strategies to combat political oppression. The Catholic church, in turn, has become the sole institutional opposition to the government, which fears its power among the poor. For example, when news of the murders of Brazilian street children began to surface, it was the church that spearheaded the campaign to stop the killing and to press charges against those responsible. Similarly, the church in Guatemala has been the key institution for community development and has stressed the teaching of political skills, consciousness-raising and self-reliance (Gondolf, 1981).

Liberation theology is not limited to Central and South America. As Hatjavivi, Fostin and Mbuende (1989) noted, Namibia's transition from a colony to a quasi-state is, in large part, due to the efforts of the church and the remaining German clerics who, under British rule, became significant figures with the local advent of liberation theology, offering hope of independence.

Given the radicalism of liberation theology and the rigid hierarchical structure of the Catholic church, opposition to the movement was inevitable. Many church leaders, especially the most conservative and those closest to the regimes in power, have attempted to undercut the influence and appeal of liberation theology. Lynch (1994), for example, noted how orthodox Catholics sought to diminish the appeal of liberation theology by accusing liberation theologists of changing sacred words and precepts used in their teaching. *Sensus Fideli*, a document issued by the magisterium (the teaching authority of the church), included practical steps on how opponents of the movement could demonstrate the weaknesses of its theological underpinnings. The liberationists have continued to espouse their traditional philosophy but have had to change some of its precepts.

Regardless of its opposition, liberation theology has been a vital force for emancipation and empowerment in Latin and South America and worldwide. It is so progressive in its tenets that many view it as a semi-Marxist movement within the church (Evans, 1992; Pottenger, 1989). In fact, Dussel (1992) argued that liberation theology and Marxism are very similar with one major difference: liberation theology universally rejects "dialectical materialism." It is not surprising then that many social work leaders today have called for adoption of liberation theology by the profession (cf., Breton, 1992; Campfens, 1988; Evans, 1992). In many ways, it complements the work begun by Saul Alinsky that laid the foundations of current day community practice. Thus, the Catholic church, through its liberation theology, has become a major contributor to personal, social, economic and political empowerment in an unprecedented manner.

CONCLUSIONS

In this chapter, I have juxtaposed empowerment, social work's most proactive principle, with the work of organized religion in America and abroad. My argument is that empowerment goes beyond the relationships of client-social worker or consumer-agency. Empowerment is necessary when there are power imbalances, and the disenfranchised have neither the perception nor the skills needed for change. As I have shown, many religious organizations and congregations are actively involved in assisting the powerless to advance their position in society. In this respect, I concur with Maton and Wells (1995) who suggested: "Concerning group empowerment, religion has the potential to facilitate groups' critical awareness of oppressive forces, to offer compelling alternative visions and cultural values, and to mobilize human and institutional resources" (p. 177).

It is important to re-emphasize that organized religion has been a source of repression and intolerance as well as empowerment. The same religious based mechanisms and structures used to empower the disenfranchised and the disadvantaged can also be harnessed to work against them. This is all too evident in church history, which is replete with instances of clerics working against the powerless and in the service of dictatorships. The forces of organized religion can also be used to deny the rights of others who disagree with church teaching. Religious sponsored, anti-abortion protests, for example, may empower those opposed to abortion, but they also are an attempt to abridge the rights of others. The new religious right is using empowerment techniques to impose their opinions and values on school boards, local government, public media and the arts. In a similar vein, Baer (1993) noted that, in African American churches, men had full access to positions of control and influence that were unavailable to women. This power imbalance empowered male members at the expense of female members. Our point is that organized religion is not a monolithic cohesive institution but rather a diversity of institutions, organizations and congregations, some of which actively support empowerment while others are neutral or even hostile.

Belonging to a proactive organization helps members learn the skills and means to advocate for change. Such a collective often maintains contact with political and community leaders, which helps members to become knowledgeable about issues and involved in protecting their interests. In this way, religious organizations form group identification and collectively engage in the process of change. Moreover, young and inactive members are encouraged to participate and become assertive members of society (Warner, 1993). When such a collective embraces a process of social change it is already equipped with personal ties, basic resources, leadership skills and a strong sense of virtue. Many religious groups from congregations to denominations have the capacity to assist in empowering the neediest members of society, but are waiting to be asked. As such they are a potential resource which social workers can tap into in order to successfully campaign for increased empowerment in society.

I have documented the efforts and contributions of organized religion to empower many groups identified by social work as in need of assistance. The groups included African Americans, Hispanics, gays and lesbians people, women and the oppressed. I have also noted that findings regarding the efforts by organized religion to empower these people have been largely under-reported and undervalued. It is my contention that religious organizations, denominations and congregations are, in fact, doing more for the powerless than many social services organizations. It is important to remember Durkheim's (1954) assertion that religion provides direction and expectations as to the meaning of human existence and defines the obligations of its members to themselves, their families and the broader society. This suggests that the efforts of organized religion to empower people should be recognized, supported and expanded. I am firmly convinced that social services organizations should not only focus on empowering clients in the consumption of services but also adopt a broader societal perspective to combat power inequalities such as that proposed by Breton (1992), Evans (1992) and Moore (1991). Social work and the religious community need to teach and learn from one another. The religious community can learn a great deal from social workers about how to care for and deal with needy people, while social work can cooperate with religious organizations in an effort to empower clients in all aspects of life, from understanding who they are and how society is treating them to their contact with service providers. By working together, social work and the religious community can help counteract the power imbalance that is so pervasive in the world today.

REFERENCES

Altman, D. (1982). *The homosexualization of America*. New York: St. Martin Press.
Ammerman, N. T. (1997). *Congregations and community*. New Brunswick, NJ: Rutgers University Press.
Baer, H. A. (1993). The limited empowerment of women in black spiritual churches: An alternative vehicle to religious leadership. *Sociology of Religion*, 54, 65-82.

Battle, V. D. (1988). The influence of Al-Islam in America on the black community. *The Black Scholar*, 19(1), 33-41.

Bear, H. A. and Singer, M. (1992). *African-American religion in the twentieth century*. Nashville: University of Tennessee Press.

Billings, D. B. (1990). Religion as opposition: A Gramscian analysis. *American Journal of Sociology*, 96, 1-31.

Blake, J. P. (1991, March 9). A man on a mission of hope. *The Philadelphia Daily News*, 17.

Boff, L. (1985). *Church, charisma and power*. London: SCM Press.

Boyte, H. C. (1984). *Community is possible: Repairing America's roots*. New York: Harper and Row.

Brady, H. E., Verba, S. and Schlozman, K. L. (1995). Beyond SES: A resource model of political participation. *American Political Science Review*, 89, 271-294.

Breton, V. L. (1989). United and slighted: Women as subordinated insiders. In W. R. Hutchison (Ed.), *Between the times: The travail of the Protestant establishment in America, 1900-1960* (pp. 143-167). Cambridge: Cambridge University Press.

Breton, M. (1992). Liberation theology, group work, and the right of the poor and oppressed to participate in the life of the community. *Social Work with Groups*, 15, 257-269.

Caldwell, C., Greene, A. D. and Billingsley A. (1992). The black church as a family support system: Instrumental and expressive functions. *National Journal of Sociology*, 6(1), 21-46.

Campfens, H. (1988). Forces shaping the new social work in Latin America. *Canadian Social Work Review*, 5 (Winter), 9-27.

Chaves, M. and Higgins, L. M. (1992). Comparing the community involvement of black and white congregations. *Journal for the Scientific Study of Religion*, 31, 425-440.

Chazanov, M. (1991, January 25). Mosque has a U.S. flavor. *Los Angeles Times*.

Clark, J. M., Brown, J. C. and Hochstein, L. M. (1989). Institutional religion and gay/lesbian oppression. *Marriage and Family Review*, 14, 265-284.

Cohen, B. J. and Austin, M. J. (1997). Transforming human services organizations through empowerment of staff. *Journal of Community Practice*, 4(2), 35-50.

Cott, N. (1977). *The bonds of womanhood: "Woman's sphere" in New England 1780-1835*. New Haven, CT: Yale University Press.

Dahl, R. A. (1961). *Who governs? Democracy and power in an American city*. New Haven, CT: Yale University Press.

DePriest, T. and Jones, J. (1997). Economic deliverance through the church. *Black Enterprise* (February), 195-197.

De Sousa, F. C. I. (1995). Discussing women's reproductive health, religion, roles and rights: Achieving women's empowerment. *Convergence*, 28(3), 45-51.

DuBois W. E. B. (1903). *The Negro church*. Atlanta: Atlanta University Press.

Durkheim, E. (1951). *Suicide, a study in sociology*. Glencoe, IL: Free Press.

Dussel, E. (1992). Liberation theology and Marxism. *Rethinking Marxism*, 5(3), 50-74.

Evans, E. N. (1992). Liberation theology, empowerment theory, and social work practice with the oppressed. *International Journal of Social Work*, 35, 135-147.

Frady, M. (1996). *Jesse: The life and pilgrimage of Jesse Jackson*. New York: Random House.

Gaventa, J. (1980). *Power and powerlessness: Quiescence and rebellion in an Appalachian valley*. Urbana, IL: University of Illinois Press.

Gite, L. (1993). The new agenda of the black church: Economic development for black America. *Black Enterprise* (December), 54-59.

Gondolf, E. (1981). Community development amidst political violence: Lessons from Guatemala. *Community Development Journal*, 16, 228-236.

Haddad, Y. Y. and Lummis, A. T. (1987). *Islamic values in the United States: A comparative study*. New York: Oxford University Press.

Hatjavivi, P. H., Fostin, P. and Mbuende, K. (1989). *Church and liberation in Namibia*. London: Pluto.

Horwitt, S. D. (1989). *Let them call me a rebel: Saul Alinsky his life and legacy*. New York: Knopf.

Larrea, G. J. (1994). The challenges of liberation theology to neoliberal economic politics. *Social Justice*, 21, 34-45.

Lehman, E. C. Jr. (1985). *Women clergy: Breaking through gender barriers*. New Brunswick, NJ: Transaction Books.

Lincoln, C. E. and Mamiya, L. H. (1990). *The black church in the African-American experience*. Durham, NC: Duke University Press.

Lincoln, C. E. and Mamiya, L. H. (1993). Challenges to the black church: The black church in the twenty-first century. In K. B. Bedwll (Ed.), *Yearbook of American and Canadian churches* (pp. 1-7). Nashville: Abington.

Lynch, E. A. (1994). Beyond liberation theology? *Journal of Interdisciplinary Studies*, 6, 147-164.

Magnuson, N. A. (1977). *Salvation in the slums: Evangelical social work, 1865-1920*. Metuchen, NJ: Scarecrow Press.

Manning, M. (1985). The black faith of W. E. B. DuBois: Sociocultural and political dimensions of black religion. *Southern Quarterly*, 23(3), 15-33.

Maton, K. I. and Rappaport J. (1984). Empowerment in a religious setting: A multivariate analysis. *Prevention in Human Services*, 3(3/4), 37-72.

Maton, K. I. and Wells, E. A. (1995). Religion as a community resource for well-being: Prevention, healing, and empowerment pathways. *Journal of Social Issues*, 51, 177-193.

Moore, T. (1991). The African-American church: A source of empowerment, mutual help, and social change. *Prevention in Human Services*, 10, 147-167.

Morris, A. D. (1984). *The origins of the civil right movement: Black communities organizing for change*. New York: Free Press.

Orsi, R. A. (1991). He keeps me going: Women's devotion to Saint Jude Thaddeus and the dialectics of gender in American Catholicism, 1925-1965. In T. Kselman (Ed.), *Brief in history: Innovative approaches to European and American religion* (pp. 137-169). Notre Dame, IN: University of Notre Dame Press.

Osborne, D. and Gaebler, T. (1992). *Reinventing government: How the entrepreneurial spirit is transforming the public sector, from schoolhouse to state house, city hall to the pentagon.* Reading, MA: Addison-Wesley.

Ozorak, E. W. (1996). The power, but not the glory: How women empower themselves through religion. *Journal of the Scientific Study of Religion*, 35, 17-29.

Parsloe, P. (1996). *Pathways to empowerment.* Birmingham, UK: Venture Press.

Pateman, C. (1970). *Participation and democratic theory.* Cambridge: Cambridge University Press.

Pena M. (1994). Liberation theology in Peru: An analysis of the role of intellectuals in social movements. *Journal of the Scientific Study of Religion*, 33, 34-45.

Perry, T. D. (1972). *The Lord is my shepard and he knows why I am gay.* Los Angeles: Nash.

Perry, T. D. and Swicegood, T. L. P. (1990). *Don't be afraid anymore: The story of Reverend Troy Perry and the metropolitan community church.* New York: St. Martins Press.

Pew Research Center for the People and the Press (1996). *Demographics and political attitudes for mainline white Protestants, evangelical white Protestants, Catholics, and others.* source: http://www.people-press.org/relgtab.htm

Pottenger, J. R. (1989). *The political theory of liberation theology: Toward a reconvergence of social values and social science.* Albany, NY: State University of New York Press.

Raboteau, A. J. (1978). *Slave religion: The invisible institution in the antebellum South.* New York: Oxford University Press.

Rappaport, J. (1987). Terms of empowerment-exemplars of prevention: Toward a theory for community psychology. *American Journal of Community Psychology*, 15, 121-145.

Reese, L. A. and Brown R. E. (1995). The effects of religious messages on racial identity and system blame among African Americans. *Journal of Politics*, 57, 24-43.

Ryle, E. J. (1989). The developments in Catholic moral theology and their promise for social workers. *Social Thought*, 15(3-4), 79-89.

Salamon, L. M. and Van Evera S. (1973). Fear, apathy, and discrimination: A test of three explanations of political participation. *American Political Science Review*, 67, 1288-1306.

Saleebey, D. (1992). Introduction: Power in the people. In D. Saleebey (Ed.), *The strength perspective in social work practice.* New York: Longman.

Sarfoh, J. A. (1986). The West African Zongo and the American ghetto: Some comparative aspects of the roles of religious institutions. *Journal of Black studies*, 17, 71-84.

Scherer-Warren, I. (1990). 'Rediscovering our dignity'—An appraisal of the utopia of liberation in Latin America. *International Sociology*, 5, 11-25.

Sherman, A. L. (1996). STEP-ing out on faith-and off welfare. *Christianity Today* (June 17), 35-36.

Shokeid, M. (1995). *A gay synagogue in New York*. New York: Columbia University Press.

Simon, B. (1990). Rethinking empowerment. *Journal of Progressive Human Services*, 1(1), 27-40.

Smith, C. (1991). *The emergence of liberation theology: Radical religion and social movement theory*. Chicago: University of Chicago Press.

Smith C. E. (1993). Black Muslims and the development of prisoners' rights. *Journal of Black Studies*, 24, 131-146.

Smith-Rosenberg, C. (1985). *Disorderly conduct: Vision of gender in Victorian America*. New York: Knopf.

Solomon, B. (1976). *Black empowerment*. New York: Columbia University Press.

Speer, P. W., Hughey, J., Gensheimer, L. K. and Adams-Leavitt, W. (1995). Organizing for power: A comparative case study. *Journal of Community Psychology*, 23, 57-73.

Stodghill II, R. (1996, August 19). Bringing hope back to the 'hood. *Business Week*, 70-73.

Strader, T., Collins, D., Noe , T. and Johnson K. (1997). Mobilizing church communities for alcohol and other drug abuse prevention through the use of volunteer church advocate teams. *The Journal of Volunteer Administration*, XV(2), 16-29.

Sweet, D. M. (1995). The church, the Stasi, and socialist integration: Three stages of lesbian and gay emancipation in the former East German Democratic Republic. *Journal of Homosexuality*, 29, 351-367.

Tapia A. (1996). How the black church responding to the urban crisis? *Christianity Today* (March 4), 26-30.

Tenenbaum, S. (1993). *Credit to their community: Jewish loan societies in the United States*. Detroit: Wayne State University Press.

Thumma, S. (1991). Negotiating a religious identity: The case of the gay evangelical. *Sociological Analysis*, 52, 333-347.

Twyman, A. S. (1993) Project means homes, jobs, and hope. *The Philadelphia Daily News* (Spring), 4, 16.

Twyman, A. S. (1995). Once again the search for "una vida major." *The Philadelphia Daily News*, (April 17, 1995), pp. 21-22.

Wallace, R. A. (1992). *They call her pastor: A new role for catholic women*. Albany, NY: State University of New York Press.

Warner, S. R. (1989). *The Metropolitan Community Church as a case study of religious change in the USA*. Paper presented at the annual meeting of the Society for the Scientific Study of Religion, Salt Lake City.

Warner, S. R. (1993). Work in progress toward a new paradigm for the sociological study of religion in the United States. *American Journal of Sociology*, 98, 1044-1093.

Wilcox, C. and Gomez, L. (1990). Religion, group identification, and politics among American Blacks. *Sociological Analysis*, 51, 271-185.

Wiltfang, G. and McAdam, D. (1991). The costs and risks of social activism: A study of sanctuary movement activism. *Social Forces*, 69, 987-1010.

Winland, D. N. (1994). Christianity and community: Conversion and adaptation among Hmong refugee women. *Canadian Journal of Sociology*, 19, 21-45.

Wuthnow, R. (1988). *The reconstructioning of American religion: Society and since World War II*. Princeton, NJ: Princeton University Press.

Xi, Lian. (1997). *The conversion of missionaries: Liberalism in American Protestant missions in China, 1907-1932*. University Park, PA: Pennsylvania State University Press.

Young, M. H. (1980). Nonviolent action in Brazil. *Social Development Issues*, 4(2), 71-93.

Section 4

Research
and Education

Chapter 19

USER CONTROLLED RESEARCH AND EMPOWERMENT

Clare Evans
Leonard Cheshire Disabled People's Forum
Wiltshire, United Kingdom
Mike Fisher
National Institute for Social Work, United Kingdom

THE CONTEXT OF EMPOWERMENT

Whenever the relationship between service users and practitioners is being reshaped, we should examine with great care the response of professionals to challenges to their expertise. A quarter of a century ago, Haug and Sussman documented what they called "the revolt of the client," and noted that the dominant reaction was co-optation:

> The objective is to socialize the dissidents into the special organizational knowledge of the professional circles.... In this way, the authority of the professional is preserved at the cost of sharing only a small proportion of his [*sic*] professional power. (Haug and Sussman, 1969, p. 158)

The central argument of this paper is that the theory and practice of empowerment is at risk of being mere co-optation, unless the key role of service users in defining the concept is acknowledged. We view empowerment as largely defined by professionals, claiming the authority of service users for its legitimacy. We argue that, above all other concepts, empowerment, which aims to enhance the lives of service users, must reflect service users' own definitions of their experiences and of the issues they face. Because of its central role in legitimating knowledge, we highlight research as a particularly important activity, and we argue that professionals have employed the power and status of research unilaterally to define the experiences and needs of service users. We argue for recognition of the role of service users as researchers in their own right, not merely as participants in research processes designed by professionals, and for the role of user controlled research as a means of increasing the power of service users over the way their experiences are defined.

Although they have differing histories and traditions, neither the UK nor the North American work on empowerment has given much attention to the role of service users in knowledge creation through research. In the UK, considerable attention has been devoted to gathering users' views of services, primarily to ensure their voice was heard in policy-making. This was strengthened by the work on anti-discriminatory practice, which emphasizes how far professional judgment embodies the assumptions, stereotypes and prejudices of dominant power groups. Recent work reflects the fact that UK social work is predominantly practised within local authority structures and within extensive legislative and procedural guidance. Thus special attention has been given to the structural factors affecting empowerment (Braye and Preston-Shoot, 1995) and to the opportunities offered by new arrangements for community care resulting from the NHS and the Community Care Act 1990 (Stevenson and Parsloe, 1993). Work at the Institute for Public Policy Research has sought to elevate the right to social welfare to the same level as civil and political rights (Bynoe, 1997; Coote, 1992). With the partial exception of anti-discriminatory approaches, however, most of this work takes for granted the right of practitioners and policy-makers to define empowerment and to research how it may be achieved.

North American thinking on empowerment has always had a stronger basis in civil rights, attributable in part to the need to find a common cause in the face of the multiplicity of welfare providers and their liberationist or benefactorial philosophies (Simon, 1994, p. 6). The fact that the civil rights movement encompassed broad social rights allowed social work theory to benefit from the re-examination of the principles of social justice, culminating in Solomon's emphasis on empowerment as a guiding principle governing users' access to resources "in a manner that enhances their self esteem as well as their problem solving capacities" (Solomon, 1976, p. 347). Another important strand in North American thinking has been the strengths perspective, in which resistance to the dominant definitions of service users' experiences is engendered by an emphasis on users' positive abilities (Rapp and Wintersteen, 1989; Saleebey, 1992). This perspective is visible in models of practice such as those proposed by Bricker-Jenkins and Cox and Parsons (Bricker-Jenkins, 1990; Cox and Parsons, 1994).

As even this brief review demonstrates, however, the question of what counts as knowledge and how it is created is a powerful undercurrent in the empowerment agenda but one which rarely surfaces to receive the direct attention of theorists. At several points, we come close to a conceptualization that would help this debate. Empowerment theorists frequently draw on Freire's concept of conscientization (see Simon, 1994, pp. 4 and 140). Rose and Black develop the related notion of critical debate (Rose and Black, 1985) and Rees uses the term biography to refer to the process of raising awareness of structures and processes which result in disempowerment (Rees, 1991). If we describe this as investigating social processes, we might find that it comes close to a concept of research. However, no specific role for service users in research is proposed and some caution is warranted because so little emphasis is accorded the knowledge and expertise of service users. Instead, the underlying conceptualization of this process is an educational one, and this runs the risk of implying that the job of the practitioner is to lead service users towards knowledge rather than supporting service users to articulate their own knowledge and expertise, which is then instrumental in educating practitioners and in influencing social structures.

Simon provides another glimpse of the relationship between knowledge and empowerment theory in her call for systematic investigation of the effects of practice (Simon, 1994, p. 192). However, she does not pursue the role of service users in such evaluation. Rapp, Shera and Kisthardt apply the lessons of empowerment practice to research and propose a role for service users in determining the scope of research, the measures used and in gathering data and disseminating the findings (Rapp, Shera and Kisthardt, 1993). Their role in analysis, however, is not explored, and the conception is primarily one of collaboration rather than research under the control of service users. If the literature on empowerment is short on recognition of the role of service users in research, the next task of this paper is to explore the literature on social research.

EMPOWERMENT AND RESEARCH

For service users, there is little doubt that research is one of the key ways in which users' experiences and needs are defined. In their review of studies on user involvement, Lindow and Morris point out that the agenda for research on disability has been primarily set by non-disabled researchers (Lindow and Morris, 1995, p. 87). In a similar vein, Beresford argues that involving service users in research is likely to change radically the purpose, process and assumptions underlying research (Beresford, 1994).

There are, however, few examples of evaluation directly under user control. Many studies employ participatory models and give a high priority to the views of users (Barnes, 1993; Marsh and Fisher, 1992), but these projects remain essentially conceived and executed by practitioners and academics. The account of user led research by Whittaker et al. shows that their project's origins in a health-care organization made it difficult to keep ownership with service users (Whittaker, Kershaw and Spargo, 1993). Several studies describe concerted attempts to return control of research to participants, but the necessity for this arises precisely because the study originated outside the control of service users (see, e.g., Bewley and Glendinning, 1994). As Davis notes, there remains the prospect of academics "subjecting users to research that we and funders deem to be in our and their best interests" (Davis, 1992, p. 46).

Whitmore describes an interesting attempt to recognize a greater role for service users when a pre-natal program for single mothers was due to be evaluated. Whitmore starts by recognizing that "ordinary people are capable of generating knowledge ... as valid as that produced by more highly structured and scientific processes" (Whitmore, 1994, p. 84). Although the evaluation was not originated by service users, the research process was constructed to involve service users in almost all aspects and to ensure a key role for service users as analysts of the data. Perhaps most importantly, Whitmore draws attention to the influence of user expertise on research processes. For example, the user researchers wanted scope to explore interviewees' reactions rather than to proceed strictly according to the interview schedule (p. 87), and they helped the author to understand the experience of being interviewed as a test of interviewees' capacity to defend themselves against possibly harmful intrusion (p. 91). Given this recognition of the quality of research arising from user involvement, it is a pity that it was not felt appropriate for the user researchers to write the final report, because the author felt that the funding body required the use of technical language seen as outside the competence of the user researchers (p. 96).

These approaches remain essentially within the frameworks of cooperative inquiry and participatory research, which recognize the benefits to the quality of knowledge and to the well-being of research participants which can arise from their active involvement in research processes (Reason, 1994, p. 41-9). Cooperative and participatory research necessarily engenders a form of empowerment since it is preferable to experience collaboration with powerful outsiders rather than exploitation. Participatory approaches, however, imply some prior activity which people may be invited to join: no matter how deliberately sketchy the activity in order to permit maximal reshaping by users, there is already a structure and a momentum which service users often feel it is their first task to change. Moreover, there is no guarantee that the issues under investigation will be those which service users would have chosen, and no guarantee that any power sharing will be maintained if service users decide a course of action which professionals oppose. In many ways, therefore, participation initiated by professionals remains conditional.

What is needed is to go beyond these models of research and find new frameworks which recognize not just the rights of service users to participate but also their right to determine the research agenda in the first place. In the UK, this issue has recently been explored by disabled activists and academics pursuing the implications for research of recognizing disability as a form of oppression. Drawing on lessons from feminist and race relations research, Oliver argues, for example, that existing models require an artificial distinction between those who do research and the researched, and that the skills and knowledge of research are attributed solely to researchers, who then decide what should be investigated (Oliver, 1992). These "social relations of research production" encourage the individual model of disability (which views the difficulties faced by disabled people as caused by their impairment), and leads directly to research practices which reflect this way of thinking. Thus government surveys ask "what is wrong with you" instead of "what is wrong with society" (p. 104). Oliver calls instead for emancipatory models of research, which confront "the power structures which resource research production," and which pursue the benefit to disabled people as a central principle (p. 110-11).

This new approach to the social relations of research production has been pursued by feminist disabled people (Keith, 1992; Morris, 1992), by deaf people (Jones and Pullen, 1992), by psychiatric system survivors (Beresford and Wallcraft, 1997) and on behalf of people with learning difficulties (Booth and Booth, 1996). It has involved methodological debate about the construction of critical surveys (Abberley, 1992), about objectivity (Barnes, 1996), about the role of qualitative methods (Barnes, 1992) and about the practices of funding bodies (Ward and Flynn, 1994). As with all such debates, it reflects diverse views within the disability movement, particularly about the role of disabled academics (Shakespeare, 1996) and the need to recognize different political positions on oppression within the disability movement (Bury, 1996). However, the direction of travel is unmistakably towards research which pursues the issues which disabled people have placed on the agenda.

Zarb characterizes participatory research as "only a first step," since "research has done little or nothing to contribute to the empowerment of disabled people," and goes on to argue that

Simply increasing participation and involvement will never by itself constitute emancipatory research unless and until it is disabled people themselves who are controlling the research and deciding who should be involved and how. (Zarb, 1992, p. 128)

In this view, much research is already participatory, in the sense that it involves people in decisions about how the research is done, and much involves a certain degree of reciprocity, in the sense that each participant (including the researcher) learns from the experience. But it is not empowering unless it results in disabled people acquiring greater power, and the key to this is placing research under the control of disabled people themselves.

User controlled research is thus a means for service users to reclaim an important source of power, the power to determine how experience and need is defined. It involves service users selecting what issues are researched, acquiring research funds, initiating the inquiry and designing and controlling the processes of research. It involves service users themselves becoming researchers, since this allows their perceptions and decisions to influence the research in a way which would otherwise be impossible (e.g., if the research were commissioned from a third party). As Whitmore found, it involves user researchers undertaking data analysis, since their knowledge and skills as users are an important resource for improving the quality of the analysis. Lastly, it involves user researchers in deciding how research findings should be recorded and disseminated, since this is a key step in using research to promote change.

USER CONTROLLED RESEARCH IN ACTION

The Context of the User Organization

The background to the user controlled research project described in this chapter is that of collective advocacy developed by people who use social services and health in Wiltshire through the development of Wiltshire and Swindon Users' Network.[1] The organization began in November 1991 with a meeting of service users and allies across the county to discuss user involvement. Part of the NHS and the Community Care Act 1990 stresses the importance of consulting with users and carers and it was a response to the feeling that this had not been appropriately developed that Clare Evans called the meeting. The management group, the majority of whom were service users, was formed and chaired by Clare. The next 18 months were spent in calling meetings of interest to service users at regular intervals with considerable outreach to support people to attend and lobbying social service departments to hear the voice of service users. In June 1993 substantial funding (sufficient to establish a proper office infrastructure and to employ staff) was given by Wiltshire Social Services to this independent organization in a service agreement. The purposes of the funding were to provide a network of support to service users in Wiltshire and to facilitate direct links between service users and the social services. As a result of a strong infrastructure underpinning the users' network, further funds were given a year later for specific projects in the fields of independent living, information and advocacy. The organization now employs 27 members of staff, over half of whom are service users, has an annual turnover of £500k and membership of several hundred service users across the county.

The emerging principles of empowerment as we developed our organization are those of collective advocacy—learning to gain confidence and empowerment through meeting together, supporting each other and collectively getting our voice heard. As we planned our organization together, developed good practice and wrote about it, we learned to value ourselves and our expertise as service users, responding both to the effect of getting services changed to be more appropriate to our needs and to the benefits of working together on our own self-esteem. The definition of empowerment we often use within the network is that of being in control of one's life and able to influence others. This is particularly appropriate for us because the individual and the collective are both identified within this definition. It relates well to the definition offered by Pinderhughes: "Empowerment requires the use of strategies that enable clients to experience themselves as competent, valuable, and worthwhile both as individuals and as members of their cultural group" (Pinderhughes, 1992, p. 111). Torre, too, calls attention to the relationship between empowerment as an individual and the opportunity to "influence events and institutions" (quoted in Cox and Parsons, 1994, p. 18).

In the users network, we achieved this by relating our own experience to all activities as we developed the organization. For example, when we organized meetings they were always chaired by a service user and the group leaders; when we broke into small group discussions, chairs were always service users even if allies were present with perhaps more experience of facilitating groups. We paid people's expenses to attend meetings to demonstrate that their expertise was being valued and we widely publicized the results of our meetings and the perspectives we brought to bear on such subjects as care management, so that the social service department was challenged from the start about empowering practice. Thus we began to feel that we could make a contribution to society and more specifically the services we received. We could break down assumptions about people speaking on our behalf and challenge professionals about the way they worked.

Prior to funding there was little demand from outside about the direction of our organization, which only had a small amount of funding in order to pay people's costs to attend meetings, thus we were very much in control of the agenda and the manner in which we enacted it. The acquisition of funding in order to employ staff to extend our activities to reach a wider group of service users might have compromised our independence. In negotiating funding, we were aware of this danger and we obtained the protection of a longer term service agreement, which meant there would be no knee-jerk reactions in relation to funding from challenges we gave social services. There was also an understanding from within the social service department that the control we had over our organization was part of good practice in user empowerment and therefore it was not in their interest to challenge our activities.

Being able to influence others—part of the definition of empowerment—we interpreted as being about the user controlled organization developing a range of activities of user involvement on a continuum (see Table 1). It wasn't always easy to plan each of these areas of participation in detail since some were more acceptable to the social service department than others. However, a policy of riddling the system with as many perspectives of service users in as many different pieces of work as possible was effective in having an impact upon the professional culture of the department. On the whole we spent less of the organizational resources and energy on consultation after pieces of work had been designed and policy proposals formulated since the level of influence on such pieces of work could be small, many decisions having already been made. This echoes the problem about participative research, where user involvement often arises after important decisions about the study have been made. Rather more attractive to us were ideas we had about developing policy proposals ourselves and participating with professionals in developing policies such as that of care management and in training staff.

As we had small successes in influencing development, our confidence grew and we had ever-increasing expectations of gaining more power to influence. Having this shared confidence operating within our own organization, and providing a comparatively safe environment from the funders' perspective, we became more confident about taking risks by moving into new areas of related work where experts' views of us as service users seemed to need challenging. This proactive approach was a characteristic of our organization as we became empowered and contrasted with the disempowering effects we experienced in the receipt of daily personal care. It also demonstrates how much the principles and experiences of the host organization influenced the

Table 1 Continuum of user involvement

Collective Examples		Individual Examples
User controlled service provision	CONTROL	Own care managers
Involvement on Users' terms, not tokenism	VETO	Refusal to use services offered, go elsewhere
Developing policy, training Professionals	PARTICIPATION	Involvement in assessment and care plan
Draft policies. Community Care Plan	CONSULTATION	Involvement in choices offered
Publicity re provision and rights to services	INFORMATION PROVISION	Leading to choice of service offered

conduct of research, in that we were collectively able to take risks which individually would have been impossible.

User Controlled Research as an Area of User Empowerment

Our interest in user controlled research grew out of our learning from three different relationships we found we had with traditional professional social science research. First, in general terms, we found many of us had the experience of being treated as passive recipients of social services and being made use of by academic researchers in order to collect our views for research which they would publish and gain credit and recognition for. We were frequently contacted as an organization by institutions of higher education wanting to develop research proposals and use our organization as a means of reaching large numbers of service users. This in itself made us feel we were being taken advantage of, plus the experience of individuals who gave up considerable amounts of time being interviewed by academic researchers whose standards of practice were such that they did not even respect the service user enough to contact them afterwards with the results of their research.

Our second reason was our growing understanding and recognition of user expertise which was relevant in the field of research. In the early days of the network, a user-led organization in the county carried out research into disabled people's views of employment and in so doing employed disabled people as interviewers and in writing up the research. Other experiences included service users interviewing other service users in a clinical audit carried out by health and social services into discharge from hospital, and service users helping to define the questions for a large-scale survey of the home-care service providing personal care. In all of these experiences and other smaller areas of work we were surprised at the difficulty that professionals had in understanding the important issues for service users and knowing how to ask them questions which would be meaningful to answer.

Our third experience was of inappropriate research evaluating user controlled projects commissioned by purchasing agencies. We had an experience of an evaluation of one of our projects, a mental health patients' council project, in which the researcher from a national research institution clearly thought that interviewing the user worker and the user line-manager of the project and a few professionals on the outside meant that she had no obligation to interview users of the service. Yet to us in the network, the views of users of any service, whoever the provider, should be paramount in any evaluation of outcomes, which should be user defined. This distinction between users of the specific service being evaluated and members and staff of an organization being service users of health and social services was an important principle underlying our commitment to user control.

These experiences of research, which showed both the way user expertise could be a resource within the research process and the inadequacy of professional research without sufficient recognition of user expertise, led us to want to demonstrate that a study entirely controlled by users was a valid way of conducting research, with its own as yet unrecognized strengths as well as shortcomings all too readily identified by professional researchers. We sought an opportunity to re-cast the principles we had learned from our own experience about the role of user expertise and user involvement in influencing services within the field of research.

Funding for User Controlled Research

On the continuum of user involvement (Table 1), user control was identified as most valued in all aspects of user participation. The concept of user controlled research is the same as that of all user controlled activities, and within the user movement in Britain there is a clear understanding of this as distinct from user led, which describes users as participating but not in the majority. User controlled research is very rare—in fact we could find no previous examples of a substantial piece of research about disabled users being funded which was completely in the control of service users. Presumably, this relates to commissioners' disregard of evaluation carried out by service users and professional researchers' views on the possible invalidity of research methods used.

The funds for this research came from some one-off funding available for development work of the Wiltshire Independent Living Fund (WILF), a third party cash payment scheme in Wiltshire. When proposals for funding were invited, it had been important to maintain the user controlled nature of the use of the funding. Because of our previous work and credibility gained and the learning about good practice in user involvement among allies within social services together with specific available funding the two page proposal for the research was adequate to gain funding. In making the proposal we were able to take for granted funders' understanding of the need for a large budget to pay users to carry out the research and manage the project. There was also a similar understanding about the high costs of bringing disabled people together. This understanding gave us the flexibility to ensure that the research was entirely user controlled and developed in the course of the project along lines we determined, based on what we felt to be appropriate.

There were therefore only two stipulations about the funding agreed with funders: that the research would collect the views of users of WILF about the services they receive, and the funding level would be £20k. It had been an important principle explicitly stated in the funding proposal written by the users' network that the research hypothesis and methodology would be determined by disabled people who formed the advisory group. The phrase "fools rush in where angels fear to tread" comes to mind as a description of not only this process of user participation but many others where thinking is developed as pieces of work progress, based on the experience of users, to be good practice. This seems the only practical way forward in an area of work where no previous models have been developed on specific aspects of participation. We did not have time to reflect about how we might undertake this research before the happy coincidence of the support of a university researcher and a network ally since December 1992, Mike Fisher, requested to spend some of his sabbatical learning how a user controlled organization carried out research. We had previously identified this as a joint area of interest, but had not been successful in obtaining funding for it. In connection with this piece of user controlled research, we were pleased to invite him to act as our research advisor.

Managing User Controlled Research

In new pieces of work we sought to push out the barriers of what both users and professionals considered appropriate for a user organization. Our assumption in the network was that carrying out user controlled research was just another piece of participation, so the principles guiding all such participation were used to set it up. Within the umbrella of our independent user controlled organization, we managed a number of projects which each had its own advisory committee of users with relevant experience. Between March and September 1995, the network advertised widely for people interested in being on the advisory committee for research to contact the network so that we could set up an initial meeting. Users were told it would be a specific time limited piece of research into WILF, that costs and the general network fee of £5 an hour would be paid to attend the advisory committee, and it was anticipated there would be further opportunities for employment in the research as it was carried out. We were somewhat disappointed that some network members with experience of participating in research as outlined earlier were not interested in joining the work, but the group who volunteered was composed of WILF users and other disabled people, two of whom did not have a physical impairment but spoke from the perspective of a mental health user and a recovering alcoholic and had some experience in carrying out research. These service users were the decision-makers on the committee we called WILFRAG (Wiltshire Independent Living Fund Research Advisory Group), and we were joined at every meeting by the research advisor and note-taker.

The format and roles of members of the group were determined by the network philosophy to empower users by enabling them to participate with the support needed at a pace dictated by their needs. The users participating in WILFRAG did much more than just attend meetings to manage research. The role of the note-taker, therefore, in addition to keeping a record of the meeting, was to welcome people to the meeting, to support users filling in their expense claim forms, make payments accordingly and to make the refreshments. People knew they could expect this service as part of their participating in the research. Although this had implications for the speed at which the research could progress, it gave an opportunity for the learning that can take place through the informal networking required to achieve these practical tasks to meet disabled people's needs.

Although there was some shared understanding of the guidelines from this group from their experience as members of the network, it was also a diverse group with people having different perspectives. The authority of the chair (CE) was based on her role as director of the network, with responsibility for maintaining the network principles in all our work and managing the use of funding. The management of the group in relation to the network philosophy was in challenging the principles underlying their assumptions about the way the research would be carried out. For example, the use of the census in traditional research as a way of defining disabled people was not based on the social model of disability and so the chair challenged it. She also emphasized the need to balance this kind of quantitative data with other data of a qualitative nature, which would help to gain an insight into the direct experience of service users. The compromise we came to on this was valuing some initial quantitative research which would add credibility to the project, provide a framework for those unfamiliar with WILF and give an overall picture of WILF users from which we could draw a sample of people to be interviewed in depth.

Designing and Executing the Research

In a group without much experience of carrying out research but with a commitment from their own experience about the value of WILF, it was difficult at times to move people on from recounting their experience of the process to using that experience to inform decisions we needed to make about research detail, such as what the areas of questioning should cover. Whitmore, too, recounts how there were days when they "accomplished very little of the 'task' but a lot of process" (1994, p. 90).

At an early stage, we had decided to explore the general patterns of service use from the records of applications kept by the body which made the actual payments to users (Wiltshire Community Foundation). One member of the group had experience of statistical work and volunteered to go through the records. This raised two immediate issues concerning confidentiality. First, the foundation stipulated that the user researcher must be bound by its rules governing access to data, which was duly agreed. Secondly, the members of WILFRAG, often themselves users of WILF, felt very strongly that all data about any individual user of WILF were owned by that user, and no data, even if made anonymous, should be used without user consent. No potential benefit from the use of aggregated, anonyous data could, in this view, justify dispensing with this consent. Lengthy steps were required to obtain this consent from all who had ever made an application. A third problem, of poor quality basic data on applicants, would surface later.

These quantitative data were essential for drawing up a sample of people to be interviewed and to understand how the pattern of applicants related to particular administrative areas of Wiltshire. However, WILFRAG wanted also to explore whether the pattern of applications related to the population of disabled people eligible for the service. This raised the question of how to define an appropriate comparison population and led to the problem described above where census data could not be used since they did not reflect definitions of disability acceptable to the users' network. In particular, the Census employed the category of "limiting, long-term illness," a concept that implied it was possible to define disability in terms of individual impairment, which was unacceptable. No appropriate comparison population was ever found. The most promising avenue was to employ the criteria used to determine initial eligibility for WILF (receipt of Disability Living Allowance at the middle or higher rate), but data on DLA recipients were not available in geographical sub-divisions corresponding to the county where the research was undertaken. Normally, some kind of quantitative framework would serve to locate a small-scale study and offer some means of assessing its generalizability. The consequence is that it may be difficult for user controlled research, which seeks to question the basis of nationally available quantitative data, to gauge the generalizability of its findings.

The research group decided to gather information directly from WILF users about their experiences. The members had little experience of designing or undertaking qualitative interviewing, although several had considerable work experience on which to draw. We decided to draw up the interview schedule as a collaborative exercise over two days, during which all members of the group had the chance to ensure the questions they thought should be asked were included. Two of the group with research experience were given the task of converting the list of areas into a four-part interview schedule, with questions and appropriate probes and with signposts to assist interviewers to follow different sequences of questions depending on the interviewee's specific experience. An important point is that the interview was highly structured, with detailed phrasing and words we hoped interviewers would use printed on the schedule and a checklist at the end to ensure that sections were not omitted. This was an attempt to minimize the pressure on interviewers relatively new to qualitative interviewing and to minimize the potential for straying too far off course.

A second sequence of two days was then devoted to training four people as interviewers. WILFRAG required interviewers to undergo training in order to protect the interests of interviewees and to ensure the quality of the research. The training was undertaken by two people in WILFRAG with research experience and quickly became an opportunity not only to practice interviewing skills but also to refine the phrasing in accordance with the knowledge of the interviewers, three of whom were themselves WILF users and all of whom were disabled. The fact that the interviewers were all users meant that they had no difficulty in acting "in role" when it came to interview practice. WILFRAG had taken a decision to audiotape and transcribe interviews, so training also covered the use of tape recorders and addressed concerns about the potential intrusiveness of this technique.

Contacting interviewees involved a great deal of care. The list of applicants gave a sampling frame to ensure those interviewed were representative of applicants as a whole. However, missing basic data in the list of applicants made this difficult. For example, age was often missing, thus we could sample only those applicants where age was recorded. WILFRAG members then wished to contact applicants directly, to invite participation in the interview stage. However, the director did not wish applicants to be approached directly by an unknown person, arguing that they were vulnerable people who would not readily respond to a direct approach and that network philosophy was that people were entitled to support from a known and trusted person in order to help them maintain control over their lives. The proposal was that those who used the support service should be approached by their support worker and others through a letter from the network's director. Some members of WILFRAG opposed this on the grounds that network philosophy enabled users to make their own decisions; one member objected on the grounds that bias might be introduced by the approach through the support service, the operation of which was under investigation. In the end, the director's decision prevailed, and it was agreed that the sample would be selected entirely independently but that members of the support service would invite users according to a carefully planned protocol which minimized variation in response that might be attributable to their influence.

Analysis and dissemination are often areas where the empowering ethos must give way to scientific expertise. We were fortunate in the fact that the statistical data could be handled by a member drawing on skills from his previous work. Handling qualitative data often involves finding a balance between understanding the stories in the interview and comparing the detail of people's responses. We decided to use this approach to shape user controlled analysis. The proposal was to have two people read all the interviews (22), while four others took responsibility for noting the responses in the four areas of the interview. This was agreed by WILFRAG, but with the important stipulation that the interviewers should be involved so that their knowledge of the interviewees could be brought to bear on analysis. Thus, user controlled research challenged the widespread practice in social scientific research of divorcing analysis from data collection. In effect, the argument was that what traditional science might call bias, user controlled research termed inside knowledge, which should be used to inform analysis. Indeed, one of the interviewers was an interviewee since her name surfaced during sampling. Having given her permission to be identified, she could not only comment on what she thought other interviewees might have meant but also on what the user researchers made of her own interview.

In other respects, the analysis of qualitative data in fact closely resembled aspects of traditional methods undertaken in a team context. The stories contained in the interviews provided a context for interpreting the meaning of specific responses. The technique of having each interviewer note responses across all interviews (on large sheets of paper, stretching sideways as far as necessary to include all interviewees) encouraged a version of constant comparison, a well-known technique in grounded theory. A week of reading was allocated to each participant in this process, and two days were set aside to meet and to exchange views about the meaning interpreted in the interviews. The two people who had read all the interviews for their stories took the major responsibility for note-taking and for writing up the section of the report concerning the qualitative data. Some members of WILFRAG also used their knowledge of related social policy issues to draw attention to the importance of some findings, which might otherwise go unremarked. For instance, in the context of studies showing that community care assessment was experienced by many users as intrusive and unskilled, the finding that WILF users found assessment a demanding experience, but one which was worthwhile and which was carried out with skill, suggested the need for close examination of this issue.

Dissemination plans were made by WILFRAG and included allocating roles to users to write up sections of the report, to design the finished product and to negotiate its printing. When the draft report was ready, another full day meeting of WILFRAG was convened to go over it in detail with all involved. Plans were also made for a presentation during the network's AGM, again given by user members of WILFRAG.

THE ROLE OF ACADEMIC RESEARCHER AS ALLY AND FACILITATOR

Service users within their own organizations can quickly distinguish between those professionals willing and able to act as allies and those who are not—phrases such as not take over, recognize user expertise, treat as people, not patronizing, being willing to learn describe allies. Probably service users imagine it is more easy for allies to know how to act in an empowering way than it really is. It certainly involves a set of attitudes based on both an intellectual and emotional commitment and a set of skills and competencies.

In carrying out this research, users expected the academic researcher to act as an ally. Thus we needed to remain in control so he was able to offer advice about research to the group, but there was no guarantee his advice would be acted on. The researcher's previous contact with the network as an associate member and university lecturer inviting users to lecture on a social work program had gained him credibility with the few members of the group who knew him. Most in the group quickly came to respect his acting as an ally, although for one user in the group not previously active in the network and therefore less able to value user expertise, the academic researcher remained, in his view, the leader of the research and in charge of the whole process.

In return for his recognition of our expertise as disabled people, we quickly recognized the academic researcher's expertise as he identified the complexity of some of the issues in achieving our goals of completing the research. On two occasions the network took particular steps in recognition of the fact that the academic researcher was a non-user. First, we stipulated that interviewer training should involve a user trainer as well as the academic. This was important because the network wished to be proactive in moving away from the stereotype of the non-user being in authority and teaching users towards a model where power is shared and learning is two-way and because only another user, with her clearer understanding of users' needs and perspectives, would be fully able to carry out the training appropriately. The second occasion for particular care was when the results were presented to a wider audience at the launch, where it was important that users presented the findings and were seen to be in control. The academic researcher played a particularly positive role in finding solutions to carrying out analysis collectively by giving us the confidence to continue with the research task and guidance about what was appropriate research practice.

IMPLICATIONS FOR EMPOWERMENT RESEARCH

The principles of user controlled research constitute a profound challenge to the social research community. Academic researchers acquire status and prestige through research grants and through publishing. In the UK, these measures are increasingly used to channel infrastructure funds selectively to academic disciplines. Academics spend long years acquiring research qualifications and reputations. In short, academics have gained power through research and probably subscribe to what might be called the quantum theory of power, namely that there is a finite amount of it and that giving power away means losing it.

The challenge is to use that power to create the conditions by which service users can empower themselves and to recognize what might be called the reciprocity theory of power, namely that by giving it away, more is created. The task is to redirect research skills into working alliances with users, to assist users get research funds and research skills themselves, and to put academic research skills under the control of service users. It involves a readiness to learn from users as researchers, in much the same way as qualitative research often requires immersion in the world of participants. It involves resisting the age-old allegation that committed research cannot be good research and that there is a hierarchy of scientific methods and values, at the top of which is a particular conception of empiricism and objectivity. Lastly, it involves a readiness to resist the academic temptation to claim ownership of the results of research and to find new measures of prestige and status.

User controlled research may also give social researchers cause to reflect on some of the difficult validity issues in research based on users' views of services. For instance, it is not uncommon in small-scale qualitative work for academic researchers to encounter substantial refusal rates among service users, sometimes as high as 30 percent (e.g., Fisher, Marsh and Phillips, 1986). In the study described here, the refusal rate was 13 percent, suggesting that the user controlled basis may have reduced reluctance to be interviewed. The question of matching interviewer to interviewee is also an issue in social research, whether to take account of gender, age, ethnicity, sexuality or disability. If, as user researchers taught Whitmore, participation in research requires that users protect themselves "from people they saw as having power to harm them" (1994, p. 91), is it possible that the quality of the data collected by service users from service users is less influenced by this power dimension, and therefore a more accurate account of their experiences and perceptions?

User controlled research is part of user empowerment, and the question remains whether this project was empowering. This assessment is complex, partly because of new legislation permitting all local authorities to make direct payments to disabled people to purchase personal care. This means we cannot assess how far the study served to maintain the existence of the scheme in Wiltshire, since it is being replaced under this legislation. We can, however, point to some of the benefits of the research for the network and for its members. We think there are particular reasons why users felt that undertaking research themselves was more empowering than choosing to commission a third party, even under a user defined contract. This is because the processes of research offer new roles and new power relationships for people whose autonomy has often been restricted in their dealings with statutory services. A viable, additional identity of researcher is offered and recognized by appropriate financial reward. Skills may be developed or re-awakened, and this represents an investment in users as people.

From the point of view of the network, the research reinforced the collective principles of the organization by offering a new opportunity to test their relevance in line with its philosophy of pushing out the boundaries of changing the way professionals perceive and define users. A risk was taken, and the network was equal to it. Within Wiltshire, the network has become involved in the social services investment in a local university's research unit and is able to offer advice on research from the perspective of having completed a substantial study of its own. The study has influenced thinking in the local social services about implementing the new direct payments legislation, by reinforcing the need for a support service to accompany access to funds and by documenting a more empowering (though no less gruelling) assessment process.

Although participative research remains somewhat limited in its empowering potential, we recognize its widespread use as a model and suggest that some of the practices of user controlled research might be usefully imported. For instance, there are good reasons to consider the involvement of service users as interviewers of other service users. With training and support, this can give an extra purchase on the validity of the users' accounts. It is also helpful and viable to involve service users in analyzing the data, since their special insights into the meaning of users' accounts will help to shape the analysis. Although similar to traditional respondent validation techniques, this approach goes beyond checking out the validity of the researchers' interpretations to involve service users in originating the interpretations. In these ways, users' expertise can improve the quality of social research and in particular the richness of the understanding achieved.

There are limits to everyone's abilities, and among service users some may be unable at times to be in control of some aspects of their lives. However, this lack of control is often reinforced by professionals' stereotypes of passive users and by the disempowering effects on users of this perception. So it is a task for empowerment-oriented researchers to find ways of returning as much control as possible to users, whatever their abilities or circumstances. For example, researchers at the Norah Fry Research Centre, University of Bristol (UK), have developed ways of involving service users with learning difficulties in analysis and dissemination of research, including developing new ways of presenting research findings suitable for service users (Bashford, Mackenzie,

Townsley and Williams, 1994; Townsley, 1994). Thornton and Tozer have also documented an extensive range of initiatives for involving older people in planning and evaluating services (Thornton and Tozer, 1994).

Lastly, we recognize that the test of user controlled research is whether it has an impact, particularly on the redistribution of power towards service users, and that small-scale, locally based research is unlikely to have major effects on policy. Indeed, this was the reason given by a major UK foundation for not funding the original proposal that gave rise to the research described here. The relationship between social research and social change is complex, however, and policy change often requires the accumulation of a body of evidence, from a variety of perspectives. Our argument is that empowerment-oriented practitioners and service users should ensure that one of these perspectives is provided by a body of user controlled research.

ENDNOTE

[1] A detailed account of how the network developed and the range of user participation activities it is involved with is available from Wiltshire and Swindon Users' Network, 7 Prince Maurice Court, Hambleton Avenue, Devizes, Wiltshire SN10 2RT, UK. The research described here ("I Am In Control") is also available from the Network (£5).

REFERENCES

Abberley, P. (1992). Counting us out: A discussion of the OPCS disability surveys. *Disability, Handicap and Society*), 7(2), 139-155.

Barnes, C. (1992). Qualitative research: Valuable or irrelevant? *Disability, Handicap and Society*, 7(2), 115-123.

Barnes, C. (1996). Disability and the myth of the independent researcher. *Disability and Society*, 11(1), 107-110.

Barnes, M. (1993). Introducing new stakeholders—user and researcher interests in evaluative research. *Policy and Politics*, 21(1), 47-58.

Bashford, L., Mackenzie, S., Townsley, R. and Williams, C. (1994). *Parallel writing: Making research accessible to people with learning difficulties*. University of Bristol: Norah Fry Research Centre.

Beresford, P. (1994). Commentary on 'Community care: Findings from department of health funded research' by Lesley Hoyes and Robin Means. *Community Care Management and Planning*, 2(2), 63-64.

Beresford, P. and Wallcraft, J. (1997). Psychiatric system survivors and emancipatory research: Uses, overlaps and differences. In C. Barnes and G. Mercer (Eds.), *Doing disability research*. Leeds: Disability Press.

Bewley, C. and Glendinning, C. (1994). *Involving disabled people in community care planning*. York: Joseph Rowntree Foundation.

Booth, T. and Booth, W. (1996). Sounds of silence: Narrative research with inarticulate subjects. *Disability and Society*, 11(1), 55-69.

Braye, S. and Preston-Shoot, M. (1995). *Empowering practice in social care*. Buckingham: Open University.

Bricker-Jenkins, M. (1990). Another approach to practice and training—clients must be considered the primary experts. *Public Welfare*, Spring, 11-16.

Bury, M. (1996). Disability and the myth of the independent researcher: A reply. *Disability and Society*, 11(1), 111-113.

Bynoe, I. (1997). *Rights to fair treatment*. London: IPPR.

Coote, A. (1992). *The welfare of citizens*. London: Rivers Oram Press.

Cox, E. and Parsons, R. (1994). *Empowerment-oriented social work practice with the elderly*. Pacific Grove CA: Brooks/Cole.

Davis, A. (1992). Who needs user research? Service users as research subjects or participants: Implications for user involvement in service contracting. In M. Barnes and G. Wistow (Eds.), *Researching user involvement* (pp. 34-47). Leeds: The Nuffield Institute.

Fisher, M., Marsh, P. and Phillips, D. (1986). *In and out of care*. London: Batsford.

Haug, M. and Sussman, M. (1969). Professional autonomy and the revolt of the client. *Social Problems*, 17, 53-61.

Jones, L. and Pullen, G. (1992). Cultural differences: Deaf and hearing researchers working together. *Disability, Handicap and Society*, 7(2), 189-196.

Keith, L. (1992). Who care wins? Women, caring and disability. *Disability, Handicap and Society*, 7(2), 167-175.

Lindow, V. and Morris, J. (1995). *Service user involvement: Synthesis of findings and experience in the field of community care*. York: Joseph Rowntree Foundation.

Marsh, P. and Fisher, M. (1992). *Good intentions: Developing partnership in social services*. York: Joseph Rowntree Foundation.

Morris, J. (1992). Personal and political: A feminist perspective on researching physical disability. *Disability, Handicap and Society*, 7(2), 157-166.

Oliver, M. (1992). Changing the social relations of research production. *Disability, Handicap and Society*, 7(2), 101-114.

Pinderhughes, E. (1992). *Understanding race, ethnicity and power: The key to efficacy in clinical practice*. New York: Free Press.

Rapp, C., Shera, W. and Kisthardt, W. (1993). Research strategies for consumer empowerment. *Social Work*, 38(6), 727-35.

Rapp, C. and Wintersteen, R. (1989). The strengths model of case management: Results from twelve demonstrations. *Psychosocial Rehabilitation Journal*, 13(1), 23-32.

Reason, P. (1994). Human inquiry as discipline and practice. In P. Reason (Ed.), *Participation in human inquiry* (pp. 40-56). London: Sage.

Rees, S. (1991). *Achieving power: Practice and policy in social welfare.* Sydney: Allen and Unwin.

Rose, S. and Black, B. (1985). *Advocacy and empowerment.* London: Routledge.

Saleebey, D. (Ed.). (1992). *The strengths perspective in social work practice.* New York: Longmans.

Shakespeare, T. (1996). Rules of engagement: Doing disability research. *Disability and Society,* 11(1), 115-119.

Simon, B. (1994). *The empowerment tradition in American social work.* New York: Columbia.

Solomon, B. (1976). *Black empowerment: Social work in oppressed communities.* New York: Columbia University Press.

Stevenson, O. and Parsloe, P. (1993). *Community care and empowerment.* York: Joseph Rowntree Foundation/Community Care.

Thornton, P. and Tozer, R. (1994). *Involving older people in planning and evaluating community care: A review of initiatives.* York: University of York: Social Policy Research Unit.

Townsley, R. (1994). *Presenting information for people with learning difficulties: An overview of current ideas and techniques.* University of Bristol: Norah Fry Research Centre.

Ward, L. and Flynn, M. (1994). What matters most: Disability, research and empowerment. In M. Rioux and M. Bach (Eds.), *Disability is not measles: New paradigms in disability* (pp. 29-48). North York, Ontario: Roeher Institute.

Whitmore, E. (1994). To tell the truth: Working with oppressed groups in participatory approaches to inquiry. In P. Reason (Ed.), *Participation in human inquiry* (pp. 82-98). London: Sage.

Whittaker, A., Kershaw, J. and Spargo, J. (1993). Service evaluation by people with learning difficulties. In P. Beresford and T. Harding (Eds.), *A challenge to change: Practical experiences of building user-led services* (pp. 109-125). London: National Institute for Social Work.

Zarb, G. (1992). On the road to Damascus: First steps towards changing the relations of disability research production. *Disability, Handicap and Society,* 7(2), 125-139.

Chapter 20

RESEARCH AS EMPOWERMENT: THE SOCIAL ACTION APPROACH

Jennie Fleming
Centre for Social Action
De Montfort University, Leicester, England
Dave Ward
Department of Social and Community Studies
De Montford University, Leicester, England

Empowerment is the social work term of the 1990s. Adams (1996) believes it represents a fundamental "paradigm shift" (p. 33) taking the practice of social work away decisively from the medical/pathological model. Others are more sceptical, seeing the term as acting as a "conceptual deodorant" (Ward, 1997) used to justify propositions which at root represent varying ideological and political positions, obscuring conflict and difference, and in the final analysis, potentially a "gilded vehicle" of social control (Davis, 1986) and professional self-interest (Page, 1992; Baistow, 1994).

Drawing from the *Dictionary of Social Work* (Thomas and Pierson, 1995) for a basic definition, empowerment is concerned with how people gain a collective control over their lives to achieve their interests and the method by which social workers seek to enhance the power of people who lack it. It represents a change of focus from social work on people to social work with people. Staples (1990, p. 30) identifies key themes in empowerment as: "participation of people in their own empowerment," "the importance of recognising existing competencies" and "building on individual and collective strengths." Empowerment is the process by which power is developed or taken by the powerless themselves. "Empowering practice ... seeks change not only through *winning* power ... but through *transforming* it" (Mullender and Ward, 1991, p. 6, our emphasis). Empowerment practice offers people the chance to experience new ways of influencing their life chances. It looks to share power between workers and service users and to challenge the both to use it non-oppressively. Breton (1994) eloquently explains the task for social workers:

In the face of more and more severe problems, the normal and understandable reaction of caring and dedicated professionals is to become more and more expert, and develop better and better technologies ... if empowerment is the goal that reaction is exactly the one professionals should not have. What social workers need to adopt in empowerment work are 'bottom-up' strategies whereby they learn from the oppressed, from whose who, more or less effectively, deal first hand with the problems of racism, poverty, sexism, ageism etc.; then bringing the best of social work knowledge and expertise, collaborate with the oppressed to build more just societies. (p. 35)

For service users there is the opportunity to break out of the debilitating sense of self-blame created by the ideological repackaging of public ills as private troubles (Wright Mills, 1970) by right wing conservative governments in America, Australasia and the United Kingdom. Especially where affiliated to groupwork, empowerment can be tremendously powerful in moving people towards more humane and emancipatory relationships. Tara Mistry's (1989) description of a group for black and white women is a classic example. She describes how a mixed race women's group run by herself and a white co-worker was able to move beyond developing an awareness that, as black and white working-class women, members shared similar problems, which have social bases outside their immediate control and are not the result of individual inadequacy; they also confronted and worked on the stereotypes of black people held by their white friends.

In the United Kingdom, these issues have begun to be played out in the arena of research, with the insistence of service users that they have a right to participate in, even to control, the definition and assessment of need and the formulation of services (Davis and Mullender, 1994); and with new legal requirements on service providers to consult widely in their planning and review processes. The consequent active involvement of service users in the research process, rather than as passive research subjects, presents new challenges for established research practice and methods.

APPROACHES TO SOCIAL RESEARCH

To state the obvious, a basic requirement of social research is to obtain data from people. However, in achieving this, social scientists and applied researchers employ different methods of data collection with a view to understanding social phenomena. These can be classified into two broad approaches: quantitative and qualitative. There are philosophical debates and competing views between these two approaches (e.g., Bryman, 1988) as to how the researcher should treat social reality: the people to be studied who live in their own worlds. The positivist tradition asserts that social phenomena can be explained scientifically, based on regularities from the data obtained. Most researchers who take this standpoint aim "not to disturb the world they are studying: their aim, instead, is to trawl their data collecting net quietly through the social world" (Graham and Jones, 1992, p. 239) and use tools such as surveys or questionnaires to depict and understand the subject matter.

In contrast to the positivist tradition is the interpretive tradition in which an understanding of the social world and the subject matter studied is generated from the people. This second tradition is more concerned with understanding social phenomena from the viewpoint of the people themselves (Denzin, 1970). The argument is that human beings are active participants who live in a changing environment. As they interact with the social world in their everyday lives, they adapt and adjust to the situation. Thus, people's active response to social reality possesses meaning that cannot be interpreted by a snapshot survey. Through a process of engaging with people, the meaning behind their reactions and actions towards certain situations can be explained.

Working along the same principle, participationists move a step further. Researchers not only aim to understand what meaning and significance the social world has for people but also explore its properties with them. These are generated and verified by and with the people themselves (Reason, 1990). Involving the respondents in the whole research process enables them to become active participants in defining and interpreting their actions collectively with the researcher and can enhance their understanding about their own living environment. Thus, the notion of empowerment is embedded in this research approach. By taking and shifting the paradigm of researching social reality from researcher centred, where the research problems are predefined or controlled by the researcher, to researched centred, where the research issues are being defined and scrutinized together through dialogue, the values and methods of empowerment come to the fore (Abu-Samah, 1996).

Social Action: An Approach to Empowerment

Over the past 20 years the Centre for Social Action has developed a model of empowerment known as social action (Williamson, 1995). The approach has been recognized as effective in a wide range of human services and to have "advanced our knowledge of practice developments and their conceptualisation" (Brown, 1996, p.92). It is also seen to have wide international currency (Jakobsson, 1995; Treu, Salustowicz, Oldenburg, Offe and Neuser, 1993; Lee 1994; and Breton, 1994).

This formulation of social action differs from its normal usage in North America as an umbrella term covering a range of forms of "professional effort to bring into public discourse issues which, according to the consensus between power holders and the public, should remain in the shadow of public debate" (Staub-Bernasconi, 1991, p. 36). Social action is practice and activity which are committed to social change and social justice (Breton, 1995). In contrast, in the UK, social action has evolved as an explicitly articulated practice theory and methodology. It sits within the radical social work tradition (Bailey and Brake, 1975) and today is making a prime contribution to the debates about empowerment and associated working practices (see, for example, Barry, 1996 and Fleming, Harrison and Ward, 1998, in response). Self-directed groupwork (Mullender and Ward, 1991) is a particular application (and, conceptually, the earliest) of this articulation of social action; social action research has evolved more recently out of this praxis.

Social action as a theoretical perspective draws on several strands of thought. It has been influenced strongly by Paulo Freire, the disability movement (see, for example, Mike Oliver, 1992), black activists and writers (see, for example, Cress-Welsing, 1991; hooks, 1992; Ahmed, 1990; and Gilroy, 1987) and the women's movement (see, for example, Hudson, 1989; Dominelli and McCleod, 1989; Langan and Day, 1992; and Evans, 1994).

Social action has two central characteristics. First, the model was specifically designed to distance from the deficit and blaming the victim approaches which we perceived to be dominating thinking around social welfare work. Models of individual pathology are no substitute for serious consideration of the collective or social condition of service users (Williamson, 1995). Thus social action is based on a commitment to people having the right to be heard, to define the issues facing them, to set the agenda for action and, importantly, to take action on their own behalf. We noted that in much existing community development and social education practice, once an issue is raised, the workers make the assumptions about how it should be addressed. Between the what? and the how? the crucial question of why? is usually left out.

Therefore, secondly, social action advocates that only through the careful understanding of the reasons "why" can the question of "how" be tackled. In asking the question "why," people participate in consideration of underlying causes and through this process they gain greater understanding of their circumstances and hence, empower themselves.

Asking this question is the key that unlocks the process. We encourage people to pursue this question until the root causes of a problem have been identified. Leaving out this stage and this way of looking at problems confines explanations and responsibilities and the scope of the solutions to the private world around people and within their existing knowledge and experience. These have been fashioned by their position on the social ladder and by the processes of social control, education and socialization, which keep this in place.

Asking the question "why" gives people the opportunity to widen their horizons of what is possible, to break out of the demoralizing and self-perpetuating narrowness of vision and introspection created by poverty, lack of opportunity and exclusion. It enables them to conceive of new explanations in the wider social, political and economic context and to consider how they can identify and engage with these, in fact to challenge the taken-for-granted victim blaming explanations in which they are trapped. It turns the spotlight round from people as a problem in themselves, to the problems they encounter, and enables them to see opportunities to develop a much wider range of options for action and change. (For further explanation and detail of this process, please see Mullender and Ward 1991; Ward and Mullender, 1991; and Kidd and Kumar, 1994).

Thus social action is about empowering service users to define their own needs and facilitating them to shape their own environment. Through pursuing the question "why," a key concern is for analyzing circumstances and developing appropriate measures for doing this, in partnership with service users. Within this process there are clear links between practice and research. Indeed, these are reinforced where the process, as action research, goes beyond investigation, analysis and evaluation to attention to plans for new and/or improved services and action to achieve these. In this respect, we are seeking to fuse traditions. Social action research recognizes the importance of a high level of social intervention skill for the researcher, but additionally it views a thorough and defensible research methodology as an essential feature for good practice. We are concerned not only about the potential for empowerment through research but also reflexively about the importance of research for empowerment practice.

SOCIAL ACTION RESEARCH—EMPOWERING INVESTIGATION

At the Centre for Social Action, methods for research and evaluation have developed alongside practice. We recognized that just as traditional methods were not adequate for good practice, so conventional research techniques did not take proper account of service users' views. The centre has developed a research approach based on the values and methods of social action.

Again, one can identify two central characteristics. First, it is the responsibility of researchers to set in motion a process of participation whereby people identify and define their needs and work on common issues that can become agendas for change. Second, this means that, although special skills and knowledge are employed, these do not accord privilege and are not solely the province of professionals. In effect, the research methods should reflect non-elitist principles and enable users to empower themselves to make decisions and control outcomes.

A key task of the researcher is to establish methods which align with the values, principles and understanding of the people involved in the research. The challenge is, "How can the professional researcher (or practitioner) make sense of that alignment and how should it be managed?" To address this, we will call upon a statement of values identified and set out for social action practice (Mullender and Ward, 1991), which has been helpfully applied to the research context (Lloyd, 1997) and critically assess its applicability through the case study that follows. As with other aspects of social action practice, these values have evolved and continue to evolve through a dialectic process of study, articulation and reflection (Kolb, 1984; Schon, 1983) in which all those associated with the Centre for Social Action in whatever capacity—practice, research or training and education—take part.

- Service providers and users formulate the issues. This is more than participation in a preshaped agenda; it is control, perhaps shared with researchers, and funders, in shaping the agenda.
- The interaction between researchers and respondents is non-hierarchical. The researchers share their personal and professional resources, including their own role in the research process—reasons for interest, hypotheses or bias about the field of study and influences on their choice of methodology.
- Data analysis and dissemination are undertaken jointly. This enables people to see the effect of their participation on the research process and facilitates further dialogue. A corollary of joint involvement in dissemination is creating a research structure which leaves respondents

stronger than previously by enabling them to act on their new knowledge and understanding. (Lloyd, 1997, p. 75)

These principles will be readily recognized both by both researchers with a qualitative orientation, particularly where contextualized within passionate scholarship (Du Bois, 1983), and by workers in a range of settings (community, social and youth work, health, housing, planning and adult education for example) who have a development orientation.

The approach draws from the practice of social education and community development work (Mullender and Ward, 1991) interpreted and complemented by feminist (Roberts, 1981), disability (Oliver, 1992; Zarb, 1992) and black (Ahmed, 1989) research insights and perspectives. Within this framework we have adopted and utilized the techniques of grounded theory (Strauss and Corbin, 1990), new paradigm research (Reason, 1990), fourth generation research (Guba and Lincoln 1989) and qualitative data analysis (Miles and Huberman, 1994) to develop an ethnographic research approach (Everitt, Hardiker, Littlewood and Mullender, 1992) that emphasizes collaboration, participation and mutual respect. Our focus is on analyzing what is happening on the basis of people's felt experience and, from this, to contribute to developing measures that can explicitly empower those involved to shape their environment and bring about improvements in their material conditions.

As far as is feasible, we work together with all the parties involved at all levels, at all stages of a research project. They participate in the refinement of the objectives, in the formulation of the questions to be addressed and the methods of information collection and, in due course, in the interpretation of the findings. This forms the basis of a collaborative research approach that draws out qualitative and quantitative data, using a range of data collection methods. Where appropriate, local people are involved and provided with training as peer researchers. They are able to elicit data and, in their own right, contribute perspectives out of reach of external information gatherers (Dyson, 1995; Dyson and Harrison, 1996).

The value of the whole method lies particularly in the depths of richness of the qualitative data gathered, providing vivid descriptions and clear insights into problems and opportunities. By using a collaborative format and a combination of methods, a range of perspectives is brought to bear on data and meanings attributed to them, achieving both sensitivity to participants and, through triangulation, research validity (Patton, 1990). Working in this way has made us well aware of the ethical dimensions of research. Concepts of confidentiality, informed consent and open and honest communication with all participants are central. The approach provides a means of directly addressing these issues with participants (Fleming and Ward, 1996).

Social action research builds on the expectations, understanding and experience of all participants to offer concepts which they can engage with and apply to their own circumstances. Findings are disseminated and shared with people in terms they can understand and use. Benefits lie in securing widespread ownership of findings and in achieving support for implementation.

The process also engenders knowledge, skills and structures that are sustained after research involvement is over. What takes place is a seamless interaction, and progression, of research and development work.

Process

Social action research usually falls into nine main phases. These are not separate and discrete; there will be some overlap between stages:

1. Orientation (including literature review)
2. Setting up of a research steering group
3. Defining the parameters of the research
4. Gathering and analyzing the data
5. Presentation and discussion of interim findings
6. Further information collection
7. Analyzing the information collected
8. Preparation and presentation of final report
9. Wide dissemination of the findings

Orientation
This is a period for the researchers to meet and establish working links and systems of communication with the key relevant people in the subject area and to familiarize themselves with:

- the range and structure of the subject area;
- geography, demography and scope of the area or locality;
- all relevant written materials;
- other relevant research literature so that the study can draw on existing knowledge and experience.

Setting up a research steering group
A research project will usually be guided by a group of people with knowledge and expertise in the subject area with relevant experience in the

field of social action research and with local knowledge. Its function is to be a forum to discuss issues arising from the research, in particular process and practice as well as method and findings. This ensures the quality and relevance of the research.

Defining the parameters of the research

Conventional research seems to be obsessed with defining research questions. Social action research works on the basis that research should not be detached from practical activities. Projects should learn from the information produced by the research, as it emerges, and should incorporate it into the process. This means that people at all levels must have close links with the research and a commitment to take on the process and its results into their own activities. Thus, all parties are involved in discussions about what information should be collected, why and from whom, how it should be collected and how it should be presented and used. What is important at this stage is not to specify a number of predetermined questions based on researchers' or funders' perspectives, but to ensure that the research methods deployed are sufficiently flexible and open for issues to be introduced by participants and to be added from emerging data.

The researchers spend time with participants to identify what the parameters of the research will be. They look at the multiplicity of interests and concerns and the consequent plurality of legitimate matters for attention (Powell and Goddard, 1996) and work with participants to establish which are the key areas, processes, practices and outcomes upon which the research will focus initially.

Gathering and analyzing the data

Data collection methods are finally decided with participants and the steering group. We believe that users have much to contribute in deciding the most successful ways of collecting information. A variety of information collection methods are available to achieve this. These include:

- a review of secondary sources, minutes of meetings, policy documents, correspondence, newspaper articles;
- direct observation;
- guided conversations with key individuals and groups;
- maps and diagrams, e.g., resource and facility maps;
- critical incident analysis to look at how certain problems areas and are dealt with;
- drama workshops;
- case studies of organizations or individuals;

- work diaries of paid and unpaid workers and community members;
- focus groups;
- SWOT analyses (looking at the strengths, weaknesses, opportunities and threats in particular situations);
- questionnaires (ranking and scoring);
- statistical data
  (see also Mikkelsen, 1995, Chapter 3)

Where appropriate, information collection is undertaken by peer researchers or by using translators All instruments are pretested to ensure their clarity and relevance. Interviews and focus groups are taped with the permission of the participants.

A purposeful sampling strategy is used with contrast sampling to ensure diversity (Patton, 1990). This allows for the identification of common patterns or variations between groups. Efforts are made to reach the opinions of the unorganized, those who are not necessarily active in groups. We have found that the snowball sampling technique is an effective way of achieving this. (Browne and Minichiello, 1990).

Data are analyzed throughout the research period by a variety of means. Thematic coding of the qualitative information can be undertaken. Coding schemes are devised as the research develops with the collaboration of those involved in the projects. Codes can be derived from research questions or evolve in the early stages of the research, using the comparison procedure suggested by Miles and Huberman (1994) to ensure adequate reliability and validity. Emergent themes are discussed with the participants and in the steering group. By having a range of people and methods of looking at the same situation, it is possible to allow for some triangulation. Computer packages can assist in the analysis of quantitative and qualitative data (for example, QSR NUD-IST and SPSS).

Presentation of and interpretation of interim findings
The consultative nature of social action research may mean that it can take longer than other research approaches. However, because of the significance to participants of the research, there is an interim presentation of progress and findings part-way through by means of a short interim report of findings and interpretation seminar(s) for participants.

Further information collection
The research process continues after the interim report and seminars. It is adapted and adjusted to take into account the discussion of the interim report. Avenues identified in the interim interpretation are further investigated.

Analyzing and interpreting all the information collected

The analysis of all the data collected is undertaken by the researchers within a framework agreed with the participants. It is intended that the interpretation of the information, after analysis, should involve as much participation as possible. This takes place through workshops, discussion groups and draft reports circulated for comment. These enable people to be involved in giving meanings to the information and discussing its implications for policy and practice.

Preparation and presentation of the final report of the research

In practice the findings of the research are fed back to the participants on an ongoing basis. This allows them to have the greatest possible influence on the development of practice and policy. In addition, the research is likely to have several written outputs.

Dissemination of the results

We are absolutely committed to the research having as wide as possible an impact. We share information and promote learning through publications, training courses and seminars.

This action research approach has been used in a wide range of research projects and evaluations, all of which have been focused towards identifying directions and processes for achieving change, on the basis of an analysis of existing circumstances. They range through health needs assessments sponsored by statutory organizations to project and service evaluations and feasibility studies on behalf of user and community groups, national and local voluntary organizations and statutory bodies.

Projects have taken place in a diverse range of ethnic and cultural environments, for example, the multicultural community of the City of Derby, the Somali community in London, disabled people in rural Derbyshire, the youth of Liverpool. Outside the UK, the methodology has been successfully utilised in a Malaysian planned village context to evaluate structures and processes of community participation within national development programs (Abu-Samah, 1996). The methodology has also been central to a training approach used extensively by the Centre for Social Action in Russia and Ukraine. The researchers invariably have left in place action and development plans and, frequently, structures and access to resources for carrying these forward. Often, the centre has been asked to continue involvement by providing consultancy and training for these next steps.

EXAMPLE AND DISCUSSION

We will now explore how we attempt to put these principles and methods into practice in research by the example of a health needs assessment we have undertaken (Fleming and Harrison, 1994). This was a study commissioned by a health forum steering group within a large urban regeneration agency to undertake a community health needs assessment in the inner city area in which they were operating. The research brief was to obtain detailed information of the views of people living in the area about the quality of their life, from a health perspective, and to generate ideas for actions to improve residents' health and well-being. The agency had already commissioned a quantitative study based on questionnaires and a tick-box methodology sent to 1300 households in the area. We were invited to do a complementary study in much greater depth, with a smaller number of participants from selected groups in the population, which it was hoped would provide a platform for informed action by residents. The health forum steering group was keen to get more detailed knowledge of what the statistical report meant in terms of impact on local people's lives and they felt our philosophy and methodology would enable them to do this.

We do not treat people as just objects to be investigated or used as sources of information. We attempt to involve them in all stages of the research process. It is assumed in all our work that the people with whom we work are the experts about their circumstances. In this research we started by asking local people and professionals, "What are the questions we should be asking people about their health?", "Who should we be asking?" and "How can we *find* the answers to these questions?" Though residents were given a central place in determining the questions, all stakeholders—those with an interest—were included. In this case, it meant the research sponsors also suggested areas to explore, as did local professionals. This process of involving all those with an interest in the research encourages as wide as possible ownership of the results and commitment to take action on the recommendations.

By taking this approach it emerged that even the concept of health had different meanings for different people. Thus, "What does 'health' mean to you?" was one of the first questions asked before we began to ask about what affected their health. It also emerged that local people did not see health as a medical concept. When asked about health they talked about "happiness," "satisfaction," "energy levels," as well as "lack of pain" and "being able to do all you need to in a day," whereas the health professionals talked of hypertension, asthma and accidents in the home. As a consequence, it was agreed to use the term "health and well-being" rather than just "health" in order to reflect more accurately the concept as understood by local people.

These early stages draw attention to matters of epistemology, that is, to the construction and definition of knowledge. Feminist and disabled researchers (e.g., Oakley, 1981; Oliver, 1992) have argued that research has been dominated by male and able-bodied people who have controlled the agenda, the questions and the findings. The agency sponsors held a medical model of health, while local people were expressing a view in which health is not an individual problem, rather one constructed by society. The dilemma this poses is, however, that to take either position implies that there is only one view of reality and, in effect, to adopt a positivist notion of objectivity. The values of empowerment rest on a perspective that all knowledge is socially constructed. Reality is multifaceted, changing and, at times, contradictory. As Fuss (1989, cited in Lloyd, 1997, p. 96) argues, we must both value and theorize experience but prevent it becoming reified. Exploring with research subjects about how to reflect their experiences can counter the danger of research packages categorizing data in predetermined ways, but it may conceivably be valid to do otherwise. We must be careful not to write out the expertise of the researcher and fall into a false equality trap (Barker, 1986). Crude juxtapositioning of qualitative and quantitative approaches may also overlook, and so undervalue, other things that can be gained from respondents' experiences. We know that quantitative data can be derived from single and different discussions though categorizing, counting and even reassembling language to produce enriched and sometimes new insights (Bailey, 1994).

The discussions with local people, local professionals and the research sponsors informed the second stage of the research—information collection. It was decided to devise a semi-structured interview schedule to ask people individually and in groups broad questions about what people considered good health to be; what factors they thought affected their health and well-being, either positively or negatively; why they thought these factors existed; and how they believed matters could be improved. Questions were also asked about people's levels of knowledge and satisfaction with medical services that they used.

This process of tackling a problem drawn from practice is one we have found very effective in research. Asking people to identify what are the issues, concerns or problems for them; to look at why they exist; and how they can be tackled is not a passive process. It actively involves local people in both the provision of information and its analysis and recognizes their knowledge, skills and experience.

The questions in the semi-structured interview were piloted with a small number of residents and they were asked for their opinions of the questions and the interview process. This resulted in some changes in the wording and ordering of the questions and some being left out altogether. An example of the latter was that the sponsors wished to have questions asked about their activities. It became apparent very early on that people did not know about the agency and so could not comment on their activities. People made it very clear that they did not like being asked questions which they did not have the information to answer.

After this phase the main information collection took place. People identified their health as being affected by many and varied factors. People felt their health and well-being benefited from the support of family and friends, getting together with people like themselves and for those that had them, jobs and financial security. People identified their health as being adversely affected by a wide variety of factors including: poor housing, financial worries, racism, fear of crime, lack of appropriate cultural and linguistic facilities, poor environment, pollution, poor transport and mobility problems and lack of jobs.

The actions suggested by residents also showed an understanding of health as a social phenomena with interpersonal, environmental and financial components and that health promotion needs to be an interagency and multi-disciplinary response. They suggested their health and well-being would be improved by more job and training opportunities, women-only fitness activities, community care assistants with specialized language skills, grants for house repairs and adaptations for home-owners and cleaner streets, among other things.

The qualitative methods used allowed for these subtleties and differences of opinion to emerge. The data collected provided rich and vivid descriptions of people's lives and the clear insights which they alone can give into the difficulties and opportunities they experience.

The participants in the research were treated as equals and as experts in their own circumstances. They were seen as subjects of the research who have the right to speak out and to be heard. The process is dynamic, the whole research was an interaction between the researcher and the respondents. The researcher played an active role in asking questions of respondents either as individuals or in groups, through prompting and probing. The information gathered was collated and subsequently shared and checked out with respondents to ascertain its accuracy and explore its meaning by focus group discussions and sharing of the draft report for comment and discussion.

The techniques of data collection were flexible and interactive. They ranged through observation, participant observation, casual conversation, informal interview, follow-up interviews and focus groups. They also included the analysis of records, reports, books, articles and other materials. All these are relatively unstructured data collection techniques with no predetermined outcomes in mind. By such a combination of methods, a range of perspectives was brought to bear on issues and the meanings attributed to them, achieving a measure of validity while remaining sensitive to participants.

It has already been described how local people participated in setting the parameters and focus of the research. They were also involved in deciding who should take part. This was done by using the community to identify groups that could be involved and also for individual interviews using the snowball technique. People who had taken part were asked to identify other people who might be willing to be interviewed. In this way we made contact with those people who do not, or cannot, take part in groups.

Keeping a consultation process going in which respondents have a real say is far from straightforward. There is the question of whose interests are being promoted by the inevitable selectivity that occurs. As outlined, we were particularly concerned to bring in people who are not usually represented, but timescales exerted one restriction on what was possible. Nevertheless, we would, like Lloyd (1997, p. 79) argue that any shortfall does not invalidate the exercise as the process itself contributes to the identification of issues to be followed through.

As practitioners we know the strength people gain from working together with others and sharing problems. The realization that one is not alone with a problem and the opportunity to share experiences can be empowering for people. Thinking of solutions in a group where people can bounce ideas off each other and develop ideas further is a major aspect of this approach. Oliver (1992, p. 105) observes that the experience of being researched can be an isolating one, reinforcing the dominant idea of problems being individual. Working in groups can combat this.

Some of the groups with which we worked were existing groups where people already knew each other and discussed things together, for example, a group of Polish elders at a social club. Others came together especially for the research, for example, a group of older Muslim men who all attended a Pakistani centre for lunch but had not worked together as a group before. This group shared common issues, such as difficulty getting interpreters, poor housing, the need for adaptations to assist elderly people with physical impairments. In sharing these issues, they realized that they were not alone and that the issues were not just their problems. In discussion actions were identified that others could try.

An example of the power of group activity from this research study is a group of Muslim young women with children. Through taking part in the study they identified loneliness and isolation as very real problems for them that detrimentally affected their feeling of well-being and thus their health. They decided they wanted to organize regular meetings for themselves and their children. They negotiated with the local Pakistani community centre to use the centre on the day the men were at the mosque. They applied to and lobbied the local authority for funding.

Experience of oppression and discrimination was clearly voiced in the report of this research through the words of the people themselves. Respondents who did not have English as their first language clearly described the consequences of not having access to people to translate medical information into their own language and the problems of having professional workers who do not understand the cultural aspects of a situation. For example, the brother of an Asian woman who had just given birth was used by the midwife to interpret, causing severe embarrassment. Gay men highlighted their experience of discrimination and the effect it had on their health and well-being. For example, members of a self-help group for people with HIV/AIDS voiced the prejudice they found when it came to the allocation of community care assistants and housing.

To enable people to say what they want to say, who interviews them can be important. Care was taken to ensure that all sections of the community could participate. Where necessary, interviewers with particular language skills were employed or interpreters used. Sometimes people indicated that a researcher was not an acceptable person to talk to and so alternatives were found. For example, the white woman researcher was not able to engage African Caribbean young men, so an African Caribbean man was employed to facilitate their involvement. He did this successfully.

Besides checking out and discussing data with specific informants, collections of data and analyses (in other words the evolving report) were presented to participants in workshops and discussion groups at successive stages. In addition there were, of course, many informal individual conversations. The group meetings and workshops had a strongly interactional format, as did the presentation of the final report to health service and city officials in which local participants were prominent. Part of the researcher/ practitioner role was to prepare participants to contribute effectively and support them on the day.

Oliver (1992) argues that it is in dissemination that the capacity of research to be empowering is most starkly revealed. Our respondents reminded us repeatedly that there had to be tangible outcomes for their quality of life. They had suspended their scepticism that researchers simply parachuted in, abused their confidences and left with no evidence of results, except, they suspected, on their own careers. Thus, following Zarb (1992), we tenaciously pursued involving participants in dissemination.

Such involvement, however, brings to the fore the question of the relationship with funders. A common feature in social action research is an anxiety on the part of funders about the early pace of the work, which emphasizes community networking and so does not meet expectations of research output and value for money. An intellectual understanding of the social action process seems to come under severe strain when it comes down to monitoring the spending of hard cash. We have found that we simply have to weather this storm until the richness and creativity of the emerging outputs become self-evident. This is reinforced by the determined commitment of respondent participants to support the process and see it through. Thus, a secondary effect is the emergence of an increasingly organized and powerful community through the process of the research. A further stand-off can arise over the findings themselves, which may not fall into the narrow categories in which the service delivery responsibilities of the funders and other agencies are framed. This, of course, opens up questions of vested interests as well as expectations of the research. In the health needs project, as in many others, it required all the facilitation skills of the researchers in the multidisciplinary steering group, as well as the contextual pressure exerted by the respondents, to ensure that the findings were faithfully expressed and a commitment to tangible outcomes secured.

The findings were available in a range of formats all of which highlighted the participatory nature of the process that had produced them. They received publicity through the media and we know that they penetrated deeply into the community. Indeed, city officials inform us two years later that they are surprised and not a little disconcerted, periodically, still to have the findings produced as evidence to support the aspirations of groups.

CONCLUSION

Genuinely empowering research entails a demanding agenda. In this paper, we have tried to outline how research and evaluation of human service delivery can be made meaningful and useful to service users and service providers. We are not saying that social action can be a panacea for all problems, indeed we must be cautious and not overestimate the impact of the approach. There is always the possibility that empowerment creates the illusion of change co-opted to the status quo. However, our experience shows that the philosophy and methods described are very effective in ensuring service users' participation. It is through their participation that they can be empowered to ensure that services which are appropriate to, and which meet, their needs will develop.

REFERENCES

Abu-Samah, A. (1996). Empowering research process: Using groups in research to empower people. *Groupwork*, 9(2), 221-252.

Adams, R. (1996). *Social work and empowerment*. London: Macmillan.

Ahmed, B. (1990). *Black perspectives in social work*. Birmingham: Venture Press.

Ahmed, S. (1989). Research and the black experience. In M. Stein (Ed.), *Research in practice: Proceedings of the fourth annual JUC/BASW research conference*. Birmingham: British Association of Social Workers.

Bailey, R. (1994). *Probation supervision: Attitudes to formalised helping*. Unpublished doctoral thesis, University of Nottingham.

Bailey, R. and Brake, M. (Eds.). (1975). *Radical social work*. London: Edward Arnold.

Baistow, K. (1994). Liberation or regulation? Some paradoxes of empowerment. *Critical Social Policy*, 42, 34-46.

Barker, H. (1986). Recapturing sisterhood: A critical look at 'process' in feminist organising and community work. *Critical Social Policy*, 16, 80-90

Barry, M. (1996). The empowering process: Leading from behind? *Youth and Policy*, 54, 1-2.

Breton, M. (1994). On the meaning of empowerment and empowerment-oriented social work practice. *Social Work with Groups*, 17(3), 23-37

Breton, M. (1995). The potential for social action in groups. *Social Work with Groups*, 18(2/3), 5-13.

Brown, A. (1996). Groupwork into the future: Some personal reflections. *Groupwork*, 9(1), 80-96.

Browne, J. and Minichiello, A. (1990). The condom: Why more young people don't put it on. *Sociology of Health and Illness*, 30, 229-245.

Bryman, A. (1988). *Quantity and quality in social research*. London: Unwin.

Cress-Welsing, F. (1991). *ISIS papers*. Chicago: Third World Press.

Davis, K. (1986). Disabling definitions: A comment on Mullender and Ward. *British Journal of Social Work*, 16(1), 97.

Davis, K. and Mullender, A. (Eds.). (1994). Key issues in disability: Rights or charity. The future of welfare [special edition]. *Social Action*, 2(1). London: Whiting and Birch.

Denzin, N. (1970). *The research act in sociology*. London: Butterworth.

Dominelli, L. and McLeod, E. (1989). *Feminist social work*. London: Macmillan.

Du Bois, B. (1983). Passionate scholarship: Notes on values, knowing and method in feminist social science. In G. Bowles and R. Duelli Klein (Eds.), *Theories of women's studies*. London: Routledge and Kegan Paul.

Dyson, S. (1995). Clients as researchers: Issues in haemoglobinopathy awareness. *Social Action*, 2(4), 4-10.

Dyson, S. and Harrison, M. (1996). Black community members as researchers: Working with community groups in the research process. *Groupwork*, 9(2), 203-220.

Evans, M. (Ed.). (1994). *The woman question*. London: Sage.

Everitt, A., Hardiker, P., Littlewood, J. and Mullender A. (1992). *Applied research for better practice*. London: Macmillan.

Fleming, J. and Harrison, M. (1994). *Derby pride health needs study*. Derby: Derby Pride Ltd..

Fleming, J., Harrison, J. and Ward, D. (1998). Social action can be an empowering process: A response to the scepticism of Monica Barry. *Youth and Policy*, 60, 46-61.

Fleming, J. and Ward, D. (1996). The ethics of community health needs assessments: Searching for a participant centred approach. In M. Parker (Ed.), *Ethics and community*. Preston: University of Central Lancashire, Centre for Professional Ethics.

Fuss, D. (1989). *Essentially speaking: Feminism, nature and difference*. London: Routledge.

Gilroy, P. (1987). *There ain't no black in the Union Jack*. London: Hutchinson.

Graham, H. and Jones, J. (1992). Community development and research. *Community Development Journal*, 24(3), 235-241.

Guba, E. and Lincoln, Y. (1989). *Fourth generation evaluation*. Newbury Park, CA: Sage.

hooks, b. (1992). *Ain't I a woman: Black women and feminism*. London: Pluto Press.

Hudson, A. (1989). Changing perspectives: Feminism, youth and social work. In M. Langan and P. Lee (Eds.), *Radical social work today*. London: Unwin Hyman.

Jakobsson, G. (Ed.). (1995). *Social work in an international perspective*. Helsinki: Helsinki University Press.

Kidd, R. and Kumar, K. (1994). Coopting Freire: A critical analysis of pseudo-Freirian adult education. *Social Action*, 2(2), 11-18. (Original work published 1981)

Kolb, D. (1984). *Experiential learning*. Eaglewood Cliffs, NJ: Prentice Hall.

Langan, M. and Day, L. (Eds.). (1992). *Women, oppression and social work*. London: Routledge.

Lee, J. (1994). *The empowerment approach to social work practice*. New York: Columbia University Press.

Lloyd, M. (1997). Partnership with service users: Considerations for research. In R. Adams (Ed.), *Crisis in the human services: National and international issues*. Kingston upon Hull: University of Lincolnshire and Humberside.

Mikkelsen, B. (1995). *Methods for development work and research: A guide for practitioners*. London: Sage.

Miles, M. and Huberman, M. (1994). *Qualitative data analysis* (2nd ed.). London: Sage.

Mistry, T. (1989). Establishing a feminist model of groupwork in the probation service *Groupwork*, 2(2), 145-158.

Mullender, A. and Ward, D. (1991). *Self-directed groupwork: Users take action for empowerment*. London: Whiting and Birch.

Oakley, A. (1981). Interviewing women: A contradiction in terms. In H. Roberts (Ed.) *Doing feminist research*. London: Routledge and Kegan Paul.

Oliver, M. (1992). Changing the social relations of research production. *Disability, Handicap and Society*, 7(2), 101-114.

Page, R. (1992). Empowerment, oppression and beyond: A coherent strategy? A reply to Mullender and Ward (CSP Issue 32). *Critical Social Policy*, 35, 89-92.

Patton, M. (1990). *Qualitative research methods*. London: Sage.

Powell, J. and Goddard, A. (1996). Cost and stakeholder views: A combined approach to evaluation services. *British Journal of Social Work*, 26(1), 93-108.

Reason, P. (Ed). (1990). *Human inquiry in action: Developments in new paradigm research*. London: Routledge and Kegan Paul.

Roberts, H. (Ed.). (1981). *Doing feminist research*. London: Routledge and Kegan Paul.

Schon, D. (1983). *The reflective practitioner*. New York: Basic Books.

Staples, L. (1990). Powerful ideas about empowerment. *Administration in Social Work*, 14(2), 29-41.

Staub-Bernasconi, S. (1991). Social action, empowerment and social work—An integrative theoretical framework for social work and social work with groups. In A. Vinik and M. Levin (Eds.), *Social action in groupwork*. Binghampton, NY: Haworth Press.

Strauss, A. and Corbin, J. (1990). *The basics of qualitative research*. London: Sage.

Thomas, M. and Pierson, J. (1995). *Dictionary of social work*. London: Collins.

Treu, H-E., Salustowicz, P., Oldenburg, E., Offe, H. and Neuser, H. (Eds.). (1993). *Theorie und Praxis der Bekamphung der Langzeitarbeitslosigkeit in der EG-* Weinheim. Germany: Deutscher Studien Verlag.

Ward, D. (1997). Groupwork: Out in the cold? In R. Adams, L. Dominelli and M. Payne (Eds.). *Social work: Themes, issues and critical debates*. London: Macmillan.

Ward, D. and Mullender, A. (1991). Empowerment and oppression: The indissoluble link. *Critical Social Policy*, 32, 21-30.

Williamson, H. (Ed.). (1995). *Social action for young people*. Lyme Regis: Russell House.

Wright Mills, C. (1970). *The sociological imagination*. Harmondsworth: Penguin.

Zarb, G. (1992). On the road to Damascus: First steps towards changing the relations of disability research production. *Disability, Handicap and Society*, 7(2), 125-138.

Chapter 21

ASSESS HELPING PROCESSES AND CLIENT OUTCOMES IN EMPOWERMENT PRACTICE: AMPLIFYING CLIENT VOICE AND SATISFYING FUNDING SOURCES

Ruth Parsons
Graduate School of Social Work
University of Denver

There is a growing consensus regarding empowerment both as a desirable goal and as a process in social work practice (See Gutiérrez, Parsons and Cox, 1998). Furthermore, there is an increasing convergence in the conceptualization, definition and operational strategies of empowerment in social work practice (Gutiérrez, DeLois and GlenMaye, 1994; Gutiérrez, 1989, 1990; Parsons, 1994, 1998; Cox and Parsons, 1994; Simon, 1994; Solomon, 1976; Saleebey, 1992; Manning, 1994; Gutiérrez, Parsons and Cox, 1998). However, there is less development and agreement regarding the assessment and measurement of empowerment, either as program principles or as expected client outcomes. In programs where empowerment principles either guide the nature of the helping process or empowerment is defined as the desired program outcome, the need for assessment is paramount (Parsons, 1998; Rapp, Shera and Kisthardt, 1993; Zimmerman, 1995; Rogers, Chamberlin, Ellison and Crean, 1997).

The importance of this concept to consumers of mental health services is evident in the efforts and writing of many consumer groups in identifying their needs. Empowerment has become a focal concept for the consumer movement in mental health that counters the negative and iatrogenic effects of both mental illness and inadequate mental health interventions. Empowerment emphasizes beliefs, attitudes and practices which promote the capacity of mental health consumers to understand their conditions and to become active participants in matters that affect their lives (Bolton and Brookings, 1996); it is a counter to oppression and professional paternalism (McClean, 1995). Empowerment in mental health has been described as a new vision of healing

(Fisher, 1994); advocacy principles in services (Rose and Black, 1985); and improving quality of life rather than curing illness (Libassi, 1992). Consumer groups are currently attempting to define and measure empowerment as a way to assess the efficacy of programs and movements that are geared toward this goal (Chamberlin, 1997).

However, assessment and evaluation of empowerment practice is a complex task. Contextual adaptations, cultural, ethnic and gender differences are critical to this process. A need to facilitate empowerment in the evaluation and research process increases the complexity of this task. Empowerment research, including evaluation research, must facilitate and create contexts in which clients, or previously silent and isolated people, gain understanding, voice and influence over the decisions that affect their lives (Rappaport, 1990; Rapp, Shera and Kisthardt, 1993; Holmes, 1992; Parsons, East and Boesen, 1994; Parsons, 1998; Sohng, 1998). Furthermore, research content and method must amplify clients' voices and represent their point of view in context, vantage point, selection of outcomes, measures, data collection and analysis and dissemination (Rapp, Shera and Kisthardt, 1993). Empowerment evaluation invites usage of both quantitative and qualitative methodologies in order to address some of these complex issues. Regardless of the methods chosen, assessment of empowerment requires thoughtful consideration of both ends and means, with the guiding principle of who is the beneficiary of the assessment. These principles of empowerment research (See Parsons, 1998) were used as guides in this research.

This paper describes the process of developing assessment instruments for both the processes (inputs) and outcomes of empowerment based practice. This is a description of the development of two assessment tools; the empowerment practice principles (EPP), which assesses strategies and helping behaviours in an empowerment based program, and the empowerment outcomes assessment (EOA), an instrument to assess change outcomes in clients. The methods utilized to create these instruments amplify the voices of oppressed people and come directly from their words that describe their experience. Clients whose voices gave words to these instruments participated in the initial creation of the words, themes, concepts and questions. The content of the instruments was constantly fed back and validated with clients as to whether the words captured their experience. In the piloting of the instruments for assessment of consumers of mental health services, consumers participated in focus groups and individual interviews to determine if the questions fit their experience and what might need to be added or changed in order for the instruments to be better measures of their experience. In the final phase, additional focus groups of clients and providers were asked to define empowerment processes and outcomes so that the revised content of the instruments could be checked for validity. In the last two phases, research trained clients/consumers assisted in all components of the development, including administering the instruments to consumers.

INITIAL GROUNDED RESEARCH

At the very beginning ground level, the author (Parsons, 1994) used group interviews and individual qualitative interviews to identify helping behaviours, program characteristics and client outcomes in five empowerment based programs. This reputational sample consisted of social work programs whose intentional mission and program philosophies are based on empowerment. These programs were selected because their definition and stated perceptions of empowerment were congruent with current social work empowerment practice concepts in the literature. The four agencies and five programs included: a shelter facility and a community support program in an agency for domestic violence survivors; an empowerment project within a residential facility for elders; a residential program for adults with severe and persistent mental illness; and a coalition of AFDC recipients whose function was to bring about policy changes in an AFDC program. The diversity in program function was deliberate in the sample selection from the standpoint of including clients and workers engaged in varied purposes of intervention with diverse populations and different needs. Functions of these programs ranged from the personal safety crises of the women in the shelter to social change and education function of the community program for domestic violence and the AFDC coalition and issues of loss and grief associated with aging in the elder women's project. While the programs differed greatly in client need, problem severity and program purpose, all shared a stated outcome goal of empowerment.

The researcher conducted five group interviews, one in each setting, 18 individual client interviews and ten staff individual interviews. Only one individual interview respondent was male. The other 17 were female, one African American, five Latinas and 11 whites, ages 25-86. Of the 45 participants in focus groups, ages ranged from 19-86, with a median age of approximately 30. The elder group ranged in ages from 58-86. Group respondents included nine African Americans, 12 Latinos, 24 whites, 43 females and two males. Research participants were informed that one of this study's objectives was to define empowerment from the perspective of clients and workers and they were asked to talk about that concept in the programs. This qualitative study included the following research questions: how did the program define empowerment; how did the clients define empowerment; in what ways did the program attempt to facilitate empowerment; how the clients experienced such programs; why clients sought help from these particular programs; what clients expected to receive in the way of help; what was the clients' experience in the helping process; and what changes could clients identify and associate with being in the program? The two following assessments of empowerment based services and outcomes were developed from the results of this qualitative study.

EMPOWERMENT PRACTICE PRINCIPLES (EPP)

The EPP is a 48-item survey intended to assess the program intervention strategies, as carried out by the workers, as to their empowerment attributes. Some of the probes used were: "What was it in this program that made you start to think or behave differently?" and, "What was it about the program and the helping process that caused you to change and begin to experience greater empowerment in your life?"

Transcripts from the group and individual in-depth interviews were analyzed together. Through a constant comparative method (Lincoln and Guba, 1985), patterns were extracted from the transcripts and were organized into categories. Common themes, generated from the categories, were defined and distinguished from each other and data which supported those themes were extracted from the transcripts and compiled into the results. The linking relationships between the themes were identified and the results represent those linked categories and themes. Then, the author searched the social work practice literature for other studies and concepts relevant to empowerment practice principles. A synthesis of this literature (Gutiérrez, DeLois and GlenMaye, 1994; Gutiérrez, 1989, 1990; Cox and Parsons, 1994; Simon, 1994; Solomon, 1976; Manning, 1994 and1998) combined with author's research provided a basis for the development of the EPP scale. The result of this synthesis of available research is contained in Figure 1.

Themes and Categories Derived from the Research

Parsons' study (1994) found in each program that both clients and staff suggested the importance of an environmental ambiance and culture that facilitate empowerment. This category (or element), named *Creation of a cohesive collective*, included these environmental themes: feeling of safety; opportunity for interaction and relationships; feeling of trust and support; the opportunity to tell personal stories and to be heard; opportunity to make mutual decisions regarding problems for work; to access resources; to build interdependence; create hope; and the opportunity to take collective action.

Figure 1: Practice Elements of Empowerment

Cohesive Collective	Collaborative Relationship with Professionals and Peers
• safety • interaction • relationship/trust • networks • being heard and validated • mutual decision-making • mutual aid • interdependence • creation of hope • collaborative action	• experiencing power • clients' perceptions honoured • clients' voices amplified • clients as teachers/helpers
Collaborative Strength Based Assessment	Educational Focus
• belief in client • coping capacities and motivation • focus on individual and environment • fostering client belief in self • challenge and confrontation • taking risks	• shared learning • critical thinking • trying new skills • consciousness-raising • conflict management • resource access • self-advocacy

The relationships between professionals and clients and between clients themselves were a second category. The themes associated with this category suggested that these relationships are collaborative, with shared power. Clients' perceptions of problems, their voices and choices are amplified in the decision-making process. Clients are expected to give and contribute as well to receive help and support. Assessment, a third category, is strength based and collaborative, with emphasis on clients' views of problems and coping. Clients are expected to take risks and are challenged and confronted to believe in themselves. A dual focus in assessment is directed toward both the client and his or her environment. A final and very key category of empowerment interventions is an educational focus, providing a place for learning and trying out new skills. The educational focus includes information regarding the socio-political context of the common problems and increases the consciousness of participants. New skills such as advocacy, brokerage, conflict management and other resource access skills are important educational goals.

Clients' words from Parsons's interviews formed the items representing these four categorical domains. A Likert-type response set of strongly disagree to strongly agree was assigned to the items. This instrument was pilot-tested with 15 individuals and five groups. In both individual and group piloting, the questions were read and respondents were asked if the question made sense, if they understood the question, could they answer the question, were there any words that were vague or needed clarity, were the responses clear. Alternative response sets were created for the questions and respondents from the pilot were asked which response set was clearer and made the questions easier to answer. More piloting and group feedback were done to see if the new shorter responses were an improvement. No substantive changes were made in the instrument as a result of the first pilot.

Survey Respondents

A final draft of this survey was further piloted with individuals to test the clarity of the items and the effects of the length of the survey. It was administered to 95 respondents who are consumers of mental health services from five diverse programs within the mental health service system, representing a variety of services and purposes. One program was a traditional mental health clinic with a residential and an independent living component. Other respondents were located in clubhouses and consumer run centres.

Sixty (63.2 percent) were in one of the traditional mental health service teams, and 35 (36.8 percent) were involved in one of the clubhouse or consumer run centre programs. The researchers obtained permission to come into the facilities from either the staff or the staff and consumers. In each facility, signs were posted informing the consumers about the research and asking for volunteer respondents. Respondents were compensated $5.00 for expenses. All respondents had a diagnosis of severe mental illness. Demographics for the respondents are shown in Table 1.

EPP

The EPP (see Appendix I) was used to assess to what extent the empowerment principles and processes are implemented in programs. This 48-item instrument is a Likert-type instrument with a 1-5 response set, with 5 indicating the greatest presence of empowerment principles. The total mean of the respondents on the EPP was 3.74, with a standard deviation of .558. The

Table 1: Demographics of Respondents

Age (mean =38.7)	20-29: 22%	30-39: 30%	40-49: 38%	50+: 10%
Marital Status	Never married: 85%	Separated: 10%	Married: 3%	
Gender	Male: 56%	Female: 43%		
Race	White: 75%	Black: 12%	Hispanic: 8%	Other: 2%
Living Arrangements	Independent: 55%	Residential or family: 40%	Other: 3%	
Education	High school (attend or finish): 67%	College (attend or finish): 30%		
Program Involvement	2 yrs or less: 35%	More than 2 yrs: 40%		
Source of Income	SSI 64%	Employment: 56%	Other 21%	

demographic variables were program, age, gender, race, marital status, education, living situation, source of income and length of time in the program. Each demographic variable was tested through analysis of variance, with the total mean score on the EEP as the dependent variable. No significant differences were found on the EEP for any demographic group. To test the inter-item reliability of this instrument, a Chronbach's Alpha was determined. The coefficient of reliability for this instrument was .9371. Removal of items whose total item correlation = .21 or less results in a 45-item instrument with an Alpha of .9411.

From the qualitative interviews with consumers of social service programs, four categorical domains, presented in Figure 1 were used to construct the EPP—environment, collaborative relationship between worker and client, strengths based assessment and education. These domains were tested as sub-scales and the result follows. The domain of environment was represented by questions 1, 10, 11, 2, 3, 4, 5, 6, 7, 8 and 9. All the questions in that sub-scale showed an item total correlation of .20 or above except for question 9, and the reliability coefficient for the 11 items was .81. The domain of collaborative relationship was represented by questions 18, 19, 26, 27, 29, 30, 31, 32, 35, 36, 37, 39 and 40. The items in this sub-scale with an item total correlation of .20 or above were only 19, 38, 35, 39 and 40, and the reliability coefficient was .60, indicating that this sub-scale did not perform as a distinct domain of this concept. The domain of strengths based assessment was represented by questions 15, 16, 17, 20, 21, 22, 24, 28, 33, 34, 41 and 42. All items in this sub-scale had item total correlation of .20 or above except question 34. The standardized item alpha for this domain was .85, indicating a distinct domain around the utilization of strengths to view client problems. The final domain in the instrument is educational focus in the interventions. This domain was represented by questions 12, 13, 14, 16, 23, 25, 43, 44, 45, 46, 47 and 48. Only questions 14 and 45 did not show an item total correlation of .20 or above and the total standardized alpha for the sub-scale was .80, indicating a distinct domain of the instrument.

These results indicate that of the four domains, three performed as distinct domains and the fourth domain of collaborative relationship did not perform as a distinct domain. Correlation coefficients derived from Pearson r procedures were as follows: education and environment—.45; education and relationship—.48; education and strengths based assessment—.66, relationship and environment—.54; strengths based assessment and environment—.49; relationship and strengths based assessment—.61. The correlation indicates strong association between the four domains, but not so strong that each is measuring the same domain. The associations provide strength for the validity of the scale as a whole.

All items were phrased in a positive direction, except items 9, 18 and 30. It was a deliberate decision to phrase all the questions in a positive direction based on the piloting of the instrument wherein consumers informed us that switching of the questions was too confusing for them. Three negative direction items were left as a test to see the results. The following questions in the scale had a total item correlation of .20 or under (as well as 18 and 30 that were in a negative direction):

> Item 14—"Sometimes I have an opportunity to do some work here to help out the staff."
>
> Item 34—"I am encouraged to take risks here, even if I sometimes make a mistake." This item was interesting in that consumers commented as they answered the question, "My case manager would never let me make a mistake," indicating a perception that the case manager is in control and will protect the consumer, an idea very contrary to empowerment.
>
> Item 36—"I am encouraged to share what I know about mental illness with the other clients or with staff."
>
> Item 37—"I feel like I get more than I give here."
>
> Item 45— "This program teaches me how to get help from agencies."

These items were eliminated from the next version of the scale.

The correlation relationships between the four domains are strong, but not so strong that each is measuring the same domain, and they provide strength for the validity of the scale as a whole. The revised scale can be found in Appendix II. It is a 33-item scale that reflects the changes indicated in this discussion.

Validity Testing

The EPP was developed from qualitative interviews regarding the helping process with clients of empowerment based programs. Items on the instrument were generated from the concepts and themes found in the qualitative interview data and relevant literature. Further refinement of the questions was done in focus groups and individual interviews with consumers of the mental health service system. During the collecting of the quantitative data, additional focus groups and individual interviews were conducted with some of the 95 consumers of mental health services. The author, her co-worker, Susan Manning, and a research-trained consumer of mental health services conducted these interviews in order to ground the data from the quantitative instruments in the experience of consumers. The research questions were: "What are the experiences that lead to empowerment? What experiences have you had which facilitated or hindered your empowerment?" The themes that emerged from those qualitative interviews suggested three important principles of empowerment based intervention. They are: consciousness—described as attitudes, values and beliefs of providers, clients and family members that view consumers of mental health as people instead of symptoms of illness; the learning environment—described as the agency culture, philosophy and design that promotes empowerment, such as governance structure, participation in decision-making, paid positions of value, the presence of group and collective, opportunities to take leadership and build skills; and specific strategies—the daily activities that promote empowerment, like education programs, full participation in treatment planning, record access, opportunities to take responsibility, to risk and fail, access to medical care, and rituals to celebrate steps in recovery (see Manning, 1998, for a detailed explanation of these findings).

A comparison of these three components with the domains of the EPP discussed earlier suggests significant overlay and congruence. Although the themes were not identified in the same categories, there are many common sub-themes. For example, the learning environment is similar to the cohesive collective domain with some overlap also with a collaborative approach to assessment. Consciousness themes are found in the assessment and relationship domain of the EPP, and strategies are similar to the educational focus domain and to cohesive collective. This research was conducted with the same population of respondents on the EPP and strongly confirms the face and content validity of this instrument.

Another source of validity for the instrument is the work of Marsha Ellison, (1996) in which she explored the meaning and measurement of empowering demedicalizing practices in mental health case management programs. Likewise, her research was conducted with consumers of case management who were asked to identify practices by professionals that promoted their citizenship rather than their patient status. Of the 25 practices that she identified, the practices, which were the most ascribed to by both professionals and clients, were also the practices that appeared to be the most similar to items on the EPP. These were the following: create a mutual relationship; client driven services; maximizing choice; give client voice; see client as a person (not a diagnosis); client strengths identified; use of group and collective strategies; and involvement of clients in service delivery. Comparison of responses on the EPP and Ellison's scale provides another content validity check for the EPP.

Further, an advisory group was formed for this pilot research and members were given the instruments to view for content. This advisory panel consisted of consumers, mental health professionals, administrators, state mental health officers and members of family and consumer advocacy groups. Feedback from this group helped to validate the content of the instrument. A panel of six experts in the area of empowerment was asked to rate the questions for their face validity in measuring empowerment principles in the helping process and expected outcomes in client. The comments from these two groups pointed out problematic questions, wording and conceptual issues. These suggestions were taken into account in the next revision of this instrument.

Summary of EPP

Three of the four domains in this instrument held up in the quantitative pilot test. Questions in the relationship domain did not perform as a sub-scale. The overall scale reliability coefficient was strong although the scores clustered heavily at the upper end of the scale which depress the viability of that alpha. Social desirability may be a factor in this scale in view of the high mean (3.7) and low standard deviation (.58). Nearly all of the questions were worded in the same direction, and the few that were worded in the opposite direction were the questions that did not correlate with the other items. The testers found many phrases in the items that needed to be changed, mostly for greater specificity. The expert panel members identified wording that they perceived to be problematic. The revised version of the scale reflects the dropping of items with low inter-item correlation and word changes for many items based on the pilot work. The final version of the scale is in Appendix II.

It would be useful to test this scale for its ability to detect variation in programs that are successful in delivering services from an empowerment base and those that are less orientated to empowerment principles. Further testing of this instrument with more and varied empowerment based program clients and staff will increase its utility for assessing interventions for empowerment principles.

THE EMPOWERMENT OUTCOMES ASSESSMENT (EOA)

The empowerment outcome assessment (EOA) is a 34-item client self-report instrument (see Appendix III). The data from the qualitative study of five programs described earlier were used to identify the major categories of empowerment outcomes. Clients who identified what it meant to them to be empowered defined the outcomes. The categories and themes from the study can be found in Figure 2. These three categorical dimensions of empowerment outcomes as identified by clients—personal, interpersonal and socio-political—are found in other similar research (Cox and Parsons, 1994; Zimmerman, 1995; Bolton and Brookings, 1996; and Chamberlin, 1997).

Figure 2: Dimensions of Empowerment Outcomes

Personal	Interpersonal	Community/Political Participation
(Self-perception) • self-awareness • self-acceptance • belief in self • self-esteem • feeling that you have rights	(Knowledge/Skills) • assertiveness • setting limits on • giving • asking for help • problem solving • accessing resources • critical thinking	(Action) • joining organizations • giving back by helping others • making a contribution • voting, writing letters, speaking in public • taking control in generalized areas of one's life

The author identified assessment measures for these dimensions, which were already in existence for the population of adults with severe and persistent mental illness and all of which were developed with clients/consumers of service programs.

The personal dimension includes themes of increased self-awareness, self-acceptance, belief in self, self-esteem and a feeling of having rights. For this dimension, 13 items were selected from Dorothy Torre's empowerment scale (See Torre, 1985). These items are similar to items in other scales that propose to measure the personal aspect of empowerment (Bolton and Brookings, 1996; Chamberlin, 1997). Torre used a structured conceptualization approach to develop this instrument with 130 participants. Her personal empowerment cluster correlates .77 with Rotter's internal-external locus of control scale (Torre, 1985).

The interpersonal dimension includes such themes as increased assertive behaviour including asking for help from others when needed, learning new or better problem solving strategies and the acquisition of critical thinking about problems and solutions. For this dimension, 11 items were selected from Paulson's (1991) client empowerment scale that he developed with consumers of mental health.

In the broader dimension of community and political participation (socio-political), such outcomes as giving back to peers and programs, joining community organizations that deal with problems clients are experiencing and taking a proactive stance to problems. These items were selected from Segal's organizational empowerment scale and extra-organizational empowerment scale (Segal, Silverman and Temkin, 1993). These scales were developed by consumers of mental health and represent behavioural actions in regards to service organizations and to the general community. These scales were tested for validity and reliability by Segal and associates and were found to meet basic criteria as valid and reliable measures of empowerment.

The above three groups of items were combined into a 40-item, single survey instrument and assigned a common response set in a Likert-type scale, and the wording for each of the items was altered for conformity and consistency. This instrument was pilot tested with 15 individuals and five groups. In both individual and group piloting, the questions were read and respondents were asked if the question made sense, if they understood the questions, could they answer the question, were there any words that were vague or needed clarity, were the responses clear. Alternative response sets were created for the questions and respondents from the pilot were asked which response set was clearer and made the questions easier to answer. More piloting and group feedback was done to see if the new shorter responses were an improvement. Language was changed as a result of the pilot testing. Some questions were eliminated. For example, a question about personal problems having a linkage to political issues was eliminated because respondents could not understand and answer the question. Some questions were added, "Do you know how to file a grievance if you believe you have not been treated fairly?" was suggested by a consumer as a necessary part of empowerment.

EOA testing with consumers of mental health

The final draft of the EOA (see Appendix III) was administered to the same 95 consumers as described above. The mean score of the population on the EOA was 2.883, with a standard deviation of .544, minimum 1.7 and maximum 4.5. All the demographic variables were tested as independent variables through analysis of variance, with the total mean score on the EOA as a dependent variable. No significance was found between the mean of EOA and any demographic variable except for length of time client was associated with the program. Clients who had been in the program over two years scored significantly higher on the EOA than clients who had been involved in their programs only two years or less (F=9.28, significance level < .003)

To test the overall reliability of the items on the EOA, a Chronbach's Alpha measure of inter-item reliability was used. The coefficient of reliability on the full 34 items was .8618. Those items, which had a total item correlation of less than .25 when deleted from the scale, raise the alpha to .8711. The relationship between consumers' scores on the EPP and the EOA was tested with a Pearson r correlation and was found to be positively correlated at .4103, and significant at .000. While this only accounts for a little over 15 percent of the variance between these two scales, it is significant in the direction of consumers who view the helping process as having empowerment type attributes also view themselves as being empowered by the program.

After the removal of these items, the EOA is a 29-item scale, with three sub-scales. These are ten personal empowerment items, nine interpersonal empowerment items, and ten socio-political participation items. The three sub-scales contained in this instrument were tested for inter-item reliability and tested for correlation to each other. The personal sub-scale contained items 1, 2, 3, 4, 5, 7, 8, 11, 13, 21, 25, 33 with a mean of 3.40. The coefficient of correlation for these items was .8344. The total item correlation for one item was less than .20 (item 11) and with that item removed from the sub-scale, the Chronbach's Alpha increased to .8450. The interpersonal sub-scale contained items 8, 12, 14, 16, 17, 18, 19, 22, 23, 30, 34, 28, with a mean of 3.05. The Chronbach's Alpha for these items was .7535. Item 28 had a total item correlation of less than .20 and the removal of that items raised the Alpha to .7602. Items on the political participation sub-scale were 6, 9, 10, 15, 20, 24, 26, 27, 29, 31, 32 with a mean of 2.13. The items yielded an alpha of .8036. No item had a total inter item correlation of less than .25.

Correlation between the sub-scales was tested by the use of Pearson r and are as follows: personal and interpersonal sub-scale yielded a Pearson r correlation of .4197, with a significant p value of .000; personal and political sub-scales yielded a Pearson r of .2146, with a significant p value at the .037; and the socio-political participation and interpersonal sub-scales had a Pearson r of .5384 and a significant p value of .000. These means and correlation suggest that respondents' personal attitudes—feeling in control of and hopeful about their lives—were stronger than their interpersonal—perception of their own knowledge and skill for solving problems or for taking control of managing their mental health services—and stronger than their socio-political participation—action taking on their own behalf and others. The strengths of the correlation between the three sub-scales suggest that these three domains of empowerment are different from one another but are, however, correlated sufficiently to be considered a single construct.

Each sub-scale was tested for significance with each demographic variable. The variable, education, was significantly correlated with the political participation sub-scale ($F = 7.3$, p <.008) and with the interpersonal sub-scale ($F = 7.3$, p <.008). Consumers who had completed an educational training level beyond secondary school were more likely to participate in organizations and community groups and take political action than consumers who had completed educational training at the secondary level or below. Likewise they were more likely to know where and how to resolve problems and to tell their service providers when their services were not satisfactory. Also, consumers who had been participants in their programs longer than two years scored higher on the political participation sub-scale than those who had participated less than two years ($F = 7.2$, p< .008). These findings are predictable in view of the skills and behaviours embedded in both the political and interpersonal sub-scale.

An advisory group for this research pilot work was formed (see earlier description of this group). The advisory group was given copies of the instruments and invited to make comments. The instruments were sent to a panel of six experts in the area of empowerment. Panel members were asked to rate the questions as to their validity as measures of empowerment outcomes. Many suggestions were made regarding the questions and suggestions for additional questions were also made. These suggestions were taken into account in the latest revision of these instruments.

Validity

The creation of the original categorical dimensions of this scale came from the words and themes of clients in the author's study. As the instruments were piloted with the 95 consumers of mental health, new focus groups and individual interviews were also conducted to check with consumers of mental health regarding their ideas about empowerment outcomes. This research was analyzed (see chapter by Susan Manning in the present volume) and themes were identified that confirmed the content of this instrument. Those themes, which made up the category of empowerment outcomes, as viewed by consumers, were: quality of life; assertiveness; self-determination; choices; self-advocacy; belonging to a community; having access to resources; meaningful work; acceptance of and openness about illness; feeling valued and respected as a human being; belief in self.

On face and content validity check, these themes derived from the qualitative interviews suggest convergence between the items in the EOA and the stated desirable outcomes by consumers.

Further opportunity for face and content validity check is available from the work of Rogers, Chamberlin, Ellison and Crean (1997) who have developed a consumer constructed scale to measure empowerment among users of mental health services. This research developed 15 attributes of empowerment developed by an advisory board of leaders of the self-help movement, which are as follows:

1. Having decision-making power
2. Having access to information and resources
3. Having a range of options from which to make choices (not just yes or no)
4. Assertiveness
5. A feeling that the individual can make a difference (being hopeful)
6. Learning to think critically, unlearning the condition, seeing things differently
7. Learning about and expressing anger
8. Not feeling alone; feeling a part of a group
9. Understanding that people have rights
10. Effecting change in one's life and one's community
11. Learning skills (e.g., communication) that the individual defines as important
12. Changing others' perceptions of one's competency and capacity to act
13. Coming out of the closet
14. Growth and change that is never-ending and self-initiated
15. Increasing one's positive self-image and overcoming stigma

These items coincide very richly with the items that make up the EOA. Both were created with input from consumers of mental health and most likely represent an accurate description of empowerment from the words of the consumer, an important principle in the development of empowerment measures. Comparing responses on the EOA and this instrument will provide a validity check for this instrument.

Summary of EOA

The conceptual domains for this instrument were derived from the initial qualitative interviews with a diverse population of clients. The questions for the conceptual areas for the population of consumers of mental health were adapted from already existing instruments and validated with focus groups of consumers of mental health services. Piloting of the instrument resulted in changes in language, change in response sets, adding and dropping questions. The quantitative testing for reliability of the scale yielded a scale with a Chronbach's Alpha of .8963. Respondents to the survey who had been associated with their programs over two years scored significantly higher on the EOA than the respondents who had been associated with their programs less than two years. Adaptation of the instrument based on quantitative and qualitative study yields a 25-item scale found in Appendix IV.

This instrument was developed on the theoretical premise that empowerment has at least three dimensions—personal, interpersonal and socio-political participation—represented by sub-scales within the instrument. These sub-scales yielded positive and significant correlation with each other. The validity testing of this instrument has been ongoing from the initial development of the questions. Further testing is needed in several areas. One is the cultural context of different populations, such as ethnicity, race, economic, gender and special problem areas.

CONCLUSIONS

The measures presented here are a beginning attempt to assess the presence of empowerment practice principles in social work practice intervention strategies and expected outcomes in clients. These measures were developed utilizing the principles of amplifying the client or consumer voice by utilizing the experience and words of clients to create the conceptual domains and items in the measures. Piloting and re-piloting kept the developmental process close to the client/consumer's experience. Other measures were adapted that utilized consumer voices as well. These measures are similar in content to the newer empowerment measures by Chamberlin (1997) and Ellison (1996). These assessments together are a good beginning for looking at outcomes in programs that matter to clients, utilizing their words and experiences to capture both process and outcome in empowerment. Empowerment should not be assessed in clients with any objective measure alone, but should always be guided by the principle of providing clients the opportunity to have voice in their own context, their own experience. These instruments can augment such qualitative approaches and help to document the desired outcomes for funding sources and administrators.

REFERENCES

Bolton, B. and Brookings, J. (1996). Development of a multifaceted definition of empowerment. *Rehabilitation Counseling Bulletin*, 39(4), 256-264.

Chamberlin, J. (1997). A working definition of empowerment. *Psychiatric Rehabilitation Journal*, 20(4), 43-46.

Cox, E. and Parsons, R. J. (1994). *Empowerment-oriented social work practice with the elderly*. Pacific Grove, CA: Brooks/Cole.

Ellison, M.L. (1996). *Empowerment and demedicalization in mental health case management: Meaning and measurement.* Unpublished dissertation, Boston University Graduate School of Arts and Sciences.

Fisher, D.B.(1994). A new vision of healing as constructed by people with psychiatric disabilities working as mental health providers. *Psychosocial Rehabilitation Journal*, 17(3), 67-81.

Gutiérrez, L. M. (1989). *Empowerment in social work practice: Considerations for practice and education.* Paper presented to the Council on Social Work Education, Annual Program Meeting, Chicago, IL.

Gutiérrez, L. M. (1990). Working with women of color: An empowerment perspective. *Social Work*, 35(2), 5-8.

Gutiérrez, L. M., DeLois, K.A. and GlenMaye, L. (1994). Understanding empowerment based practice: Building on practitioner based knowledge. *Families in Society*, 76(9), 534-542.

Gutiérrez, L. M., Parsons, R.J. and Cox, E.O. (1998). *Empowerment in social work practice: A sourcebook*. Pacific Grove: Brooks/Cole Publishing Co.

Holmes, G. E. (1992). Social work research and the empowerment paradigm. In D. Saleeby (Ed.), *The strengths perspective in social work practice* (pp. 158-168). New York: Longman.

Libassi, M. F. (1992). The chronically mentally ill: A practice approach. In S.M. Rose (Ed.), *Case management and social work practice* (pp. 77-90). New York: Longman.

Lincoln, Y. S. and Guba, E.G. (1985). *Naturalistic inquiry*. Beverley Hills, CA: Sage Publications.

Manning, S. S. (1994). *Colorado mental health consumer and family development project: Program evaluation report.* Denver. CO: Colorado Division of Mental Health.

Manning, S. S. (1998). Empowerment in mental health programs: Listening to the voices. In L. M. Gutiérrez, R. J. Parsons and E. O. Cox (Eds.), *Empowerment in social work practice: A sourcebook*. Pacific Grove, CA: Brooks/Cole Publishers.

McClean, A. (1995). Empowerment and the psychiatric consumer/ex-patient movement in the United States: Contradictions, crisis and change. *Social Science and Medicine*, 40(8), 1053-1071.

Parsons, R. J. (1994). *Empowerment based social work practice: A study of process and outcomes.* Paper presented to the 41st Annual Program Meeting, Council on Social Work Education, San Diego, CA: March.

Parsons, R. J. (1998). Evaluation of empowerment practice. In L. M. Gutiérrez, R. J. Parsons and E. O. Cox (Eds.), *Empowerment in social work practice: A sourcebook.* Pacific Grove, CA: Brooks/Cole Publishers.

Parsons, R. J., East, J.F. and Boesen, M.B (1994). Empowerment: A case study with AFDC women. In L. M. Gutiérrez and P. Nurius (Eds.), *Education and research for empowerment practice.* Seattle, WA: Center for Policy and Practice Research, University of Washington, School of Social work.

Paulson, R. (1991). Professional training for consumers and family members: One's road to empowerment. *Psychosocial Rehabilitation Journal,* 14(3), 69-80.

Rapp, C. A., Shera, W. and Kisthardt, W. (1993). Research strategies for consumer empowerment of people with severe mental illness. *Social Work,* 38(6), 727-735.

Rappaport, J. (1990). Research methods and the empowerment social agenda. In P. Tolan, C. Keys, F. Chertok and L. Jason (Eds.), *Researching community psychology,* (pp. 51-63). Washington, D.C.: American Psychological Association.

Rogers, E. S., Chamberlin, J., Ellison, M. L. and Crean, T. (1997). A consumer-constructed scale to measure empowerment among users of mental health services. *Psychiatric Services,* 48 (8), 1042-1047.

Rose, S. M. and Black, B. L. (1985). *Advocacy and empowerment: Mental health care in the community.* Boston: Routeledge and Kegan Paul.

Saleebey, D. (Ed.). (1992). *The strengths perspective in social work practice.* New York: Longman.

Segal, S. P., Silverman, C. and Temkin, T (1993). Empowerment and self-help agency practice for people with mental disabilities. *Social Work,* 38(6), 705-712.

Simon, B. L. (1994). *Empowerment traditions: History of empowerment in social work.* New York: Columbia University Press.

Sohng, L. (1998). Research as an empowerment strategy. In L.M. Gutiérrez, R. J. Parsons and E. O. Cox (Eds.), *Empowerment in social work practice: A sourcebook.* Pacific Grove, CA: Brooks/Cole Publishers.

Solomon, B. (1976). *Black empowerment: Social work in oppressed communities.* New York: Columbia University Press.

APPENDIX 1

Consumer Version—Service Program Characteristics
Empowerment Practice Principles (EPP)

Likert Scale used:

Strongly Disagree   Disagree   Not Sure   Agree   Strongly Agree

FOR EACH STATEMENT, CIRCLE THE ANSWER THAT FITS BEST WITH YOUR EXPERIENCE HERE IN THIS PROGRAM.

1. This place feels safe to me.

2. When I talk about my own story and my life here, I know that staff will listen.

3. You can say what you want to say here to your therapist or other staff and not feel judged.

4. I feel like the staff and other clients here accept me for who I am.

5. It is OK to express an opinion here that is different from the staff and other clients.

6. This is a supportive place to talk about your feelings.

7. Staff here seem good at working through their own problems in the organization.

8. Staff here seems good at working through their own problems in the organization.

9. There is not much support here for clients like me.

10. This place feels like a community to me.

11. I know most of the staff here.

12. This program teaches me to speak out to others when I think things are not right.

13. This program teaches me to handle conflict with others in a better way.

14. Sometimes I have the opportunity here to do some work to help out the staff.

15. The staff works hard to be my advocate (someone on my side who fights for my rights).

16. I learn here to stand up for myself.

17. The staff here really believes in me.

18. The staff makes me feel powerless and not important.

19. Staff believes I have something to offer to my own treatment and to that of others.

20. Staff recognizes my strengths and abilities.

21 Staff challenges me to move beyond my current situation.

22. Staff believes that I can accomplish much in my life with the right support.

23. This program helps me to learn how my personal situation is affected by government politics.

24. I am encouraged by the staff to make my own decisions.

25. This program helps me to talk to other clients.

26. There are many people you can call upon here when you need help.

27. Clients help each other here.

28. Staff here are honest enough to tell you the truth about yourself even when you don't want to hear it.

29. Clients here work together and make decisions as a group.

30. I don't have much hope for the other clients here.

31. Staff shares with me how their own lack of power affects services.

32. I tell the staff when I am unhappy with the services here.

33. The mental health team lets me decide how to manage my money.

34. I am encouraged to take risks, even if I sometimes make a mistake.

35. I believe the staff listens to me.

36. I am encouraged to share what I know about mental illness with the other clients or with staff.

37. I feel like I get more than I give here.

38. I sometimes know as much as the staff knows about what to do about my problems.

39. The staff here shows me respect.

40. Decision-making about my life and plans are shared between me and the staff.

41 Staff encourage me to try to solve my own problems.

42. Staff helps me see that my problems are not always my fault.

43. This program teaches me to be a problem solver here.

44. This program teaches me about the mental health system.

45. This program teaches me how to get help from agencies.

46. This program teaches me how a lack of power could affect my situation.

47. This program has provided me opportunities to take leadership roles.

48. The staff helps me find the basic services I need, like food and transportation.

APPENDIX 2

Consumer's Perception of Service-Program Characteristics
Empowerment Practice Principles (EPP)

Likert Scale used:

    Strongly Disagree   Disagree   Not Sure   Agree   Strongly Agree

CIRCLE THE ANSWER THAT FITS BEST WITH YOUR EXPERIENCE HERE IN THIS PROGRAM.

1.   This place feels safe to me.

2.   When I want to talk about my own story and my life here, the staff is willing to listen.

3.   You can say what you want to say to the staff and not feel that they are judging you.

4.   I feel like the staff and other clients here accept me for who I am.

5.   I don't feel free here to express opinions that are different from others.

6.   This is not a good place to talk about your feelings.

7.   Staff seems uncomfortable with people who have mental illness.

8.   This place feels like a community to me.

9.   This program teaches me to speak out to others when I think things are not right.

10. This program teaches me to work out disagreements with others.

11. The staff works hard to be my advocate (someone on my side who fights for my rights).

12. I learn here to stand up for myself.

13. The staff really believes in me.

14. The staff makes me feel powerless (like I can't accomplish anything).

15. The staff believes that I should be actively involved in my own treatment.

16. The staff does not help me to recognize my strengths and abilities.

17. Staff challenges and pushes me to work hard on my goals.

18. Staff believes that I can accomplish my goals with the right support.

19. This program helps me to learn how government and politics affect my personal situation.

20. The staff encourages me to make my own decisions.

21. Clients in this program try to pull together and solve our common problems.

22. I don't tell the staff when I am unhappy with the services here.

23. The mental health team lets me decide how to manage my own money.

24. The staff encourages me to take risks, even if I sometimes make a mistake.

25. The staff encourages me to tell others what I know about mental illness (other clients or the staff).

26. The staff does not show respect for clients.

27. My case manager and I plan together how I can best meet my goals.

28. Staff encourages me to try to stand on my own as much as possible.

29. Staff helps me not to always blame myself for my mental illness.

30. This program teaches me to be a good problem solver.

31 This program does not teach me about the mental health system.

32 This program teaches me how to get help from other agencies (like food, employment).

33. This program does not provide me opportunities to learn leadership.

APPENDIX 3

Empowerment Outcomes Assessment (EOA)

Likert Scale used:

      never   seldom   sometimes   often   almost always

Please circle the response that best describes how you feel, think or behave.

1. Do you feel you can get what you want from life?

2. Do you feel you can accomplish your goals in the long run?

3. Do you feel most things in your life are out of your control?

4. Do you feel that life offers you many choices?

5. Do you feel that you have enough power to be listened to by others?

6. Have you led or helped to lead a discussion group in the mental health centre or other community organization?

7. Can you do most things you set out to do?

8. Do you believe you can have an influence on mental health services?

9. How often have you attended a local, state or national conference?

10. How often do you join organizations or clubs (a member or board member)?

11. Do you feel important as a member of groups you belong to?

12. Do you know where you can get basic services when you need them (like food, transportation, etc.)?

13 Do you feel overall that you are free to live as you choose?

14. Do you make suggestions to the administrationn of this or another agency about how mental health services could be improved?

15. Have you written or had someone to help you write a letter to the editor of a newspaper, newsletter or magazine?

16. Do you tell mental health professionals what you think of the services being provided to you?

17. Do you know about what rights mental health clients have under the law?

18. Do you know the steps to take when you are concerned about receiving poor mental health services?

19. Do you make sure mental health professionals understand your opinions about the services you receive?

20. Have you spoken at a high school, college, university or community group?

21. How often do you feel confident about things in your life?

22. Do you have ideas about how the mental health service system should work?

23. How much do you know about agencies in the community that will help mental health clients with grievances and complaints?

24. Have you worked in any group (like a board or advisory committee) which makes funding decisions about mental health service or a program?

25. Do you feel valued by the people who matter to you the most?

26. Have you attended a meeting of the city council, local government, state legislature, Congress or taken other social actions?

27. Do you look (on your own) for mental health services when you need them?

28. How much do you understand the mental health services that you are involved in?

29. Do you get in touch with your legislators about important bills or issues concerning mental health?

30. How much do you know about how to get mental health agency administrators, legislators or people in power to listen to you?

31. Do you volunteer in the community (mental health or general community projects)?

32. Have you been a part of a group that decides on rules and policies in your mental health centre or community program?

33. Do you have many freedoms in life?

34. Do you know what to do when problems arise in your life?

Personal Domain Items—1, 2, 3, 4, 5, 7, 11, 13, 21, 23, 25, 33, 34
Interpersonal Domain Items—8, 12, 14, 16, 17, 18, 19, 22, 23, 27, 28, 30
Organizational/Community Domain Items—6, 9, 10, 15, 14, 20, 24, 26, 27, 29, 31, 32

APPENDIX 4

Empowerment Outcomes Assessment (EOA)

Likert Scale used:

Strongly Disagree   Disagree   Not Sure   Agree   Strongly Agree

Below are a number of statements that describe how a consumer of mental health services may view his or her situation. Please circle the response that best describes how you feel, think or behave.

1. Overall, I can get what I want from life.

2. In the long run, I am responsible for whether or not I accomplish my goals.

3. Most things in my life are out of control.

4. Life offers me many choices.

5. It doesn't really matter what I say because only the people with power are heard.

6. I have led or helped to lead a discussion group in the mental health centre or other community organization.

7. I usually cannot do most things I set out to do.

8. I believe that together with others I can have an influence on the mental health services I receive.

9. I do not participate in local, state or national conferences.

10. I have joined or kept membership in an organization.

11. I usually cannot get basic services (food, transportation, housing) when I need them.

12. Overall, I would say that I am free to live as I choose.

13. I make suggestions to the administration of this mental health centre about what I think might be improved.

14. I have written or had someone help me write a letter to the editor of a newspaper, newsletter or magazine.

15. I tell mental health professionals what I think of the services being provided to me.

16. I know what rights mental health clients have under the law.

17. I don't usually speak up when I have a grievance or complaint about receiving poor mental health services.

18. I am confident about most things in my life.

19. I have taken part in deciding how much money should be spent on a mental health service or program.

20 I get in touch with legislators about important matters concerning mental health.

21. I don't know how to get mental health agency administrators, legislators or people in power to lsiten to me.

22. I don't volunteer in the community (mental health or general community projects).

23. I have taken part in deciding what rules and policies people have to follow in a mental health program or other community agency.

24. I don't have many freedoms in my life.

25. I don't usually know where to turn when problems arise in my life.

Personal items—1, 2, 3, 4, 5, 7, 12, 18, 24
Interpersonal items—8, 11, 13, 15, 16, 17, 21, 25
Socio-political participation items—6, 9, 10, 14, 19, 20, 22, 23

Chapter 22

THE CONNECTION BETWEEN UNIVERSAL VALUES AND EMPOWERMENT: IMPLICATIONS FOR SOCIAL WORK PRACTICE

Haya Itzhaky
School of Social Work
Bar Ilan University, Israel
Pinchas Gerber
School of Social Work
Bar Ilan University, Israel

Over the last three decades, empowerment has become an accepted concept in the field of social work (Guttiérrez, GlenMaye and Delois, 1995; Hansenfeld, 1987; Parson, 1991, 1998; Pinderhughes, 1983; Richan, 1989; Saleebey, 1996; Solomon, 1976). Empowerment practice has emerged as a theory for clinical practice, community action and social change. Its aim is to assist people of colour, minorities and other oppressed groups better understand and address the role that powerlessness plays in perpetuating personal and social problems (Breton, 1994; Cowger, 1994; Goldstein, 1983; Gutiérrez, Glen May and Delois, 1995; Hepworth and Larsen, 1986; Kondrat, 1995; Parsons, 1991, 1998; Saleebey, 1996). Few studies (Pinderhughes, 1983) discussed the importance of social workers becoming self-empowered while Richan (1989) and Pinderhughes (1983) discussed the need for social work students and workers to become self-empowered in order to, and before, they can empower their clients.

Frans (1993) related that empowerment has grown out of social action ideology and self-help perspectives. Relating this concept to social workers' empowerment, he emphasized the workers' ability to change events in their lives, to share goals and aspirations of a meaningful social system, to be an active participant in this system and to initiate action for oneself or for others. Gutiérrez, GlenMaye and Delois (1995) defined self-empowerment as a psychological process, and Spreitzer (1995), who examined various types of workers, also suggested that empowerment is a psychological process and further defined it as a motivational concept which includes four different cognitive styles. These styles incorporate the meaning and importance of work performed, worker competence, self-determination and autonomy, and workers' impact on their professional environment.

Leslie, Holzhalb and Holland (1998) discussed social work staff's empowerment within social service organizations and stressed the match between worker characteristics and organizational needs. Expanding on issues emphasized in human resource literature, their worker empowerment scale dealt with three sub-scales including empowerment and personal orientation, empowerment and work environment and empowerment and work relationship.

In Frans's empowerment scale (1993), empowerment is composed of five central concepts: a perception of self that includes a sense of self-validation; a critical awareness of one's place in the world; a perception of possessing knowledge and skills sufficient to influence events in one's life or in others'; an individual propensity to act or to initiate effective action; and a sense of collective identity where one shares the goals and aspirations of a meaningful social system.

Frans stressed empowerment as it applies to social workers in their practice, while Spreitzer discussed workers' empowerment within the confines of a work environment. Leslie, Holzhalb and Holland dealt with social workers in terms of their agency staff. The common theme that these researchers suggest is that empowerment combines the personal development and functioning of the worker but also is concerned with the dynamic relationship between the workers and their social and work environment. According to these definitions, worker empowerment is a multidimensional concept.

Since values are the standards that guide people's behavior they should affect worker's self-empowerment (Pinderhughes, 1983). The literature (Pinderhughes, 1983; Richan, 1989, Wodarski, Pippin and Daniels, 1988), and specifically Frans and Moran (1993), in discussing the value orientation of social workers, suggests that there is a connection between values and empowerment though it does not examine it. Frans and Moran pursue this theme in their empowerment study and indicate that while providing quality service to clients, social workers must possess a humanistic value system that supports social justice, individual freedom, and a positive view of human nature, in addition to being personally empowered. Though the connection between these two theories has not been sufficiently researched (Frans and Moran, 1993), we accept this as a challenge and goal for our study since these two fields are accepted as being important for the professional development of social work practitioners (Frans and Moran, 1993; Richan, 1989).

The purpose of this study is to determine if more universal values, can be associated with empowerment. In other words, we concur that humanistic values are essential to social work practice, but we believe that they represent a fraction of the values (Segal, 1993; Timms, 1983) that are required and essential to become an empowered social worker (Horner and Whitbeck, 1991). We suggest that there may be other values that social workers utilize, and that in order to properly evaluate the specific values that affect social workers, values need to be considered in a context "wider than that supplied by social work" (Timms, 1983, p. 1).

Previous value researchers (Kidneigh and Lundberg, 1958; McLeod and Meyer, 1967; Rockeach, 1973; Varley, 1963) attempted to define a common base for values. Many of these researchers lacked a theoretical base to their work (Schwartz, 1994). In contrast, Schwartz's (1994) value study is based on the convergence theory of modernization (Einsenstadt, 1973; Inkeles and Smith, 1974; Levy 1976), which suggests that as structures of modern societies become more homogeneous, a convergence in the value systems of the members of such societies is created (Sage, 1993, p. 8). Based on this theory, Bilsky and Schwartz (1994, p. 164) suggest that "values (a) are concepts or beliefs, (b) are about desirable end states or behaviors, (c) transcend specific situations, (d) guide selection or evaluation of behavior and events, and (e) are ordered by relative importance."

The goal of this study is to examine if universal values correlate to empowerment components. Specifically, we will examine if there are different values that correlate to different empowerment components.

METHODS

Sample

The sample population of this study included social workers that were enrolled in various continuing education programs at Bar Ilan University's School of Social Work (Israel) during the 1996-1997 academic year. Many of these social workers were recent graduates, whereas others were social workers employed in several government social service agencies. The social workers were asked to fill out questionnaires during class time. From the original 250 questionnaires, 206 were returned. Four questionnaires were discarded because they were not completed. Thus 202 questionnaires, 80.8 percent of the total distributed questionnaires, were included in this study.

The educational and or professional tracks of the social workers were: 83 percent casework and 12 percent community-group work. Ninety-one percent of the population was female and 9 percent was male. Fifty nine point two percent were single and 40.8 were married. The respondents' ages were: up to and including age 30, 56 percent; 31-40, 35 percent; 41-55, 9 percent. All of the population was Jewish with 32.5 percent describing themselves as being Orthodox, 15.1 percent Conservative and 52.4 percent as non-practising in their religious observance.

Study Instrument

The social worker empowerment scale was developed by Frans (1993). It is based on a five-point Likert scale ranging from 1 (Strongly Disagree) to 5 (Strongly Agree) and is comprised of five factors (34 items) which measure social workers' perceptions of personal and professional empowerment: These factors are:

1. Knowledge and skills (nine items such as "know responses to situations," "education prepared me for job," "read professional journals" and "attend conferences and training seminars") define a worker's perception in being able to sufficiently change events in their lives or in the lives of their clients.
2. Collective identity (seven items such as "spend time with other professionals," "believe that workers have common purpose," "identify strongly with profession") refers to the sense of sharing goals, resources and aspirations of a meaningful social system.
3. Critical awareness (five items such as "know who has power," "place in world is clear" and "know where I stand") is defined as an ability to recognize one's place in the world as it relates to larger systems. As such, the underlying assumption is that one is cognizant of the various political, economic, cultural and social factors that make up one's environment.
4. The self-concept (seven items such as "important to people," "feel competent as anyone" and "sure of self") is one's sense of self-appraisal and self-esteem and refers to the individual as an active participant in the social environment.
5. Finally, propensity to act (six items such as "when aware, try to get involved," "initiate response to problems" and "organize co-workers") describes a perception of the ability to initiate effective action on behalf of self or others. In other words, as social workers, we assist our clients mobilize their emotional and intellectual resources in order to change their environment.

The reliability test revealed that the correlation of each item within each component ranged from: 0.37 to 0.52 for collective identity; 0.42 to 0.67 for propensity to act; 0.52 to 0.69 for self-concept; 0.68 to 84 for critical awareness; and 0.42 to0.69 for knowledge and skills. In our study, this scale reported relatively high Cronbach Alpha reliability scores and are presented along with those received by Frans in Table 1.

Table 1: Comparison of Frans's and Current Study's Cronbach Alphas

EMPOWERMENT	FRANS CRONBACH ALPHA	CURRENT STUDY CRONBACH ALPHA
COLLECTIVE IDENTITY	.71	.75
KNOWLEDGE and SKILLS	.75	.81
SELF-CONCEPT	.86	.85
CRITICAL AWARENESS	.76	.78
PROPENSITY to ACT	.78	.84

The value scale was developed by Schwartz (1992). This ten-factor value scale (57 items) is a result of a massive 44-country, cross-cultural research study. This study demonstrated that there are ten types of cross-cultural values:

1. Power (five items such as "social power" and "authority").
2. Achievement (five items such as "ambitious" and "successful").
3. Hedonism (two items—"pleasure" and "enjoying life").
4. Stimulation (three items—"an exciting life," "varied life" and "daring").
5. Self-direction (six items such as "independent" and "choosing own goals").
6. Universalism (nine items such as "equality," "social justice" and "a world at peace").
7. Benevolence (nine items such as "helpful," "loyal" and "true friendship").
8. Tradition (six items such as "accept portion in one's life" and "moderate").
9. Conformity (four items such as "obedient" and "politeness").
10. Security (seven items such as "national security," "sense of belonging" and "social order").

The respondents were asked to rate each of the 57 items with a seven-point Likert scale ranging from 1 (Against My Guiding Principles in Life) to 7 (Major Guiding Principle in My Life). The reliability test for items reported a correlation in each item from 0.16 to 0.56. The reliability estimates (Cronbach Alpha) for each of the ten values in this study ranged from 0.47 to 0.70 and are reported in Table 2.

Table 2: Cronbach Alpha Results —Current Study

VALUES	CRONBACH ALPHAS
CONFORMITY	0.65
TRADITION	0.47
BENEVOLENCE	0.67
SECURITY	0.61
UNIVERSALISM	0.68
ACHIEVEMENT	0.70
STIMULATION	0.62
SELF-DIRECTION	0.70
POWER	0.55
HEDONISM	0.65

RESULTS

Table 3 shows the correlations between values and the empowerment components. The data demonstrate that the four values of stimulation, achievement, universalism and self-direction have a positive correlation with all five components of empowerment. This indicates that the more values social workers utilize, the more empowerment they will have.

The two values of power and dedonism have a significant positive correlation to four empowerment components. Power correlates with knowledge, self-concept, awareness and propensity to act, but did not represent a significant positive correlation to collective identity. Hedonism correlates significantly with collective identity, knowledge, self-concept and awareness, but did not have a significant correlation to propensity to act.

The two values of security and tradition have positive correlations with only two empowerment components. Security positively correlates to knowledge and awareness whereas tradition positively correlates to collective identity, as well as to awareness. Conformity and benevolence have significant positive correlations only with the awareness empowerment component.

It is interesting to point out that all ten value factors have a positive and significant relationship to the empowerment component of Awareness. Seven

Table 3: Pearson Correlations Between Values and Empowerment

VALUES	Collective identity	Knowledge	Self-concept	Awareness	Propensity to act
			EMPOWERMENT		
Conformity	.1298	.1034	.576	.1746	.0689
	p = .066	p = .141	p = .414	p = .013	p = .0329
Tradition	.0800	-.0085	-.0133	.1753	.0410
	p = .024	p = .904	p = .873	p = .012	p = .561
Benevolence	.0810	.0095	.0711	.2002	.1169
	p = .253	p = .892	p = .314	p = .004	p = .097
Security	.1247	.1425	.0791	.1713	.0666
	p = .078	p = .042	p = .262	p = .015	p = .345
Universalism	.2379	.2552	.2512	.1991	.1762
	p = .001	p = .000	p = .000	p = .004	p = .012
Achievement	.2914	.3523	.3721	.3121	.3421
	p = .000	p = .000	p = .000	p = .000	p = .000
Stimulation	.2329	.1917	.2674	.2223	.1802
	p = .001	p = .006	p = .000	p = .001	p = .010
Self-direction	.2338	.3371	.39946	.3377	.2585
	p = .001	p = .000	p = .000	p = .000	p = .000
Power	.1350	.2094	.2749	.2017	.1748
	p = .056	p = .003	p = .000	p = .004	p = .013
Hedonism	.2269	.2120	.2805	.2468	.0990
	p = .001	p = .002	p = .000	p = .000	p = .160

values (stimulation, achievement, conformity, tradition, Universalism, hedonism and self-direction) have a positive and significant relationship to the empowerment component of collective identity. Six values (stimulation, achievement, universalism, power, hedonism and self-direction) have a positive and significant relationship with the empowerment components of knowledge/ skills and self-concept. Five values (stimulation, achievement, universalism, power and self-direction) had a positive correlation to the empowerment component of propensity to act.

In analyzing the results, we tried to determine if there is a similar value content to all value dimensions that were found to be related to all or most of the empowerment components.

We divided the ten value factors into more homogeneous groups that would express similar value properties. By using factor analysis, we found two distinct factor groups of values with their eigenvalue greater than one. These two value factors explain 61.84 percent of the variance. The loading of the different value types on these two factors is presented in Table 4.

Table 4: Factor Analysis

VALUE	FACTOR ONE (SPIRITUALITY)	FACTOR TWO (MATERIALISM)
CONFORMITY	**.8076**	(.2308)
TRADITION	**.8050**	(.0588)
BENEVOLENCE	**.7560**	(.2782)
SECURITY	**.6907**	(.4452)
UNIVERSALISM	**.5963**	(.5199)
HEDONISM	(.1148)	**.7650**
ACHIEVEMENT	(.3671)	**.6974**
STIMULATION	(.1447)	**.6954**
POWER	(.1982)	**.6913**
SELF-DIRECTION	(.4333)	**.6662**

The first factor we called spirituality (Table 4) represents the four value types of conformity, tradition, benevolence and security. The second factor, which we call materialism, is composed of the remaining six value types that include hedonism, achievement, stimulation, power, self-direction and universalism. We included universalism in material values because of its content relevance in addition to its high loading in both factors (0.59 in factor one and 0.52 in factor two).

DISCUSSION

The goal of this study was to identify which values act as a resource for empowerment among social workers. Until recently, previous researchers discussed the theoretical and empirical relationship between values and empowerment but did not establish its empirical relationship. In this study, we examined this specific empirical relationship between values and the components of empowerment.

The findings of this study indicate that there is a clear empirical relationship between most universal values and social workers' self-empowerment. The findings of our study suggest that four values (stimulation, achievement, self-direction and universalism) have a significant and positive correlation to all five components of empowerment and that two values (power and hedonism) have a significant and positive correlation to four components of empowerment. The remaining four values (benevolence, tradition, conformity and security) have a significant and positive relation to one or two empowerment components.

In an attempt to categorize and classify these values according to content, we were able to find two distinct value groups. The first group, which is significantly correlated to empowerment, is related to material values. The second group, which for the most part does not have significant correlations to empowerment, is related to spiritual values. This division is similar to the findings of Schwartz (1994) who found four subgroups for these values: self-transcendence (universalism, benevolence), conservation (conformity, tradition and security), self-enhancement (power and achievement) and openness to change (hedonism, stimulation and self-direction). The first two subgroups are related to spiritual values and the last two subgroups are related to material values.

The importance of spiritual values in social work practice was noted by Siporin (1985) and Canda (1988), but the question remains as to how values related specifically to materialism are more significantly correlated to social workers' empowerment than spiritual values. We believe that the answer can be found in economic psychology theory. According to Richins and Rudmin (1994), materialism has both a positive and negative influence on culture, economy, society and man. Specifically, it can be seen in the application of this theory in finance, work motivation, material gratification and quality of life where individual interests stress personal power, independence and satisfy individual needs. Material values are primarily individual in nature and are related to the world of work. In this environment, individuals have the opportunity to earn capital that can be used to make their material desires and aspirations become a reality. Also, Western society's material goal orientation has additional relevance in defining social identity and social levels of communication. Materialism has become a social norm and accepted way of life. Financial success translates into social status and acceptance, and material wealth provides a basis for social prestige. This holds true for social workers as well as other workers in different sectors where material values have become the norm. Therefore, their connection to workers' empowerment can be understood in this context.

Spiritual values are dependent on culture and religion (Schwartz, 1992, 1994). According to Schwartz, people living in a religious environment or subscribing to a higher source out of traditional belief have a preference toward spiritual values. These individuals will willingly adapt themselves to this society, which in their view promotes spiritual beliefs and values. In this study, spiritual values are correlated only to empowerment components that relate to being part of a social environment (collective identity, awareness and knowledge) more than empowerment components that deal with individual development and ability (self-concept and propensity to act).

It can be understood from this that although social work education and supervision does lead workers in socializing several professional core values (Frans and Moran, 1993), religious values are based on society and relate only to those empowerment components that relate to society. Material values that are not related to society but lead to the development of the individual are related to all empowerment components, both those related to the individual and to society.

Additionally, instead of looking horizontally at how values correlate with empowerment, we noted that vertically, the single empowerment component of critical awareness positively and significantly correlates with all values. This suggests that all spiritual and material values are related to the workers' self-awareness of their place in the world as it relates to larger social systems. It further suggests that supervisors who wish to develop worker empowerment should concentrate on critical awareness, which has the most influence on universal values.

Our findings have direct implications for social work practice. We suggest that the practice of social work is simultaneously influenced by two factors: agency environment and supervision.

In the agency environment, administrators need to create an organizational climate and environment where material values such as work motivation, work gratification and quality of life are stressed. Administrators need to examine their workers' individual needs and the conditions that influence their personal and professional satisfaction. Specifically, administrators need to create an environment that encourages achievement and self-direction while also embracing universalism. Additionally, administrators need to adopt agency policy that supports workers' continuing education based on learning material values and those spiritual values that were found to correlate to workers' self-empowerment.

Supervision also plays a prominent role in the value-empowerment relationship. The supervisor integrates the ability to learn and to internalize professional knowledge with the ability to use this knowledge in the agency and in the field. The supervisor also reflects personal awareness of the social workers themselves and assists them in prioritizing their work (Itzhaky and Aloni, 1996). Consequently, we suggest that supervisors need to help their workers learn, internalize and prioritize material values over spiritual values. This will not only broaden their value repertoire but also increase their level of self-empowerment.

Our study examined Jewish social workers, most of whom were under 30 years old and enrolled in continuing education programs. We suggest that further studies be conducted to examine the relationship between values and empowerment among a more mature and experienced social work population from additional cultural or ethnic groups in order to determine if similar results can be found. Finally, we suggest that the relationship between material values and empowerment among our clients should also be examined. Should these values correlate to an increased level of self-empowerment among the client population, new strategic treatment plans will need to be developed, and social workers will need to be trained on how best to advance those material values that significantly correlate with their clients' self-empowerment.

REFERENCES

Bilsky, W. and Schwartz, S.H. (1994). Values and personality. *European Journal of Personality*, 8, 3, 183-181.

Breton, M. (1994). On the meaning of empowerment and empowerment-oriented social work practice. *Social Work With Groups*, 17(3), 23-35.

Canda, E. R. (1988). Spirituality, religious diversity, and social work practice. *Social Casework*, 69, 238-47.

Cowger, C. D. (1994). Assessing client strengths: Clinical assessment for client empowerment, *Social Work*, 39, 3, 262-267.

Eisenstadt, S. N. (1973). *Tradition, change and modernity*. New York: John Wiley and Sons.

Frans, D. (1993). A scale for measuring social work empowerment, *Research on Social Work Practice*, 3, 312 -328.

Frans, D. and Moran, J. (1993). Social work education's impact in students' humanistic values and personal empowerment. *Arete*, 18(1), 1-11.

Goldstein, H. (1983). Starting where the client is. *Social Casework*, May, 267-275.

Guttiérrez, L., GlenMaye, L. and DeLois, K. (1995). The organizational context of empowerment practice: implications for social work administration, *Social Work*, 40, 249-257.

Hansenfeld, Y. (1987). Power in social work practice, *Social Service Review*, 61, 469-483.

Hepworth, D. and Larsen, J. A. (1986). *Direct social work practice: Theory and skills*. (2d ed.). New York: The Free Press.

Horner, W. C. and Whitbeck, L. B. (1991). Personal versus professional values in social work: A methodological note. *Journal of Social Science*, 14, 21-43.

Inkeles, A. and Smith, D. H. (1974). *Becoming modern*. Cambridge, MA: Harvard University Press.

Itzhaky, H. and Aloni, A. (1996). The use of didactic teaching for developing mechanisms of coping with resistance in supervision, *Clinical Supervisor*, 14, 1, 65-77.

Kidneigh, J.C. and Lundberg, H. W. (1958). Are social work students different? *Social Work*, 3, 57-61.

Kondrat, M. E. (1995). Concept, act, and interest in professional practice: Implications of an empowerment perspective. *Social Service Review*, 69, 405-428.

Leslie, D.R., Holzhalb, C.M. and Holland, T.P. (1998). Measuring staff empowerment: Development of a worker empowerment scale. *Research on Social Work Practice*, 8, 212-222.

Levy, S. C (1976). *Social work ethics*. New York: Human Services Press.

McLeod, D. L. and Meyer, H. J. (1967). A study of the values of social workers. In E. S. Thomas (Ed.), *Behavioral sciences for social workers*. New York: Free Press.

Parsons, R. (1991). Empowerment as purpose and practice principle in social work, *Social Work with Groups*, 14, 7-21.

Parsons, R (1998). Evaluation of empowerment practice. In L. M. Guttiérrez, R. Parsons and E. P. Cox (Eds.), *Empowerment in social work practice*. Pacific Groves: Books/Cole Publication Company.

Pinderhughes, E. (1983). Empowerment for our clients and for ourselves. *Social Casework*, 68, 331-338.

Richan, W. C. (1989). Empowering students to empower others: A community-based field practicum. *Journal of Social Work Education*, 25, 276- 283.

Richins, M. L. and Rudmin, F. W. (1994). Materialism and economic psychology. *Journal of Economic Psychology*, 15, 217-231.

Rockeach, M. (1973). *The nature of human values*. New York: The Free Press.

Sage, G. (1993). *Measuring and understanding cross-national differences in value consensus*. Unpublished master's thesis, Hebrew University, Jerusalem, Israel. (Hebrew).

Saleebey, D. (1996). The strengths perspective in social work practice: extensions and precautions. *Social Work*, 41, 296-305.

Schwartz, S. H. (1992). Universals in the content and structure of values: Theoretical advances and empirical tests in 20 countries. In M. Zanna (Ed.), *Advances in experimental and social psychology*, (pp. 1-69). Orlando, Fl: Academic Press.

Schwartz, S. H. (1994). Are there universal aspects in the structure and contents of human values? *Journal of Social Issues*, 50, 19- 43.

Schwartz, S. H. and Bilsky, W. (1990). Toward a theory of the universal context and structure of values: Extensions and cross-cultural replications. *Journal of Personality and Social Psychology*, 58, 878-891.

Segal, U. A. (1993). Cross-cultural values, social work students and personality. *International Social Work*, 36, 61-73.

Siporin, M. (1985). Morality and immorality in working with clients. *Social Thought*, 9, 10-28.

Solomon, B. B. (1976). *Black empowerment: Social work in oppressed communities.* New York: Columbia University Press.

Spreitzer, G. M. (1995). Psychological empowerment in the workplace: Dimensions, measurement, and validation. *Academy of Management Journal*, 38, 1442-1465.

Timms, N. (1983). *Social work values: An inquiry.* London: Routledge and Kegan Paul.

Varley, B. K. (1963). Socialization in social work education. *Social Work*, 8, 102-109.

Wodarski, J. S., Pippin, J. A. and Daniels, M. (1988). The effects of graduate social work education on personality, values and interpersonal skills. *The Journal of Social Work Education*, 24, 266-277.

Chapter 23

WIDENING PARTICIPATION: EMPOWERMENT OF NON-TRADITIONAL LEARNERS

Imogen Taylor
School for Policy Studies
University of Bristol

Empowerment is both an elusive and a compelling concept. On an individual and collective level it is beguiling in its promise, yet under scrutiny it both disappoints at the theoretical level and in understanding of its application. It has suffered from being hijacked by the New Right and the tendency of government to view empowerment as a panacea "increasingly becoming an ethical obligation of the new citizenry ... empowerment is not only good for you: it seems to be becoming essential to leading a better life" (Baistow, 1994/5, p. 37). As it becomes all things to all people, empowerment has also suffered from being decontextualized, and its meaning in relation to specific contexts lost.

One possible response to this situation is to abandon the concept of empowerment. Yet, issues of power and empowerment in professional education and practice, both in relation to students and to users of professional services, undoubtedly have a significance which demands analysis and understanding if as educators and practitioners we are to advance our thinking and practice. In this chapter, using findings from a small empirical study carried out at a British university, I explore the empowerment of non-traditional learners. These students have been both disempowered in the wider society and specifically in education where typically they are ignored and invalidated:

> When one is forced to learn and to be a learner in a framework
> which is dominated by the dominant value system, one's

identity as a learner and one's capacity as a learner within
that system, may be put at risk. (Weil, 1986, p. 232)

Accepting the premise that empowerment can only be understood in relation to the context surrounding its use and the discourse in which it is embedded (Gore, 1992, p. 56), I begin by highlighting features of the higher and professional education context which have become increasingly significant in the shape and direction of professional education. I then briefly examine the discourse of empowerment in education. I introduce the concept of non-traditional learners and review research into what we know about them. In the second part of the chapter, I cite research into the experience of empowerment of non-traditional learners in an innovative social work education program at Bristol University in England and identify elements of the approach to teaching and learning which appear central to the empowerment of students. I suggest that aspects of the structure of the program and its underpinning philosophy combat those processes of disempowerment inevitable in a traditional Western university, which represents a hierarchical and privileged structure of power and domination, and in a professional education course, which is shaped by external regulation and surveillance.

THE HIGHER AND PROFESSIONAL EDUCATION CONTEXT

In the UK, both social work practice and education are becoming increasingly proscribed and prescribed. In higher and professional education, we are buffeted by competing ideologies of the purpose of education. Jarvis (1993) identifies four existing models of education. The market model with an emphasis on competition, efficiency and education as a commodity. The progressive liberalism model where education is viewed as enriching the individual. The welfare model where education puts right social injustices. And the social control model where education has become part of the political agenda of the New Right and policies redirect education away from individual needs to those of an industrialized and commercial society.

The balance in higher education has shifted towards the merging of market and social control models, producing a powerful force for change in professional education and consequently in professional practice. Higher education has come to be viewed as a marketable commodity with an emphasis on standardization, it is "being colonised by the state, with unifying agendas being urged onto the academic community" (Barnett, 1992, p. 7). This is typified by developments such as modularization, credit accumulation and transfer, and accreditation of prior experience and learning. Perhaps for professional education, of most significance is the increasing pervasiveness of the competence approach and the attempts to map professional competence on a continuum from the developing systems of national vocational qualifications (NVQs) though the diploma in social work to the post qualifying stages. An effective curriculum is seen as one which trains individuals to act in an instrumental way on the environment:

> With competence there is closure; all learners are tied into a centrally determined predefined set of goals, whose meaning and practice are circumscribed. The goal of learning is competence demonstrated in a specific set of ways, nothing more, nothing less. (Edwards and Usher, 1994, p. 12)

This would not appear to offer much scope for empowerment.

CONCEPTUALIZING EMPOWERMENT IN EDUCATION

The concept of empowerment in education is not new, and among the first to promote it in the early 1970s was Freire (1981). However, as a concept its application to higher education is generally undeveloped in its contribution to our understanding of how to structure education so that it provides the opportunity for an empowering experience for students. The power-knowledge formulation is typically presented as important: "Individuals are regulated and governance secured through power-knowledge formulations" (Edwards and Usher, 1994, p. 3). Foucault's (1980) thesis that propositional knowledge and power are linked, where knowledge does not represent the truth of what is but rather constructs what is taken to be true, is influential in this perspective. Professional educators exercise disciplinary power through the discourse of education and training. Professionals are accorded the status of truth because they uphold dominant discourses in society.

Gore (1992, p. 59) critiques the vision of empowerment as too often construed as a simplistic dualism between empowerment or oppression. Also drawing on the work of Foucault (1980), Gore suggests empowerment is the exercise of power to help others exercise power. Hence she frames "what *can* 'we' do for 'you'?" as the appropriate question rather than "what we can do for you!" The latter assumes that we know what would be empowering for others and that power is a commodity to be dispensed. However, neither is "what *can* 'we' do for 'you'?" fully satisfactory as it implies a student-led approach and risks denying expertise on the part of the teacher. Also, a student-led approach is untenable within professional education where the accrediting body determines a set of outcomes to be achieved prior to qualifying.

"What *can* 'we' do for 'you'?" can be extended beyond the teacher-student (Gore, 1992) to the education program infrastructure. A schema developed by Rees (1992) in his work on power in social welfare, identifies steps in the process of empowerment that suggest features of an infrastructure key to supporting empowerment:

STEPS IN ACHIEVING POWER

I. Understanding themes
II. Evaluating self-image and knowledge
III. Specifying problems
IV. Developing awareness of policies
V. Developing the notion of choice
VI. Experiencing solidarity with others
VII. Acquiring and using language
VIII. Resisting a return to powerlessness
IX. Developing interactive and political skills
X. Evaluation
     (Rees, 1992, p. 89)

Rees emphasizes that these stages are not as clear-cut or straightforward as such a representation might suggest.

Later in this chapter, I return to these empowerment concepts in relation to the experience of non-traditional learners at Bristol University, but first it is important to examine what is meant by non-traditional learner.

WHO ARE THE NON-TRADITIONAL LEARNERS?

Non-traditional learners are those students who did not achieve a standard school leaving qualification and enter university through a variety of routes, including access routes (access courses are designed to facilitate entry to further and higher education for non-traditional students). There is a noticeable absence of a developed discourse about these students and terms such as drop-out, non-standard and disadvantaged all reflect their marginalization. Whereas the term non-traditional also risks marginalizing them by comparing them against the traditional norm, the term is preferred here because it conveys a notion of the richness and diversity of this group of students (Weil, 1986).

Recently in the UK, the profile of non-traditional learners has been given significant impetus by two much publicized government reports. The first was "Learning Works," the report by the Further Education Funding Council into promoting "access to further education for people who do not participate in education and training but who could benefit from it" (Kennedy, 1997, p. iii). This report comments that recent policies to increase participation and achievement have mainly provided opportunities for those who have already achieved to continue to do so rather than reach those who are disadvantaged economically and socially. The report concludes that

> We must widen participation not simply increase it. Widening participation means increasing access to learning and providing opportunities for success and progression to a much wider cross-section of the population than now (p.15).

Secondly, widening participation in higher education was a key focus of the report into higher education in the learning society (known as the "Dearing Report" after its chairperson Sir Ron Dearing):

> Despite the welcome increase in overall participation, there remain groups in the population who are under-represented in higher education notably those from socio-economic groups III to V, people with disabilities and specific ethnic minority groups. Many of the causes lie outside higher education itself, although we recognise that higher education can contribute to improving the situation. (Dearing, 1997, p. 3).

Increasing the participation of non-traditional learners is particularly crucial to professional education where we have a moral obligation to widen the participation of students and consequently of qualified practitioners to more closely reflect the population with whom they work.

Gender, ethnicity, class and disability continue to significantly influence access to higher education. Whereas in the UK gender inequalities have decreased rapidly over the past two decades, women remain more likely than men to be educated in less prestigious institutions, are less likely to be awarded degrees and are more likely to qualify at a later age (Halsey, 1993). Although significant advances have also been made in increasing access of ethnic minority groups, there remain important differences between groups, between institutions and between subjects selected for study (Modood, 1993). For example, in the ex-polytechnics or new universities, all ethnic minority groups, with the exception of Bangladeshis, are over-represented, but in the old university sector they are there in half the proportion of the other sector, and African-Caribbeans and Bangladeshis are significantly under-represented. Class inequalities remain the most intractable to change. Astonishingly, whereas the chances of working-class students entering higher education have increased in absolute terms, class inequalities, measured in relative terms, have apparently remained stable for the past three generations (Halsey, 1993).

Disability has more recently emerged as factor restricting access to higher education (Barnes, 1991). Here there is evidence of barriers in the literal sense. Barnes (1991) found that most British colleges and universities are inaccessible. Phillips, Stalker and Baron (1995), in their study of disabled social work students in Scotland, identify five barriers to disabled people training as social workers: a disabling environment, problems of stereotyping, a failure of application of equal opportunities policies, assumptions about non-disablement, which underpin selection and training, and self-limitation by applicants, including a reluctance to disclose impairments.

For well over a decade there has been a profusion of schemes designed to increase access to higher education. However, these have had shamefully little impact on increasing the access of non-traditional students. There is a surprising dearth of national data about who attends access courses, and neither the relative importance of access routes or information about students on access courses is well documented. However, one study (Wakeford, 1992) demonstrates that expansion of access courses does not necessarily mean proportionately increasing participation in higher education by those groups under-represented as a whole. Not only have the policies and strategies adopted to widen participation been ineffective, there is a developing critique that they have also kept attention focused on access rather than on accessibility, diverting attention from the need for "the transformation of higher education in such ways as to make it more attractive, relevant and open to all sections of the population" (Wright, 1991, p. 7.)

In the next section of this chapter, I go on to discuss enquiry and action learning (EAL), an approach to teaching and learning social work which I suggest has features which make it more accessible than traditional programs.

ENQUIRY AND ACTION LEARNING

Enquiry and action learning (EAL), was introduced in 1990 at Bristol University into the teaching and learning of social work. EAL is described in full elsewhere (Burgess, 1992), but for purposes of this paper, I briefly refer here to its core features and link them to the Rees (1992) schema introduced earlier.

The Bristol program is a two-year, full-time course leading to the professional social work qualification, the diploma in social work (DipSW) awarded by the validating body, the Central Council for Education and Training in Social Work (CCETSW). A combined total of about 70 graduate and non-graduate students are admitted each year, and the course may also lead to an academic award of either a diploma, a degree or a masters degree, depending on the route taken. For purposes of our discussion here, it is significant that the Bristol DipSW course includes both graduates and non-graduates in the same classes.

The name "enquiry and action learning" was chosen to emphasize the process of learning through discovery and action. The EAL curriculum includes four linked elements: a problem based approach, learning in groups, strategies to encourage self-directed learning, and a balance between propositional, process and personal knowledge (Eraut, 1994).

Problem based learning has been introduced throughout the curriculum. Lectures and seminars have largely been replaced by study themes built around situations drawn from practice. Each theme lasts on average about two weeks and is introduced by a lecture with the aim to provide a conceptual map to the theme. A series of themes together comprise a unit or module and is designed to meet the learning objectives specified by CCETSW (1995).

Students work in study groups of about 12. Membership remains constant for a term, and in the first term includes a mix of graduates and non-graduates. Membership is also determined to ensure a balance of race and gender, and students who come from groups oppressed in society, including disabled, gay and lesbian students, are not knowingly isolated. Groups are chaired by students with help and guidance from the facilitator. In the interests of encouraging student self-directedness as well as economy of resources, facilitators attend half the meetings. The facilitator role is a central one initially and becomes increasingly peripheral as the course progresses. Study groups provide the opportunity for students to acquire and use language, develop interactive and political skills and experience solidarity with others (Rees, 1992).

Where possible, students assume responsibility both individually and in groups for what they learn and how they learn. Each group decides on and prioritizes the issues presented by the problem, identifies the knowledge and skills required to work on it and decides how to tackle the work in the time available. Students may select learning activities from suggestions provided or may design their own. In engaging in these learning activities, students move through the Rees (1992) steps of specifying problems, developing awareness of policies and developing notions of choice. Also, by reflecting together on the process of learning and evaluating whether they have achieved their objectives, they are developing the process knowledge of evaluation (Rees, 1992).

EAL incorporates different kinds of knowledge, mapped in a model of professional knowledge by Eraut (1994). Propositional knowledge includes discipline based concepts, generalizations and practice principles. Personal knowledge may remain at the impression level, and a challenge for professional education is to bring this to the surface so that it can be examined for its impact on professional practice. Process knowledge includes knowing how to conduct the various processes that contribute to professional action. EAL attributes significance to each area of knowledge with a planned, specific emphasis on students identifying and building on their pre-course experience through the use a variety of strategies. In doing this students are mapping the themes (Rees, 1992) important in their lives.

THE EXPERIENCE OF NON-TRADITIONAL STUDENTS IN HIGHER EDUCATION

We know remarkably little about the experiences of non-traditional students in higher education generally, or in social work education specifically. Existing studies tend to focus on attrition or the relative success of non-traditional learners and to discuss increasing staff support as a solution. A British study of non-standard students in social work found that they lack self-confidence and "reassurance and competent guidance need to be offered in generous quantities" including some attention to study skills (Mills and Malloy, 1989, p. 52). Rosen (1993) in her study of black access students on a London social work course comments on the importance of personal contact with staff to facilitate learning. A study of retention in an undergraduate social work program in New York City (Berger, 1992) found that two variables were associated with student success: the past history of marks; and student age, with relatively older and relatively younger students most likely to graduate. Berger also focuses on supports needed to help students adapt to the system rather than revision of the system.

The most relevant study for our purposes here was completed by Weil (1989). Weil carried out a multi-site qualitative study of non-traditional learners in England and developed a framework of disjuncture and integration to explain their experience of returning to higher education. Disjuncture involves issues of identity and arises from mutually interacting influences and the feeling of being at odds with oneself. If disjuncture interacts with miseducation, then the overall sense of identity of the learner is undermined. The students experienced disjuncture in relation to their expectations of and initial encounter with the learning context, their expectations of teaching and learning approaches, the ways in which social and power differences were managed, the extent to which core aspects of identity felt threatened, the management of multiple and conflicting roles and the kinds of knowledge allowed and disallowed. Alternatively disjuncture can be anticipated and managed and result in integration. Of particular importance to integration is the active use and appreciation of different kinds of knowledge, making connections across different kinds of disciplinary boundaries and the positive valuing and use of personal and social differences within the group.

Weil's framework has been useful in understanding findings from my own small exploratory study of non-traditional learners. In 1991, within the context of a larger scale evaluation of EAL (Taylor, 1997), I began a two-year study looking at the experience of twelve non-traditional learners on the Bristol course. All had very negative early experiences with education and had left school at 16 or earlier with minimal qualifications. Seven had since completed access courses with the objective of gaining entry to social work education. The sample was predominately working class, three students were African-Caribbean, the average age was 35. I look first at their experiences of disempowerment, particularly early in the program, I then look at strategies to support empowerment.

Disempowerment of Non-traditional Learners

My focus on the barriers that disempower students is primarily on those embedded in higher education itself. However, it is important first to acknowledge student poverty and the multiple roles carried by non-traditional learners, two elements that students bring with them to learning but are essentially beyond the influence of an individual program. These barriers emerge from the economically and socially oppressed positions of non-traditional students and contribute to their experience of powerlessness.

Poverty is increasingly an issue for all students in the UK. It will be a particular problem for students from economically disadvantaged backgrounds. There is evidence that the amount of student debt increases significantly with age (*Association of University Teachers Bulletin*, January 1995) and this has become worse as grants decrease in real value and secondment or paid educational leave becomes a rarity. Funding problems significantly reduce choices available to non-traditional students. As Home (1997) found in her study of Canadian social work, nursing and adult education students, low income is linked with role stress, particularly in relation to child-care responsibilities. All the Bristol students, with the exception of three, were carrying significant caring responsibilities for family members, including children, partners and aging parents. Yvonne, an African-Caribbean single parent mother described her situation:

> You can't shut off your life outside. You're worrying about
> the kids, you're worrying about this, you're worrying about
> that, you're too tired to study because you've been up the
> night before.

Closely linked with role stress is lack of time. "Perhaps the most intractable situational problem facing mature students is that of time and family commitments" (Woodley, Wagner, Slowey, Hamilton and Fulton, 1987, p. 177). As this Bristol student said:

> It's very hard to find your own space. When you leave here
> and you go home you haven't got time to study. By the time
> you've got home from school, you've cooked, you've tidied
> up, it's time to go to bed. When do you have time to study?
> Weekends are even worse, you're on your feet twenty-four
> hours a day then.

Home (1997) also found that multiple role students have difficulty realistically assessing the time needed for study and consequently do not make sufficient preparation for child-care coverage. Family support reduces vulnerability to stress although it plays a less important part than expected (Home, 1997). However, families are not always supportive. One African-Caribbean woman described being told by both her mother and her husband that in entering university she was "getting beyond herself" and going to become "one of them." Similarly Rosen (1993) describes the strain on family relationships of ethnic minority students being perceived as joining the establishment.

The Bristol students did not experience disjuncture between expectations of and initial encounter with the learning context (Weil, 1989). On the contrary, they expected to feel daunted, intimidated and out of place. These expectations were heightened by their negative earlier experiences of education and they had left school feeling demoralized and devalued. One student described how even "nicking off" (truancy) did not generate enthusiasm from the school to bring her back. Entering university, they had minimal expectations of success. Students were indeed "entering unknown territory and feeling their way blindfolded through what they understood to be a minefield, intended to explode their aspirations at the first chance" (Rosen, 1993, p. 12).

The experience of alien territory is strengthened by hierarchical university structures that reinforce social differences and power relations. "The university classroom is never free from domination; hierarchy, paternalism, and systems of threat and exclusion structure our practice" (Rossiter, 1993, p. 77). A focus on propositional knowledge as the truth risks further disempowering non-traditional learners as such knowledge typically omits their experience or pathologizes it and supports the thesis that propositional knowledge and power are linked (Foucault, 1980). Propositional knowledge may devalue the students own language, as the spoken and written language of non-traditional students may not meet conventional academic norms. As this African-Caribbean student said, "I didn't have confidence in my own language, I felt I wasn't good enough." Weis (1985), in her study of black students in a community college, found that "dominated groups must become familiar with the discourse of dominant groups if they are to challenge the class structure effectively" (p. 166). This is compounded by the requirement that students on professional courses must be ready to practise using language that will not disadvantage the service users they will be working with.

This experience of disjuncture is reinforced by the kinds of knowledge allowed and disallowed (Weil, 1989). Dialogue is crucial to process in the classroom, yet for dialogue to be possible, classroom participants must trust each other. Dialogue with staff about the dilemmas facing non-traditional students is perceived to be risky and "acting as if the classroom was a safe space in which dialogue is possible and happening does not make it so" (Ellsworth, 1989, p. 315). Dialogue is difficult because of a fear of being misunderstood, of disclosing too much and becoming vulnerable. As this Bristol student said, "I've got this thing about appearing as stupid if I have to ask questions, so I don't ask too much." Precisely those students who may need additional support, perhaps in the form of study skills, find it difficult to reveal this and to seek help.

Higher education offers the opportunity to improve students' life chances yet it threatens their sense of identity, heightening the fear of failure. This is reinforced by assessment practices which, as I discuss elsewhere (Taylor, 1997), present one of the most impermeable barriers to empowerment:

> We cannot underestimate the power of the formal system—
> to define and undermine identity and status (or lack of it), to

frame the criteria by which success should be judged, to influence the extent to which learning is allowed to be a process rather than just a means to an end. (Weil, 1986, p. 232)

Failure is terrifying, as this white, working-class woman said, "Each piece of work is frightening because we've come such a long way. If I fail, what would I go back to?" An African-Caribbean woman poignantly described the dilemma of failure, of not being able to return to where she had been, yet feeling that what she had achieved brought with it a new set of problems: "One part of me wishes I never came here and the other part of me is glad I did ... I can't go back because of what I know, I can't go back where I was three years ago."

Activities that Support Empowerment

Weil (1989) proposes integration occurs when the new situation compensates for the prior feeling of disjuncture and identifies three different approaches that are significant to this: the appreciation and active valuing of different kinds of knowledge, positive valuing and making connections across disciplinary boundaries. Based on the Bristol study, I propose an adaptation to the Weil framework. It was clear at Bristol that active learning was an important element and that this included, among other activities, making connections across disciplinary boundaries.

Weil's focus is on integration rather than empowerment. However, I propose here that by building on and linking Weil's framework, which is essentially about outcomes, with Rees's (1992) model of steps in the process of empowerment, we can begin to identify those aspects of the EAL philosophy and structure that support the student experience of empowerment.

Appreciation and Active Valuing of Different Kinds of Knowledge

Conceptualizing professional knowledge as including personal, process and propositional knowledge (Eraut, 1994) and the active valuing of different kinds of knowledge appears central to the experience of empowerment, "On this course I feel I do know things and I've got things to offer from my own experience and that experience has been valuable." Rita, who had completed an Access course and arrived at university apprehensive she was going to find a culture of us and them, instead found that her pre-course personal and process knowledge were valued and "qualifications don't really come into it."

The expectation in the curriculum of building on pre-course experience requires students to begin perhaps for the first time to understand the themes of their biography (Rees, 1992). Rees suggests that it is integrating those themes that depict power and powerlessness which are crucial. In the first term, students work on a required unit about anti-oppressive practice. In other units throughout the course there is also a strong emphasis on understanding structural oppression. In this way students are linking personal with propositional knowledge, evaluating self-image and knowledge (Rees, 1992) and learning to specify problems as symptoms of wider structural issues rather than of personal deficiencies. Rees suggests people with a long history of powerlessness are used to having their problems defined for them. Bristol students telling their stories were learning to identify and conceptualize problems as well as manage the impact of experience and gain a measure of control over it, important elements of process knowledge (Eraut, 1994).

Another empowering aspect of valuing personal knowledge is that students begin, perhaps for the first time, to give voice to their experience of being disadvantaged and oppressed: "Where language and naming are power, silence is oppression, is violence" (Belenky, Clinchy, Goldberger and Tarule, 1986, p. 23). Weil (1989) describes students "unlearning not to speak" (p. 121). The development of a voice is given much attention in the empowerment literature. Rees refers to the stage of acquiring and using language. Rosen (1993) found that students "began to argue and discover their own powers. They perceived teachers prepared to listen to them and take their ideas seriously" (p.179). Others, including facilitators and students may support this process by providing the public language to describe a private experience (Thompson, 1995).

Belenky et al. (1986) drew our attention to the importance for women of voice in learning by identifying five stages in the epistemological development of women learners. At the first stage women are silent and "experience themselves as mindless and voiceless and subject to the whims of external authority." At the next stage of received knowledge "women conceive of themselves as capable of receiving, even reproducing, knowledge from the all-knowing external authorities but not capable of creating knowledge on their own" (p. 15). At the third stage women begin to question external knowledge, and in the final two stages they achieve "real talk" and create knowledge. As discussed earlier, the Bristol students were initially reluctant to risk speaking out. Yvonne said early in the course, "You daren't open your mouth for fear of saying something stupid." However, by the end of the course, Yvonne had learned not to take all theory as the truth and to value her own voice and power:

I've got a voice and I'm going to make sure I'm heard ... I've learned about people, I've learned about organizations, I've learned about theories and even though I may not believe some of them I can understand them. I know how to present myself and not present myself. I know how to read people a bit more. I know how to survive.

Other educators (Ellsworth, 1989; Rossiter, 1993) also describe the possibility of empowerment for students as they are supported to express subjugated knowledge and assume authority over their own learning. Rees's (1992) step of acquiring and using language is undoubtedly of central importance in the process of empowerment.

The case studies that form the hub of the EAL problem based curriculum further supported non-traditional learners to give voice to their experience. These are carefully designed to include the experience of minorities and have been amended to integrate feedback from students on this issue. For example, there have been very active groups of gay and lesbian students and disabled students who have provided constructive criticism about the representation of minority issues in curriculum content.

Bringing different kinds of knowledge into the learning group provides another benefit for non-traditional learners. The knowledge being shared combines both a cognitive and an affective meaning and has an impact rarely achieved in a lecture. It is also shared in accessible language as opposed to academic discourse which can be exclusive and excluding, "It's (sharing) sort of easier to take in than reading books and trying to remember for myself. It's easier to listen to other people and how they put it into context." Developing interactive and political skills in the learning group can have quite a practical outcome, important in a context of ever-decreasing resources for learning.

Active Learning

The EAL emphasis on active learning was an important feature of the non-traditional students' experience of empowerment. As an African-Caribbean student commented, "If I don't get up and do it, I'm not going to get it. Because EAL makes me go out and research and do things, I'm learning more things." Non-traditional learners are likely to have a history of being very competent in a diverse range of activities prior to entering the course. Among the Bristol students was a builder, a secretary, a care assistant and a chef. However, in the traditional blank slate (Freire, 1981) approach to education, students are not generally expected to transfer the often considerable process skills associated with these activities to the education context. Yet the Bristol students knew how to be active and "go out and research and do things," including making choices about what is relevant and determining what is appropriate for their audience in the learning group.

Rees (1992) identifies the activities of developing notions of choice and deliberating over what might be possible as an important stage in empowerment,

> to develop ability in choosing involves assertiveness and a familiarity with the importance of choice. It requires moving from the assumption that there is no alternative to accepting one's lot, to deliberation over what might be possible. (p. 93)

The Bristol students became very competent with the complexities of making choices, both individually and collectively.

Taking an active role rather than being passive recipients of learning requires students to develop competence in process knowledge. Breton (1994) suggests that "recognising oneself and being recognised as competent" (p. 26) is a necessary component of empowerment, which involves

> The willingness to recognise both one's competence and the limits of one's competence, it involves trusting oneself and one's knowledge and abilities (including one's ability to learn) and being ready to risk demonstrating (i.e., acting on) one's knowledge and abilities. (p.27)

In a curriculum that requires active learning, the process described here by Breton is one which students rehearse many times.

The problem based approach also provides the opportunity for making connections across disciplinary boundaries which Weil (1989) found was an important integrating feature for students in her study. For the Bristol students, problem based learning required the integration of knowledge from different disciplines. However, crucially it also meant that they experienced learning as highly relevant to practice. Woodley et al. (1987) found that two out of three mature students in qualifying courses were studying for instrumental reasons connected with career improvement.

Positive Valuing

The socio-emotional context for learning is crucial (Boud, Keogh and Walker, 1993). There is evidence to suggest that positive valuing by staff is particularly important for non-traditional learners (Mills and Malloy, 1989; Rosen, 1993). Weil found positive valuing to be of key importance in managing disjuncture and achieving integration,

> Enabling teachers and groups can go a long way to counteract the impact of disjunction arising from forces that seem to be outside the bounds of one person's agency, and to create an oasis of integration in which the experience of other kinds of disjunction can be made sense of and effectively managed. (Weil, 1989, p. 143)

For Bristol students, support from enabling teachers was also crucial, particularly early in the course. There was evidence of an access-oriented culture and of staff available to support student needs (Mills and Malloy, 1989).

However, the structure of learning groups was equally if not more significant to the experience of being positively valued. A central tenet of EAL philosophy is that students are a rich resource for one another (Knowles, 1984) and learning is structured in groups to enable students to draw on each other's resources. The non-traditional learners were almost without exception very positive about learning in groups, and often connections made in the first term provided a base which remained significant for the rest of the course. Learning collectively is a new experience for many students whose previous experiences of education have been characterized by individualized competition,

> Student one (white): "EAL reduces competitiveness."
> Student two (white): "It encourages sharing."
> Student three (black): "It takes away inequalities as well."

This excerpt from a group discussion at the end of the first term illustrates Rees's (1992) stage of experiencing solidarity with others and the confidence and trust which sharing can bring.

Ellsworth (1989) emphasizes her own limitations as an educator in finding ways to support the expression of the student voice, in particular she feels she can only have partial knowledge because of her own subjectivity, "I as professor could *never know* about the experiences, oppressions, and understandings of other participants in the class" (p. 310). Yet an advantage of the learning group is that it includes diverse voices with many intersections of race, class, gender, sexuality and disability. Learning in groups also allows for the empowering possibilities described by Rees (1992) of evaluating self-image and addressing students' disparaging views of themselves. For the Bristol students this often took place in the regular group activity of evaluation and feedback.

Such diversity does not inevitably provide a positive experience and at worst may replicate the students' pre-course experience with lack of power and control. The small group is a microcosm of society, and patterns of social oppression will be replicated here unless steps are actively taken to counteract this tendency (Brown and Mistry, 1994). Certainly one Bristol student felt that middle-class articulate students in her group were inclined to make non-traditional students feel less able. Another described feeling that other group members were talking over her head. Efforts are made to structure group membership, particularly in the first term, to reduce the possibility of replicating patterns of oppression. Members of minorities are not knowingly placed by themselves in groups. Facilitators are expected to intervene if patterns of oppression are replicated.

Alongside the learning groups is a structure of support groups. Existing support groups are for black, ethnic minority, gay, lesbian and disabled students. These groups are provided time in the schedule to meet, allocated a meeting space and appropriate consultants are paid to facilitate. Typically consultants are drawn from people from the minority group concerned and do not include course staff, with the intent of providing students with a safe place to explore course issues and a base from which to advocate for their needs.

Structuring opportunities for positive valuing by other students is crucial in today's context of diminishing staff resources. It is also an opportunity to prepare for professional practice in a workplace where intensive individual supervision is a fast diminishing commodity.

"What *can* 'We' do for 'You'?"

Finally, I return to the question of "what *can* 'we' do for 'you'?" (Gore, 1992) and the role of the teacher. EAL frames the teacher as a facilitator and one aspect of the learning environment, albeit early in the course a crucial aspect. What are the key aspects of the facilitator role in an empowerment framework?

Facilitating does not mean abdication of responsibility, "it is the subtle art of creating conditions within which people can exercise full self-determination in their learning" (Heron, 1989, p. 17). This is boundaried by the professional context, where, in the cooperative mode, the facilitator, where possible, shares power over the learning process and negotiates outcomes, collaborating in managing the learning process (Heron, 1989).

Facilitation is essentially a transactional dialogue between students and staff where each bring experiences and knowledge (Brookfield, 1986). Like the student, the facilitator is also not expected to be a blank slate. The facilitator brings expertise as a planner and evaluator, resource person and instrument of social action and change (Boud, 1987). Being empowering as a facilitator means offering a sense of authenticity and helping students to voice and make meaning of their own experiences (Rossiter, 1993). Supporting students individually and collectively to voice and make meaning of their experiences requires the facilitator to be clear about the political and ethical obligations of the position, about the power she or he holds and how to exercise it constructively (Taylor, 1996; Taylor, 1997).

Bristol facilitators support the students to manage learning dilemmas and the competing pulls of student led and profession led learning; of propositional, process and personal knowledge; of formative and summative assessment; of the learning needs of the individual and the group; and of the pressures towards acknowledging homogeneity and providing support rather than addressing difference and critical thinking (Taylor, 1997).

However, the question "what 'we' can do for 'you'?" may equally be asked by other students as well as course planners, researchers and managers in the quest to construct a context that enables non-traditional learners to exercise power and to make the educational context truly more accessible. By learning in this way, it is also possible that non-traditional social work students will transfer the personal and process knowledge of empowerment from the educational context into practice.

REFERENCES

Association of University Teachers (1995, January). Making demands: Mature students and higher education. *AUT Bulletin.*

Baistow, K. (1994/5). Liberation and regulation? Some paradoxes of empowerment. *Critical Social Policy*, 42, 35-46.

Barnes, C. (1991). *Disabled people in Britain and discrimination: A case for anti-discrimination legislation.* Hurst: Calgary.

Barnett, R. (1992). *Learning to effect.* Buckingham: SRHE and Open University Press.

Belenky, M., Clinchy, B., Goldberger, N. and Tarule, J. (1986). *Women's ways of knowing: The development of self, voice and mind.* New York: Basic Books.

Berger, R. (1992). Student retention: A critical phase in the academic careers of minority baccalaureate students. *Journal of Social Work Education*, 28, 85-97.

Breton, M. (1994). On the meaning of empowerment and empowerment-oriented social work practice. *Social Work with Groups*, 17(3), 23-37.

Boud, D. (1987). A facilitator's view of adult learning. In D. Boud and V. Griffin (Eds.), *Appreciating adults learning: From the learners perspective.* London: Kogan Press.

Boud, D., Keogh, R. and Walker, D. (1993). *Using experience for learning*. Buckingham: SRHE and Open University Press.

Brookfield, S. (1986). *Understanding and facilitating adult learning*. San Francisco: Jossey Bass.

Brown, A. and Mistry, T. (1994) Groupwork with 'mixed membership groups: issues of race and gender. *Social Work with Groups*, 17, 5-23.

Burgess, H. (1992). *Problem-led learning for social work: The enquiry and action approach*. London: Whiting and Birch.

Central Council for Education and Training in Social Work. (1995). *Assuring quality in the diploma in social work—1, rules and requirements for the diploma in social work*. London: CCETSW.

Dearing, R. (1997). National committee of inquiry into higher education (Dearing Report). *Higher Education in the Learning Society, Report of the National Committee*. Norwich: HMSO.

Edwards, R. and Usher, R. (1994). Disciplining the subject: The power of competence. *Studies in the Education of Adults*, 26(1), 1-14.

Ellsworth, E. (1989). Why doesn't this feel empowering? Working through the repressive myths of critical pedagogy. *Harvard Education Review*, 59(3), 297-324.

Eraut, M. (1994). *Developing professional knowledge and competence*. London: Falmer.

Foucault, M. (1980). Truth and power. In C. Gordon (ed.), *Power/knowledge: Selected interviews and other writings 1972-1977*. New York: Pantheon.

Freire, P. (1981). *Pedagogy of the oppressed* (2nd ed.). New York: Herder and Herder.

Gore, J. (1992). What can we do for you! What can "we" do for "you"?: Struggling over empowerment in critical and feminist pedagogy. In C. Luke and J. Gore (Eds.), *Feminism and critical pedagogy* (pp. 54-73). London: Routledge.

Halsey, A. H. (1993). Trends in access and equity in higher education: Britain in international perspective. *Oxford Review of Education*, 19, 129-140.

Heron, J. (1989). *The facilitator's handbook*. London: Kogan Press.

Home, A. (1997). Learning the hard way: Role strain, stress, role demands and support in multiple-role women students. *Journal of Social Work Education*, 33(2), 335-346.

Jarvis, P. (1993). *Adult education and the state: Towards a politics of adult education*. London: Routledge.

Kennedy, H. (1997). *Learning works: Widening participation in further education*. Coventry: Further Education Funding Council.

Knowles, M. and Associates. (1984). *Andragogy in action*. San Francisco: Jossey-Bass.

Mills, A. J. and Malloy, S. T. (1989). Experiencing the experienced: The impact of non-standard entrants upon a programme of higher education. *Studies in Higher Education*, 14, 41-53.

Modood, T. (1993). The number of ethnic minority students in British higher education: Some grounds for optimism. *Oxford Review of Education*, 19, 187-192.

Phillips, R., Stalker, K. and Baron, S. (1995). *Barriers to training disabled social work students: A study in the Tayforth area.* Stirling: University of Stirling.

Rees, S. (1992). *Achieving power: Practice and policy in social welfare.* Australia: Allen and Unwin.

Rich, A. (1977). Conditions for work: The common world of women. In S. Ruddick and P. Daniels (Eds.), *Working it out.* New York: Pantheon.

Rosen, V. (1993). Black students in higher education. In M. Thorpe, R. Edwards and A. Hanson (Eds.), *Culture and processes of adult learning.* Routledge and Open University Press.

Rossiter, A. (1993). Teaching from a critical perspective: Towards empowerment in social work education. *Canadian Social Work Review*, 10, 1.

Taylor, I. (1996). Facilitating reflective learning. In N. Gould and I. Taylor (Eds.), *Reflective learning for social work: Research, theory and practice* (pp. 79-96). Aldershot: Arena.

Taylor, I. (1997). *Developing learning in professional education: Partnerships for practice.* Buckingham: Open University Press.

Wakeford, N. (1992). Beyond educating Rita: Mature students and access courses. *Oxford Review of Education*, 19, 217-230.

Weil, S. (1989). Access: Towards education or miseducation? Adults imagine the future. In O. Fulton (Ed.), *Access and institutional change.* Buckingham: SRHE and Open University Press.

Weil, S. (1986). Non-traditional learners within higher education institutions: Discovery and disappointment. *Studies in Higher Education*, 11, 219-235.

Weis, L. (1985) *Between two worlds: Black students in an urban community college.* London: Routledge.

Woodley, A., Wagner, L., Slowey, M., Hamilton, M. and Fulton, O. (1987). *Choosing to learn: Adults in higher education.* Buckingham: SRHE and Open University Press.

Wright, P. (1991). Access or accessibility? *Journal of Access Studies*, 6, 6-15.

Chapter 24

EMPOWERMENT AND SOCIAL WORK EDUCATION: RECLAIMING OUR VOICES AS TEACHERS

Michael Kim Zapf
Faculty of Social Work
The University of Calgary

Empowerment has become a familiar word in the social work literature, discussed regularly in our generalist practice theories and specific applications. Inherent in the notion of empowerment is a sense of demystification of the helping process; power is shared as the worker moves away from the elevated status of expert towards a true collaboration with the client as equal partner. Some beginning steps have been taken to suggest a similar collaborative process for social work education. Much of the attention, however, has focused on empowering students while largely ignoring the challenges facing teachers. This paper opens with a brief overview of the characteristics of empowerment as found in the current generalist social work theory. Implications for social work education are then examined, with particular attention to the concepts of narrative surrender and reclaiming of voice by social work instructors.

EMPOWERMENT AND THE SOCIAL WORK LITERATURE

Social work theory has long espoused the tenet of client self-determination, yet this principle has come under recent attack for its inability to fully recognize issues of power and oppression. Arguing for the sharing of power with clients, Hartman (1993) concluded that "self-determination was a hollow promise sharply limited by lack of access to resources, to opportunity, to power" (p. 365). Improved access to resources, opportunity and power appears to be the essence of the term empowerment as it appears in the recent social work literature.

In their overview of direct practice theory, Hepworth and Larsen (1993) defined empowerment as "enabling clients to gain the capacity to interact with the environment in ways that enhance their need gratification, well-being, and satisfaction" with the goal of assisting the poor and oppressed "to develop their latent powers and to exert these powers to obtain needed resources" (p. 495). Miley, O'Melia and DuBois (1995) presented two dimensions of empowerment as a guide for social work practitioners: a conceptual dimension and a process dimension. As a concept or state of mind, empowerment involves feelings such as worthiness, competence, mastery, perceived control and strength; as a process, empowerment involves reallocation of power and resources (p. 68-69). Building on this framework of sharing power with oppressed groups and victims of injustice, Kirst-Ashman and Hull (1997) recently concluded that empowerment can be considered "a legitimate goal for generalist social workers ... consistent with our commitment to improve social conditions, assist populations-at-risk, and restore the capacity of people to solve their own problems" (p. 379).

In addition to mainstream generalist textbooks, empowerment is being discussed in many areas of social work, including: research (Rappaport, 1990; Ristock and Pennell, 1996; Whitmore, 1990); administration (Dodd and Gutiérrez, 1990); cross-cultural practice (Green, 1995; Gutiérrez, 1990; Hirayama and Cetingok, 1988; Inglehart and Becerra, 1995); feminist practice (Van Den Bergh, 1992); and several related fields such as community health (Katz, 1984; Labonte, 1989) and community psychology (Price, 1990; Rappaport, 1987).

Much of the Canadian literature on empowerment actually comes from the relatively new specialization of northern or remote practice. Collier (1984) argued that the northern practitioner could not avoid power issues and must make a choice to align with the community against the outside development interests. Wharf (1985) also stressed the importance of a partnership between the northern worker and the community, a partnership featuring a blurring of professional boundaries and a risky sharing of authority with the community. McKay (1987) argued that a conflict perspective had to be added to the ecosystems approach to adequately recognize the power issues inherent in northern practice. Dacks and Coates (1988) collected readings on the importance of empowerment for planning, management and community development in Canada's north. Zapf (1991) argued that the hidden urban bias underlying conventional generalist social work theory was a major obstacle to empowerment for northern regions. Ricks (1991) advanced an empowerment training model to overcome the "subordinate power relationships" experienced by many northern Native social workers. The Canadian Circumpolar Institute developed an annotated bibliography of literature relevant to local control and empowerment of northern communities (Stevenson and Hickey, 1995).

COLLABORATIVE PARTNERSHIPS AND EXPERT KNOWLEDGE

Whatever the source, a major component of the empowerment literature in social work appears to be the necessity of a worker-client relationship that "should approach equality as much as possible" (Zastrow, 1995, p. 523). Part of showing genuine respect for the client and moving beyond conventional power roles is an understanding of "the helping relationship as one of collaboration wherein the client will be an equal partner in searching for and developing solutions to the problems" (Hepworth and Larsen, 1993, p. 496). For Miley, O'Melia and DuBois (1995) as well, an active application of the empowerment concept to social work practice compels workers and clients "to collaborate as partners" (p. 71).

Some have carried over this model of collaborative partnership to the activities of social work education. Leonard (1994) advocated a "dialogical education" where "teachers and students together build the different knowledges necessary for practice" (p. 24). Miley, O'Melia and DuBois (1995) similarly suggested a joint learning process which they called "collaborative teaching" which "transforms educational processes so that learners become users rather than simply recipients of education" (p. 373). Rossiter (1993) also wanted mutuality in social work education, "the engagement of both students and teachers in the process of change inherent in learning ... a relationship of mutual empowerment" (p. 87). Most of this new work on collaborative education acknowledges the foundation work of Friere (1971) with his notion of a "problem-posing" model of adult education to replace the dominant "banking" model.

From a practice perspective, Kirst-Ashman and Hull (1997) identified several specific sources of power that can hinder collaboration and inhibit the overall sharing of power with clients. Along with the often discussed social control function and professional mystique, they pointed to expert knowledge as a clear obstacle to empowerment because of the distance created between worker and client. Regarding the worker as an expert can create a dangerous hierarchy of action and dependency.

> Proficient experts have the knowledge, foresight, insight, ideas, and action plans which are then bestowed on inept clients who lack insight, ideas, and action plans. Proactive professionals take charge of passive clients. Masterful experts commence action and ineffectual client systems are acted upon. (Miley, O'Melia and DuBois, 1995, p. 71)

Returning to the needs of social work education, Rossiter (1993) agreed that the notion of expert knowledge can be "fundamentally oppressive" (p. 79) within a university system that she saw as a "structure of domination" featuring "hierarchy, paternalism, and systems of threat and exclusion" (p. 77). Leonard (1994) related the concept of expert knowledge in social work education directly to the underlying power issues, pointing out that what we consider as expert knowledge is merely the "dominant paradigm" or the "consensus of dominant forces" (p. 22). Powerful forces have resulted in certain sources of knowledge gaining a status of privilege or truth, to the exclusion of outside knowledge. He encouraged social work education to "renounce a commitment to privileged, objective knowledge" and to "search for alternative sources of knowledge" by exploring "alternative accounts, histories, and experiences of our social world" (p. 22- 23).

Another perspective on expert knowledge and social work education can be derived from the earlier work of Maslow (1964). In a critique of organized religion, he argued that the original experiences of mystics and prophets cannot easily be conveyed to the general population. Meaning gets lost when mystical experiences are concretized into words, rituals and ceremonies. Maslow (1964) cautioned that we as audience come to worship the words and symbols themselves, turning them into sacred objects and ceremonies, thereby distancing ourselves even further from the original experience. In his words, teachers are often engaged in

> an effort to communicate peak-experiences to non-peakers, to teach them, to apply them, etc. Often, to make it more difficult, this job falls into the hands of non-peakers.... The peak-experiences and their experiential quality are no transmittable to non-peakers, at least not by words alone, and certainly not by non-peakers. (p. 24)

While there may not be exact parallels between organized religion and social work education, the warnings advanced by Maslow can be helpful in understanding the difficulties in moving toward a collaborative process with students. Leading social work authors have developed conceptual frameworks and models of practice from their own very real experiences in the field and the library. These experiences are then written down and organized carefully into the textbooks from which most of us teach and structure our courses. Students expect us to package and deliver discrete modules from the textbook and related literature, coherent units of knowledge that they can master or manipulate for the examination or required papers. Our own practice skills and academic efforts may be irrelevant to this process. To return to Maslow's (1964) terminology, instructors and students may be "worshipping" the authors of textbooks by turning their "concretized symbols" into "sacred things and sacred activities" (p. 24) through lectures and graded assignments. As social work instructors, we may be trying to communicate someone else's peak experiences to non-peakers, with little or none of our own insights or struggles in the process. Instructors concretize expert knowledge from the literature and the given curriculum; students concretize expert knowledge from the texts and lectures. In this way, all participate in reproducing the hierarchy of the university. As instructors, we seldom work together with students to develop our own models from our own shared experiences.

NARRATIVE SURRENDER

Seeking to replace the medical model in social work practice, Weick (1983) argued that a culture based on expert knowledge results in persons no longer having confidence in their own judgments or experiential knowledge unless validated by an expert.

> The result is that their knowledge about themselves becomes partially or wholly hidden. In addition, whatever information they give to the professional is without meaning until the professional confers meaning on it. What is seen, therefore, at the base of the giving over process, is a willingness to give someone else power to define one's personal reality. (p. 468)

This process, labelled by Weick as "giving over," has been further developed in medical sociology where Frank (1995) describes a moment of "narrative surrender" where a person with an illness agrees

> to tell her story in medical terms. "How are you?" now requires that personal feeling be contextualized within a secondhand medical report. The physician becomes the spokesperson for the disease, and the ill person's stories come to depend heavily on repetition of what the physician has said. (p. 6)

Frank (1995) traces the illness experience through periods of differing "fundamental assumptions" showing how the folk medicine and family care of "premodern" times gave way to "modern" technical expertise with highly trained medical specialists and complex treatment institutions where "the chart becomes the official story of the illness" (p. 5).

Kleinman and Kleinman (1996) use similar language to depict the transformation of persons who have suffered traumatic violence. As their very real memories are converted into "trauma stories," the person moves from "one who experiences" to become "one who is a victim" and finally "one who is sick." "These trauma stories then become the currency, the symbolic capital, with which they enter exchanges for physical resources and achieve the status of political refugee" (p. 10).

Such cultural appropriation of real experience is described by deMontigny (1995) from a social work perspective. He argues that modern social agencies have created an institutional reality through documentation where the elite professionals can buffer themselves from the messy daily lives of clients/ consumers. The case file has become the defining story of the client's experiences; diagnostic categories and labelled interventions are the official narrative as documented by those with the power to apply the labels. In a sense, this is an extreme example of the distancing effect of expert knowledge. There is a tremendous power differential between those who have the power to generate and impose stories (through case files, court reports, agency policy, journal articles, etc.) and those who are subject to the stories which are created about them. Returning to deMontigny's (1995) words, "social workers rework material that they extract from people's lives to fit the concerns of an institutional reality" (p. 58). With specific reference to child protection work, Stanford (1995) also denounced "the domesticating narratives provided by simplistic ideas on empowerment" describing such files as "empty" and "hostile to creativity" (p. 148).

DeMontigny (1995) illustrated a similar pattern of narrative surrender from his own experiences with social work education. As a social work student, he encountered confusion and frustration as he was forced to

> bridge the gap between the world of my experience and the world that denied my experience, a world of my thoughts and beliefs and a world that demanded that I perform other people's thoughts and beliefs—spoken through operational directives, policies, and legislation.... In the process of becoming professional, I learned how to reframe, rename, and re-experience. (p. 12)

In her experiences as a new teacher, Rossiter (1993) described this same sense of narrative surrender within social work education:

> As an inexperienced teacher operating without a concrete conception of a critical teaching practice, I felt I lacked

authenticity in the class. Because I felt unable to authorise my own version within the academic structure, I could not offer students a genuine partnership in learning. I was constantly aware of the contradictions inherent in talking about relations of dominance while perpetuating them. (p. 82)

SOCIAL WORK EDUCATORS AND THE RECLAIMING OF VOICE

There is evidence in the literature of an emerging postmodern experience of "reclaiming voice," the regained ability to tell one's own story. From his medical perspective, Frank (1995) depicted the ill person coming to realize that medical records cannot capture the full experience and meaning of their illness, instead perceiving

> a need for what would now be called her own voice, a personal voice telling what illness has imposed on her and seeking to define for herself a new place in the world. What is distinct in postmodern times is people feeling a need for a voice they can recognize as their own. (p. 7)

From a feminist standpoint, Belenky, Clinchy, Goldberger and Tarule (1986) strongly advocated this reclamation of voice for teachers in adult education. They want students to see that teachers are "groping too," participating with students in learning processes which are "human, imperfect, and attainable" (p. 216, 217). The authors put forward a model of "connected teaching" to overcome the distance created by expert knowledge in the current system:

> The teacher does not wish to deposit his words in the students' notebooks, but the students insist upon storing them there. They treat his words as sacrosanct. He cannot understand why they will not risk a response.
>
> But the teacher himself takes few risks. True to the banking concept, he composes his thoughts in private. The students are permitted to see the product of his thinking, but the process of gestation is hidden from view. The lecture appears as if by magic. The teacher asks his students to take risks he is unwilling—although presumable more able—to make himself. He invites the students to find holes in his

argument, but he has taken pains to make it airtight.... So long as teachers hide the imperfect processes of their thinking, allowing their students to glimpse only the polished products, students will remain convinced that only Einstein—or a professor—could think up a theory. (p. 215)

Within social work education, much of the attention given to reclaiming voice has focused on only one partner in the desired collaborative learning relationship—the student. Pennell and Ristock (1997) described classroom exercises developed to "encourage the students to check the theories in their ... textbook and other readings against their own experiences" within a macro-level course with a goal of students "constructing theories on community out of class members' experiences of their home communities" (p. 31). In advocating a "renewed working partnership" (p. 17) between instructors and students in social work education, Moffat and Miehls (1997) also shared classroom vignettes where students in courses on diversity have encountered very real instances of power relations, oppression and privilege. They explained the assignment of a reflective paper, a subjective piece of writing requiring that "students consider aspects of their own identity and how their identity might influence the nature of their social work practice" (p. 10).

Rossiter (1993) also described specific social work course revisions designed to help students focus on their own learning process. Arguing that many students have actually been injured intellectually from their past encounters with expert knowledge in the education system, she wanted to keep students focused on their "own process of interacting with the material," actively engaged in the struggle "to develop their own theories-as-metaphors" (p. 84). Her students were also required to write subjectively in the first person and "to use writing as a way of raising questions to which they have no answers" (p. 85).

This focus on students may be important, but how can social work instructors go about reclaiming their personal and authentic voices which may have been surrendered through professional training and institutional realities? There have been some suggestions in the literature for developing such a collaborative teaching partnership with students. In the 1970s, a strong relationship between content and process in social work education was advocated by Brigham (1977). He argued that empowerment of social work students would require instructors to move away from the authoritative stance of expert knowledge towards respectful dialogue. In the 1980s, Schon (1988) called again for professional education to abandon the outdated hierarchical model of expert/student in favour of new roles based on partnership and mutual learning. Dore (1993) further argued the importance of the social work instructor modelling his or her learning behaviours and processes for the students. Pietroni (1995) identified the following among the aims of professional social work education:

To provide a containing environment in which individual practitioners are given the opportunity of recovering or establishing creative individual thought;
To offer a partnership in learning between educators and learners;
To provide a learning environment in which the log-jams and messiness of day-to-day practice can be faced and scrutinised in detail. (p. 48)

Haynes and Beard (1998) recently proposed a collaborative teaching model using a professional practitioner and a professional educator together in the classroom. They distinguish this collaboration from the simple mechanics of team teaching with its sequential division of course responsibilities:

Collaborative teaching is the joint teaching by a professional educator and a professional practitioner who share a common commitment to build practice competency and to work together in ongoing course design, planning, teaching and evaluation. (p. 36)

Why must such collaboration involve two different persons? Most social work educators began their careers as practitioners and we have extensive field experience to draw upon, as well as our immediate involvement with the messy and often chaotic process of using frameworks to make sense of what we did (or didn't do!) in the field. This integration of our practice and academic selves may be a valuable ongoing activity to share with our students, empowering them to do the same and modelling the process. As Taylor (1997) reminds us in her discussion of partnerships in professional education, "the personal is professional." Reclaiming voice for social work educators probably begins with that recognition and the taking of responsibility for active integration.

Rossiter (1993) explained how she began to resolve her teaching dilemma by learning to "enter the learning relationship from my own standpoint ... as opposed to being the representative of the curriculum" (p. 88), arguing strongly that a crucial component of the empowering dialogue between teacher and students is that "the teacher *relearns* alongside the student" (p. 80). From the literature, another example of an attempt to use voice in the social work classroom:

> Many of my courses are centred around cross-cultural issues. In the first class, I often show an overhead projection of a black and white photograph taken around 1955 depicting myself, my brother, and my mother standing in front of a train station about to take a 350-mile train trip across the prairies. I am pre-school and I look very serious wearing my twin pearl-handled cap revolvers and my cowboy boots. It would be my job on that trip to protect my mother from Indians as we rode the train across the prairie!
>
> Now I had never met a real Aboriginal person in my life to that point. But I had a strong sense of the imminent danger, acquired from the comics, television, and movies of my day. Of course, I also had images of "good Indians" such as Tonto and L'il Beaver.
>
> What impact do those powerful cultural categories still have on me today? If I am trying to work with a First Nations resource person or community leader today, do I still expect Tonto, a "good Indian" who is loyal but not as smart, who looks up to me, who relies upon his or her association with me for status in the larger community, who walks close but a few feet behind me, who does not speak English as well as I do, who can be trusted with most things but not the really important decisions? If I am still bound by the categories passed on by my culture in childhood, how can I possibly learn from and enjoy a relationship of respect with my First Nations friends or co-workers today?
>
> When I stand at the front of the class beside that life-size photograph of me from some 40 years ago, students are confronted with the reality of the changes I have had to make and continue to work on. I can then share specific incidents in my struggle, and the influence of people who have helped me. Overall, this sharing appears to have much greater impact on students than my standard lecture on the processes of unlearning and reframing. (Zapf, 1997, p. 90-91)

This approach appears to fit within the constructivist teaching/learning paradigm of social work education identified by Graham (1997).

Such accounts may indicate an overall direction, but the literature still offers few concrete guidelines for the reclaiming of voice. As Leonard (1994) cautioned, "dialogical education is not a fully established alternative form of learning within Western countries: rather it is a set of social practices to be struggled for in a spirit of revolutionary optimism" (p. 24). Beginning attempts to reclaim voice have been described as "halting, self-doubting, and often inarticulate" (Frank, 1995, p. 7), and as "celebrating the equivocal, the confusing, the chaos, and the mystery of the everyday" (deMontigny, 1995, p. 221). For social work educators attempting to reclaim voice, Tuson (1996) demanded "at the very least an allowance of incoherence, space for the chaotic, within the ordered realm of academic writing" (p. 74). Solas (1992) referred to this style of teaching as

> personal both in its selection of events and in its expression or style. As such, the search for unity and coherence (order), characteristic of traditional forms of educational enquiry, gives way to disunity and incoherence (chaos) in life ... so that unified arguments are replaced by itineraries of topics. (p. 212)

CONCLUSION

Crucial to the notion of empowerment in social work practice is a collaboration between worker and client as partners in the change process. Expert knowledge has been identified as a major hindrance to such power sharing. Within social work education, there have been calls for a similar transformation to a model of collaborative teaching whereby teachers and students engage in a mutual learning process. Once again, expert knowledge and the distance it creates between student and teacher emerge as oppressive obstacles to any notion of shared power.

Through a process of narrative surrender, social work educators may disguise our own individual chaotic learning processes to become simple conveyors of expert knowledge. Such things as the polished lecture, the edited assignment and the transcript have become the currency of the education process. As an empowering alternative, social work educators are encouraged to reclaim our voice by working to integrate our professional and personal selves, taking active personal ownership of our ongoing efforts to organize and attribute meaning to course material and sharing this process as part of our involvement with students.

It would appear that reclaiming of voice can be a difficult and risky task for social work educators, yet we are beginning to demand those very risks from our students. If we stop there, hiding behind expert knowledge while expecting students to risk an authentic voice, we may be guilty of what Serrano-Garcia (1984) labelled "the illusion of empowerment," when oppressed groups are offered community development within a colonial context. In a truly empowering collaborative learning partnership with students, we can demand no less of ourselves than we expect from them.

REFERENCES

Belenky, M. F., Clinchy, B. M., Goldberger, N. R. and Tarule, J. M. (1986). *Women's ways of knowing: The development of self, voice, and mind.* USA: Basic Books.

Brigham, T. (1977). Liberation in social work education: Applications from Paulo Friere. *Journal of Education for Social Work,* 13(3), 5-11.

Collier, K. (1984). *Social work with rural peoples.* Vancouver: New Star.

Dacks, G. and Coates, K. (Eds.). (1988). *Northern communities: The prospects for empowerment.* Edmonton: Boreal Institute for Northern Studies.

deMontigny, G.A.J. (1995). *Social working: An ethnography of front-line practice.* University of Toronto Press.

Dodd, P. and Gutiérrez, L. (1990). Preparing students for the future: A power perspective on community practice. *Administration in Social Work,* 14, 63-78.

Dore, M. (1993). The practice-teaching parallel in educating the micropractitioner. *Social Work,* 29(2), 181-190.

Frank, A. (1995). *The wounded storyteller: Body, illness, and ethics.* Chicago: University of Chicago Press.

Friere, P. (1971). *Pedagogy of the oppressed.* New York: Seaview.

Graham, M. A. (1997). Empowering social work faculty: Alternative paradigms for teaching and learning. *Journal of Teaching in Social Work,* 15(1/2), 33-49.

Green, J. W. (1995). *Cultural awareness in the human services* (2nd ed.). Boston: Allyn and Bacon.

Gutiérrez, L. H. (1990). Working with women of color: An empowerment perspective. *Social Work,* 35, 149-153.

Hartman, A. (1993). The professional is political. *Social Work,* 38, 365-366.

Haynes, D. T. and Beard, N. C. (1998). A collaborative teaching model to build competence. *Journal of Teaching in Social Work,* 16(1/2), 35-55.

Hepworth, D. H. and Larsen, J. A. (1993). *Direct social work practice: Theory and skills* (4th ed.). Pacific Grove: Brooks/Cole.

Hirayama, H. and Cetingok. (1988). Empowerment: A social work approach for Asian immigrants. *Social Casework,* 69, 41-47.

Inglehart, A. P. and Becerra, R. M. (1995). *Social services and the ethnic community.* Boston: Allyn and Bacon.

Katz, R. (1984). Empowerment and synergy: Expanding the community's healing resources. *Prevention in Human Services,* 3, 201-226.

Kirst-Ashman, K. K. and Hull, G. H., Jr. (1997). *Generalist practice with organizations and communities.* Chicago: Nelson-Hall.

Kleinman, A. and Kleinman, J. (1996). The appeal of experience; the dismay of images: Cultural appropriation of suffering in our times. *Daedalus,* 125(1), 1-23.

Labonte, R. (1989). Community empowerment: The need for political analysis. *Canadian Journal of Public Health,* 80, 87-88.

Leonard, P. (1994). Knowledge/power and postmodernism: Implications for the practice of a critical social work education. *Canadian Social Work Review,* 11, 11-26.

Maslow, A. H. (1964). *Religions, values, and peak-experiences.* New York: Viking Press.

McKay, S. (1987). Social work in Canada's north: Survival and development issues affecting aboriginal and industry-based economies. *International Social Work,* 30, 259-278.

Miley, K. K., O'Melia, M. and DuBois, B. L. (1995). *Generalist social work practice: An empowering approach.* Boston: Allyn and Bacon.

Moffat, K. and Miehls, D. (1997). *Development of identity in the classroom: Social work students' evolution from neutrality to subjectivity.* Paper presented at the Learned Societies' Conference, St. John's, Newfoundland.

Pennell, J. and Ristock, J. R. (1997). Feminist links, postmodern interruptions: Toward a critical social work education. In P. Sachdev (Ed.), *Social work discussion papers: Trends in social work education.* St. John's: Memorial University School of Social Work.

Pietroni, M. (1995). The nature and aims of professional education for social workers: A postmodern perspective. In M. Yelloly and M. Henkel (Eds.), *Learning and teaching in social work: Towards reflective practice* (pp. 34-56). London: Jessica Kingsley Publishers.

Price, R.H. (1990). Whither participation or empowerment? *American Journal of Community Psychology,* 18, 163-167.

Rappaport, J. (1987). Terms of empowerment/exemplars of prevention: Toward a theory for community psychology. *American Journal of Community Psychology,* 15, 121-148.

Rappaport, J. (1990). Research methods and the empowerment social agenda. In P. Tolan, C. Keys, F. Chertok and L. Jason (Eds.), *Researching community psychology: Issues of theory and methods* (pp. 51-63). Washington: American Psychological Association.

Ricks, F. (1991). Native sexual abuse counsellor: An empowerment training and healing model. *The Northern Review*, 7, 112-129.

Ristock, J. L. and Pennell, J. (1996). *Community research as empowerment: Feminist links, postmodern interruptions*. Don Mills: Oxford University Press.

Rossiter, A. B. (1993). Teaching from a critical perspective: Towards empowerment in social work education. *Canadian Social Work Review*, 10, 76-90.

Schon, D. (1988). *Educating the reflective practitioner*. San Francisco: Jossey-Bass.

Serrano-Garcia, I. (1984). The illusion of empowerment: Community development within a colonial context. *Prevention in Human Services*, 3, 173-200.

Solas, J. (1992). Investigating teacher and student thinking about the process of teaching and learning using autobiography and repertory grid. *Review of Educational Research*, 62, 205-225.

Stanford, R. (1995). Creativity and child protection social work. In M. Yelloly and M. Henkel (Eds.), *Learning and teaching in social work: Towards reflective practice* (pp. 136-149). London: Jessica Kingsley Publishers.

Stevenson, M. G. and Hickey, C. G. (1995). *Empowering northern and Native communities for social and economic control: An annotated bibliography of relevant literature*. Edmonton: Canadian Circumpolar Institute.

Taylor, I. (1997). *Developing learning in professional education: Partnerships for practice*. Buckingham: Open University Press.

Tuson, G. (1996). Writing postmodern social work. In P. Ford and P. Hayes (Eds.), *Educating for social work: Arguments for optimism* (pp. 61-75). Hants: Ashgate Publishing Company.

Van Den Bergh, N. (1992). Feminist treatment for people with depression. In K. Corcoran (Ed.), *Structuring change* (pp. 95-110). Chicago: Lyceum Books.

Weick, A. (1983). Issues in overturning a medical model of social work practice. *Social Work*, 28, 467-471.

Wharf, B. (1985). Toward a leadership role in human services: The case for rural communities. *The Social Worker*, 53, 14-20.

Whitmore, E. (1990). Empowerment in program evaluation: A case example. *Canadian Social Work Review*, 7, 215-229.

Zapf, M. K. (1991). Educating social work practitioners for the north: A challenge for conventional models and structures. *The Northern Review*, 7, 35-52.

Zapf, M. K. (1997). Voice and social work education: Learning to teach from my own story. *Canadian Social Work Review*, 14(1), 83-97.

Zastrow, C. (1995). *The practice of social work* (5th ed.). Pacific Grove: Brooks/Cole.

Future Directions

Chapter 25

EMPOWERMENT:
LESSONS LEARNED AND FUTURE DIRECTIONS

Wes Shera
Lilian Wells
Faculty of Social Work
University of Toronto

This book captures a dialogue among a group of authors and engages the reader in appreciating the many dimensions of empowerment practice in social work. There are common themes which emerge from the various chapters, but discontinuities and contradictions are also evident. This final chapter reviews and reflects on each of the chapters in the four sections and concludes with some overall observations.

The first section of the book includes chapters that describe a range of theoretical approaches that have been employed as frameworks for empowerment. They also identify important conceptual challenges in moving forward. Miley and Dubois present a comprehensive framework for generalist social work practice, representing the "mainstream" American perspective of empowerment. It is based on theories of human systems, social change and empowerment. They state that a philosophical orientation is necessary but not sufficient for empowerment-oriented practice. They operationalize empowerment practice emphasizing three critical, inter-related strategies: activating resources, creating alliances and expanding opportunities. They identify a danger in the labelling of clients as "oppressed" and "disenfranchised," highlighting instead the importance of challenging oppressive and discriminating social systems. With the widespread use of their textbooks, this framework is probably the most broadly disseminated approach in North America. It is also useful to note how their conceptualization has developed over time.

Barry and Sidaway bring an analysis of theories of participation and of multidimensional theories of power as essential elements in the foundation of empowerment-oriented social work practice. They propose a partnership model that includes elites and non-elites and point to the need for evaluation that incorporates the perspectives of all stakeholders. Their operationalization of practice stresses the importance of strategies for change and the practice skills of negotiation, facilitation and conflict resolution. Drawing on environmental planning and rural and international development, they illustrate how knowledge from various disciplines and areas of practice can cross-fertilize our conceptualization of empowerment practice.

Ramon, taking a social science perspective, examines the similarities and differences between collective and individual empowerment and suggests that the concept of interdependence, rather than autonomy, is characteristic of both. She notes that the ideological sources of these two aspects of empowerment differ, the former arising from a conflict model of society, the latter from a liberal tradition. She argues that the emerging prominence of empowerment is a reaction to the New Right but is found more in professional discourse than in practice. Ramon contributes the concept of "hybrid identity" arising from client empowerment and involvement. She criticizes the focus on individual empowerment in the Anglo-Saxon world in comparison to southern Europe and South America and raises issues regarding transcultural transferability. The potential of collective empowerment is socio-political, to generate collective thought, action and research. It requires that social workers use groupwork and community work, support people to obtain employment or education and focus on connecting people to networks.

MacDonald and MacDonald amplify the debate with a detailed examination of the concept of power, concluding that empowerment cannot be treated as a simple intrinsic good. The consequences of empowerment must be considered and evaluated. They raise questions about situations where divergence of interests and conflictual interests cannot be resolved. They also argue that in the situation where, for example, a person rationally prefers an expert to make a decision, the user is rejecting empowerment. We would suggest that the incorporation of concepts developed by ethicists regarding the differences between decisional and executional choice and the right to delegate might have modified their conclusion. They emphasize the importance of the professional's technical competence, sensitively applied with "the provision of knowledge as the only defensible route to empowerment."

Imbrogno, from a socio-political perspective, identifies two paradigms of empowerment: incremental and rational consensus. He proposes that strategies of dialectic discourse can lead to qualitative social change rather than be limited to incremental change that is serial, remedial and fragmentary. Using a world view that sees a clash of values as inevitable in human and social activity, he describes a Socratic process leading to a rational consensus to produce social change in the redistribution of power relations and in the dissemination of social goods and benefits.

The chapters in section two examine how empowerment practice is operationalized in different fields of practice. A major focus of the contributions is on identifying context specific and transferable components of empowerment practice. Common themes in this section are the importance of a strengths perspective; attention to the special needs and the context of population groups; the importance of collectivity and groups; and the need for an understanding of the history of stigma, discrimination and oppression. Partnerships with clients and the voice of the consumers/clients in defining empowerment are central concepts. While the overall strategies and techniques are similar, the priorities, context, the particular strengths and challenges faced by each population and their unique history of stigma, discrimination and oppression require particular knowledge and skills.

Manning argues most explicitly that empowerment takes different forms for different people and for different contexts. Population-specific understandings of empowerment that are located in the context of people's experience are needed. Based on a series of participatory research projects, she documents a model of empowerment practice in the field of mental health. She identifies a constellation of experiences with power and powerlessness encountered by people in the mental health system. These include the impact of a psychiatric disability with a "loss of self," diminished quality of life (often exacerbated by poverty), institutionalization and "learned helplessness" plus stigma from society and the care-provider system itself. These experiences influence the philosophy and strategies required to practice with this population.

Manning raises the issue of people with severe mental illness who experience more than one source of oppression, such as, people of colour, the physically disabled, women and the elderly. She highlights the necessity to identify their special needs and work to develop appropriate models of empowerment. She also identifies the paradox of facilitating the development of consumer power within the mental health system—seen by so many as oppressive.

Staples addresses this paradox in more detail. His chapter is based on a study of a member-run consumer self-advocacy organization and assesses the capacity of service providers and the mental health bureaucracy to facilitate and sanction consumer empowerment. Drawing on the literature, he outlines practice principles and techniques for professionals and guidelines for mental health organizations. He highlights that empowerment transcends self-perception and cannot be confined to the acquisition of knowledge, capacities and skills—it should also include substantial results and benefits.

He identifies a range of difficulties at the personal and structural levels, noting, for example, the complexities involved with the disempowerment of staff due to budget cuts and re-structuring and the problem of organizations using the rhetoric of empowerment but not the practice. Civil rights legislation and clear grievance procedures are two of the ways identified to counteract such problems.

East's chapter integrates feminist theory and a postmodern perspective into a multi-level model of practice with low-income women. She describes the challenges in using these constructs, concluding that they are important for women and especially women of colour. She incorporates self-in-relation theory and spirituality as vital components for personal empowerment. Stress management is an important factor for interpersonal empowerment for this population as is leadership training for political empowerment. She also highlights the characteristics of empowering settings within which the model functions.

Beaulaurier and Taylor describe how a critical mass of people with physical disabilities was able to influence the general public, legislators and services to recognize the civil rights of the disabled and to gain opportunities and resources for independent and self-determined lifestyles in the community. In addition to the impact of the physical condition and its meaning to the individual, people with physical disabilities face stigma and isolation plus environmental factors that restrict opportunities. Attention is focused on environmental change to increase accessibility and resources to maximize choice. They suggest that the disabled rights movement was launched more in spite of rather than in conjunction with health and social work professionals, and they identify a model of practice for work with people with disabilities. They specify the knowledge and skills required and highlight strategies such as consciousness-raising, community liaison, education and social change.

Cox examines empowerment as it relates to the frail elderly with physical and/or mental disabilities. She identifies two overall challenges: the need to cope with care needs and stigma and how to find meaning and valued roles. She describes how the feminist movement and the disability movement make important contributions to this field of practice but that the development, implementation and evaluation of interventions are limited. Barriers include the current hostile political climate and the intergenerational equity debate, reduction of services, the social construction of aging as a medical problem, individualism and the disempowerment of social workers. Nonetheless, she does see a growing enthusiasm about the potential of frail older people.

MacKenzie brings knowledge from the child welfare field, where social control is a feature. His study of an Aboriginal child and family service agency illuminates empowerment in a situation where First Nations now have jurisdictional control. Empowerment of staff, attention to structural issues such as colonization, racism and the effects of residential schools are important, unique factors for this population. General principles that emerge are the concept of voice and the right to make responsible choices, the emphasis on culturally appropriate services as a means to personal and cultural empowerment and the need to provide a range of services within a holistic perspective.

The third section expands on a number of critical issues in empowerment practice, groupwork, empowering and empowered organizations, spirituality and religion, issues of culture and ethnicity, and the competing discourses on empowerment by service users and providers. The first three chapters elaborate on the special role of social work with groups for empowerment-oriented practice. Each also highlights the impact of context, specifically, the political, economic or cultural dimensions of society. Breton pulls together the common themes of socio-political context, the importance of groupwork in empowerment practice and the need for explicit strategies and techniques. She asserts that social work must rise to take on the challenge of a post-empowerment, neo-conservative era and proposes a six-step groupwork model. Home identifies the challenges and dilemmas when one tries to implement empowerment groups in today's agency environment. She finds the constraints imposed by reduced resources and by agency pressures to provide only short-term service may contribute to unsuccessful outcomes. In the face of cultural imperatives, Hirayama and Hirayama examine a range of issues involved in the cross-cultural application of empowerment practice. They also describe strategies of empowerment in a Japanese context and compare them to those that would be appropriate in America.

The next two chapters examine the interrelated roles of social work practitioners, service organizations and consumers. Beresford critiques current empowerment practice as being limited by its neglect of the users' perspective. The dominant discourse in social work continues to be the professional one, tied to the service system and professional objectives. Service users are primarily concerned about transforming people's lives and capacities, enhancing their rights, choices and opportunities and battling exclusion. He argues for reforming social work practice by learning from service users and their movements. Nagdna, Harding and Holley focus on the organizational level and integrate a multicultural dimension. They provide an historical analysis of American social policy and direct practice in terms of diversity and oppression. They articulate three propositions that characterize an empowered and empowering multicultural human service organization and test these in two case studies. From this analysis they identify several challenges (the tension between a social service and social change agenda, issues of funding and of legitimization), and propose possible strategies to address these problems.

The concept of spirituality has not been incorporated in the empowerment literature of developed countries. Ortiz and Smith make compelling arguments for addressing this gap. They describe the nature of spirituality, how it may differ from organized religion and identify how spirituality and empowerment are companion forces. Examples from South Africa, Haiti, the African American church, feminist communities and Christian based communities illustrate their thesis. In a similar area, Cnaan, while acknowledging disempowering actions by religious bodies, analyzes the role of organized religion in fostering empowerment. He gives examples related to the African American community, the Haitian community, the gay community and women, drawing on the application of theories of social action and liberation theology.

The chapters found in the fourth section of this book focus on the role of research in empowerment and the utility of an empowerment perspective in the process of teaching. Involving consumers in research and using concepts of empowerment in research and education are the central themes of this section.

Evans and Fisher argue that unless service users are centrally involved in defining the concept of empowerment, there is a real danger of empowerment practice being a process of co-optation by professionals. Service users are seen as having the right to establish research agendas rather than just be participants in research. They argue for the importance of user controlled research as a means of increasing the power of service users over the way their experiences are defined. The academic researcher is viewed as ally and facilitator. User controlled research is seen as both empowering users and providing an important, often neglected perspective in policy debates.

Flemming and Ward describe a social action approach to research and explain how respondents can be empowered through participating in the entire research process. The focus of the research shifts from the being researcher-centred to being researched-centred. Service providers and users formulate the issues, their interactions are non-hierarchical and data analysis and dissemination are undertaken jointly. They warn that social action cannot be considered a panacea. However, with its inclusion of users, it does promote a process to develop services responsive to the needs and priorities of users. The insistence of users that they be involved and the new legal requirements in the United Kingdom add strength to this idea.

Parsons describes the process of developing assessment instruments for both the processes and outcomes of empowerment based practice. The two instruments, the empowerment practice principles (EPP) assessment tool and the empowerment outcomes assessment (EOA) outcomes measure were intended to amplify the voices of consumers and the words, themes, concepts and questions used in the instruments emerged from an extensive process of collaboration. Additional focus groups of clients and providers were involved in assessing the validity of the measures.

The chapter by Itzhaky and Gerber, based on a study of over 200 social workers, found that the more values social workers utilize, the higher will be their level of self-empowerment. Specifically, it was determined that material values, as opposed to what they term spiritual values, have more significant and positive correlation with workers' self-empowerment. The authors suggest that social work agencies can use this information to develop and strengthen social workers' self-empowerment by creating an organizational climate and environment where material values such as work motivation, work gratification and quality of life are stressed. They also maintain that supervision plays a critical role in the value-empowerment relationship.

Taylor examines how concepts of empowerment can be employed in working with non-traditional learners. She examines how this group has been oppressed by the hierarchical and privileged structure of the university context. She describes how a teaching innovation, inquiry and action learning, uses strategies of empowerment to counteract some of the disempowering features of higher education.

Zapf explores how we can use principles of empowerment in the process of social work education. Traditional approaches using expert knowledge are seen as a hindrance to power sharing and collaborative teaching in which teachers and students engage in a mutual learning process. He argues that a process of narrative surrender can be used by social work educators to reclaim their voice and integrate their professional and personal selves. This results in an enhanced sense of personal ownership of efforts to organize and attribute meaning to course material.

CONCLUSION

The diverse and rich contributions contained in this volume capture some of the innovative conceptual and applied work being practised in the world today. Empowerment practice has made an impact on social work in general, and most progressive practice models exhibit some of its characteristics. Rather than being viewed as a precise model of practice it is seen as a framework with principles that operationalize the best intent of our social work code of ethics. It speaks, in particular, to the marginalized and disempowered. It also questions the appropriateness of an expert model of practice and suggests that collaboration to establish working alliances with those we serve is more effective and appropriate. It incorporates the best of what we know works in assisting individuals, groups and communities. Focusing on strengths, negotiating partnerships, addressing issues of power and oppression and respecting the voice of consumers are central concepts in this approach.

While most writers agree that the construct is multi-level, we are only beginning to understand the interdependencies that connect the various levels. We are also, based on recent literature including the contributions found in this volume, beginning to appreciate how feminist, postmodern and constructivist perspectives are infusing the approach with new vitality and addressing the social, structural and systemic issues which act as impediments to the empowerment process.

Empowerment practice as an organizing framework lends itself to different interpretations. On the one hand, empowerment practice has been critiqued because of its imprecise nature and operationalization, and this has led to either its lack of adoption or abuse by neo-conservatives. On the other hand, it does provide a framework that allows the infusion of rich and diverse theoretical perspectives. This ensures that it is a dynamic evolving framework that is responsive to emerging realities and conceptual challenges. It is also very interesting to note how empowerment is understood and practised in different contexts. The exchange of scholarship among colleagues from Britain, Canada, the US and Israel has been a rare opportunity for comparative analysis. Operationalizing empowerment practice within specific cultural contexts and service parameters such as social control is also instructive.

While many authors suggest that some aspects of empowerment practice are field specific, there is ample opportunity to examine transferability across areas of practice. We are also reminded that many disciplines have experimented with ways of understanding and applying empowerment and there is much to be learned by examining their respective experiences.

The social, economic and political context has a tremendous influence on the way we are able to practice. In many developed democracies the neo-conservative agenda of eroding the welfare state has a devastating impact on both those who receive and those who provide social services. The development of legislation that supports civil rights, restores self-governance to Native peoples or requires the active involvement of users in evaluation of service can promote empowerment. While it has been a long time coming, recent efforts of the British and Canadian governments to reinvest in our social safety net are encouraging and may provide a more convivial climate in the future.

A major impediment to empowerment has been the relative paucity of research on this approach. Recent efforts to develop, with the assistance of consumers, appropriate instruments for measuring both the process and outcomes of empowerment are encouraging. The area also lends itself to a wide variety of studies employing a diversity of research methods, from tests of interventions to narrative studies. An emerging theme of this research is the importance of modelling the process of empowerment in the conduct of the research. This development is congruent with increasing experience and scholarship in the area of participatory research and empowerment evaluation.

The expectation that we model what we preach also impacts the teaching enterprise. Teaching is not only an opportunity to talk about practice but also is a rich venue for modelling for students. The core concepts of empowerment are clearly translatable to the classroom situation. The use of the Internet has also contributed to empowerment. It has opened up a new world of information and connections. Increasingly, both in practice and education, professionals are taking on the role of coach and supporter rather than expert and monitor.

As we approach the millennium, we must strive to preserve the values that underpin social work practice and education. Empowerment practice provides us with a dynamic, value-focused framework that is inclusive, consumer-focused and addresses the structural inequities that impact so many people today. This is exactly the approach needed to ensure a civil society and a healthy future for individuals, families and communities.